CHINA'S BANKING LAW AND THE NATIONAL TREATMENT OF FOREIGN-FUNDED BANKS

This is a timely, thorough assessment of an important aspect of China's WTO obligations. The analysis ranges from national treatment under the Qing to the 2012 US-PRC WTO dispute over China UnionPay, noting not only when unequal treatment hurts foreign-funded banks vis-à-vis local banks, but also when it helps them.

Jane K. Winn, University of Washington School of Law, USA

To my wife

China's Banking Law and the National Treatment of Foreign-Funded Banks

中国银行法与外资银行国民待遇

WEI WANG (王伟), Ph.D.
Associate Professor of Fudan University Law School
Shanghai, China

LONDON AND NEW YORK

First published 2013 by Ashgate Publishing

2 Park Square, Milton Park, Abingdon, Oxfordshire OX14 4RN
52 Vanderbilt Avenue, New York, NY 10017

Routledge is an imprint of the Taylor & Francis Group, an informa business

First issued in paperback 2020

British Library Cataloguing in Publication Data
Wang, Wei.
China's banking law and the national treatment of foreign-funded banks.
1. Banking law – China. 2. Banks and banking, Foreign – Law and legislation – China.
3. General Agreement on Trade in Services (Organization) 4. World Trade Organization.
I. Title
346.5'1082–dc23

The Library of Congress has cataloged the printed edition as follows:
Wang, Wei, 1970 July–
China's banking law and the national treatment of foreign-funded banks / by Wei Wang.
pages cm
Includes bibliographical references and index.
ISBN 978-0-7546-7084-1 (hardback)
1. Banks and banking, Foreign—Law and legislation—China. 2. Banks and banking, International—Law and legislation—China. I. Title.
KNQ942.5.W36 2013
346.51'08215–dc23

2012043462

ISBN 13: 978-0-7546-7084-1 (hbk)
ISBN 13: 978-0-367-60161-4 (pbk)

Contents

List of Tables

List of Abbreviations

ABC	Agricultural Bank of China Limited
APEC	Asia-Pacific Economic Cooperation
BISD	Basic Instruments and Selected Documents
BIT	Bilateral Investment Agreement
BOC	Bank of China Limited
CBRC	China Banking Regulatory Commission
CEPA	Closer Economic Partnership Arrangement
CIRC	China Insurance Regulatory Commission
CSRC	China Securities Regulatory Commission
CCB	China Construction Bank Limited
CCP	Chinese Communist Party
CMBC	China Minsheng Banking Corp., Ltd.
CUP	China UnionPay Co., Ltd.
DRI 2004	Detailed Rules for Implementation of the Regulation on Administration of Foreign-Funded Financial Institutions of 2004
DRI 2006	Detailed Rules for Implementation of the Regulation on Administration of Foreign-Funded Banks of 2006
DSB	The Dispute Settlement Body
DSU	Understanding on Rules and Procedures Governing the Settlement of Disputes
EC	European Communities
ECFA	Cross-Strait Economic Cooperation Framework Agreement
EPS	Electronic Payment Services
FBSEA	Foreign Bank Supervision Enhancement Act of 1991
FFB	Foreign-Funded Banks
FFFI	Foreign-Funded Financial Institutions
FTA	Free Trade Agreement
GAO	General Accounting Office of the United States
GATS	The General Agreement on Trade in Services
GATT	The General Agreement on Tariffs and Trade
GLBA	Gramm-Leach-Bliley Act of 1999
GNG	Group of Negotiations on Goods
GNS	Group of Negotiations on Services
HKEx	Hong Kong Exchanges and Clearing Limited
HKSAR	Hong Kong Special Administrative Region
HSBC	Hongkong and Shanghai Banking Corporation
IBA	International Banking Act of 1978
ICBC	Industrial and Commercial Bank of China Limited

ILC	International Law Commission of the United Nations
IMF	International Monetary Fund
MFN	Most-Favoured-Nation
MOFCOM	Ministry of Commerce of the People's Republic of China
MOFTEC	Ministry of Foreign Trade and Economic Cooperation of the People's Republic of China
NAFTA	North American Free Trade Agreement
NDRC	National Development and Reform Commission of the People's Republic of China
NPC	National People's Congress of the People's Republic of China
OCC	Office of the Comptroller of the Currency
OECD	The Organization for Economic Co-operation and Development
PBC	The People's Bank of China
PRC	People's Republic of China
RMB	Renminbi
ROC	Republic of China
SAFE	State Administration of Foreign Exchange of the People's Republic of China
SSE	Shanghai Stock Exchange
TPRM	Trade Policy Review Mechanism
TRIMs	Agreement on Trade-Related Investment Measures
TRIPS	Agreement on Trade-Related Aspects of Intellectual Property Rights
TRM	The Transitional Review Mechanism
UOB	United Overseas Bank
US	The United States
USSR	The Union of the Soviet Socialist Republics
USTR	United States Trade Representative
WTO	The World Trade Organization
XIB	Xiamen International Bank

Foreword

The Chinese economy is a power-house and one of its component parts is the banking sector. As with other parts of the power-house, foreign institutions have sought access to the gubbins. Over the last decade foreign banks have established over two hundred foreign representative offices in China, and some forty wholly owned banks with nearly two hundred and fifty branches and subsidiaries. This splendid book tells the story of how this happened. The focus is on China's membership of the World Trade Organization (WTO) but the book also provides an invaluable account of the law and practice of Chinese banking law today.

The book begins with an historical overview of the treatment of foreign banks in China from 1840. In its wider context of the West's interaction with China it forms an important backdrop to the relationship today. We learn that from the First Opium War to the end of the Qing Dynasty, foreign-funded banks enjoyed extraterritorial rights in China. In particular they had the right to issue paper currency and to deal in foreign exchange, and had special lending rights for special projects. Then, for many years there were restrictions, indeed, exclusions.

Professor Wei Wang then moves to an examination of the WTO and China's banking industry. China's WTO accession agreements and non-discrimination treatment commitments are outlined. His careful study of the GATS will be of more general interest with its references to the current literature and the case law of the appellate body. Attention is given to China's banking law framework. Among the points made is its susceptibility to violation of GATS/WTO national treatment obligations. There are chapters on the Chinese treatment of foreign banks, whether more or less favourable than that of Chinese banks. Less favourable treatment is not insignificant and Professor Wei Wang explores how this is prima facie incompatible with WTO national treatment obligations. He argues that China should eliminate less favourable treatment unless it is prudential.

Perhaps of greatest interest to the foreign lawyer will be the chapters on foreign-funded banks in China. The discussion begins with the history from 1983, when the banking commission issued its first foreign banking rule for the establishment of permanent representative offices. It continues with a discussion of the various permissible forms of foreign bank and their legal status. Professor Wei Wang explains that the three general banking laws enacted by the national people's congress and its standing committee are applicable to foreign-funded banks only in name and that they are regulated mainly by regulations. He contends that this treatment of foreign-funded banks means a lower status for them and less stability. There is a useful table of how foreign banks have fared in the Chinese courts with a particular discussion of cases such as that involving Citibank's Shanghai Branch in 2002. The special legal Status of Hong Kong and Macao Banks on the mainland is addressed.

This is a timely book. China has been a member of the WTO for over a decade. In 2012, the WTO panel issued a report on the case of *China – Certain Measures Affecting Electronic Payment Services*, which raised the issue of whether China was in breach of its national treatment obligations since only China UnionPay, a Chinese entity, was permitted to supply electronic payment services for payment card transactions denominated and paid in renminbi. But it is more than a primer of how the GATS/WTO affects foreign banks in China. It offers an invaluable and authoritative account of Chinese banking law when, as Professor Wei Wang explains, books seeking to identify the scope of Chinese banking law are thin on the ground.

This is no lifeless account. Professor Wei Wang reveals himself as a constructive critic and reformer. China's banking laws are, in his view, in a mess. He suggests that at the present China's banking law framework is unstable. An overall policy framework is absent. That is not good for China or for foreign banks. Professor Wei Wang proposes a framework which would integrate the laws, horizontally and vertically, so that China's banking law as a whole would apply equally to both Chinese-funded banks and foreign-funded banks.

This is a well-researched and thorough account, which will appeal to a wide range of readers. It deserves careful attention by the Chinese authorities. It will go a long way to quenching the thirst for knowledge about China's banking and commercial laws. Professor Wei Wang has done foreign lawyers and scholars an enormous service by setting out the current state of play in such a clear and through manner.

Sir Ross Cranston FBA
Royal Courts of Justice, London
November 7, 2012.

Foreword

China's embarkation on its historically unprecedented "Great Economic Experiment" of "Reform and Opening-up" under the rubric of a move toward "market socialism with Chinese characteristics" was launched by Deng Xiaoping in 1978 and continues through to the present. As an integral part of this reform process from the start was the governmental awareness that China would need to develop a banking system conducive to economic modernization. However, the fundamental, initial hurdle was that in 1978 a "banking system" in any modern sense did not exist in China: there existed a "mono-bank" structure centered on the People's Bank of China (PBC) functioning in conjunction with the Ministry of Finance. But in reposturing the PBC into a modern central bank, the PRC government created four "commercial" banks that were burdened with the "policy" financing of the multitude of state-owned enterprises (SOEs) and with the attendant mass of non-performing loans (NPLs).

It was not until the 1990s that the PRC undertook a series of major financial sector reform initiatives: (i) restructuring these commercial banks so as to "depoliticize" them and to create a separate asset management structure to begin to deal with the NPLs; (ii) engaging in a gradual liberalization of its financial markets and the provision of financial services; and (iii) the creation of a suitable bank regulatory and supervisory system that would foster principles of prudential operation and good governance with respect to the evolving banking system and banking institutions. Attendant to these separate, and not well-coordinated, reforms was the ultimate realization that significant domestic legal reforms within the banking/financial system would be needed; that financial system/services liberalization would require China's entry into the global WTO trade system; and that, as made evident by the Asian Financial Crisis (in which the PRC's MoF and PBC acted most responsibly on a regional basis), China would need to align itself with the adoption of "international banking standards" as being developed by the Basel Committee. In a most scholarly and insightful manner, Professor Wang Wei provides us, in *China's Banking Law and the National Treatment of Foreign-Funded Banks*, a special "analytical window" through which to better understand and to evaluate these reforms in a coordinated and useful manner that significantly advances an understanding of these reforms on a practical, policy and scholarly level.

Professor Wang is one of a few young, economic law scholars coming out of the 1990s who began to explore the interconnections between economic and legal reforms, domestic and international reforms, and trade and financial liberalization. This new multi-dimensional and interdisciplinary analytical approach was truly ground-breaking as scholars, policymakers and practitioners tended to operate within their own comfortable "pigeonholes". Economists did not talk to lawyers;

domestic policymakers were driven by domestic and not international concerns; and, trade people did not talk to financial services people. Professor Wang in his scholarship since the late 1990s has understood and explored these interconnections. This understanding has resulted in the very special treatise before us.

Though the "window" appears to be narrow (i.e., the WTO "national treatment" standard as to China's banking law), the author most skillfully and meticulously takes the reader through China's rich history of dealing with foreign-funded enterprises; thus, providing the reader with a needed perspective for better understanding China's struggle in dealing with foreign-funded banks. Also, the author provides one of the best discussions of the highly complicated and multi-dimensional aspects of the notion of the national treatment standard within China, and additionally of the much neglected and misunderstood linkage between the WTO/GATS financial services liberalization and the WTO "prudential carve-out" and related provisions. Further, the author's exploration of the application of the WTO to China as to financial services provides a special insight into how potentially the WTO's rule-based structure and its related Dispute Settlement Understanding is "nudging" China domestically toward a more rule-based and economic, rule of law approach in its financial sectors.

In tackling these most complicated interconnections, Professor Wang shows himself to be the first-rate legal financial and economic law scholar he is. He lays out as clearly as one can the current practical and legal "mess" in which the current state of China's banking laws rest (as a US academic, I am well-familiar with a statutory and regulatory "mess" in the financial services arena). As a banking law academic, the undersigned greatly appreciates the author's critical estimation, with suggestions for further reform, of China's present banking structure/system.

In addition, Professor Wang's detailed analysis of key, relevant WTO cases (including the recent US-China case over the China bank card monopoly) is most impressive and helpful, as is his exhaustive analysis of the "national treatment" quandary within China's law and practice. Professor Wang conducts all his analysis in a balanced, but objectively critical manner. Effectively, he provides us with a foundation for ongoing study and consideration for those within and without China.

Obviously, from a practical context, this exceptional volume should be of primary interest to foreign bankers, investors and observers seeking a better understanding of the entry and treatment of foreign-funded banks/financial institutions within China, and of the evolving Chinese banking/financial systems and laws/regulations. Perhaps, more significantly, there is a wealth of insights in this volume to stimulate further thought and debate for domestic and international policy-makers, regulators/supervisors and academics. This is a most substantial volume of timely significance, written by a first-rate legal scholar. First-rate in all respects!

Prof. Joseph J. Norton, SJD, DPhil., LLD
January 6, 2013
Formerly Sir John Lubbock Professor of Banking Law (London) (1993–2004);
James L. Walsh Professor of Financial Institutions Law (SMU, Dallas)

Preface

The legal status and treatment of foreigners in China were first studied by Dr. Wellington V.K. Koo in his history-making book *The Status of Aliens in China* (Columbia University Press, 1912). Since then, more and more people have paid great attention to the topic. Different from Dr. Koo's book written one hundred years ago, my book centres on the legal status and treatment of foreign-funded banks in China of the present time. Today's China is also different from Mao's China, when foreign banks were forced to leave this country.

There is not a guideline or a legislative philosophy concerning the application of Chinese banking law. When people look at Chinese banking law, some may pay attention to the so-called laws enacted by the National People's Congress or its Standing Committee, some to the regulations issued by the State Council, some to the rules made by the People's Bank of China, some to the rules made by the China Banking Regulatory Commission, like a few blind men touching a big elephant. Is there a framework for Chinese banking law? If so, where is the position of foreign-funded banks in the framework? What is the treatment of foreign-funded banks in the framework? Is the framework compatible with national treatment obligations of the World Trade Organization? These questions are the focus of this book.

In my view, China's banking law framework is a four-tiered and tripartite framework, under which the treatment of foreign-funded banks is the mixture of more favourable treatment, less favourable treatment and identical treatment, compared with the treatment of Chinese domestic-funded banks. I suggest that China integrate its existing banking law framework. For this purpose, I propose to integrate China's banking law framework horizontally and vertically. The vertical integration is to upgrade the foreign banking regulations and rules, and to change the four-tiered banking law framework to a three-tiered framework. The horizontal integration includes the internal integration between domestic banking law to create *tertium comparationis*, and the external integration between foreign banking law and domestic banking law. As a result, China's banking law as a whole will apply equally to both Chinese-funded banks and foreign-funded banks.

Wei Wang
Shanghai
January 5, 2013

Acknowledgments

Many people supported me during the past ten years in which this book took shape. I would like to thank Professor Joseph J. Norton, the former Sir John Lubbock Professor in Banking Law at the Centre for Commercial Law Studies, Queen Mary, University of London. Professor Norton provided me not only academic guidance on law, but also financial support in the form of the John and Joan Jackson Scholarship, which enabled me to further my research in London. I would like to thank Professor Douglas Arner at the University of Hong Kong, and Professor Zhou Zhongfei of Shanghai University of Finance and Economics, whose criticisms and comments helped enormously.

I wish to thank the Asian Development Bank for providing me the opportunities to take part in two Chinese banking law projects as a consultant, in which I worked with the People's Bank of China (PBC) and the China Banking Regulatory Commission (CBRC) in Beijing and had the chance to know China's banking laws and regulations and their problems in practice. I also wish to thank Professor Lou Jianbo of Peking University Law School, Professor Berry Hsu, Professor Zhang Xianchu of the University of Hong Kong, Professor George Walker of the CCLS of Queen Mary, University of London, Professor Kang Rui of Shanghai Maritime University, Mr Liang Honglie, Dr. Zhang Xin, Dr. Mamiko Yokoi, and Dr. Mohamed Gad. I am greatly obliged to the librarians of the Institute of Advanced Legal Studies (IALS), Queen Mary College, the School of Oriental and African Studies, the London School of Economics and Political Science, the University of Hong Kong, the National Library of China, Nanjing Library, and Jinling Library.

I also wish to thank the person who is as yet unknown to me, namely, the reviewer who offered a number of detailed comments which have contributed a great deal toward the betterment of this work.

Lastly, I thank my parents, my wife and my daughter for their love and support, without which I could never have finished this book.

Wei Wang

Introduction

Look at one spot on a leopard and then you can visualize the whole animal
[*guan zhong kui bao, ke jian yi ban*].

Liu Yiqing, Essays and Criticism [*Shi Shuo Xin Yu*]
Liu Song Dynasty (420 AD–479 AD)

Background

The People's Republic of China (PRC)[1] became a Member of the WTO on December 11, 2001.[2] According to the Marrakesh Agreement Establishing the World Trade Organization (WTO Agreement),[3] "[e]ach Member shall ensure the conformity of its laws, regulations and administrative procedures with its obligations as provided in the annexed Agreements".[4] China also confirmed, in paragraph 68 of the Report of the Working Party on the Accession of China (Working Party Report),[5] that the Chinese central government would revise or annul administrative regulations or departmental rules if they were inconsistent with China's obligations under the WTO agreements[6] and the Protocol on the Accession of the PRC (China Accession

---

[1] In this book, for the sake of convenience, unless otherwise stated, China generally refers to mainland China, i.e., the PRC, not including the Hong Kong Special Administrative Region (HKSAR), the Macao Special Administrative Region and Taiwan, all of which have different legal systems.

[2] Protocol on Accession of the People's Republic of China Done at Doha on November 10, 2001, Notification of Acceptance and Entry into Force, WT/LET/408 (November 20, 2001).

[3] The WTO Agreement, in The Legal Texts: the Results of the Uruguay Round of Multilateral Trade Negotiations 4–14 (Cambridge Univ. Press 1999) [hereinafter The Legal Texts].

[4] Id. art. XVI:4.

[5] Working Party Report, WT/ACC/CHN/49 (October 1, 2001), in Compilation of the Legal Instruments on China's Accession to the World Trade Organization 755–847 (Law Press China 2002).

[6] In this book, the WTO agreements generally refer to the Multilateral Trade Agreements annexed to the WTO Agreement. According to Article II:2 of the WTO Agreement, the Multilateral Trade Agreements under the WTO refer to the agreements and associated legal instruments in Annexes 1, 2 and 3 of the WTO Agreement. Annex 1A is "Multilateral Agreements on Trade in Goods", including mainly the General Agreement on Tariffs and Trade 1994 [hereinafter the GATT]; Annex 1B is "General Agreement on Trade in Services" [hereinafter the GATS]; Annex 1C is "Agreement on Trade-Related Aspects

Protocol).[7] Therefore, China's laws, regulations and other rules must comply with WTO obligations.

WTO Members watch China's laws, regulations, and rules in many other ways. For example, the United States (US) is paying a good deal of attention to what commitments China has made under the WTO and whether China complies with those commitments. In October 2002, the US General Accounting Office (GAO) submitted a special report to Congressional Committees, analysing China's WTO commitments in detail.[8] At the same time, according to section 421 of the US-China Relations Act of 2000,[9] the United States Trade Representative (USTR) shall report *annually* to the US Congress on compliance by China with its WTO commitments. To the end of 2011, the USTR had issued nine reports on China's WTO compliance.[10] Obviously, China's laws, regulations, and rules are under the watchful eye of the WTO Members.

The real threat for China comes from the dispute settlement mechanism of the WTO. For example, if a WTO Member takes the view that China's law, regulation, rule or any measure violates the WTO obligations, it may start the dispute

of Intellectual Property Rights [hereinafter TRIPS]; Annex 2 is the Understanding on Rules and Procedures Governing the Settlement of Disputes [hereinafter the DSU]; Annex 3 is Trade Policy Review Mechanism [hereinafter TPRM].

7 China Accession Protocol, WT/L/432 (November 23, 2001), in COMPILATION OF THE LEGAL INSTRUMENTS ON CHINA'S ACCESSION TO THE WORLD TRADE ORGANIZATION 1–14 (Law Press China 2002).

8 GAO, Report to Congressional Committees, *World Trade Organization: Analysis of China's Commitments to Other Members*, October 2002, GAO-03-4, http://www.gao.gov/cgi-bin/getrpt?GAO-03-4.

9 22 U.S.C. § 6951.

10 See USTR, 2002 Report to Congress on China's WTO Compliance, December 11, 2002, http://www.usvtc.org/trade/wto/China_WTO_compliance_report.pdf; 2003 Report to Congress on China's WTO Compliance, December 11, 2003, http://www.ustr.gov/assets/Document_Library/Reports_Publications/2003/asset_upload_file425_4313.pdf; 2004 Report to Congress on China's WTO Compliance, December 11, 2004, http://www.ustr.gov/assets/Document_Library/Reports_Publications/2004/asset_upload_file281_6986.pdf; 2005 Report to Congress on China's WTO Compliance, December 11, 2005, www.ustr.gov/assets/Document_Library/ Reports_Publications/2004/; 2006 Report to Congress on China's WTO Compliance, December 11, 2006, http://ustraderep.gov/assets/Document_Library/Reports_Publications/2006/asset_upload_file688_10223.pdf; 2007 Report to Congress on China's WTO Compliance, December 11, 2007, http://www.ustr.gov/sites/default/files/asset_upload_file625_13692.pdf; 2008 Report to Congress on China's WTO Compliance, December 2008, http://www.ustr.gov/sites/default/files/asset_upload_file192_15258.pdf; 2009 Report to Congress on China's WTO Compliance, December 2009, http://www.ustr.gov/webfm_send/1572; 2010 Report to Congress on China's WTO Compliance, December 2010, http://www.ustr.gov/webfm_send/2596; 2011 Report to Congress on China's WTO Compliance, December 2011, http://www.ustr.gov/webfm_send/3189; 2011 Report to Congress on China's WTO Compliance, USTR, December, 2011, http://www.ustr.gov/webfm_send/3189.

settlement mechanism of the WTO against China, and if China loses the case, China must implement the adopted rulings of the WTO Dispute Settlement Body (DSB) by amending or repealing the relevant law, regulation, rule or measure inconsistent with WTO obligations. The rulings of the DSB have legally binding force on WTO Members.[11]

In the above context, it is very important to continually undertake a thorough study of WTO obligations and China's WTO commitments on the one hand, China's laws, regulations and rules on the other, and evaluate the consistency between the former and the latter, and then search for ways for China to enhance the observance of the international law while maintaining proper flexibility. For this book, I choose national treatment from the former, and China's banking law from the latter. The essence of this book is to address the relationship between WTO national treatment and China's banking law, especially the impact of the GATS/WTO national treatment obligations on China's banking law framework. It must be noted that this book itself is not a general research on China's banking law, but a specific research on China's banking law from the perspective of international trade law.

Why National Treatment?

It is generally recognized that the principle of non-discrimination is the cornerstone of the WTO.[12] In the world trading system, national treatment and most-favoured-nation (MFN) treatment are two types of non-discriminatory treatment.[13] The purpose of MFN treatment is to ensure equal competition opportunities provided by one country are available to other countries, whereas the fundamental purpose of national treatment is to ensure equal treatment between a host country and foreign countries. Georg Schwarzenberger called MFN treatment "foreign parity", [14] and

---

[11] The Understanding on Rules and Procedures Governing the Settlement of Disputes, art. 22, in The Legal Texts, supra note 3, at 354–79.

[12] Matthew Kennedy, *Services Join GATT: An Analysis of the General Agreement on Trade in Services*, 1 Int'l T.L.R. 11, 16 (1995); see also Bernard M. Hoekman and Michel M. Kostecki, The Political Economy of the World Trading System: the WTO and Beyond 252 (Oxford Univ. Press 2nd edn, 2001); Communication from Japan, Non-Discrimination, ¶ 2, WT/WGTI/W/124 (June 28, 2002).

[13] See OECD Secretariat, Core Principles in a Trade and Competition Context, 20, WT/WGTCP/W/221 (February 6, 2003); Communication from the EC and Its Member States, ¶ 11, WT/WGTCP/W/222 (November 19, 2002); Communication from India, 1, WT/WGTI/W/149 (October 7, 2002); Non-Discrimination: Most-Favoured-Nation Treatment and National Treatment, Note by the Secretariat, ¶ 10, WT/WGTI/W/118 (June 4, 2002).

[14] Georg Schwarzenberger, International Law and Order 157 (Stevens & Sons 1971).

national treatment "inland parity".[15] National treatment, which becomes more and more important in international trade,[16] is always one of the main issues among WTO Members.[17] In *US – Section 211 Omnibus Appropriations Act*,[18] the Appellate Body held that MFN treatment and national treatment obligations are cornerstones of the world trading system.[19] Jackson pointed out that national treatment is "more quickly embroiled in domestic politics" and "often breached" because it "affects internal government actions so directly".[20]

In service trade, national treatment attracts much more attention than MFN treatment does. This phenomenon may be partly due to the differences between goods and services. There are no customs duties for services because services are intangible. But with regard to goods, which are tangible, customs duties are very suitable. In Schwarzenberger's view, under the circumstances of customs duties, national treatment has no opportunities to compete with MFN treatment, but after border crossing, in some internal fields, national treatment means more than MFN treatment.[21] Another reason for the importance of national treatment over MFN treatment in service trade is the pivotal position of specific commitments in the GATS.[22] Owing to the key function of specific commitments in services, national treatment and market access, as principal parts of specific commitments, are the main issues for trade in services. From the experience of the nine rounds of transitional reviews (2002–2009, 2011) after China's accession to the WTO, the focus of the reviews, especially for financial services, was on national treatment and market access obligations.[23] It is not surprising that national treatment in

---

15 Id.

16 Don Wallace, Jr, and David B. Bailey, *The Inevitability of National Treatment of Foreign Direct Investment with Increasingly Few and Narrow Exceptions*, 31 Cornell Int'l L.J. 615, 630 (1998).

17 John H. Jackson, The World Trading System: Law and Policy of International Economic Relations 213 (MIT Press 2nd edn, 1997).

18 Appellate Body Report, *US – Section 211 Omnibus Appropriations Act*, WT/DS176/AB/R, adopted January 2, 2002.

19 Id. ¶ 297.

20 John H. Jackson, World Trade And The Law Of GATT 274 (Bobbs-Merrill Company 1969); see also John H. Jackson, *National Treatment Obligations and Non-Tariff Barriers*, 10 Mich. J. Int'l L. 207, 208 (1989).

21 Schwarzenberger, supra note 14, at 157–58.

22 GATS, in The Legal Texts, supra note 3, at 284–307.

23 See generally, WTO Committee on Trade in Financial Services, Report of the Meeting Held on October 21, 2002, S/FIN/M/37 (October 24, 2002); Report of the Meeting Held on December 1, 2003, S/FIN/M/43 (December 4, 2003); Report of the Meeting Held on November 23, 2004, S/FIN/M/47 (November 26, 2004); Report of the Meeting Held on September 19, 2005, S/FIN/M/50 (September 23, 2005); Report of the Meeting Held on November 27, 2006, S/FIN/M/53 (November 30, 2006); Report of the Meeting Held on November 12, 2007, S/FIN/M/55 (December 16, 2007); Report of the Meeting Held on December 1, 2008, S/FIN/M/57 (December 4, 2008); Report of the Meeting Held on

financial service trade should be sufficiently recognized, observed and responded to by the Chinese government.

In 2006, the China Banking Regulatory Commission (CBRC) issued the Detailed Rules for Implementation of the Regulation on Administration of Foreign-Funded Banks of 2006 (DRI 2006). The three principles for formulating DRI 2006 were as follows:

1. To comprehensively fulfil China's commitments to the WTO, and eliminate geographic and client limitations.
2. To embody the national treatment principle so as to create a legal environment for fair competition between Chinese-funded and foreign-funded banks.
3. To abide by international supervision practice.[24]

In 2012, the WTO panel issued a report on the case of *China – Certain Measures Affecting Electronic Payment Services* [hereinafter referred to as *China – Electronic Payment Services*]. One of the main issues in the case was whether China broke its national treatment obligations by allowing only a Chinese entity (China UnionPay) to supply electronic payment services for payment card transactions denominated and paid in renminbi in China.[25]

The core role of national treatment has long been noted by the United States. In history, the US government attached great importance to national treatment.[26] The United States strongly insisted on the inclusion of a national treatment clause during the negotiation of a Sino-US Bilateral Investment Treaty (BIT) from 1983.[27] In fact, the failure of the Sino-US BIT negotiation was due to the conflict between the American insistence on national treatment and Chinese objection to it.[28] It is noteworthy that the US government pays particular attention to national treatment in financial services. The US Department of Treasury presented six National

November 2 and 9, 2009, S/FIN/M/61 (March 4, 2010); Report of the Meeting Held on October 31, 2011, S/FIN/M/71(November 4, 2011).

24 CBRC Replies to Reporters on DRI 2006, available at http://www.cbrc.gov.cn/chinese/home/docView/2877.html (published November 28, 2006).

25 *China-Electronic Payment Services*, WT/DS413/R (July 16, 2012).

26 For the early treaties with a national treatment clause concluded by the United States, see Wallace McClure, *German-American Commercial Relations*, 19 Am. J. Int'l L. 689, 692 (1925) (stating that national treatment of shipping appeared in a treaty between the United States and the Hanseatic Republics of Bremen, Hamburg and Lübeck concluded on December 20, 1827).

27 See Xu Chongli, *Shilun Woguo dui Waizi Shixing Guomin Daiyu Biaozun de Wenti* [On the Issue of National Treatment Standards for Foreign Investment in China], 1 Guoji Jingjifa Luncong [Chinese J. Int'l. Econ. L.] 175, 193 (Chen An (ed.), Law Press China 1998).

28 Id.

Treatment Study Reports to Congress, i.e. in 1979, 1984, 1986, 1990, 1994 and 1998.[29] Furthermore, in the United States, there are numerous private sources providing such information on national treatment.[30] It must be noted that *China – Electronic Payment Services* was also raised by the United States against China.

Conversely, in China, there are few national treatment studies on trade in financial services sponsored by governmental or non-governmental institutions. This is due to the weakness of WTO research in China. Although thousands of books on the WTO have been published in China in recent years, few books or journal articles focus on a special obligation under the WTO, such as national treatment.[31]

Sources

China's laws, regulations, and rules used in this book mainly come from the following sources: (1) Gazette of the Standing Committee of the National People's Congress (Gazette of the NPC);[32] (2) Gazette of the State Council;[33] (3) Collection of the Laws of the PRC;[34] (4) Gazette of the Ministry of Commerce of the PRC;[35]

---

[29] Letter from Robert E. Rubin, to Al Gore, then president of the US Senate, and to Newt Gingrich, then Speaker of the US House of Representative, November 30, 1998, in US Department of the Treasury, *National Treatment Study Report 1998*, http://www.treas.gov/offices/international-affairs/nts/.

[30] Id.

[31] In 2005, Wang Yi wrote a book on WTO national treatment rules. This is China's first book specifically concerning WTO national treatment. See Wang Yi, WTO Guomin Daiyu de Falü Jiqi zai Zhongguo de Shiyong [WTO National Treatment Rules and Their Application in China] (China Social Sciences Press and the People's Court Press 2005).

[32] PRC Legislation Law [*Lifafa*], art. 52, ¶ 3, adopted at the Third Session of the Ninth NPC on March 15, 2000, effective July 1, 2000, in Falü Huibian 2000, at 2–23 (People's Publishing House 2001) (providing that the text of a law published in the Gazette of the Standing Committee of the NPC shall be the standard text).

[33] Id. art. 62, ¶ 2 (providing that the text of an administrative regulation published in the Gazette of the State Council shall be the standard text).

[34] Collection of the Laws of the PRC [*Zhonghua Renmin Gongheguo Falü Huibian*, hereinafter Falü Huibian] is edited by the Legislative Affairs Commission [*Fazhi Gongzuo Weiyuanhui*] of the Standing Committee of the NPC and published once a year, or sometimes published in a bound volume by the People's Publishing House [*Renmin Chubanshe*].

[35] Gazette of the Ministry of Commerce of the PRC [*Zhonghua Renmin Gongheguo Shangwubu Wengao*, hereinafter Gazette of the MOFCOM] is edited by the Ministry of Commerce [hereinafter the MOFCOM], which replaced the former Gazette of the Ministry of Trade and Economic Cooperation [hereinafter the MOFTEC] in 2003 after the MOFTEC became the MOFCOM. See Decision of the First Session of the Tenth NPC on the Plan of Reforming the State Council Institutions [*Di Shijie Quanguo Renmin Daibiao Dahui Diyici Huiyi guanyu Guowuyuan Jigou Gaige Fang'An de Jueding*], March 10, 2003, Gazette of

(5) Gazette of the People's Bank of China [*Zhongguo Renmin Yinhang Wengao*, hereinafter Gazette of the PBC]. All of the sources are listed in the Working Party Report.[36] In addition, I use the Gazette of the China Banking Regulatory Commission (Gazette of the CBRC),[37] Gazette of the Supreme People's Court [*Zuigao Renmin Fayuan Gongbao*]. I also refer to China's laws, regulations and rules translated into English for reference, including those notified by China to the WTO as required by GATS Article III:3,[38] and those provided by China to the WTO under Section 18 of the China Accession Protocol.[39] However, it is worth noting that only Chinese versions are authentic. If there is any conflict or difference

---

The NPC 190–94 (2003, no. 2); see *also* Circular of the State Council on Establishment of Agencies [*Guowuyuan guanyu Jigou Shezhi de Tongzhi*], *Guofa* [2003] No. 8, March 21, 2003, Gazette of the State Council 10–11 (2003, no. 12); Circular of the General Office of the State Council on Performance by the Ministry of Commerce of Certain Responsibilities Prescribed in Administrative Regulations and Documents of the State Council in Force [*Guowuyuan Bangongting guanyu Shangwubu Lüxing Xianxing Xingzheng Fagui, Guowuyuan Wenjian zhong Xiangying Zhize de Tongzhi*], *Guobanfa* [2003] No. 87, October 20, 2003, Gazette of the State Council 9 (2003, no. 35).

36 Working Party Report, supra note 5, ¶ 330.

37 Gazette of the CBRC [*Zhongguo Yinhangye Jiandu Guanli Weiyuanhui Gongbao*] is edited by the China Banking Regulatory Commission [hereinafter the CBRC] established in 2003, which obtained most supervisory powers from the central bank, i.e., the People's Bank of China [hereinafter the PBC]. See Decision of the First Session of the Tenth NPC on the Plan of Reforming the State Council Institutions, supra note 35; Decision of the Standing Committee of the NPC on the Performance by the CBRC of the Supervisory and Administrative Duties Originally Performed by the PBC [*Quanguo Renmin Daibiao Dahui Changwu Weiyuanhui guanyu Zhongguo Yinhangye Jiandu Guanli Weiyuanhui Lüxing yuanyou Zhongguo Renmin Yinhang Lüxing de Jiandu Guanli Zhize de Jueding*], adopted at the Second Meeting of the Standing Committee of the Tenth NPC on April 26, 2003, Gazette of The NPC 326 (2003, no. 3). In 2011, the CBRC edited Compendium of China Banking Regulations and Supervisory Rules (3 vols., Law Press China, 2011). The Compendium does not provide an exhaustive list of Chinese banking law. On the one hand, it contains few banking rules of the PBC. On the other hand, it contains many non-banking laws, such as Accounting Law, Trust Law, Negotiable Instrument Law, Enterprises Bankruptcy Law, Criminal Law, etc.

38 GATS Article III:3 states: "Each Member shall promptly and at least annually inform the Council for Trade in Services of the introduction of any new, or any changes to existing laws, regulations or administrative guidelines which significantly affect trade in services covered by its specific commitments under this Agreement."

39 Section 18 of the China Accession Protocol stipulates: "... China shall provide relevant information, including information specified in Annex 1A, to each subsidiary body in advance of the review ...." Moreover, in accordance with Annex 1A:V(a) of the China Accession Protocol, China should annually provide information for transitional review purpose, including, inter alia, "regularly updated lists of all laws, regulations, administrative guidelines and other measures affecting trade in each service sector or sub-sector ...".

in the meaning of words between Chinese versions and English versions, Chinese versions shall prevail.[40]

With regard to WTO materials, I take advantage of the official "Documents Online" database provided by the WTO,[41] and some authoritative publications edited by the WTO,[42] or edited by the MOFCOM.[43] In addition to the WTO agreements, the book examines and analyses a number of treaties concerning national treatment, which are mainly from the Collection of the Treaties of the PRC [*Zhonghua Renmin Gongheguo Tiaoyue Ji*] edited by the Ministry of Foreign Affairs of the PRC, the Collection of the Multilateral Treaties of the PRC edited by the Department of Treaty and Law of the Ministry of Foreign Affairs of the PRC,[44] the Compilation of Old Sino-Foreign Treaties and Agreements edited by Wang Tieya,[45] the Compilation of Archives of the History of the Republic of China edited by the Second Historical Archives of China,[46] and other supplementary sources.

Structure

The focus of the book is to study the treatment of foreign-funded banks in comparison with that of Chinese-funded banks in China's banking law framework, in the context of GATS/WTO national treatment obligations, which constitutes the "four corners" of the book. The structure of this book is as follows:

Chapter 1 introduces the history of national treatment in China, which originated from the late Qing Dynasty (1840–1911), rose in the period between 1912 and 1949, fell in the early People's Republican period (1949–1978), and rose again from 1979. Chapter 1 also analyses the reasons for the fall and rise of national treatment in China, and gives an overview of the history of foreign-funded banks and their treatment in China.

---

40 Such statement is in each notification provided by China pursuant to Article III:3 of the GATS, see, e.g., S/C/N/213, S/C/N/215, S/C/N/221, S/C/N/222, S/C/N/223, S/C/N/224, S/C/N/225.

41 Http://docsonline.wto.org/?language=1.

42 See, e.g., The Legal Texts, supra note 3.

43 See, e.g., Compilation of the Legal Instruments on China's Accession to the World Trade Organization (Law Press China 2002).

44 See, e.g., Collection of the Multilateral Treaties of the prc [*Zhonghua Renmin Gongheguo Duobian Tiaoyue Ji*] (Law Press China 2002).

45 Compilation of Old Sino-Foreign Treaties and Agreements [*Zhongwai Jiuyuezhang Huibian*], vols 1, 2 and 3 (Wang Tieya (ed.), Joint Publishing House 1957, 1959, 1962, reprinted in 1982) [hereinafter Old Sino-Foreign Treaties].

46 Compilation of Archives of the History of the Republic of China [*Zhonghua Minguoshi Dang'An Ziliao Huibian*], vols 1–5 (The Second Historical Archives of China, Jiangsu Ancient Books Publishing House (ed.) 1991, 1994, 1997) [hereinafter Archives of the History of the roc].

Chapter 2 examines China's WTO commitments in respect of national treatment, including general national treatment commitments in the China Accession Protocol and Working Party Report, and specific banking commitments in China's service schedule. Chapter 2 provides detailed analysis of China's GATS/WTO-plus obligations, which shall prevail over GATS/WTO national treatment obligations.

Chapter 3 discusses the market access, forms and legal status of foreign-funded banks in China. In this book, unless otherwise specified, foreign-funded banks refer to foreign-funded commercial banks, including foreign bank branches, foreign bank subsidiaries (wholly-foreign-funded banks), Sino-foreign equity joint venture banks, and representative offices of foreign banks in China. Thus, China's foreign banking law in this book generally refers to China's foreign-funded banking law. One of the issues in this chapter is the complicated relationship between market access and national treatment, between GATS Article XVI and XVII, illustrated by the first case on this issue in the history of the WTO dispute settlement, i.e. *China-Electronic Payment Services*. Chapter 3 also explores the special preferential status of Hong Kong banks, Macao banks and Taiwan banks under the FTA arrangement, that is, the CEPA and the ECFA. Such preferential treatment of Hong Kong banks, Macao banks and Taiwan banks does not conflict with China's MFN treatment commitments to other WTO members.

Chapter 4 focuses on different treatment of foreign-funded banks and Chinese-funded banks in China's banking law framework.[47] In this book, Chinese-funded banks refer to Chinese-funded commercial banks, including state-owned commercial banks, joint-stock commercial banks, city commercial banks, and rural commercial banks. They do not include policy banks, city credit cooperatives, rural credit cooperatives, rural cooperative banks, trust and investment companies, finance companies, foreign bank branches, wholly-foreign-funded banks or Sino-foreign equity joint venture banks.[48] In this chapter, I draw a conclusion that China's existing banking law framework is a four-tiered and tripartite law framework, under which a number of shortcomings exist, including especially susceptibility to violation of GATS/WTO national treatment obligations discussed in Chapter 2.

Chapter 5 examines more favourable treatment of foreign-funded banks under China's existing banking law framework. I argue that more favourable treatment of foreign-funded banks is compatible with WTO national treatment obligations,

---

[47] For the framework of China's banking financial institutions, see http://www.cbrc.gov.cn/chinese/jrjg/index.html.

[48] In 2007, the CBRC issued the Interim Measures for Administration of Village Banks [*Cunzhen Yinhang Guanli Zanxing Guiding*], CBRC *Yinjianfa* [2007] No. 5. According to Article 2 of the Interim Measures, village banks are banking institutions providing financial services to local peasants, agriculture and rural economy. The investors for village banks include domestic or overseas financial institutions, domestic non-financial institutions, or domestic natural persons. Therefore, whether a village bank is Chinese-funded or foreign-funded depends on its investors.

although China has begun to reduce and repeal more favourable treatment of foreign-funded enterprises.

Chapter 6 examines less favourable treatment of foreign-funded banks, which is also the key issue in WTO's TRM meetings for China. I argue that less favourable treatment is *prima facie* incompatible with WTO national treatment obligations. China should eliminate less favourable treatment of foreign-funded banks unless less favourable treatment is prudential.

Chapter 7 discusses identical treatment between foreign-funded banks and Chinese-funded banks. There is a trend that more and more Chinese banking laws, regulations, and rules equally apply to all commercial banks in China, no matter whether they are Chinese-funded or foreign-funded.

In Chapter 8, with the comparison to a single banking law framework and a dual banking framework, I suggest that China adopt an integrated banking law framework to restructure its four-tiered and tripartite banking law framework. China may integrate its banking law framework through horizontal integration and vertical integration, internal integration and external integration. As GATS/WTO national treatment does not mean identical treatment, the integrated banking law framework does not mean a single framework. Under the integrated banking law framework, prudential banking rules relating to foreign-funded banks, including some less favourable treatment and more favourable treatment, may be placed in special chapters or articles of the integrated banking laws, regulations, and rules. To strengthen the option, Chapter 8 also analyses the economic and political bases of the integrated banking law framework.

The book ends with a conclusion.

Methodology

The book uses qualitative methodology to analyse the types of foreign-funded banks, meanings of national treatment in the WTO and its changes in China's WTO commitments. Meanwhile, for the purpose of tracing the origin of foreigners' treatment in China, the book makes reference to a number of historical materials. For instance, chapter 1 discusses the evolutionary history of foreigners' treatment, especially national treatment, in China, including, inter alia, certain treaties signed by governments of the Qing Dynasty, the Republic of China, and the PRC. Chapter 1 also gives an overview of the history of foreign-funded banks and their treatment in China. On the whole, the book attaches great importance to historical methodology.[49]

---

[49] According to the Vienna Convention on the Law of Treaties of 1969 [hereinafter the Vienna Convention], the historical preparatory work of the treaty may be used as supplementary means of interpretation of the treaty. The Vienna Convention, art. 32, effective January 27, 1980, applicable to China from October 3, 1997, in 7 COLLECTION OF THE MULTILATERAL TREATIES OF THE PRC 174–99 (Law Press China 2002). In some WTO

Furthermore, this book adopts the comparative study method. For example, I compare treatment of Chinese-funded banks and that of foreign-funded banks in chapters 5, 6, 7, the US banking law framework and the dual banking law framework in chapter 8.

Lastly, the book uses both the Bluebook [50] and the Chicago Manual of Style[51] as style and citation guide. It must be noted that there are some differences between the two books and there are few guidelines for citing Chinese legal materials in the Bluebook and the Chicago Manual of Style.[52] To overcome the weaknesses, I put information as much as possible in relevant footnotes and bibliography. For Chinese laws, regulations, rules or other normative documents, as well as Chinese books, journal articles, Chinese special names, terms, etc., I express them bilingually, first Chinese (by the pinyin romanization system), then English translation, or first English, then Chinese pinyin so as to avoid misconception or misunderstanding. Even though the Chinese names, terms, or titles are mainly expressed by the pinyin romanization system, under special circumstances, some place-names, personal names, and dynasty names long familiar in the Western world retain their old spellings in the older Wade-Giles system or the Postal Atlas system, together with the pinyin spellings.

---

cases, the Panels and the Appellate Body took into account negotiating history of relevant GATT/WTO documents. See Panel Report, *US – Anti-Dumping Act of 1916*, WT/DS136/R, adopted September 26, 2000, ¶¶ 6.201–202 (discussing one historical document relating to the negotiation of the Havana Charter and the GATT, i.e., the Report of the Working Party on Modifications to the General Agreement, which was adopted by the CONTRACTING PARTIES on September 1–2, 1948); *Korea – Measures Affecting Imports of Fresh, Chilled and Frozen Beef*, WT/DS161/R, adopted January 10, 2001, ¶¶ 539–562 (discussing the negotiating history of the 1989 GATT Committee on Balance-of-Payments Restrictions Consultations and other historical documents); Panel Report, *US – Measures Relating Exports Restraints as Subsidies*, WT/DS194/R, adopted August 23, 2001, ¶ 8.64 (stating that negotiating history can be invoked as supplementary means of interpretation), ¶ 8.65 (discussing the negotiating history of the *SCM Agreement*); Appellate Body Report, *US – Definitive Safeguard Measures on Imports of Circular Welded Carbon Quality Line Pipe from Korea*, WT/DS202/AB/R, adopted March 8, 2002, ¶¶ 174–75, n.171 (looking to the GATT *acquis* and the relevant negotiating history of some treaty provisions); Appellate Body Report, *US – Countervailing Duties on Certain Corrosion-Resistant Carbon Steel Flat Products from Germany*, WT/DS213/AB/R, adopted December 19, 2002, ¶ 90 (Recourse to the negotiating history of the SCM Agreement); Panel Report on *EC – Trade Description on Sardines*, WT/DS231/R, adopted October 23, 2002, ¶¶ 7.134–7.136 (analysing the historical documents of the Codex Committee on Fish and Fishery Products and the Codex Alimentarius Commission); Appellate Body Report, *EC – Conditions for the Granting of Tariff Preferences to Developing Countries*, WT/DS246/AB/R, adopted April 20, 2004, ¶¶ 107, 108 (reviewing the history of the Enabling Clause).

50 The Bluebook: A Uniform System of Citation (Columbia Law Review Ass'n et al. (eds), 17th edn 2000) [hereinafter the Bluebook].

51 The Chicago Manual of Style (The University of Chicago Press 15th edn 2003).

52 See, e.g., The Bluebook, supra note 50, T.2, at 257–58.

CHAPTER 1
History of National Treatment in China

Historically and internationally, national treatment originated from treaties,[1] which is also the case for China. In the search for an understanding of treatment of foreign-funded banks in today's China, an exploration of the history of national treatment in China, especially in China's treaties, can be of immense value.[2] To study the history of national treatment in China is useful, and in many instances indispensable. Through the historical analysis, one can discover the origins and the evolution of national treatment in China and the reasons for its fall and rise, thus developing an historical interpretation of national treatment in China's present, which lays a foundation for further study of the relations between national treatment and China's existing banking law.

---

1 See SCHWARZENBERGER, INTERNATIONAL LAW AND ORDER 130 (Stevens & Sons 1971) (stating that national treatment and MFN clauses first appeared in the commercial treaties concluded during the twelfth century between England and Continental Powers); see also ARTHUR NUSSBAUM, A CONCISE HISTORY OF THE LAW OF NATIONS 33 (The Macmillan Company, rev. 1958) (stating that the national treatment clause is found in franchises granted by medieval rulers and early treaties); H. NEUFELD, THE INTERNATIONAL PROTECTION OF PRIVATE CREDITORS FROM THE TREATIES OF WESTPHALIA TO THE CONGRESS OF VIENNA (1648–1815) 112–13 (A.W. Sijthoff, Leiden, 1971) (mentioning several early treaties containing national treatment – the Treaty of Nijmwegen of 1679, the Treaty of France with the Cities of the Hanseatic League of 1716, the Treaty of France with Hungary and Bohemia of 1766, the Pinckney Treaty between the United States and Spain of 1795, the Russian-Swedish Treaty of 1801, and the Swedish-Danish Treaty of 1809).

2 But the study of the history of national treatment in China's treaties has long been neglected. Indeed, the study of the history of MFN treatment in China's treaties outweighs that of national treatment. For the history of MFN treatment in China's treaties, see Huang Jing, *Zuihuiguo Tiaokuan zhi Youlai yu Bianqian* [Origin and Evolution of the MFN Clause], in 6 MINGUO FAXUE LUNWEN JINGCUI: GUOJI FALÜ PIAN [THE CREAM OF LEGAL PAPERS OF THE REPUBLICAN PERIOD: INTERNATIONAL LAW] 411–22 (He Qinhua and Li Xiuqing (eds), Law Press China 2004); WANG TIEYA, *1943 Nian Zhongmei Xinyue yu Zuihuiguo Tiaokuan* [1943 Sino-US New Treaty and the MFN Clause], in WANG TIEYA WENXUAN [SELECTED PAPERS OF WANG TIEYA] 594–99 (Deng Zhenglai (ed.), China Univ. of Political Science and Law Press 2003); Wang Yi, *Zhonghua Renmin Gongheguo zai Guoji Maoyi zhong de Zuihuiguo Daiyu Wenti* [The PRC's MFN Treatment in International Trade], in 1990 CHINESE Y.B. INT'L L. 125–51.

I. Pre-1840

In general, China was an open country before the Ming Dynasty (1368–1644). Normal foreign communication and foreign trade had been continuous for more than one thousand years after the Silk Road was made in the Han Dynasty (206 BC–220 AD). During that period, China did not exclude outsiders, but treated them equally without discrimination.[3] There were so many foreign merchants in China that the Tang Dynasty (618 AD–907 AD) even made special rules to deal with foreign-related cases.[4] However, the Ming Dynasty officially banned maritime trade with foreign countries,[5] and this closed-door policy was maintained by the Qing [*Ch'ing*] Dynasty (1644–1911). Under the closed-door policy,[6] the Qing Dynasty, which was able to support itself in an autarky system, formulated many rules, most of which were excessively strict, to restrain foreigners and foreign trade.[7] This situation continued till 1840.

1840 is a watershed year in China's history. It was the beginning of modern Chinese history, and the end of traditional relations between China and foreign countries. From the fourteenth century to 1840, the relationship between China and foreign countries was a tribute [*chaogong*] relationship.[8] China was the receiver

---

3 See Guo Tingyi [Kuo Ting-Yee], 1 Jindai Zhongguo Shigang [A Short History of Modern China] 3 (Hong Kong Chinese University Press, 3rd edn, 1986).

4 According to the *Yonghui* Law [*Yonghuilü*] (651 AD) of the Tang Dynasty, the cases between foreigners from the same country should apply to that country's law, and the cases between foreigners of one country and those of another country should apply to Chinese law, i.e., the law of the Tang Dynasty [*zhu huawairen, tonglei zixiang fanzhe, geyi benshufa; yilei xiangfanzhe, yi falü lun*], see ZhangSun Wuji, Tanglü Shuyi [Commentary on the Law of the Tang Dynasty] 133 (Zhonghua Book Company 1983); see also Chongtufa Lun [Study on Law of Conflict] 38 (Ding Wei and Chen Zhidong (eds), Law Press China 1996).

5 See generally Chao Zhongchen, Mingdai Haijin Yu Haiwai Maoyi [Ban on Maritime Trade and Overseas Trade During the Ming Dynasty] (People's Publishing House 2005).

6 For the "closed-door" policy adopted by the Qing Dynasty, see Lin Zengping, 1 Zhongguo Jindai Shi [The History of Modern China] 17–18 (Hunan Peoples' Publishing House 1979); Bainian Zhongguo Duiwai Guanxi: 1840–1940 [China's Foreign Relations of the One Hundred Years: 1840–1949] 6–10 (Zong Chengkang ed., Nanjing Univ. Press 1993).

7 For example, foreign merchants could not employ Chinese servants, and foreigners could not ride in a sedan chair (an ordinary transportation mode for people at that time). More importantly, foreign merchants could not decide the price of their goods and they were also blackmailed by government officials. Hosea Ballou Morse, 1 Zhonghua Diguo Duiwai Guanxishi [The International Relations of the Chinese Empire] 78–81, 89, 98–99 (Zhang Huiwen et al. (trans.), Shanghai Bookstore Press 2000).

8 There are different opinions on the period of the tribute system. John King Fairbank considered that China's tribute system originated from the Zhou Dynasty (from about 1100 BC–221 BC); Morris Rossabi was of the view that it was from the Han Dynasty;

of foreign tribute, foreign countries were the tributary countries, and foreigners were usually considered barbarians [*yi*].[9] With traditional prejudice, the last feudal dynasty in Chinese history, the Qing Dynasty, regarded itself as superior to foreign states and foreigners, and was not willing to provide equal treatment to them.

II. 1840–1911

A. Prerogative Treatment

In 1840, the First Opium War (1840–1842) broke out between China and Britain.[10] After China's defeat, foreign countries were unwilling to provide equal treatment to China.[11] The Western powers obtained a large number of special rights in China through a series of unequal treaties with the Qing Dynasty. For example, the Treaty of Nanjing [*Nanking*] (1842) provided that China should negotiate with Britain regarding China's tariffs and charges, the so-called "negotiated tariffs" [*xieding guanshui*], under which China was deprived of its tariffs autonomy.[12] Furthermore, China partly lost its jurisdiction by the imposition of "consular jurisdiction" [*lingshi caipanquan*],[13]

Henry Serruys tended to think that it stemmed from the Ming Dynasty. See JAMES L. HEVIA, CHERISHING MEN FROM AFAR 10 (Deng Changchun (trans.), China Social Science Archives Press 2002) (originally Duke Univ. Press 1995). Even if there was a tribute system before the Ming Dynasty, the tribute was usually a system in name only. See XIE HAIPING, TANGDAI LIUHUA WAIGUOREN SHENGHUO KAOSHU [STUDY ON THE LIFE OF FOREIGNERS IN CHINA DURING THE TANG DYNASTY] 209 (Taiwan Commercial Press 1978) (stating that "tribute" and "frontier trade" [*hushi*] had the same meaning during the Tang Dynasty); for the ancient tribute system relations between China and foreign countries, see Gretchen Harders-Chen, *China MFN: A Reaffirmation of Tradition or Regulatory Reform*? 5 MINN. J. GLOBAL TRADE 381, 383–87 (1996).

9 But see L. TUNG, CHINA AND SOME PHASES OF INTERNATIONAL LAW 58 (Oxford Univ. Press 1940) (arguing that *yi* does not mean "barbarian", but "foreign country").

10 For the history of the First Opium War, see 1 LIN ZENGPING, supra note 6, at 1–61.

11 JIANG TINGFU, ZHONGGUO JINDAISHI [MODERN HISTORY OF CHINA] 9 (Shanghai Classics Publishing House 1999).

12 See ZHONGGUO FAZHISHI GANGYAO [OUTLINE OF CHINESE LEGAL HISTORY] 287 (Zhang Jinfan (ed.), China Univ. of Political Science and Law Press 1986).

13 The concept of "consular jurisdiction" was first described in the Jiangnan Agreement Dealing with Problems Arising from the Treaty of Nanjing [*Jiangnan Shanhou Zhangcheng*] (1842). GUO WEIDONG, ZHUANZHE: YI ZAOQI ZHONGYING GUANXI HE "NANJING TIAOYUE" WEI KAOCHA ZHONGXIN [A TURNING POINT: FOCUSING ON THE EARLY SINO-BRITISH RELATIONS AND THE TREATY OF NANJING] 482–83 (Hebei People's Publishing House 2003). But see Cheng Daode, *Shishu Zhonghua Minguo Zhengfu Feichu Lieqiang Zaihua Lingshi Caipanquan de Duiwai Jiaoshe* [On the Negotiations over the Abrogation of Consular Jurisdiction in China by the Chinese Republican Government], REPUBLICAN ARCHIVES 86,

i.e., extraterritoriality.[14] In total, there were nineteen countries which enjoyed "consular jurisdiction" in China.[15] In most situations, foreign defendants in China were not subject to Chinese laws and jurisdiction, but to those of their home state, and foreign-related litigation was dealt with by foreign consuls in China,[16] or by mixed courts [*huishen gongxie*] composed of foreign consuls and Chinese judges.[17] Britain and the United States even established courts in China, i.e., His Britannic Majesty's Supreme Court for China (1865) and the United States Court for China (1906).[18] Under the unequal treaty system, China's superior status under the old tribute system was reversed completely. During the late Qing Dynasty, foreigners in China enjoyed prerogatives beyond Chinese law and were, in most cases, granted more favourable treatment than that accorded to the native Chinese.

B. Unilateral National Treatment

Throughout the Qing Dynasty, there were few national treatment articles in Sino-foreign treaties, and a clear concept of national treatment had not been developed.

---

86 (1986, no. 1) (stating that consular jurisdiction in China originates from the Sino-British Commerce Agreement of the Five Ports [*Wukou Tongshang Zhangcheng*] (1843).

14 Generally speaking, there is little difference between "consular jurisdiction" and "extraterritoriality". See ZHOU GENGSHENG, 1 GUOJIFA [PUBLIC INTERNATIONAL LAW] 296–98 (Commercial Press 1976). For extraterritoriality in China, see SHIU SHUN LIU, EXTRATERRITORIALITY: ITS RISE AND ITS DECLINE (Columbia University 1925); U.S. DEPARTMENT OF STATE, REPORT OF THE COMMISSION ON EXTRATERRITORIALITY IN CHINA, Peking, September 16, 1926 (Government Printing Office 1926); G.W. KEETON, THE DEVELOPMENT OF EXTRATERRITORIALITY IN CHINA (Longmans, Green and Co. 1928); THOMAS F. MILLARD, THE END OF EXTERRITORIALITY IN CHINA, 2 vols (The A.B.C. Press 1931); JOHN CARTER VINCENT, THE EXTRATERRITORIAL SYSTEM IN CHINA: FINAL PHASE (East Asian Research Center, Harvard University 1970); WESLEY R. FISHEL, THE END OF EXTRATERRITORIALITY IN CHINA (Octagon Books 1974); Harold Scott Quigley, *Extraterritoriality in China*, 20 AM. J. INT'L L. 46–68 (1926); Crawford M. Bishop, *American Extraterritorial Jurisdiction in China*, 20 AM. J. INT'L L. 281–99 (1926).

15 YE ZUHAO, FEICHU BUPINGDENG TIAOYUE [ABOLISHING THE UNEQUAL TREATIES] 40 (Zhengzhong Press 1967).

16 See, e.g., Article 13 of the Sino-British Commerce Agreement of the Five Ports (1843) and Article 21 of the 1844 Sino-US Wangxia Treaty (or the Treaty of Wanghia), in ZHONGGUO JINDAI BUPINGDENG TIAOYUE XUANBIAN YU JIESHAO [COMPILATION AND INTRODUCTION OF THE UNEQUAL TREATIES OF MODERN CHINA] 28–30, 33–38 (Liang Weiji and Zheng Zemin (9eds), China Radio and Television Publishing House 1993) (hereinafter UNEQUAL TREATIES OF MODERN CHINA).

17 Chinese judges' role in the mixed courts was only nominal. See CHINESE LEGAL HISTORY 349 (Zhang Jinfan et al. (eds), Qunzhong Press 1982).

18 FEI CHENGKANG, ZHONGGUO ZUJIESHI [THE HISTORY OF CONCESSION IN CHINA] 127 (Shanghai Academy of Social Sciences Press 1991); WANG LIMIN, SHANGHAI FAZHISHI [SHANGHAI'S LEGAL HISTORY] 275 (Shanghai People's Press 1998).

For instance, the term "national treatment" does not appear in an authoritative book on the status of foreigners in China during the late Qing Dynasty.[19] It was virtually unnecessary for foreigners to demand equal status with the Chinese because of their already superior position. Nevertheless, the superior status of foreigners was not absolute or omnipresent, and neither the extraterritoriality nor the "negotiated tariffs" forbade the Chinese government to levy inland taxes and charges on foreigners in China. As an offset of the prerogatives enjoyed by foreigners, the Qing Dynasty tried to restrict the activities of foreigners as much as possible.[20] For example, although the Western powers obtained inland navigation rights in China, China levied more taxes on cargoes carried by foreign commercial ships on China's inland rivers than on cargoes carried by Chinese domestic ships.[21] Thus, the Western powers found that, under some circumstances, they needed to obtain equal rights with the Chinese, which gave rise to national treatment content in Sino-foreign treaties.

The first Sino-foreign treaty including national treatment content is the Supplemental Treaty between the United States and China concluded on November 17, 1880,[22] providing that China and the United States shall not levy higher duties on vessels and cargoes of the other party than those imposed on its own vessels and cargoes.[23] This national treatment article was once successfully used by the British Minister at Beijing as a reason to protest at an exemption measure

---

19 See generally WELLINGTON KOO, THE STATUS OF ALIENS IN CHINA (Columbia Univ. Press 1912).

20 FEI CHENGKANG, supra note 18, at 10–11.

21 See the arguments on the different treatment of foreign ships and Chinese domestic ships during the negotiations of the Sino-British Treaty for the Extension of the Commercial Relations, in XINCHOU HEYUE DINGLI YIHOU DE SHANGYUE TANPAN [COMMERCIAL TREATY NEGOTIATIONS POST THE BOXER PROTOCOL] 24–25, 33–34, 116–18 (Research Office of the Customs General Administration of the PRC (ed.), Zhonghua Book Company 1994).

22 Supplemental Treaty Between the United States and China, signed on November 17, 1880, effective on July 19, 1881, 1 OLD SINO-FOREIGN TREATIES 380–81 (Wang Tieya (ed.), Joint Publishing House 1957, reprinted in 1982).

23 Id, art. 3, providing reciprocally as follows:

The United States hereby promise and agree that *no other kind or higher rate of tonnage dues or duties* for imports shall be imposed or levied in the ports of the United States upon vessels wholly belonging to the subjects of His Imperial Majesty and coming, either directly or by way of any foreign port, from any of the ports of China which are open to foreign trade, to the ports of the United States; or returning therefrom, either directly or by way of any foreign port, to any of the open ports of China; or upon the produce, manufactures, or merchandise imported in the same from China or from any foreign country, than are imposed or levied on vessels of other nations which make no discrimination against the United States in tonnage dues or duties on imports, exports, or coastwise trade; *or than are imposed or levied on vessels and cargoes of citizens of the United States* (emphasis added).

adopted by the Qing Dynasty to subsidize China's domestic merchants.[24] National treatment obligations in this treaty were bilateral and reciprocal, but the reciprocity did not spread to other treaties during the late Qing Dynasty. In other treaties with national treatment content, national treatment obligations were unilateral and only in favour of foreign countries.

First, the Sino-Japanese Protocol (1896) provided that the tax China imposed on the articles manufactured by the Japanese subjects shall neither be other than that payable by the Chinese subjects, nor higher.[25] Second, according to the Sino-British Treaty for the Extension of Commercial Relations (1902),[26] and the Sino-Japanese Treaty for the Extension of Commercial Relations (1903),[27] houses and small piers rented by British merchants and Japanese merchants were to be taxed on an equal footing with the Chinese.[28] Third, according to the Sino-US Treaty for the Extension of Commercial Relations (1903),[29] machine-made cotton yarn and cloth manufactured in China, whether by foreigners or by Chinese, was to be taxed on an equal footing.[30] Fourth, in the Sino-British Conditions on Banning Opium concluded in 1911,[31] there was an article about uniform tax on the opium trade before its final elimination, requiring that the tax on the British opium trade should be the same as the tax on the Chinese domestic opium trade.[32]

---

24 See GEORGE N. CURZON, PROBLEMS OF THE FAR EAST 337 (Archibald Constable and Co. 1896).

25 Sino-Japanese Protocol [Zhongri Gongli Wenping], art. 3, signed on October 19, 1896 in Beijing, 1 OLD SINO-FOREIGN TREATIES, supra note 22, at 685–86.

26 Sino-British Treaty for the Extension of Commercial Relations [*Zhongying Xuyi Tongshang Xingchuan Tiaoyue*], signed at Shanghai, September 5, 1902, in 2 OLD SINO-FOREIGN TREATIES 101–114 (Wang Tieya (ed.), Joint Publishing House 1959, reprinted in 1982).

27 Sino-Japanese Treaty for the Extension of Commercial Relations [*Zhongri Tongshang Xingchuan Xuding Xiaoyue*], signed at Shanghai, October 8, 1903, in 2 OLD SINO-FOREIGN TREATIES, supra note 26, at 192–200.

28 Sino-British Treaty for the Extension of the Commercial Relations, supra note 26, Annex 3, art. 3; Sino-Japanese Treaty for the Extension of Commercial Relations, supra note 26, Annex 1, art. 3.

29 Sino-US Treaty for the Extension of Commercial Relations [*Zhongmei Tongshang Xingchuan Xuding Tiaoyue*], signed at Shanghai, October 8, 1903, in UNITED STATES RELATIONS WITH CHINA, Department of State Publications 3573, Far Eastern Series 30, 417–26 (released in August 1949) [hereinafter U.S. RELATIONS WITH CHINA].

30 Id. art. 4.

31 2 OLD SINO-FOREIGN TREATIES, supra note 26, at 711–14. For the background of 1911 Sino-British Conditions on Banning Opium, see 3 MORSE, supra note 7, at 465.

32 1911 opium-banning agreement, art. 6, in 2 OLD SINO-FOREIGN TREATIES, supra note 26, at 712; see also CHEN ZHIQI, ZHONGGUO JINDAI WAIJIAOSHI [FOREIGN RELATIONS HISTORY OF MODERN CHINA] 1167 (Nantian Book Press 1993); YAN HUIQING, YAN HUIQING ZIZHUAN: YIWEI MINGUO YUANLAO DE LISHI JIYI [EAST-WEST KALEIDOSCOPE 1877–1944: AN AUTOBIOGRAPHY BY W.W. YEN] 84 (Wu Jianyong et al. (trans.), Commercial Press 2003).

Three main characteristics of the emergence of national treatment in the late Qing Dynasty can be summarized as follows. In the first place, the scope of national treatment was very narrow. Each article only concerned one specific item, e.g. tonnage dues or duties, cotton yarn and cloth, houses and small piers, or the opium trade. In the second place, national treatment obligations in most of the treaties were unilateral and binding only on China, not on foreign countries. Under such unilateral national treatment, China promised that foreigners in China could enjoy some form of national treatment, but the Western states did not promise that the Chinese in foreign countries could obtain the same treatment. During the nineteenth century, the general practice of national treatment obligations in treaties of the world was bilateral and reciprocal,[33] but this was not the case for China's treaties during the nineteenth century and at the beginning of the twentieth century. One writer stated that the rights of reciprocity were so few in number during that period that the term "reciprocity" was almost like a misnomer.[34] The unilaterality of national treatment further indicates that the treaties were unequal.[35] In the third place, national treatment was imposed by Western powers, not granted by the Qing Dynasty on a voluntary basis. The conclusion of the three treaties on the extension of commercial relations with Britain, the United States and Japan was

---

[33] See, e.g., Article V of the Treaty of Amity, Commerce and Navigation between Great Britain and Colombia (1825), http://www.austlii.edu.au/au/other/dfat/treaties/1901/120.html; Article XI of the Convention of Commerce and Navigation between Great Britain and Sweden (including Norway) (1826), http://www.austlii.edu.au/au/other/dfat/treaties/1901/78.html; Article III of the Treaty of Friendship and Commerce between Great Britain and Liberia (1848), http://www.austlii.edu.au/au/other/dfat/treaties/1901/67.html; Article V of the Treaty of Friendship, Commerce and Navigation between Great Britain and Peru (1850), http://www.austlii.edu.au/au/other/dfat/treaties/1901/83.html; Article VI of the Treaty of Commerce and Navigation between Great Britain and Russia (1859), http://www.austlii.edu.au/au/other/dfat/treaties/1901/92.html; Article VI of the Treaty of Commerce and Navigation between Great Britain and Italy (1883), http://www.austlii.edu.au/au/other/dfat/treaties/1901/65.html; Article X of the Treaty of Commerce and Navigation between Great Britain and Japan (1894), http://www.austlii.edu.au/au/other/dfat/treaties/1901/66.html.

[34] Min-Chien Tiz. Tyau, The Legal Obligations Arising out of Treaty Relations Between China and other States 189 (Ch'eng-Wen Publishing Company 1966).

[35] While for most part the unilateral obligation was imposed by Western powers, it also partly resulted from the Qing Dynasty's ignorance of the world outside China and its ignorance of the importance and protection of overseas Chinese. See Li Hongzhang's annotations and commentaries on the draft of the Sino-Japanese Commerce and Navigation Agreement (Li Hongzhang was in charge of China's diplomacy for a long period in the late Qing Dynasty), in Wang Ermin, Wanqing Shangyue Waijiao [The Diplomacy of the Commercial Treaties Between China and Foreign Powers During the Late Qing Dynasty] 113, 114 (Hong Kong Chinese Univ. Press 1998); see also Li Changchuan, Zhongguo Zhimin Shi [China's History of Colony] 292–93 (Commercial Press 1937).

the direct consequence of the unequal Boxer Protocol [*Xinchou Tiaoyue*] (1901)[36] that resulted from the war of the eight Western powers against China for the Boxer Movement.[37] This characteristic can also be illustrated with the negotiations of the Sino-US Treaty for the Extension of Commercial Relations.[38] For example, the US representative, John Goodnow, asked China to exempt all export taxes on machine-made cotton yarn and cloth manufactured in China.[39] To keep the right to levy the export taxes, China was forced to make a compromise by agreeing to levy the taxes on an equal footing.[40]

C. Appearance and Treatment of Foreign-Funded Banks during 1840–1911

In the Chinese language, the word for bank [*yinhang*] made its first appearance in the Southern Tang Dynasty (AD 937–975).[41] However, it did not refer to a bank in a modern sense,[42] but to a gold and silver smith [*yinpu*]. There was not a modern bank in China until Western powers opened the Chinese door with their strong armour and sharp weapons. From modern history of Chinese finance, one can find that the birth of China's domestic banks was later than the arrival of foreign-funded banks in China.

The Oriental Bank [*Liru Yinhang*], one of the British banks, was the first foreign bank in China.[43] In 1847, it opened a branch in Shanghai.[44] Following the Oriental Bank, some other British banks started to enter China. For example, in 1851, the

---

36 The Boxer Protocol was concluded between China and eleven foreign states (Germany, Austria, Belgium, Spain, the United States, France, Britain, Italy, Japan, Holland and Russia) in Beijing on September 7, 1901, in UNEQUAL TREATIES OF MODERN CHINA, supra note 16, at 427–46.

37 For the history of the Boxer Movement (1899–1901), see 2 LIN ZENGPING, supra note 6, at 480–550.

38 For the negotiating history of the treaties, see generally COMMERCIAL TREATY NEGOTIATIONS POST THE BOXER PROTOCOL, supra note 21.

39 Id. at 163, 166.

40 Id. at 177–78.

41 YE SHICHANG AND PAN LIANGUI, ZHONGGUO GUJINDAI JINRONG SHI [THE ANCIENT AND MODERN HISTORY OF CHINESE FINANCE] 78 (Fudan Univ. Press 2001).

42 For the history of modern banks, see RICHARD HILDRETH, THE HISTORY OF BANKS (Routledge/Thoemmes Press 1996).

43 ZHONGGUO JINRONG SHI [HISTORY OF CHINA'S FINANCE] 144 (Hong Jiaguan (ed.), Southwestern Univ. of Finance and Economics Press 2nd edn, 2001) [hereinafter HISTORY OF CHINA'S FINANCE]. The Oriental Bank changed its name to Oriental Banking Corporation in 1851. See LINSUN CHENG, BANKING IN MODERN CHINA: ENTREPRENEURS, PROFESSIONAL MANAGERS, AND THE DEVELOPMENT OF CHINESE BANKS, 1897–1937, at 17, n.31 (Cambridge Univ. Press 2003).

44 WANG JINGYU, WAIGUO ZIBEN ZAI JINDAI ZHONGGUO DE JINRONG HUODONG [FINANCIAL ACTIVITIES OF FOREIGN CAPITAL IN MODERN CHINA] 18 (People's Publishing House 1999).

Commercial Bank of India [*Huilong Yinhang*] set up a branch in Guangzhou.[45] In 1854, the Agra and United Service Bank [*Hejiala Yinhang*], whose head office was in London, established a branch in Shanghai.[46] In the same year, the Mercantile Bank of India, London and China opened a representative office in Shanghai, and one year later it set up another representative office in Guangzhou.[47] In 1857, the Mercantile Bank of India, London and China merged with the Chartered Bank of Asia and changed its name to the Chartered Mercantile Bank of India, London and China [*Youli Yinhang*].[48] In 1858, the Chartered Bank of India, Australia and China [*Maijiali Yinhang,* or *Zhada Yinhang*], also a British bank, set up a branch in Shanghai.[49] During the 1840s and the 1850s, foreign banking capital in China was only from Britain. In 1864, the Hongkong and Shanghai Banking Corporation [*Huifeng Yinhang*, hereinafter the HSBC] was established in Hong Kong.[50] In 1865, the HSBC commenced business[51] and opened a branch in Shanghai.[52]

After 1860, banks from other states began to enter China. In 1860, Compotoir d'Escompte de Paris [*Falanxi Yinhang*] opened a Shanghai operation, mainly engaging in discount business of negotiable instruments.[53] In 1894, Banque de L'Indochine [*Dongfang Huili Yinhang*], another French bank, established a branch in Hong Kong, and in 1899 it set up a branch in Shanghai.[54] In 1890, the Deutsche-Asiatische Bank [*Dehua Yinhang*], a German capital bank, was set up, and its head office was located in Shanghai.[55] In 1893, a Japanese bank, the Yokohama Specie Bank [*Hengbin Zhengjin Yinhang*] set up a branch in Shanghai, which achieved support from the Japanese government.[56] Russia also positively participated in China's financial market. In 1895, the Russo-Asiatic Bank [*Hua'e Daosheng Yinhang*] was established in St Petersburg and set up branches in Shanghai,

---

45 Id.

46 Id. at 19.

47 Id. at 19–20.

48 Id. at 20.

49 History of China's Finance, supra note 43, at 148; Zhaojin Ji, A History of Modern Shanghai Banking: The Rise and Decline of China's Finance Capitalism 44 (M.E. Sharpe 2003).

50 History of China's Finance, supra note 43, at 228.

51 Maurice Collis, Wayfoong, The Hongkong and Shanghai Banking Corporation 24–28 (Faber and Faber 1965).

52 History of China's Finance, supra note 43, at 150.

53 Zhang Guohui, 2 Zhongguo Jinrong Tongshi: 1840–1911 [General History of China's Finance: 1840–1911) 227 (Li Fei et al. (eds), China Financial Publishing House 2003).

54 Id. at 272.

55 Id. at 263.

56 Id. at 265. For the history of the Yokohama Specie Bank in China, see Riben Hengbin Zhengjin Yinhang Zai Hua Huodong Shiliao [Historical Materials of Activities of the Japanese Yokohama Specie Bank in China] (Fu Wenling (ed.), China Finance Publishing House 1992).

Tianjin and Hankou a year later.[57] The first American bank to enter China was the International Banking Corporation, which opened a Shanghai branch in 1902.[58]

In the whole nineteenth century, there were twenty-one foreign-funded banks in China, spreading to twenty big cities.[59] In contrast to the prosperity of foreign-funded banks in China, during that period, there was only one Chinese domestic bank, i.e. the Imperial Bank of China [*Zhongguo Tongshang Yinhang*], a joint-stock bank established in 1897,[60] more than 50 years later than the establishment of the first foreign bank in China. As a matter of fact, China's financial market was in the hands of foreign-funded banks during the late Qing Dynasty.[61]

From the First Opium War to the end of the Qing Dynasty, foreign-funded banks in China enjoyed special treatment, such as the right of issuing paper currency,[62] right

---

[57] Id. at 267.

[58] Id. at 273. It must be noted that the International Banking Corporation was acquired by the National City Bank of New York in 1915. See PETER STARR, CITIBANK: A CENTURY IN ASIA 30, 45 (Editions Didier Millet 2002). For the history of the Citybank in China, see MEIGUO HUAQI YINHANG ZAI HUA SHILIAO [HISTORICAL MATERIALS OF THE AMERICAN CITYBANK IN CHINA] (Financial Institute of the People's Bank of China (ed.), China Finance Publishing House 1990).

[59] WANG JINGYU, supra note 44, at 299.

[60] HISTORY OF CHINA'S FINANCE, supra note 43, at 168. The application for establishing the Imperial Bank of China was approved by the Emperor *Guangxu* of the Qing Dynasty in 1896. See Approval Document of the Council of State on Shengxuanhuai's Application for Opening a Bank [*Junjichu guanyu Shengxuanhuai Kaiban Yinhang de Piwen*], promulgated by the Council of State on November 12, 1896, in 5 SHENG XUANHUAI'S ARCHIVES: THE IMPERIAL BANK OF CHINA 8 (Chen Xulu et al. (eds), Shanghai People's Publishing House 2000); see also LINSUN CHENG, supra note 43, at 25–29. It must be noted that the bank had another English name, Commercial Bank of China. See BARN ELMER LEE, MODERN BANKING REFORMS IN CHINA 31 (1941) (PhD dissertation, Columbia University) (UMI, printed in 2002).

[61] 1 ZHONGGUO JINDAI JINGJISHI [ECONOMIC HISTORY OF MODERN CHINA] 193–98 (Politics and Economics Department of Beijing Normal Univ. (ed.), People's Publishing House 1976).

[62] WANG JINGYU, supra note 44, at 170–75. It must be noted that the unequal treaties in the late Qing Dynasty did not authorize foreign banks to issue paper currency in China. However, the Qing Dynasty did not prevent foreign banks from issuing paper currency. So issuing paper currency became a practice [*xiguan*] of foreign banks in China. See Yao Chuanjü, *Jinrong Zhidu Siyi* [Personal Opinions on Financial System] (1924), in 3 COMPILATION OF ARCHIVES OF THE HISTORY OF THE REPUBLIC OF CHINA [*Zhonghua Minguoshi Dang'An Ziliao Huibian*], "Finance", part 1, at 224, 231 (The Second Historical Archives of China (ed.), Jiangsu Ancient Books Publishing House 1991).

of foreign exchange, special lending right for special projects.[63] As foreign entities, they also enjoyed extraterritorial rights in China.[64]

Chinese banking legislation started from 1904 with the appearance of the Thirty-Two Provisions for Pilot Banking [*Shiban Yinhang Zhangcheng Sanshier Tiao*].[65] In 1908, the Qing Dynasty promulgated the General Banking Regulation,[66] Regulation the Da Qing Bank,[67] Regulation on Savings Banks,[68] Regulation on Industry and Agriculture Banks,[69] which are early banking laws in China's history.[70] The banking regulations covered the activities of banks,[71] conditions and requirements for establishment and operation of banks, etc.[72] However, owing to the existence of extraterritorial rights, foreign-funded banks were not subject to the Chinese banking regulations.[73] In fact, China did not have any foreign banking law before and during the Qing Dynasty.

---

63 The Qing Dynasty raised a huge amount of loans from foreign banks, e.g. Russia-France Borrowing (1895), Britain-Germany Borrowing (1896), Second Britain-Germany Borrowing (1898), Railway Borrowing (1898–1911). *See* HISTORY OF CHINA'S FINANCE, supra note 43, at 163–66.

64 WESTEL W. WILLOUGHBY, FOREIGN RIGHT AND INTERESTS IN CHINA 354 (Wang Shaofang (trans.), Beijing Joint Publishing House 1957); LEE, supra note 60, at 15.

65 Zhu Sihuang, *Minyuanlai Woguo zhi Yinhangye* [*Chinese Banking from the Beginning of the Republic of China*], in Minguo Jingjishi: Yinhang Zhoubao Sanshi Zhounian Jiniankan [ECONOMIC HISTORY OF THE REPUBLIC OF CHINA: A SPECIAL ISSUE FOR THE THIRTIETH ANNIVERSARY OF THE BANKING WEEKLY] 28, 49 (Shanghai Banking Society 1947).

66 General Banking Regulation [*Yinhang Tongxing Zeli*], issued by the Ministry of Revenue [*Duzhi Bu*] of the Qing Dynasty on January 16, 1908, in Huangchao Xu Wenxian Tongkao, vol 65, Guoyongkao San, Yinhang [SUPPLEMENTARY DOCUMENTS OF THE DYNASTY, vol 65, Banking].

67 Regulation the Da Qing Bank [Da Qing Yinhang Zeli], issued by the Ministry of Revenue of the Qing Dynasty on January 16, 1908, in SUPPLEMENTARY DOCUMENTS OF THE DYNASTY, vol 65, Banking.

68 Regulation on Savings Banks [*Chuxu Yinhang Zeli*], issued by the Ministry of Revenue of the Qing Dynasty on January 16, 1908, in SUPPLEMENTARY DOCUMENTS OF THE DYNASTY, vol 65, Banking.

69 Regulation on Industry and Agriculture Banks [*Zhiye Yinhang Zeli*], issued by the Ministry of Revenue of the Qing Dynasty on January 16, 1908, in SUPPLEMENTARY DOCUMENTS OF THE DYNASTY, vol. 65, Banking.

70 XIE ZHENMIN, ZHONGHUA MINGUO LIFASHI [LEGISLATIVE HISTORY OF THE REPUBLIC OF CHINA], Part II, 851 (China Univ. of Political Science and Law Press 2000) (Zhengzhong Press 1937).

71 General Banking Regulation of 1908, supra note 66, art. 1.

72 Id. arts. 2, 3, 4, 5, 6, 7, 8, 9.

73 CHENG LIN, ZHONGGUO JINDAI YINHANG ZHIDU JIANSHE SIXIANG YANJIU: 1859–1949 [STUDIES ON THOUGHTS OF BUILDING THE BANKING SYSTEM IN MODERN CHINA: 1859–1949] 59 (Shanghai Univ. of Finance and Economics Press 1999); see also LINSUN CHENG, supra note 43, at 18; LEE, supra note 60.

III. 1912–1949

A. Bilateral National Treatment in the 1920s and 1930s

The Qing Dynasty was overthrown by the 1911 *Xinhai* Revolution [*Xinhai Geming*][74] led by Dr *Sun Zhongshan* [*Sun Yat-Sen*].[75] On January 1, 1912, the Republic of China (ROC) [*Zhonghua Minguo*] was founded, and the new government, in exchange for recognition from Western powers,[76] succeeded to all treaties between the Qing Dynasty and foreign states,[77] and recognized foreigners' prerogatives based on those treaties.[78] After the First World War (1914–1918), China, as one of the victors of the war,[79] proposed to repeal foreign state prerogatives, such as "negotiated tariffs" and "consular jurisdiction" at both the Paris Peace Conference (1919) and the Washington Conference (1921–1922).[80] But the two Conferences did not satisfy the demands from China.[81]

---

[74] For the history of the Xinhai Revolution, see XINHAI GEMING SHI [THE XINHAI REVOLUTION HISTORY], 3 vols. (ZHANG KAIYUAN AND LIN ZENGPING (eds), People's Publishing House 1980–1981).

[75] See generally SHANG MINGXUAN, SUN ZHONGSHAN BIOGRAPHY (Beijing Publishing House 2nd edn, 1981).

[76] Wang Liangbin, *Zhonghua Minguo Jianli Zhichu guanyu Chengren Wenti de Jiaoshe* [Negotiations on Recognition Issue during the Early Days of the Founding of the ROC], in JINDAI ZHONGGUO WAIJIAO YU GUOJIFA [DIPLOMACY IN MODERN CHINA AND INTERNATIONAL LAW] 93–110 (Cheng Daode (ed.), Xiandai Publishing House 1993).

[77] Open Telegram of the Foreign Ministry of the ROC to Diplomatic Representatives of Foreign States and the International Peace Conference on the Establishment of the Interim Government of the ROC [*Waijiaobu guanyu Minguo Tongyi Linshi Zhengfu Chengli Zhi ge Waijiao Daibiao bing Wanguo Baohehui Tongdian*], March 11, 1912, in 3 COMPILATION OF ARCHIVES OF THE HISTORY OF THE REPUBLIC OF CHINA, "Diplomacy", at 26 (The Second Historical Archives of China (ed.), Jiangsu Ancient Books Publishing House 1991).

[78] Yuan Shikai [*Yüan Shih-K'ai*], *President's Inaugural Declaration,* 10 Ocotober 1913, in 2 ZHONGGUO JINDAI FAZHISHI ZILIAO XUANBIAN [SELECTIONS OF MATERIALS OF CHINA'S MODERN LEGAL HISTORY] 2, 3 (Legal History Unit of the Law Faculty of China Renmin University, 1980); see also ZHOU GUCHENG, 2 ZHONGGUO TONGSHI [GENERAL HISTORY OF CHINA] 445 (Shanghai People's Publishing House 1957).

[79] China declared war against Germany and Austria on August 14, 1917, see Note of the Foreign Ministry of the ROC on China's Entering the War Addressed to the Ambassadors [*Waijiaobu guanyu Zhongguo Canzhan zhi Geguo Gongshi Zhaohui*], August 14, 1917, in 3 COMPILATION OF ARCHIVES OF THE HISTORY OF THE REPUBLIC OF CHINA, "Diplomacy", at 393 (The Second Historical Archives of China (ed.), Jiangsu Ancient Books Publishing House 1991).

[80] Cheng Daode, supra note 13, at 89–90.

[81] Id. see also Jiang Xiangze, *Zhongguo he Huashengdun Huiyi* [China and the Washington Conference], in ZHONGMEI GUANXISHI LUNWENJI [TREATISES ON THE SINO-US RELATION HISTORY] 272, 272–88 (Chongqing Publishing House 1985).

Sino-German Treaty (1921)

Although China failed to repeal "consular jurisdiction" at the Paris Peace Conference and the Washington Conference, China did repeal Germany's prerogative of "consular jurisdiction" after the end of the First World War through the Sino-German Treaty [*Zhongde xieyue*].[82] Paragraph 2 of Article 3 of the Sino-German Treaty states that:

> Life and property of the people of the two parties shall be under the jurisdiction of the place where they are located. The people of the two parties shall abide by the law of the place where they are located. Taxes and charges that one party levies on the people coming from another party shall not exceed what it should levy on its own people.

Unquestionably, the last sentence of the paragraph could be regarded as a national treatment clause. It is noteworthy that the early use of the term of national treatment in the Chinese language also followed the 1921 Sino-German Treaty.[83]

Moreover, in 1925, China and Austria signed the Sino-Austrian Commercial Treaty,[84] providing national treatment to one another with respect to court access rights,[85] labour protection,[86] inland taxes and charges,[87] heritage taxes,[88] housing taxes,[89] etc.

Compared to the rudimentary form and the narrow scope of national treatment articles in treaties signed during the late Qing Dynasty, the national treatment articles in the 1921 Sino-German Treaty and the 1925 Sino-Austrian Commercial

---

[82] Sino-German Treaty, signed on May 20, 1921, in 3 Compilation of Archives of the History of the Republic of China, "Diplomacy", at 954–55 (The Second Historical Archives of China (ed.), Jiangsu Ancient Books Publishing House 1991); also available in 3 Waijiao Wendu [Diplomatic Documents] 963–64 (Chinese National Library Documentary Microfilm Reproduction Centre 2004).

[83] See Zheng Bin [*Cheng Pin*], Zhongguo Guoji Shangyue Lun [A Treatise on Commercial Treaty Relations Between China and Other States] 185–86 (The Commercial Press 1925) (translating national treatment into Chinese as "*nei guomin daiyu*"). At that time, some Chinese scholars confused the treaty articles providing equal treatment between foreigners and Chinese with MFN treatment. See Min-Ch'ien T.Z. Tyau, Zhongguo Guoji Tiaoyue Yiwu Lun [The Legal Obligations Arising out of Treaty Relations Between China and Other States], ch. 3, at 33 (Commercial Press, 4th edn, 1927).

[84] Sino-Austrian Commercial Treaty, in 3 Compilation of Old Sino-Foreign Treaties and Agreements [*Zhongwai Jiuyuezhang Huibian*], at 570–73 (Wang Tieya (ed.), Joint Publishing House 1962, reprinted in 1982) [hereinafter 3 Old Sino-Foreign Treaties].

[85] Id. art. 4.

[86] Id. art. 5.

[87] Id. art. 8.

[88] Id. art. 10.

[89] Id. art. 11.

Treaty have a relatively broader scope and more closely resemble a modern national treatment clause. Moreover, unlike the unilateral national treatment obligations in the treaties signed during the late Qing Dynasty, national treatment obligations in the Sino-German Treaty and the Sino-Austrian Commercial Treaty were bilateral and reciprocal, so the national treatment clauses in the two treaties were equal clauses. Indeed, the Sino-German Treaty is generally recognized as the first equal treaty between China and a foreign country after the First Opium War.[90]

Tariffs Treaties (1928)

In order to regain tariffs autonomy from the Western powers, in 1928, the ROC signed seven tariffs treaties [*Guanshui Tiaoyue*] with the United States, Germany, Norway, Holland, Sweden, Britain and France, all of which contained bilateral national treatment articles.[91] China agreed to provide national treatment to foreign states in the tariffs treaties in exchange for recognition of China's tariffs autonomy that had been forfeited after the First Opium War.[92] The inclusion of national treatment in the treaties was criticized by some Chinese, such as Zhou Gengsheng,

---

[90] Yan Huiqing, supra note 32, at 150; see also Ye Zuhao, supra note 15, at 77; Qian Yishi, Zhongguo Waijiao Shi [Chinese Diplomatic History] 163–66 (Shenghuo Bookstore 1947).

[91] See, e.g., The Treaty between the United States and China Regulating Tariff Relations, July 25, 1928, art. 1, in U.S. Relations with China, supra note 29, at 445–46 reads:

The nationals of neither of the High Contracting Parties shall be compelled under any pretext whatever to pay within the territories of the other Party any duties, internal charges or taxes upon their importations and exportations other or higher than those paid by nationals of the country or by nationals of any other country.

Strictly speaking, this article is a mixture of national treatment and MFN treatment. See also Sino-German Tariff Treaty (signed at Nanjing, August 17, 1928), art. 1, in 3 Old Sino-Foreign Treaties, supra note 84, at 630–31; Sino-Norwegian Tariff Treaty (signed at Shanghai, November 12, 1928), art. 1, in 3 Old Sino-Foreign Treaties, supra note 84, at 641–42; Sino-Dutch Tariff Treaty (signed at Nanjing, December 19, 1928), art. 1, in 3 Old Sino-Foreign Treaties, supra note 84, at 653–54; Sino-Swedish Tariff Treaty (signed at Nanjing, December 20, 1928), art. 1, in 3 Old Sino-Foreign Treaties, supra note 84, at 668–69; Sino-British Tariff Treaty (signed at Nanjing, December 20, 1928), art. 2, in 3 Old Sino-Foreign Treaties, supra note 84, at 661–62; Sino-French Tariff Treaty (signed at Nanjing, December 22, 1928), art. 2, in 3 Old Sino-Foreign Treaties, supra note 84, at 670–71.

[92] Tan Shaohua, *Tan Shaohua Ni Woguo xiang Yingmei Liangguo Tichu Xiuyue zhi Jingguo yu Yuezhong Zhongyao Wenti zhi Tantao* [The History of China's Initiation to Revise Treaties with Britain and the United States and the Discussion of Important Issues in Those Treaties by Tan Shaohua], May 15, 1934, in 5 (1) Compilation of Archives of the History of the Republic of China, "Diplomacy", part 1, 73, 80, 83 (The Second Historical Archives of China (ed.), Jiangsu Ancient Books Publishing House 1994).

a famous public international law scholar,[93] who mainly argued that Chinese economic strength was not as great as that of the Western powers.[94] Indeed, from the outset of national treatment in the ROC, the criticism did not stop because of its potential impact on the national economy and the people's livelihood.[95]

Sino-USSR Commerce Treaty (1939)

It is interesting to note a dispute on national treatment between the ROC central government and one of the local governments. In 1931, the Xinjiang provincial government signed the Interim Commerce Measure with the Union of Soviet Socialist Republics (USSR, or the Soviet Union) [*Xinjiang yu Sulian Linshi Tongshang Banfa*] that included a unilateral national treatment article where the Xinjiang provincial government promised to levy tariffs and other taxes and charges on the Soviet people "not higher or heavier than those on Chinese merchants and people".[96] This unilateral national treatment article was reprimanded by the ROC central government because it did not have a reciprocal paragraph for the Soviet Union to provide national treatment to the Chinese people.[97] Although the 1931 Interim Commerce Measure was not recognized by the ROC, in 1939 the ROC and the Soviet Union concluded the Sino-USSR Commerce Treaty [*Zhongsu Tongshang Tiaoyue*] that contained a relatively mature and reciprocal national treatment article.[98] Article 4 of the 1939 Sino-USSR Commerce Treaty stated that

93 Zhou Gengsheng, Geming De Waijiao [Revolutionary Diplomacy] 186 (Shanghai Pacific Bookshop 3rd edn, 1929) (arguing that China could not endlessly be bound by the national treatment principle and it was questionable whether China should recognize national treatment in treaties).

94 *Yu Beijing Zhengfu Tongyi Bikong Chuqi de Dangguo Waijiao* [Party-Nation Diplomacy, Breathing Through the Same Nostrils with the Beijing Government], in Florilegium of Chinese Modern Foreign Relation History: 1840–1949,Vol II, part 1, at 166–170 (Modern History Unit of the History Department of Fudan University (ed.), Shanghai People's Publishing House 1977).

95 See Tan Shaohua, supra note 92; Liu Yan, Bei Qinhai Zhi Zhongguo [China Under Infringement] 113 (Wenhai Press 1987) (1928).

96 1931 Interim Commerce Measure between Xinjiang Province and the USSR, art. 5, in 5 (1) Compilation of Archives of the History of the Republic of China, "Diplomacy", part II, at 1417–1418 (The Second Historical Archives of China(ed.), Jiangsu Ancient Books Publishing House 1994).

97 Opinions of the Foreign Ministry on the Interim Commerce Agreement between Xinjiang Province and the USSR [*Waijiaobu Duiyu Xinsu Linshi Tongshang Xieding zhi Yijian*], November 4, 1933, in 5 (1) Compilation of Archives of the History of the Republic of China, "Diplomacy", part II, at 1421, 1423 (The Second Historical Archives of China (ed.), Jiangsu Ancient Books Publishing House 1994).

98 Sino-USSR Commerce Treaty (June 16, 1939), in 5 (2) Compilation of Archives of the History of the Republic of China, "Diplomacy", at 275–82 (The Second Historical Archives of China (ed.), Jiangsu Ancient Books Publishing House 1997).

one party should accord imported products from the other party the same treatment as like products of its own country with respect to all local taxes and charges.

In addition to the seven tariffs treaties and the Sino-USSR Commerce Treaty, China also concluded eight friendship and commerce treaties with Belgium and Luxembourg (1928), Italy (1928), Denmark (1928), Portugal (1928), Spain (1928), Poland (1929), Greece (1929), and Czechoslovakia (1930) during the 1920s and the 1930s, all of which included bilateral national treatment articles with respect to taxation.[99]

From the denial of unilateral national treatment obligations to the support of bilateral obligations in the 1920s, China began to attach great importance to the equal and reciprocal principle when considering providing national treatment to foreigners. In fact, the equal and reciprocal principle was applicable not only to national treatment clauses, but also to other clauses (e.g. MFN clauses) in the treaties China concluded in the 1920s and the 1930s. From then on, the unilateral national treatment clause in China was gone, never to return.

B. Extension of National Treatment in the 1940s

New Treaties in the 1940s

Although in the 1920s and the 1930s there were some treaties containing national treatment clauses, they mainly were concerned with tariffs and taxes. The extension of national treatment in China occurred in the 1940s,[100] accompanied by the final and complete repeal of "consular jurisdiction".[101] During the Second World War,

---

[99] Sino-Belgian and Luxembourg Friendship and Commerce Treaty, art. 1, in 3 OLD SINO-FOREIGN TREATIES, supra note 84, at 642–43; Sino-Italian Friendship and Commerce Treaty, art. 1, in 3 OLD SINO-FOREIGN TREATIES, supra note 84, at 646–47; Sino-Danish Friendship and Commerce Treaty, art. 1, in 3 OLD SINO-FOREIGN TREATIES, supra note 84, at 649–50; Sino-Portuguese Friendship and Commerce Treaty, art. 1, in 3 OLD SINO-FOREIGN TREATIES, supra note 84, at 655–56; Sino-Spanish Friendship and Commerce Treaty, art. 1, in 3 OLD SINO-FOREIGN TREATIES, supra note 84, at 675–76; Sino-Polish Friendship, Commerce and Navigation Treaty, art. 5, in 3 OLD SINO-FOREIGN TREATIES, supra note 84, at 719–24; Sino-Greek Friendship and Commerce Treaty, art. 3, in 3 OLD SINO-FOREIGN TREATIES, supra note 84, at 726–27; Sino-Czechoslovakian Friendship and Commerce Treaty, arts. 7, 12, in 3 OLD SINO-FOREIGN TREATIES, supra note 84, at 766–69.

[100] The prevalence of national treatment in China during the period of the 1940s synchronized with the extensive application of national treatment in the US treaties, see Robert R. Wilson, *Postwar Commercial Treaties of the United States*, 43 AM. J. INT'L L. 262, 265 (1949); see also WOLFGANG FRIEDMANN, THE CHANGING STRUCTURE OF INTERNATIONAL LAW, 227–28 (Stevens & Sons 1964) (stating that according national treatment was a "basic principle" in those FCN treaties between the United States and some countries).

[101] The ROC government once tried to unilaterally repeal the "consular jurisdiction" under the influence of revolutionary diplomacy, and it did announce the repeal of the "consular jurisdiction" on December 28, 1929, without negotiation with relevant foreign states, and issued the first law governing foreigners in China, i.e., Regulations Relating to

China, as a US ally, proposed to revise the treaties based on the principles of equality and reciprocity.[102] This proposal received a positive response from the United States.[103] And in 1943, China and the United States signed the Treaty for the Relinquishment of Extraterritorial Rights in China and the Regulation of Related Matters (Sino-US New Treaty).[104] Its main aim was to relinquish the United States' extraterritorial rights (i.e., consular jurisdiction) in China. The 1943 Sino-US New Treaty also contained a national treatment article as follows:

---

the Exercise of Jurisdiction over Foreign Nationals in China [*Guanxia Zaihua Waiguoren Shishi Tiaoli*]. Nevertheless, this attempt was stopped by Japan's invasion of China on September 18, 1931 (the Mukden Incident). See Special Order of the Republican Government [*Guomin Zhengfu Teling*] (December 28, 1929), in 5(1) COMPILATION OF ARCHIVES OF THE HISTORY OF THE REPUBLIC OF CHINA, "Diplomacy", part 1, at 52 (The Second Historical Archives of China (ed.), Jiangsu Ancient Books Publishing House 1994); The Announcement of Repealing Some Treaties of the Ministry of Foreign Affairs of the Republic of China [*Waijiaobu guanyu Feiyue de Xuanyan*] (December 30, 1929), in 5(1) COMPILATION OF ARCHIVES OF THE HISTORY OF THE REPUBLIC OF CHINA, "Diplomacy", part 1, at 52–53 (The Second Historical Archives of China (ed.), Jiangsu Ancient Books Publishing House 1994); The Official Letter from the Civilian Office of the Republican Government concerning the General Application of Chinese Law to All Foreigners in China [*Guomin Zhengfu Wenguanchu wei Zaihua Wairen Yilv Shiyong Zhongguo Falü zhi Xingzhengyuan Gonghan*] (December 30, 1929), in 5(1) COMPILATION OF ARCHIVES OF THE HISTORY OF THE REPUBLIC OF CHINA, "Diplomacy", part 1, at 53 (The Second Historical Archives of China (ed.), Jiangsu Ancient Books Publishing House 1994); see also LI ENHAN, JINDAI ZHONGGUO WAIJIAO SHISHI XINYAN [NEW STUDY OF THE DIPLOMACY HISTORY OF MODERN CHINA] 276–77 (Taiwan Commercial Press 2004); TUNG, supra note 9, at 74. For the history of the Mukden Incident of September 18, 1931, see YI XIANSHI ET AL., "JIU YIBA" SHIBIAN SHI [HISTORY OF THE "MUKDEN INCIDENT OF SEPTEMBER 18"] (Liaoning People's Publishing House 1981); "JIU YIBA" SHIBIAN ZILIAO HUIBIAN [A COLLECTION OF DOCUMENTS ON THE "MUKDEN INCIDENT OF SEPTEMBER 18"] (Sun Bang (ed.), Jinlin Literature and History Publishing House 1991).

[102] Telegram of the ROC Foreign Minister on the Discussion of Making a New Treaty with the Secretary of State of the United States, April 29, 1941, in ZHONGHUA MINGUO ZHONGYAO SHILIAO CHUBIAN: DUIRI KANGZHAN SHIQI [INITIAL COMPILATIONS OF IMPORTANT HISTORY MATERIALS OF THE REPUBLIC OF CHINA: PERIOD OF THE WAR OF RESISTANCE AGAINST JAPAN], Vol. 3, "Diplomacy in Wartime" (3), 707 (Qin Xiaoyi (ed.), Zhongguo Guomindang Zhongyang Weiyuanhui Dangshi Weiyuanhui 1981) [hereinafter COMPILATIONS OF HISTORY MATERIALS OF THE ROC].

[103] Telegram of Exchange of Notes on Repealing the Unequal Treaty between China and the United States, May 25, 1941, in COMPILATIONS OF HISTORY MATERIALS OF THE ROC, supra note 102, at 708–10.

[104] Sino-US New Treaty [*Zhongmei Xinyue*], signed at Washington on January 11, 1943, effective on May 20, 1943, in U.S. RELATIONS WITH CHINA, supra note 29, at 514–17; also available in 3 OLD SINO-FOREIGN TREATIES, supra note 84, at 1256–62; TREATIES BETWEEN THE REPUBLIC OF CHINA AND FOREIGN STATES (1927–1957) 659–69 (Ministry of Foreign Affairs of the ROC (ed.), Taipei Commercial Press 1958).

> Each of the two Governments will endeavour to have accorded in territory under its jurisdiction to nationals of the other country, in regard to all legal proceedings, and to matters relating to the administration of justice, and to the levying of taxes or requirements in connection therewith, treatment not less favourable than that accorded to its own nationals.[105]

A similar national treatment article was incorporated in the Treaty between Great Britain and China for the Relinquishment of Extraterritorial Rights in China and the Regulation of Related Matters (Sino-British New Treaty) (1943).[106] With coverage for both nationals [*renmin*] and companies [*gongsi*], the scope of national treatment in the Sino-British New Treaty was broader than that of the Sino-US New Treaty.

In addition, from 1943 to 1947, in order to relinquish extraterritorial rights of other Western powers, China concluded a series of "New Treaties" with Belgium and Luxembourg,[107] Norway,[108] Canada,[109] Sweden,[110]

---

105 Id. art. 5.

106 Sino-British New Treaty [*Zhongying Xinyue*], signed at Chongqing [*Chungking*] on January 11, 1943, entered into force on May 20, 1943, art. 6, in 37 SUPPLEMENT TO AM. J. INT'L L. 57–62 (1943) (English version); also available in 3 OLD SINO-FOREIGN TREATIES, supra note 84, at 1262–66 (Chinese version); TREATIES BETWEEN THE REPUBLIC OF CHINA AND FOREIGN STATES (1927–1957), supra note 104, at 589–94.

107 Traite Entre La Republique de Chine et L'Union Economique Belgo-Luxembourgoise Relatif A L'Abolition Des Droits D'Exterritorialite en Chine et au Reglement des Questions s'y Rapportant [hereinafter Sino-Belgian New Treaty], signed on October 20, 1943, entered into force on June 1, 1945, in TREATIES BETWEEN THE REPUBLIC OF CHINA AND FOREIGN STATES (1927–1957), supra note 104, at 33–40; also available in 3 OLD SINO-FOREIGN TREATIES, supra note 84, at 1278–82.

108 Treaty between the Republic of China and the Kingdom of Norway for the Relinquishment of Extraterritorial Rights in China and the Regulation of Related Matters [hereinafter Sino-Norwegian New Treaty], signed on November 10, 1943, entered into force on June 13, 1944, in TREATIES BETWEEN THE REPUBLIC OF CHINA AND FOREIGN STATES (1927–1957), supra note 104, at 356–61 (bilingual version); also available in 3 OLD SINO-FOREIGN TREATIES, supra note 84, at 1282–85 (Chinese version).

109 Sino-Canadian Treaty for the Relinquishment of Extraterritorial Rights in China and the Regulation of Related Matters [hereinafter Sino-Canadian New Treaty], signed on April 14, 1944, entered into force on April 3, 1945, in TREATIES BETWEEN THE REPUBLIC OF CHINA AND FOREIGN STATES (1927–1957), supra note 104, at 50–54 (bilingual version); also available in 3 OLD SINO-FOREIGN TREATIES, supra note 84, at 1292–95 (Chinese version).

110 Treaty between the Republic of China and the Kingdom of Sweden concerning the Relinquishment by Sweden of Its Extraterritorial and Related Special Rights in China [hereinafter Sino-Swedish New Treaty], signed on April 5, 1945, entered into force on November 18, 1946, in TREATIES BETWEEN THE REPUBLIC OF CHINA AND FOREIGN STATES (1927–1957), supra note 104, at 448–51 (bilingual version); also available in 3 OLD SINO-FOREIGN TREATIES, supra note 84, at 1307–09 (Chinese version).

Holland,[111] France,[112] Switzerland,[113] Denmark,[114] and Portugal,[115] most of which contained national treatment articles granting "no less favourable treatment" to nationals or companies of both sides.[116]

Ironically, one day before the signing of the Sino-US New Treaty, the puppet regime headed by Wang Jingwei [*Wang Ching-Wei*] but supported by Japan, that

---

[111] Treaty between the Republic of China and the Kingdom of the Netherlands for the Relinquishment of Extraterritorial Rights in China and the Regulation of Related Matters [hereinafter Sino-Dutch New Treaty], signed on May 29, 1945, entered into force on December 5, 1945, in TREATIES BETWEEN THE REPUBLIC OF CHINA AND FOREIGN STATES (1927–1957), supra note 104, at 332–37 (bilingual version); also available in 3 OLD SINO-FOREIGN TREATIES, supra note 84, at 1314–17 (Chinese version).

[112] Traite Franco-Chinois de Renonciation A L'Exterritorialite en Chine et Aux Droits y Relatifs [hereinafter Sino-French New Treaty], signed on February 28, 1946, entered into force on June 8, 1946, in TREATIES BETWEEN THE REPUBLIC OF CHINA AND FOREIGN STATES (1927–1957), supra note 104, at 152–60 (bilingual version); also available in 3 OLD SINO-FOREIGN TREATIES, supra note 84, at 1362–67 (Chinese version).

[113] Echange de Notes Entre la Chine et la Suisse Relatif a la Renonciation par la Suisse a ses Droits D'Exercer la Juridiction Consulaire en Chine et Aux Droits Speciaux y Afferents [hereinafter Sino-Swiss New Treaty], signed and exchanged on March 13, 1946, entered into force at same date, in TREATIES BETWEEN THE REPUBLIC OF CHINA AND FOREIGN STATES (1927–1957), supra note 104, at 459–63 (bilingual version); also in 3 OLD SINO-FOREIGN TREATIES, supra note 84, at 1375–76 (Chinese version).

[114] Treaty between the Republic of China and the Kingdom of Denmark for the Relinquishment of Extraterritorial Rights in China and the Regulation of Related Matters [hereinafter Sino-Danish New Treaty], signed on May 20, 1946, entered into force provisionally on May 20, 1946, ratifications exchanged on April 14, 1947, in TREATIES BETWEEN THE REPUBLIC OF CHINA AND FOREIGN STATES (1927–1957), supra note 104, at 83–89 (bilingual version); also available in 3 OLD SINO-FOREIGN TREATIES, supra note 84, at 1390–94 (Chinese version).

[115] Exchange of Notes between China and Portugal for the Relinquishment by Portugal of Its Rights Relating to the Consular Jurisdiction in China and the Adjustment of Certain Other Matters [hereinafter Sino-Portuguese New Treaty], signed on April 1, 1947, entered into force at same date, in TREATIES BETWEEN THE REPUBLIC OF CHINA AND FOREIGN STATES (1927–1957), supra note 104, at 412–13 (bilingual version); also available in 3 OLD SINO-FOREIGN TREATIES, supra note 84, at 1475–77 (Chinese version).

[116] See Sino-Belgian New Treaty, supra note 107, art. 5; Sino-Norwegian New Treaty, supra note 108, art. 4; Sino-Canadian New Treaty, supra note 109, art. 5; Sino-Swedish New Treaty, supra note 110, art. 4; Sino-Dutch New Treaty, supra note 111, art. 6(2); Sino-French New Treaty, supra note 112, art. 6(2); Sino-Danish New Treaty, supra note 114, art. 5. There was no national treatment clause in the Sino-Swiss New Treaty or Sino-Portuguese New Treaty, but both treaties contained MFN treatment, which could be interpreted to indirectly include national treatment of other New Treaties, see Sino-Swiss New Treaty, supra note 113, art. 2; Sino-Portuguese New Treaty, supra note 115, art. 4.

claimed that it was the official ROC government,[117] also signed an agreement with Japan under which the latter would "agree" to abandon its extraterritoriality rights in China, and, as an exchange, the former would "give" national treatment to the Japanese.[118] This puppet treaty became waste paper with the collapse of the puppet regime following the surrender of Japan at the end of the Second World War.[119] When comparing the puppet treaty with those "New Treaties", one can find that the former had a unilateral national treatment article that favoured only Japan, while the latter had bilateral national treatment articles that favoured both China and foreigners.

In the "New Treaties", China compromised by accepting national treatment in order to repeal consular jurisdiction, which was what China had done fifteen years before when it had to give national treatment to seven states as part of the price to pay for tariffs autonomy. It was not China that initiated the incorporation of national treatment in the "New Treaties". Rather, the original drafts of the Sino-US New Treaty and the Sino-British New Treaty were presented by the United States and Britain, both of which contained national treatment articles.[120] Although

---

117 The ROC government led by Jiang Jieshi [*Chiang Kai-Shek*] was forced to move to Chongqing in November 1937, and one month later, Nanjing fell into Japan's hands. The puppet regime was established in Nanjing on March 30, 1940. See 2 ZHONGGUO XIANDAISHI [CHINA'S CONTEMPORARY HISTORY] 23, 42, 90 (The Teaching and Research Group on China's Contemporary History of the Department of History of Beijing Normal University (ed.), Beijing Normal Univ. Press 1983).

118 Treaty on Returning Leased Territories and Repealing Extraterritoriality Right Between Japan and Wang Jingwei Government [*RiWang Guanyu Jiaohuan Zujie ji Chefei Zhiwai Faquan zhi Xieding*], January 9, 1943, art. 7, in ZHONGGUO JINDAI DUIWAI GUANXISHI ZILIAO XUANJI 1840–1949 [SELECTED MATERIALS OF CHINA'S MODERN FOREIGN RELATIONS HISTORY 1840–1949], Vol. II (2), at 196–97 (Teaching and Research Group on China's Modern History of the Department of History of Fudan University (ed.), Shanghai People's Publishing House 1977); also available in WANGWEI ZHENGQUAN [WANG PUPPET REGIME] 871–72 (The Central Archives of China & The Second Historical Archives of China & Jilin Province Social Academy (eds.), Zhonghua Book Company 2004). It is noteworthy that Japan shifted the planned signature date (January 15, 1943) of the treaty with the Wang Jingwei regime to an earlier date (January 9, 1943) in order to conclude the agreement ahead of the conclusion of the agreement between the United States/Britain and the Jiang Jieshi government with a provisional capital at Chongqing, see FEI CHENGKANG, supra note 18, at 417.

119 Japan declared its surrender in the middle of August 1945. See The Imperial Edict on Armistice issued by Japanese then Emperor Hirohito on August 14, 1945, in RIBEN DIGUO ZHUYI DUIWAI QINLUE SHILIAO XUANBIAN 1931–1945 [COMPILATION OF THE HISTORICAL MATERIALS ON JAPANESE IMPERIALISM AGGRESSION 1931–1945] 549–50 (Japanese History Group of the Department of History of Fudan University (ed., trans.), Shanghai People's Publishing House 1975).

120 Draft of Sino-US Relation Treaty, art. 5, in COMPILATIONS OF HISTORY MATERIALS OF THE ROC, supra note 102, at 716–19; Draft of Sino-British Relation Treaty, art. 6, in COMPILATIONS OF HISTORY MATERIALS OF THE ROC, supra note 102, at 752–56.

China argued that the national treatment articles should be replaced by the MFN treatment articles,[121] China had to accept the opinions of the United Sates and Britain. Thus, national treatment was added to the "New Treaties" in exchange for the abolition of the consular jurisdiction.[122]

Nevertheless, the inclusion of national treatment in the "New Treaties" should not be deemed an imposition like the treaties signed by the late Qing Dynasty. First, the national treatment articles in the "New Treaties" were bilateral, and contained the word "endeavour" [*jinli*] as a limit to national treatment,[123] meaning that the national treatment articles in the two treaties were by no means unconditional. With this limit, China reserved the right to set off potentially disadvantageous implications of national treatment. Moreover, throughout the negotiation of the "New Treaties", China insisted on the exclusion of business from the scope of national treatment. In the drafts made by the United States and Britain, business was in the scope of national treatment,[124] which was strongly opposed by China,[125] and the final documents did not contain business in the scope of national treatment. The last reservation made by China with respect to national treatment was that the coasting trade and inland navigation were excepted from national treatment.[126] By these limitations and reservations on national treatment, China reduced the potential negative impact of national treatment on the Chinese domestic business and industry sectors.

---

[121] Opinions of the ROC Foreign Ministry on the Draft of the Sino-US Relation Treaty, October 30, 1942, in COMPILATIONS OF HISTORY MATERIALS OF THE ROC, supra note 102, at 722–24; Opinions of the ROC Foreign Ministry on the Draft of the Sino-British Relation Treaty, December 7, 1942, in COMPILATIONS OF HISTORY MATERIALS OF THE ROC, supra note 102, at 768–70.

[122] The exchange of national treatment for the abolition of consular jurisdiction was not unique to China. For example, in 1937, Egypt signed a treaty with a few countries, mainly the Western powers, and in this treaty, as a price for the abolition of capitulations in Egypt, Egypt had to promise that it would not discriminate against foreigners or foreign-funded companies. See Convention concerning the Abolition of Capitulations in Egypt [hereinafter the Montreux Convention 1937], May 8, 1937, art. 2, in JASPER YEATES BRINTON, THE MIXED COURTS OF EGYPT 261–68 (Yale University Press 1968).

[123] See Sino-US New Treaty, supra note 104, art. 5; Sino-British New Treaty, supra note 106, art. 6; Sino-Norwegian New Treaty, supra note 108, art. 4; Sino-Canadian New Treaty, supra note 109, art. 5; Sino-Dutch New Treaty, supra note 111, art. 6(2); Sino-French New Treaty, supra note 112, art. 6(2).

[124] Article 5 of the Draft of Sino-US Relation Treaty, supra note 120; Article 6 of the Draft of Sino-British Relation Treaty, supra note 120.

[125] Opinions of the ROC Foreign Ministry on the Draft of the Sino-British Relation Treaty, supra note 121, at 771.

[126] See *Letter of Secretary Hull to the Chinese Ambassador* (*Wei Tao-ming*), January 11, 1943, in U.S. RELATIONS WITH CHINA, supra note 29, at 517–18.

Sino-US FCN Treaty (1946)

According to Article VII of the 1943 Sino-US New Treaty, China and the United States would enter into negotiations for a modern treaty of friendship, commerce and navigation after the end of the Second World War. In 1946, the Treaty of Friendship, Commerce and Navigation Between the United States of America and the Republic of China (Sino-US FCN Treaty) [*Zhongmei Youhao Tongshang Hanghai Tiaoyue*] was concluded,[127] containing a good deal of national treatment clauses to provide no less favourable treatment than that accorded or to be accorded to its own nationals, corporations and associations with respect to inland taxes, sales, distribution of goods from the other party, as well as court access rights and legal protection rights, copyrights, patents, trade marks.[128] Such national treatment clauses were an extension of the national treatment article in the 1943 Sino-US New Treaty. One characteristic of the 1946 Sino-US FCN Treaty is that it supplemented the national treatment article in the 1943 Sino-US New Treaty by granting national treatment to both nationals (i.e., persons) and corporations of the two contracting parties.[129] The extension of national treatment from nationals to corporations is a salient characteristic of the post Second World War treaties.[130] The second characteristic of the Sino-US FCN Treaty is its general adherence "to the principle of national treatment".[131] Such wording, which stresses the important status of national treatment, had never been used in any prior treaty. The third characteristic of the Sino-US FCN Treaty is the exclusion of finance from the scope of national treatment. In the draft of the Sino-US FCN Treaty, the United States proposed to incorporate finance into the treaty as an aspect to be covered by national treatment obligations, but China categorically refused this proposal.[132] As a result, finance was deleted from the final version of the Sino-US FCN Treaty.

In the 1940s, China also concluded eleven amity treaties with Dominica (1940), Iraq (1942), Cuba (1942), Afghanistan (1944), Costa Rica (1944), Mexico (1944), Ecuador (1946), Thailand (1946), Saudi Arabia (1946), Philippines (1947), and

---

127 Sino-US FCN Treaty, in 3 Old Sino-Foreign Treaties, supra note 84, at 1429–51 (Chinese version); 43 Supplement to Am. J. Int'l L. 27–51 (1947) (English version).

128 Id. at arts. 4(2), 9, 13, 16(2), 18(1)(2), 19(3), 24(1).

129 The Sino-US FCN Treaty is the first commercial treaty in which US corporations gained the right to conduct business in other countries on a national treatment basis. See Todd S. Shenkin, *Trade-Related Investment Measures in Bilateral Investment Treaties and the GATT: Moving Toward a Multilateral Investment Treaty*, 55 U. Pitt. L. Rev. 541, 571 (1994).

130 See Herman Walker, Jr, *Provisions on Companies in United States Commercial Treaties*, 50 Am. J. Int'l L. 373, 385 (1956); see also Robert R. Wilson, *Editorial Comment: A Decade of New Commercial Treaties*, 50 Am. J. Int'l L. 927, 928–29 (1956).

131 Sino-US FCN Treaty, supra note 127, art. 3(3).

132 A Diplomatic History of China: the Period of the Republic of China 1911–1949, at 692 (Wu Dongzhi (ed.), Henan People's Publishing House 1990).

Italy (1949), four of which contained national treatment articles.[133] In short, the concept of national treatment was gradually accepted by China during the 1920s to the 1940s through bilateral treaties.

C. Appearance of Multilateral National Treatment in China: GATT 1947

In 1947, China became one of the twenty-three original contracting parties of the GATT.[134] Thus, national treatment obligations in the GATT became applicable to China as multilateral treaty obligations. The ROC government paid special attention to the national treatment article, i.e., GATT Article III, because it realized that "national treatment may impede the protection of domestic industry and commerce".[135] In spite of the apprehension, the ROC government accepted the GATT because it recognized that "the advantages exceed the disadvantages".[136] From then on, China's national treatment obligations evolved into a mixture of bilateral and multilateral obligations.

By analysing the national treatment clauses in the ROC's treaties, one can find that the scope of national treatment during that period became broader and broader, that is, from only one aspect, taxes and charges,[137] to many aspects, such as legal proceedings, administration of justice, and finally to patent right, copyright, trademark, and business rights. Moreover, the beneficiaries of national treatment were extended to include legal persons (companies). Meanwhile, the ROC government had realized the importance of limiting national treatment in order to protect domestic interests and to balance the broad scope of the national treatment clauses. As a result, national treatment changed from an unconditional national treatment with a narrow scope to a conditional national treatment with a broad scope. These changes, together with the evolution from unilateral treatment

---

[133] The four Friendship Treaties are Sino-Brazilian Friendship Treaty, art. 4, para. 2, in 3 OLD SINO-FOREIGN TREATIES, supra note 84, at 1276–77; Sino-Thailand Friendship Treaty, art. 5, in 3 OLD SINO-FOREIGN TREATIES, supra note 84, at 1353–54; Sino-Philippine Friendship Treaty, art. 7, in 3 OLD SINO-FOREIGN TREATIES, supra note 84, at 1478–80; Sino-Italian Friendship Treaty, art. 6, in 3 OLD SINO-FOREIGN TREATIES, supra note 84, at 1653–55.

[134] GATT 1947, pmbl, in THE LEGAL TEXTS, supra note 3, at 423–93; see also Yang Guohua and Cheng Jin, *The Process of China's Accession to the WTO*, 4 J. INT'L. ECON. L. 297, 297 (2001).

[135] Introduction of International Trade Charter Draft and the General Agreement on Tariffs and Trade [*Guanyu Shijie Maoyi Xianzhang Cao'An ji Guanshui ji Maoyi Zongxieding zhi shuotie*], issued by the Ministry of Foreign Affairs, the Ministry of Finance and the Ministry of Economy of the Republic of China in 1948, REPUBLICAN ARCHIVES [Minguo Dang'An] 40, 41 (2003, no. 2).

[136] Id. at 43.

[137] E.g., article 7 of the Sino-Czechoslovakia Friendship and Commerce Treaty (1930) states that "such taxes and charges [paid by nationals of one party in the other party] shall not be higher than those paid by nationals of the other party."

to bilateral and multilateral treatment, reflect, to some extent, that China awakened after a sleep of over one hundred years in bondage to the unequal treaties.[138]

D. Development and Treatment of Foreign-Funded Banks during 1912–1949

After the establishment of the ROC Government in 1912, foreign-funded banks in China continued to operate without any regulation, and they continued to try to control China's finance.[139] However, with the development of Chinese domestic banks from the period of the First World War,[140] the development of foreign-funded banks in China gradually fell into a stagnant stage. In 1936, there were one hundred and sixty-four Chinese banks, but only thirty-two foreign banks.[141] In 1949, foreign banks in China were reduced to fifteen.[142] Although foreign banks' business was not as prosperous as in the late Qing Dynasty, foreign banks still enjoyed prerogative treatment in China, such as settlement procedures, circulation of negotiable instruments.[143] After the 1911 *Xinhai* Revolution, in addition to the right of keeping China's tariffs, foreign banks even obtained the right of keeping China's salt tax.[144]

As to banking legislation, in the beginning of the ROC period, i.e., the period of the Northern Warlords (1912–1927), the ROC Government succeeded to the General Banking Regulation and other banking rules of the Qing Dynasty as temporary banking law,[145] applicable only to Chinese domestic banks. Although

---

[138] It must be noted that some Chinese historians view the 1946 Sino-US FCN Treaty as an unequal treaty due to a wide economic gap between China and the United States, notwithstanding the apparent equality. See A Diplomatic History of China: the Period of the Republic of China 1911–1949, supra note 132, at 689; Tao Wenzhao, Zhongmei Guanxi Shi [History of the Sino-US Relations] (1911–1949) 320 (Shanghai People's Publishing House 2004); Zhongguo Duiwai Tiaoyue Cidian [Dictionary of China's Foreign Treaties] 386–87 (Zhu Huan and Wang Hengwei (eds), Jilin Education Press 1994).

[139] See *Note on the Organization of a Control of China's Finance by the Hong Kong & Shanghai Bank* [*Huifeng Yinhang Guanyu Zuzhi Kongguan Zhongguo Caizheng de Yijian*], Chen Huifen trans., Republican Archives 38–40 (2003, no. 4).

[140] For reasons for the development of China's domestic banks during that period, see History of China's Finance, supra note 43, at 221–23; see also Linsun Cheng, supra note 43, at 39–41 (mentioning two factors for the expansion of the modern Chinese banks, i.e., government's encouragement and stimulation of the First World War).

[141] History of China's Finance, supra note 43, at 252.

[142] Id. at 369.

[143] Yang Yinpu, Shanghai Jinrong Zuzhi Gaiyao [Outlines of Financial Institutions in Shanghai] 232, 233 (Commercial Press 1930).

[144] See History of China's Finance, supra note 43, at 187.

[145] Interim Application of All Kinds of Banking Regulations of the Qing Dynasty, Decree of the Ministry of Finance of the ROC, September 18, 1912, in 3 Compilation of Archives of the History of the Republic of China, "Finance", part I, at 19 (The Second Historical Archives of China (ed.), Jiangsu Ancient Books Publishing House 1991).

the ROC Ministry of Finance promulgated the Rule on Supervisors for Provincial Banks,[146] the Rule on Supervisors' Service for the Bank of China,[147] the Rule on Disqualifying Banking Staff,[148] the Banking Examination Rule,[149] and the Interim Rule on Banking Registration,[150] none of them applied to foreign banks in China. During that period, the ROC government discussed the drafts of the General Banking Law [*Yinhang Tongxingfa*] and the Detailed Rules for Implementation of the General Banking Law [*Yinhang Tongxingfa Shixing Xize*], and intended to cover both domestic banks and foreign banks,[151] but those efforts bore no fruit.[152]

In 1931, the ROC government promulgated the Banking Law [*Yinhangfa*, hereinafter the Banking Law 1931],[153] which was intended to apply to both Chinese domestic banks and foreign banks.[154] However, due to strong objections from China's banking, the Banking Law 1931 did not take effect.[155] In 1947, the

---

146 Rule on Supervisors for Provincial Banks [*Gesheng Guanyin Qianhao Jianliguan Zhangcheng*], promulgated by the Ministry of Finance of the ROC, February 23, 1913, amended, March 4, 1914, in JINRONG FAGUI HUIBIAN [COMPILATION OF FINANCIAL LAWS AND REGULATIONS] 105–06 (Economic Research Division of the Central Bank (eds), Commercial Press 1937).

147 Rule on Supervisor Service for the Bank of China [*Zhongguo Yinhang Jianliguan Fuwu Zhangcheng*], promulgated by the Ministry of Finance of the ROC, April 28, 1913, in 3 COMPILATION OF ARCHIVES OF THE HISTORY OF THE REPUBLIC OF CHINA, "Finance", part I, at 41–42 (The Second Historical Archives of China (ed.), Jiangsu Ancient Books Publishing House 1991).

148 Rule on Disqualifying Banking Staff [*Qudi Yinhang Zhiyuan Zhangcheng*], promulgated by the Ministry of Finance of the ROC, August 24, 1915, in COMPILATION OF FINANCIAL LAWS AND REGULATIONS, supra note 146, at 104.

149 Banking Examination Rule [*Yinhang Jicha Zhangcheng*], promulgated by the Ministry of Finance of the ROC, December 11, 1916, in COMPILATION OF FINANCIAL LAWS AND REGULATIONS, supra note 146, at 101–04.

150 Interim Rule on Banking Registration [*Yinhang Zhuce Zanxing Zhangcheng*], promulgated by the Ministry of Finance of the ROC, February 7, 1927, in 3 COMPILATION OF ARCHIVES OF THE HISTORY OF THE REPUBLIC OF CHINA, "Finance", part I, at 74–75 (The Second Historical Archives of China (ed.), Jiangsu Ancient Books Publishing House 1991). According to Article 10 of the Interim Rule on Banking Registration, it replaced the Banking Registration Rule of the Qing Dynasty (1908) temporarily used by the ROC Government.

151 CHENG LIN, supra note 73, at 117.

152 XIE ZHENMIN, supra note 70, at 852.

153 The Banking Law 1931, promulgated on March 28, 1931, in COMPILATION OF FINANCIAL LAWS AND REGULATIONS, supra note 146, at 37–44; also available in LIU GUANYING, XIANDAI YINHANG ZHIDU [MODERN BANKING SYSTEM] 221–32 (Commercial Press 1936); 2 CHINA BANKS YEARBOOK, ch. 20, T1-5 (Research Department of the Bank of China, 1937).

154 XIE ZHENMIN, supra note 70, at 858; but see YE SHICHANG AND PAN LIANGUI, supra note 41, at 268 (arguing that the Banking Law 1931 was not applicable to foreign banks).

155 For the controversy on the Banking Law 1931, see LEE, supra note 60, at 177–91.

ROC government promulgated the Banking Law 1947,[156] containing a special chapter regulating foreign banks.[157] The Banking Law 1947 applied to domestic and foreign banks in mainland China for only two years owing to China's civil war, which resulted in the establishment of the PRC in 1949.[158]

During the one hundred year history from the 1840s to the 1940s, foreign banks in China enjoyed special treatment beyond the Chinese banking law. Only after 1947, did foreign banks begin to be subject to Chinese banking law. The application of Chinese banking law to foreign banks did not mean that foreign banks were granted national treatment. On the contrary, the Banking Law 1947 failed to grant national treatment to foreign banks. Furthermore, all financial areas were not in the scope of national treatment during the ROC period. Although national treatment was generally introduced into the Chinese treaties concluded during the 1940s, China rejected the idea of providing national treatment in the area of finance.[159]

IV. 1949–1978

A. Decline of National Treatment in China during 1949–1978

After winning the war against the Chinese Nationalist Party (KMT) [*Guomindang or Kuomintang*], the leading party of the ROC government,[160] the Chinese Communist Party (CCP) established the Government of the People's Republic of China (PRC government) in October 1949. According to the 1949 Common

---

[156] The Banking Law 1947, promulgated on September 1, 1947, effective at the same day, in 3 ZHONGHUA MINGUO LIUFA LIYOU PANJIE HUIBIAN [A COMPILATION OF THE SIX CODES OF THE REPUBLIC OF CHINA] 541–59 (Wu Jingxiong (ed.), Guo Wei revised, Huiwentang Xinji Shujü 1947).

[157] Id. ch. 8, arts. 99–109. In addition to the special foreign banking chapter, some articles in the Banking Law 1947 applied *mutatis mutandis* to foreign banks in China, i.e., arts. 48, 49, 57, 58, 109.

[158] The Banking Law 1947 and other ROC laws were completely repealed by the Chinese Communist Party in 1949. See Guidelines of the Chinese Communist Party on Repealing Guomindang's Six Codes of Law and Establishing Judicial Principles in the Liberation Areas [*Zhonggong Zhongyang Guanyu Feichu Guomindang de Liufa Quanshu yu Queding Jiefangqu de Sifa Yuanze de Zhishi*] (Feb. 1949), in COMPILATION OF MATERIALS OF CHINA'S LEGAL HISTORY 1187–89 (Qunzhong Press 1988).

[159] See A DIPLOMATIC HISTORY OF CHINA: THE PERIOD OF THE REPUBLIC OF CHINA 1911–1949, supra note 132.

[160] For the general history of the Chinese Nationalist Party, see ZHONGGUO GUOMINDANG DANGSHI [CHINESE NATIONALIST PARTY HISTORY] (Song Chun (ed.), Jilin Literature and History Publishing House 1990).

Creed [*Gongtong Gangling*],[161] an interim constitutional document of the PRC, the PRC government was to examine treaties concluded by the ROC government with foreign countries in order to determine whether to recognize or repeal them, implying that the PRC government did not necessarily succeed to treaties of the ROC government.[162] Obviously, the PRC government did not recognize those treaties signed by the ROC government from the 1920s to the 1940s that granted foreigners national treatment. For instance, the 1946 Sino-US FCN Treaty was viewed by the CCP as "a hypocritical smokescreen" and "an utterly unequal treaty".[163] The CCP's hostile attitude towards the treaties signed by the ROC government was demonstrated in a declaration made by the CCP in 1947.[164] In fact, the hostility was not directed at the ROC treaties or the national treatment articles in those treaties, but rather at the then enemies of the CCP, i.e., the so-called US Imperialism and the KMT-controlled ROC government. Owing to political reasons, the PRC government did not succeed to the national treatment articles in ROC's bilateral treaties.[165]

The national treatment articles in the GATT 1947 were not applicable to the PRC after 1949. In 1950, the ROC government, which had moved to Taiwan Island,

---

161 The Common Creed, adopted at the First Plenary of the Chinese People's Political Consultancy Conference [*Zhongguo Renmin Zhengzhi Xieshang Huiyi*] on September 29, 1949, in 7 ZHONGGONG DANGSHI CANKAO ZILIAO [REFERENCE MATERIALS ON THE HISTORY OF THE CCP] 17–27 (Teaching and Research Section of the CCP History of the China Communist Party School (ed.), People's Publishing House 1980) [hereinafter MATERIALS ON THE HISTORY OF THE CCP].

162 See id. art. 55.

163 Comment on Jiangmei Commerce Treaty [*Ping Jiangmei Shangyue*], an editorial of the Liberation Daily [*Jiefang Ribao*] on November 26, 1946, in 6 MATERIALS ON THE HISTORY OF THE CCP, supra note 161, at 190–92 (1979). The United States also considered that the 1946 Sino-US FCN Treaty did not control the relationship between the United States and mainland China after 1949. See 59 AM. J. INT'L L. 390, 391 (1965).

164 Declaration of the Central Committee of the CCP on Disavowal of All Traitorous Agreements Made by Jiang's Government [*Zhonggong Zhongyang guanyu Bu Chengren Jiang Zhengfu Yiqie Maiguo Xieding de Shengming*], February 1, 1947, http://www.people.com.cn/BIG5/33831/33836/34138/34257/2569028.html (stating that the CCP would never recognize or undertake responsibility for any treaty made by the ROC government, humiliating the nation and forfeiting its sovereignty and other similar agreements concluded after January 10, 1946). Although the CCP declared that it would never recognize treaties made after January 10, 1946, it did not imply that it would recognize treaties concluded before that date.

165 For the different views on treaties between the ROC and the PRC, see Hungdah Chiu, *Comparison of the Nationalist and Communist Chinese Views of Unequal Treaties*, in CHINA'S PRACTICE OF INTERNATIONAL LAW: SOME CASE STUDIES 239–67 (Jerome Alan Cohen (ed.), Harvard Univ. Press 1972) (stating that Communist China's view on treaties is flexible and largely determined by political considerations).

notified the GATT of its withdrawal (in the name of China) from the GATT.[166] Because some Western countries, especially the United States, imposed an embargo on goods originating from the PRC after the outbreak of the Korean War in 1950,[167] the PRC opposed the United States[168] and relevant international trade and financial organizations, such as the International Monetary Fund (IMF) and the GATT, which were deemed by the PRC government to be infringement tools of the imperialist countries.[169] The embargo was one of the reasons the PRC government neither challenged the legality of Taiwan's withdrawal from the GATT nor showed any interest in the GATT during that period,[170] although some contracting parties of the GATT questioned the legality of Taiwan's withdrawal.[171] Therefore, the PRC government did not succeed to the GATT obligations. Consequently, national treatment obligations of the GATT 1947 were not applicable to China.

Moreover, the PRC government claimed that the prerogatives enjoyed by imperialist countries would be purged.[172] This is the so-called policy of "starting all over again" [*lingqi luzao*].[173] For this reason, it was believed that it was necessary to clean up imperialist remains in China, which is the so-called policy of "cleaning out the house before inviting a guest" [*dasao ganjing wuzi zai qingke*].[174] As a result, the number of foreign enterprises in China was sharply reduced from 1104 in 1949 to 66 in 1956.[175]

The normal trade relations with foreign states were also interrupted after the establishment of the PRC in 1949. From 1949 to 1978, the PRC government

---

166 Yang Guohua and Cheng Jin, supra note 134, at 298; Sylvia A. Rhodes and John H. Jackson, *United States Law and China's WTO Accession Process*, 2(3) J. INT'L ECON. L. 497, 499 (1999).

167 COMPILATIONS OF SINO-US RELATION DOCUMENTS: 1940–1976, at 83–84 (Hong Kong 70's Monthly, 1977).

168 Decree of the PRC Government Administration Council on Controlling American Properties in China and Freezing American Deposits in China [*Zhengwuyuan guanyu Guanzhi Meiguo zaihua Caichan Dongjie Meiguo zaihua Cunkuan de Mingling*], December 28, 1950, in 7 MATERIALS ON THE HISTORY OF THE CCP, supra note 161, at 118 (1980).

169 See FENG YUSHU, GUOJI MAOYI TIZHI XIA DE GUANMAO ZONGXIEDING YU ZHONGGUO [GATT AND CHINA] 215 (China Foreign Economic and Trade Publishing House 1992).

170 Yang Guohua and Cheng Jin, supra note 134, at 297, 298; Rhodes and Jackson, supra note 166, at 499.

171 For example, Czechoslovakia raised this question. See Yang Guohua and Cheng Jin, id. at 298.

172 The Common Creed, supra note 161, art. 3.

173 Zhou Enlai, *Our Foreign Policies and Missions*, April 30, 1952, in 1 DIPLOMATIC CHRONICLES OF THE PRC, October 1949–December 1956, Annex Five, at 318 (Song Enfan and Li Jiasong (eds), World Affairs Press 1997).

174 Id. at 320.

175 ZHANG HANFU BIOGRAPHY 146–51 (Writing Group of Zhang Hanfu Biography (eds), World Affairs Press 2003).

adopted the "protectionism trade policy" and strictly controlled foreign trade.[176] After the establishment of the PRC, China's main trading partners were socialist countries, such as the Soviet Union.[177] From the beginning of the 1960s, the warm relations with some socialist countries were cooled down due to the political disputes between China and the Soviet Union.[178] Under the hostile relations with most imperialist countries and some socialist countries, the PRC government overemphasized the self-reliance principle so that a normal and necessary foreign economic transaction was labelled "an act of worship to foreigners" [*chongyang meiwai*].[179]

Although the PRC government may disagree, it indeed adopted another round of "closed-door" policy from 1949 to 1978.[180] This "closed-door" policy was also reflected in China's laws. The PRC government had enacted three constitutions within thirty years from 1949 to 1978, i.e, the PRC Constitution 1954,[181] the PRC Constitution 1975[182] and the PRC Constitution 1978,[183] none of which provided any protection or treatment to foreigners in China.[184] Under the PRC's political and economic environment from 1949 to 1978, granting general national treatment to foreign countries, especially the United States, was out of the question.[185] Thus, national treatment became a victim of the political struggles.

---

176 The Common Creed, supra note 161, art. 37.

177 ZHANG ZHENGXIONG, DUIWAI MAOYI JICHU ZHISHI [BASIC KNOWLEDGE OF FOREIGN TRADE] 14 (Foreign Trade Education Press 1988).

178 For information on the Sino-Soviet split, see, e.g., IMMANUEL C.Y. HSÜ , THE RISE OF MODERN CHINA 671–87 (Oxford Univ. Press 6th edn, 2000).

179 GUOJI JINGJIFA ZONGLUN [GENERAL REVIEW OF INTERNATIONAL ECONOMIC LAW] 70–71 (Chen An ed., Law Press China 1991).

180 JOHN KING FAIRBANK, THE UNITED STATES AND CHINA 306 (Zhang Lijing (trans.), World Affairs Press 4th edn, 2003).

181 PRC Constitution 1954, adopted at the First NPC, September 20, 1954, in ZHONGHUA RENMIN GONGHEGUO XIANFA JI YOUGUAN ZILIAO HUIBIAN [COMPILATION OF PRC CONSTITUTIONS AND RELEVANT DOCUMENTS] 64–83 (Liaison Bureau of the General Office of the Standing Committee of the NPC (ed.), China Minzhu yu Fazhi Publishing House 1990).

182 PRC Constitution 1975, adopted at the First Session of the Fourth NPC, January 13, 1975, in THE CONSTITUTION OF THE PEOPLE'S REPUBLIC OF CHINA (Commercial Press 1975).

183 PRC Constitution 1978, adopted at the First Session of the Fifth National People's Congress, March 5, 1978, in THE CONSTITUTION OF THE PEOPLE'S REPUBLIC OF CHINA (People's Publishing House 1978).

184 There was only one article concerning foreigners in China in the PRC Constitutions of 1954, 1975, 1978, stating: "The PRC grants the right of residence to any foreign nationals persecuted for supporting a just cause, for taking part in revolutionary movements or for engaging in scientific activities." PRC Constitution 1954, art. 99, supra note 181; PRC Constitution 1975, art. 29, supra note 182; PRC Constitution 1978, art. 59, supra note 183.

185 In early commerce and shipping treaties with a few socialist countries, national treatment, if any, was applicable only in a special circumstance, i.e., salvage at sea. See Article 9 of the Commerce and Shipping Treaty between the PRC and the USSR (1958),

B. Foreign Banks and Their Treatment during 1949–1978

The CCP was extremely hostile to foreign banks. In the eyes of Mao Zedong, foreign banks were financial tools of the imperialist powers to "monopolize China's finance" and "clutch at China's throat".[186] From the early period of the CCP, one can find that one of the goals of the CCP was to "restrain" or even "confiscate" foreign-funded banks.[187] Thus, after the establishment of the PRC in 1949, the environment of foreign banks in China became worse and worse, especially after the outbreak of the Korean War. The policy of the PRC government for foreign banks was to repeal their prerogatives, narrow their business scope,[188] and supervise and urge the discharge of their debts. This policy made it difficult for foreign banks to carry over their business in China.[189] For example, from 1949 to 1953, the HSBC had no choice but to make an application to shut down its branches in Beijing, Tianjin, Shantou and Shanghai.[190] However, in the very

---

in 7 Zhonghua Renmin Gongheguo Tiaoyue Ji [Collection of the Treaties of the PRC] 42–46 (Law Press China 1959), also available in Treaties of the People's Republic of China, 1949–1978: An Annotated Compilation 123–28 (Grant F. Rhode and Reid E. Whitlock (eds), Westview Press 1980) [hereinafter TREATIES OF THE PRC] ; Article 10 of the Commerce and Shipping Treaty between the PRC and the Democratic Republic of Germany (1960), in 9 Collection of the Treaties of the PRC 134–39 (Law Press China 1961; Article 10 of the Commerce and Shipping Treaty between the PRC and Albania (1961), in Treaties of the PRC, supra, at 128–133; Article 9 of the Commerce and Shipping Treaty between the PRC and the People's Democratic Republic of Korea (1962), in 11 Collection of the Treaties of the PRC 92–97 (Law Press China 1963); Article 9 of the Commerce and Shipping Treaty between the PRC and the Democratic Republic of Vietnam (1962), in Treaties of the PRC, supra, at 142–47.

186 Mao Zedong, *Zhongguo Geming yu Zhongguo Gongchandang* [Chinese Revolution and the Chinese Communist Party], in 2 Selected Works of Mao Zedong 629 (People's Publishing House, 2nd edn, 1991); but see Shizuya Nishimura, *International Banking in China 1890–1913*, in BANKING, TRADE AND INDUSTRY 378–95 (Alice Teichova et al. (eds), Cambridge Univ. Press 1997) (arguing that the international banks in China were material in facilitating the growth of China's foreign trade).

187 Draft of the Party Programme of the CCP [*Zhongguo Gongchandang Danggang Cao'an*], June 1923, in 1 Zhonggong Zhongyang Wenjian Xuanji: 1921–1925 [Selected Documents of the Central Committee of the CCP: 1921–1925] 107, 112 (Central Archives (ed.), Press of the Party School of the Central Committee of the CCP, 1982); Manifesto of the Chinese Communist Party on the Current Political Situation [*Zhongguo Gongchandang Dui Shijü Xuanyan*], September 20, 1928, made by the Central Executive Council of the CCP, in 4 Zhonggong Zhongyang Wenjian Xuanji: 1928,at 405, 411 (1983).

188 Yang Xitian et al., 6 Zhongguo Jinrong Tongshi: 1949–1996 [General History of China's Finance: 1949–1996] 21 (Li Fei et al. (eds), China Financial Publishing House 2002).

189 Collis, supra note 51, at 246.

190 Aron Shai, The Fate of British and French Firms in China (1949–1954): Imperialism Imprisoned 99 (Zhang Pin et al (trans.), China Social Sciences Press 2004)

beginning, the PRC government neither allowed the closure of those branches, nor issued departure permits to foreigners employed by the foreign banks.[191] In the end, most foreign banks were allowed to leave China at the cost of giving up almost all their assets in China.[192] Through this approach, foreign banks' profits gained in China during the last one hundred years were, at least in part, returned to China.[193] Under the hostile environment, it was extremely difficult for foreign banks to find a place to do business in China. To most foreign banks, there was only one issue, i.e., how to leave China without being confiscated. Compared with the matter of to be or not to be, national treatment was of no consideration. After the middle of the 1950s, only four foreign banks, i.e. the HSBC, the Chartered Bank, the Overseas Chinese Banking Corporation, and the Bank of East Asia, stayed in China,[194] and these banks' operation in China was only nominal during the following thirty years.[195]

V. Post-1978

A. National Treatment in PRC's Laws post-1978

PRC's "closed-door" policy was replaced by a "reform and open" [*gaige kaifang*] policy adopted at the end of 1978.[196] China's relations with the United States were normalized on January 1, 1979.[197] Also in 1979, China promulgated the Sino-Foreign Equity Joint Venture Law [*Zhongwai Hezi Jingying Qiyefa*] to encourage

---

(original published by Macmillan Press 1996).

191 Id. at 91.

192 Id. at 139.

193 Id. at 49.

194 See PAUL D. REYNOLDS, CHINA'S INTERNATIONAL BANKING AND FINANCIAL SYSTEM 78 (Praeger 1982) (stating that the PRC government allowed the two British banks to exist in China as a result of a deal between the United Kingdom and China whereby the Bank of China was permitted to maintain its London branch); YANG XITIAN ET AL., supra note 188, at 21; see also JI, supra note 49, at 244 (stating that the reason for the existence of the HSBC in the PRC was that the Birtish government established a diplomatic liaison office in the PRC in 1950).

195 ZHU ZHENHUA, ZHONGGUO JINRONG JIUSHI [CHINA'S FINANCIAL MATTERS OF THE PAST] 31 (China Radio and Television Publishing House 1991).

196 Communiqué of the Third Plenum of the Eleventh Central Committee of the CCP, December 22, 1978, 1 Shiyijie Sanzhong Quanhui yilai Zhongyao Wenxian Xuandu [Selections of Important Documents since the Third Plenum of the Eleventh Central Committee of the CCP] 1–14 (Document Study Office of the Central Committee of the CCP (ed.), People's Publishing House, 1987).

197 Joint Communiqué on Establishment of Diplomatic Relations between the United States of America and the PRC, December 15, 1978, 18 I.L.M. 272 (1979).

and protect foreign investment in China.[198] The 1979 Sino-Foreign Equity Joint Venture Law itself did not contain a national treatment article, but it did provide legal protection to foreign investors for the first time in PRC's legislative history, and laid the foundation for subsequent national treatment legislation.

The history of national treatment legislation in the PRC shows that national treatment legislation began from procedural law and was extended to substantive law; within substantive law, national treatment was extended from civil law to trade law. Indeed, PRC's national treatment legislation started from court access rights of foreigners, rather than their equal trade rights. PRC's first law with a clear national treatment article is the Interim Civil Procedure Law promulgated in 1982[199] that stated that foreigners should have the same litigation rights and obligations as Chinese citizens.[200] Foreign enterprises and institutions had the litigation rights and obligations provided by the Interim Civil Procedure Law.[201] From the different expressions, it seems that China only granted national treatment with respect to civil procedure to foreign individuals, not to foreign enterprises or institutions. This discrimination between foreign individuals and foreign enterprises was gradually eliminated after the enactment of the PRC Constitution 1982[202] that allowed foreigners and foreign enterprises to invest in the territory of China and provided legal protection to both.[203] From then on, national treatment got a new lease on life in China.

In 1989, China promulgated the Administrative Procedure Law.[204] Paragraph 1 of Article 71 of the Administrative Procedure Law states that "[f]oreigners, stateless persons and foreign institutions that are engaged in administrative

---

198 Sino-Foreign Equity Joint Venture Law [*Zhongwai Hezuo Jingying Qiyefa*], adopted at the Second Session of the Fifth NPC on July 1, 1979, effective July 1, 1979, Falü Huibian 1979–1984, at 168–71 (People's Publishing House 1985); Amended in 1990 and 2001, Falü Huibian 2001, at 58–62 (People's Publishing House 2002).

199 PRC Interim Civil Procedure Law (1982), adopted at the 22nd meeting of the Standing Committee of the Fifth NPC on March 8, 1982, effective October 1, 1982, Falü Huibian 1979–1984, at 283–324. But see Private International Law 107 (Han Depei, Ren Jisheng and Liu Ding (eds), Wuhan Univ. Press rev. edn, 1989) (arguing that the Invention Encouragement Regulation [*Faming Jiangli Tiaoli*] contained a national treatment article). See the Invention Encouragement Regulation, art. 12, *Guofa* [1978] No. 279, issued by the State Council on December 28, 1978, revised in 1984, 1993, repealed in 1999, http://www.gdstc.gov.cn/zhengce/three1.htm.

200 PRC Interim Civil Procedure Law, id. art. 186, ¶ 1.

201 Id. art. 186, ¶ 2.

202 PRC Constitution 1982, adopted at the Fifth Session of the Fifth NPC on December 4, 1982, effective December 4, 1982, amended in 1988, 1993, 1999, 2004, in Falü Huibian 2004, at 1–34 (People's Publishing House 2005).

203 Id. arts. 18, 32.

204 PRC Administrative Procedure Law, adopted at the Second Session of the Seventh NPC on April 4, 1989, effective October 1, 1990, Falü Huibian 1989, at 23–39 (People's Publishing House 1990).

suits in the PRC shall have the same litigation rights and obligations as citizens and institutions of the PRC". This law grants national treatment to both foreign individuals and institutions with respect to administrative court access rights.

In 1991, the PRC Civil Procedure Law[205] replaced the Interim Civil Procedure Law and broadened the beneficiaries of national treatment to include foreign individuals, stateless persons, foreign enterprises and foreign institutions.[206] In 2007 and 2012, the PRC Civil Procedure Law was amended twice, but the article according national treatment to foreigners and foreign institutions remained. [207]

In addition to the above national treatment concerning procedural rights, some Chinese substantive laws also applied to foreigners, foreign-funded enterprises and foreign enterprise branches in the territory of China,[208] despite a lack of wording that would seem necessary to grant them, such as "the same rights and obligations".

In the PRC's legislative history, the term "national treatment" first appeared in the Foreign Trade Law.[209] Article 6 of the Foreign Trade Law states that:

> [t]he People's Republic of China shall, under international treaties or agreements to which the People's Republic of China is a contracting party or a participation party, grant the other contracting parties or participating parties, or on the principles of mutual benefit and reciprocity, grant the other party most-favoured-nation treatment or *national treatment* within the field of foreign trade (emphasis added).

Article 24 of Foreign Trade Law is specifically applicable to international trade in services, which directly stipulates that:

---

[205] PRC Civil Procedure Law [*Minshi Susongfa*], adopted at the Fourth Session of the Seventh NPC on April 9, 1991, effective April 9, 1991, GAZETTE OF THE STATE COUNCIL 481–520 (1991, no. 13).

[206] Id. art. 5.

[207] PRC Civil Procedure Law 2012, art. 5, http://www.npc.gov.cn/huiyi/cwh/1128/2012-09/01/content_1736001_2.htm.

[208] See, e.g., General Principles of Civil Law of the PRC [*Zhonghua Renmin Gongheguo Minfa Tongze*], art. 8, adopted at the Fourth Session of the Sixth NPC on April 12, 1986, effective January 1, 1987, Falü Huibian 1986, at 24–56 (People's Publishing House 1987); PRC Corporation Law [*Gongsifa*], arts. 2, 194–98, 218, adopted at the Fifth Meeting of the Standing Committee of the Eighth NPC on December 29, 1993, effective July 1, 1994, firstly amended in 1999, secondly amended in 2004, GAZETTE OF THE NPC 485–506 (2004, no. 6), thirdly amended in 2005, http://www.law-lib.com/law/law_view.asp?id=102906.

[209] PRC Foreign Trade Law of 1994, adopted at the Seventh Meeting of the Standing Committee of the Eighth NPC on May 12, 1994, effective July 1, 1994, GAZETTE OF THE STATE COUNCIL 423–29 (1994, no. 11); amended in 2004, adopted at the Eighth Meeting of the Standing Committee of the Tenth NPC, April 6, 2004, effective July 1, 2004, GAZETTE OF THE NPC 247–53 (2004, no. 4).

> [w]ith respect to international trade in services, the People's Republic of China, pursuant to the commitments made in international treaties or agreements to which the People's Republic of China is a contracting party or a participating party, grants the other contracting parties and participating parties market access and national treatment.[210]

Based on the Foreign Trade Law, one can find the contemporary attitude of the PRC government to national treatment with respect to foreign trade. The first understanding is that national treatment should be based on treaties or agreements, which means that China has no duty to grant national treatment to foreigners without a treaty or an agreement. The second understanding is that national treatment must, at the very least, be based on the principle of reciprocity, implying the impossibility of unilateral national treatment. The third understanding is that China's national treatment is not unconditional, but rather subject to China's reservations under treaties or agreements.

B. National Treatment in PRC's Treaties post-1978

PRC's early agreements with other countries emphasized MFN treatment.[211] In regard to national treatment, the PRC was fairly prudent in making such a commitment. Arguably, one article in the 1979 Agreement on Trade Relations between the People's Republic of China and the United States[212] was a national treatment article, despite lacking the term "national treatment" or other symbolic words such as "no less than" or "the same".[213] On March 19, 1985, China became a member of the Paris Convention for the Protection of Industrial Property (Paris Convention).[214] As a result, the national treatment article in the multilateral treaty (i.e., Article 2 of the Paris Convention) has been applicable to China since that date.

---

210 It must be noted that Article 24 of the Foreign Trade Law (amended 2004) is the same as article 23 of the Foreign Trade Law of 1994.

211 See, e.g., Article 2 of the Commerce and Shipping Treaty between the PRC and the USSR (1958); Article 2 of the Commerce and Shipping Treaty between the PRC and the Democratic Republic of Germany (1960); Article 2 of the Commerce and Shipping Treaty between the PRC and Albania (1961); Article 2 of the Commerce and Shipping Treaty between the PRC and the People's Democratic Republic of Korea (1962); Article 2 of the Commerce and Shipping Treaty between the PRC and the Democratic Republic of Vietnam (1962), supra note 185; see also the Exchange Note on MFN Treatment Concerning Tariffs and Navigation Between China and Denmark (1957), in 6 Zhonghua Renmin Gongheguo Tiaoyue Ji 45–47 (Law Press China 1958).

212 Agreement on Trade Relations between the PRC and the United States, art. 6, ¶ 2, signed on July 7, 1979, entered into force on February 1, 1980, in 26 Zhonghua Renmin Gongheguo Tiaoyue Ji 121–26 (World Affairs Press 1983).

213 Private International Law, supra note 199, at 107.

214 For the Paris Convention, see http://www.wipo.int/treaties/en/ip/paris/trtdocs_wo020.html. For the Chinese version of the Paris Convention, see 1 Collection of the

National Treatment in China's BITs

During the 1980s, China began to enter into bilateral investment treaties (BITs) with foreign states, providing for fair and equitable treatment [*gongping heli daiyu*] and MFN treatment.[215] In contrast to the US BITs Program launched at the end of the 1970s[216] and accompanied by a Model Text containing a standard national treatment clause,[217] China does not have a BIT model text that includes a standard national treatment clause.[218] China's first BIT was signed in 1982, but a national treatment clause was not introduced into China's BITs until four years later by the conclusion of the Sino-British BIT (1986). From 1982 to 2011, the PRC had signed about 129 BITs with countries of Asia, Europe, Africa, North America, South America, and Oceania.[219] Of these 129 BITs, national treatment clauses appear in at least 48 BITs. The 48 BITs are shown in the following table:

Table 1.1 National treatment clauses in China's BITs

No.	BIT	National treatment clause	Year
1	Sino-British BIT	art. 3(3)	1986
2	Sino-Japanese BIT	arts. 3 (2) and 4	1988
3	Sino-Slovenia BIT	art. 3(2)	1993
4	Sino-Icelandic BIT	art. 3(3)	1994
5	Sino-Moroccan BIT	art. 3(1)	1995
6	Sino-Yugoslavian BIT	art. 3(2)	1995
7	Sino-Saudi Arabian BIT	art. 3(2)	1996

continued ...

MULTILATERAL TREATIES OF THE PRC, 10–41 (The Department of Treaty and Law of the Ministry of Foreign Affairs of the PRC (ed.), Law Press China 1987).

215 Li Shishi, *Lun Zhongguo Dijie de Shuangbian Touzi Baohu Xieding* [On Bilateral Investment Protection Treaties Entered by China with Other Countries], 1990 CHINESE Y.B. INT'L. L. 109, 115–16; see also Chen Xuebin, *Towards Post-establishment National Treatment of Foreign Investment Enterprises in China – From BITs to TRIMs*, in THE WTO AND THE DOHA ROUND: THE CHANGING FACE OF WORLD TRADE 187, 189 (Ross P. Buckley (ed.), Kluwer Law International 2003).

216 Kenneth J. Vandevelde, *U.S. Bilateral Investment Treaties: The Second Wave*, 14 MICH. J. INT'L L. 621, 624 (1993).

217 Article II:1 of the 1984 Revised United States Model Bilateral Investment Treaty, 1 BASIC DOCUMENTS OF INTERNATIONAL ECONOMIC LAW 657 (Stephen Zamora and Ronald A. Brand (eds), CCH 1990).

218 It must be noted that fair and equitable treatment is different from national treatment. The former is "absolute" or "non-contingent" treatment, while the latter is "relative" treatment. See OECD, Fair and Equitable Treatment Standard in International Investment Law, Working Papers on International Investment, No. 2004/3, at 2, September 2004, www.oecd.org/dataoecd/22/53/33776498.pdf.

219 See China's Peaceful Development, Information Office of the State Council, September 2011, Beijing, http://www.scio.gov.cn/zfbps/ndhf/2011/201109/t1000031.htm.

No.	BIT	National treatment clause	Year
8	Sino-Cameroonian BIT	art. 3(1)	1997
9	Sino-Macedonian BIT	art. 3(3)	1997
10	Sino-Gabonese BIT	art. 3(1)	1997
11	Sino-South African BIT	art. 3(3)	1997
12	Sino-Yemeni BIT	art. 3(1)	1998
13	Sino-Botswana BIT	art. 3(2)	2000
14	Sino-Irani BIT	art. 4(1)	2000
15	Sino-Sierra Leonean BIT	art. 3(2)	2001
16	Sino-Myanmar BIT	art. 3(2)	2001
17	Sino-Nigerian BIT	art. 3(2)	2001
18	Sino-Cypriot BIT	art. 3(3)	2001
19	Sino-Bosnian-Herzegovinian BIT	art. 3(1)	2002
20	Sino-Cote d'ivoirian BIT	art. 3(2)	2002
21	Sino-Trinidad and Tobago BIT	art. 4(2)	2002
22	Sino-Guyanese BIT	art. 3(2)	2003
23	Sino-German BIT	art. 3(2)	2003
24	Sino-Beninese BIT	art. 3(1)	2004
25	Sino-Latvian BIT	art. 3(2)	2004
26	Sino-North Korean BIT	art. 3(2)	2005
27	Sino-Finnish BIT	art. 3(2)	2005
28	Sino-Spanish BIT	art. 3(2)	2005
29	Sino-Portuguese BIT	art.3(2)	2005
30	Sino-Czech BIT	art.3(1) (2)	2005
31	Sino-Equatorial Guinean BIT	art. 3(2)	2005
32	Sino-Madagascan BIT	art. 4(1)	2005
33	Sino-Belgian-Luxemburg BIT	art. 3(1)	2005
34	Sino-Indian BIT	art. 4(1)	2006
35	Sino-Vanuatuan BIT	art. 3(2)	2006
36	Sino-Russian BIT	art. 2(2)	2006
37	Sino-Indian BIT	art. 4(1)	2006
38	Sino-Seychellois BIT	art. 5(1)	2007
39	Sino-South Korean BIT	art. 3(1)	2007
40	Sino-Bulgarian BIT	art. 3(1)	2007
41	Sino-French BIT	art. 4	2007
42	Sino-Mexican BIT	art. 3(1)	2008
43	Sino-Colombian BIT	art. 3(1)	2008
44	Sino-Maltese BIT	art. 3(2)	2009
45	Sino-Malian BIT	art. 3(2)	2009
46	Sino-Swiss BIT	art. 4(2)	2009
47	Sino-Uzbekistan BIT	art. 3	2011
48	Sino-Canadian BIT	art. 6	2012

Note: compiled by the author based mainly on data from http://tfs.mofcom.gov.cn/aarticle/Nocategory/201111/20111107819474.html

Return of GATT National Treatment to China

After the "reform and open" policy, China became more and more interested in the GATT. In 1982, China, as an observer, attended the thirty-eighth GATT Conference.[220] And in July 1986, China applied to resume its contracting party status in the GATT.[221] Unfortunately, China did not reach an agreement with the GATT by the end of 1994, so it had to initiate the process to get access to the WTO in 1995.[222] The decision on China's WTO accession was made by consensus at the Doha Ministerial Conference on November 10, 2001.[223] The PRC government accepted the China Accession Protocol after only one day, and China became a WTO Member on December 11, 2001. From then on, national treatment obligations of the WTO, together with other WTO obligations, began to bind China as international law obligations. Thus, national treatment of the GATT returned to China after half a century.

Changes of National Treatment in China's BITs in the Twenty-first Century

From 1982 through the end of 2001, the PRC concluded about 100 BITs, among which only 18 BITs have national treatment clauses. But from 2002 to 2012, the PRC signed more than 30 BITs, almost all of which contained national treatment clauses. This trend likely indicates that more and more BITs to be concluded by China with foreign countries will contain national treatment clauses. The change is reflected in not only the increase in number of BITs that include national treatment clauses, but also in the decrease of limitations in national treatment clauses.

In the 48 BITs with national treatment clauses as shown in Table 1.1, there are a variety of limitations on the application of national treatment. First, in the Sino-British BIT, the Sino-Slovenia BIT, the Sino-Icelandic BIT, the Sino-Yugoslavian BIT, and the Sino-Macedonian BIT, national treatment is based on the conditions of "endeavour" and "in accordance with its laws and regulations". Such limitations could downgrade national treatment obligations to best-effort duties and subject national treatment obligations in the bilateral treaties to domestic laws. Second, in the Sino-Moroccan BIT, the Sino-Saudi Arabian BIT, the Sino-Cameroonian BIT, the Sino-Nigerian BIT, the Sino-Irani BIT, the Sino-Gabonese BIT, and the Sino-Yemeni BIT, the limitation on national treatment is "in accordance with its laws and regulations". Third, in the Sino-Botswana BIT, the Sino-Sierra Leonean BIT, the Sino-North Korean BIT, the Sino-Russian BIT, and Sino-Vanuatuan BIT, the limitation on national treatment is "without damaging its laws and regulations".

---

220 Yang Guohua and Cheng Jin, supra note 134, at 301.

221 Id, at 302.

222 In December 1995, China applied for accession to the WTO according to Article XII of the WTO Agreement. WT/ACC/CHN/1.

223 Accession of the PRC, Decision on November 10, 2001, WT/L/432 (November 23, 2001).

Fourth, in the Sino-Cote d'ivoirian BIT, the Sino-Guyanese BIT, the Sino-Beninese BIT, and the Sino-Latvian BIT, all of which were concluded after 2002, the limitation on national treatment is "without being inconsistent with its laws and regulations". Finally, although the Sino-Japanese BIT, the Sino-Korean BIT, the Sino-Bosnian-Herzegovinian BIT and the Sino-German BIT do not uniformly contain direct limitations on national treatment, the Protocols of the BITs do include some limitations on national treatment.[224]

Strictly speaking, the national treatment clauses with the limitations of "endeavour" are only nominal and lack legally binding force. This conclusion may also apply to those clauses with the limitation of "in accordance with its laws and regulations" because it implies that there will be no national treatment obligations without relevant domestic laws and regulations.[225] However, with the beginning of the twenty-first century, and especially after China's entry to the WTO, there have been fewer limitations on national treatment in China's BITs, which have also become less demanding. If national treatment in China's pre-WTO BITs was not attractive to foreign investment,[226] the post-WTO national treatment in China's BITs is evolving to be an attractive factor because all of China's BITs contain MFN treatment clauses.[227] These clauses allow pre-WTO BITs without national treatment clauses to incorporate such clauses, and pre-WTO BITs with heavily limited national treatment clauses to incorporate national treatment clauses with relaxed limitation. This is the MFN's automatic adaptation function or, in other words, automatic generalization.[228]

C. Foreign Banks and Their Treatment post-1978

Although there were several national treatment articles in some Sino-foreign BITs concluded during the 1980s and the 1990s, the limitations on the national

---

224 Article 3 of the Protocol of Sino-Japanese BIT states that a party may provide discriminatory treatment when necessary, in accordance with its laws and regulations, for the purpose of maintaining public order, national security or national economic development; see also Article 4 of the Protocol of the Sino-German BIT, and the Protocol of the Sino-Bosnian-Herzegovinian BIT.

225 See Vandevelde, supra note 216, at 661.

226 GUOJI TOUZI FAXUE [INTERNATIONAL INVESTMENT LAW] 432–35 (Zheng Huaqun ed., Peking Univ. Press 1999).

227 See id, at 435 (stating that a national treatment clause appears in each of China's BITs).

228 Georg Schwarzenberger, *The Most-Favoured-Nation Standard in British State Practice*, 1945 BRIT. Y.B. INT'L L. 96, 99, 119; see also NEUFELD, supra note 1, at 113; N.A. MARYAN GREEN, INTERNATIONAL LAW 93 (3rd edn, Pitman Publishing 1987); UNCTAD, BILATERAL INVESTMENT TREATIES IN THE MID-1990s, UNCTAD/ITE/IIT/7, at 61 (United Nations 1998) (stating that the generalizing effect of an MFN provision applies to a national treatment provision of a BIT).

treatment articles, such as "endeavour" and "in accordance with its laws and regulations", actually prevented national treatment from applying to China's banking law. The concept of national treatment was not introduced in the area of PRC's banking services until the PRC got access to the WTO in 2001. After 2001, the treatments of foreign-funded banks were adjusted based on PRC's WTO commitments in banking services, and the State Council promulgated the Regulation on Administration of Foreign-Funded Financial Institutions of 2001 (FFFI Regulation 2001).[229] In 2006, FFFI regulation 2001 was replaced by the Regulation on Administration of Foreign-Funded Banks [*waizi yinhang guanli tiaoli*] (hereinafter FFB Regulation 2006).[230] FFB Regulation 2006 and China's other banking laws, regulations and rules are further addressed in chapters 3, 4, 5, 6, and 7.

VI. Concluding Remarks

In the foregoing sections I have examined the history of national treatment in China's treaties and laws in an effort to find out whether and how the concept of national treatment has been accepted by the Chinese legal system. I have also deliberated on the history of foreign banks and their treatment in China. The following is an attempt to summarize the findings.

The treatment of foreigners during the Qing Dynasty and the ROC period progressed as follows: from inferior treatment to prerogative treatment, from prerogative treatment to national treatment, from unilateral national treatment to bilateral national treatment, and then finally, to multilateral national treatment. The movement from inferior treatment to prerogative treatment was the result of, at least in part, China's unwise "closed-door" policy and China's arrogant attitude towards the outside world, as well as the aggression of the Western powers.[231] The movement from prerogative treatment to national treatment, along with the movement from unilateral national treatment to bilateral national treatment and multilateral national treatment, reflect the movement of Chinese people's revolution from a quasi-colonial [*banzhimindi*] and semi-feudal [*banfengjian*] country to an independent and modern country. Also reflected is the development of a Western civilization that gradually recognized that the opium trade, consular jurisdiction,

---

[229] FFFI Regulation 2001, State Council Decree 340, promulgated on December 20, 2001, effective February 1, 2002, void on December 11, 2006, Gazette of the State Council 18–22 (2002, no. 3).

[230] FFB Regulation 2006, State Council Decree 478, promulgated on November 11, 2006, effective as of December 11, 2006, art. 73, Gazette of the State Council 13–19 (2007, no. 1).

[231] For the nature of aggression of the expansion of Western powers to China, see Fairbank, supra note 180, at 156.

negotiated tariffs, and the like, were in violation of human civilization.[232] Indeed, in Nussbaum's view, national treatment is the basis of the so-called "international bill of rights".[233] Thus, the historical evolution of national treatment in Modern China (1840–1949) is a miniature of the history of Modern China and the history of Western civilization.

The early development of national treatment in China was not the direct result of eliminating or reducing the barriers of trade to foreigners, but rather the consequence of repealing the prerogatives of foreigners caught by a series of unequal treaties or, in other words, the price that China had to pay in exchange for repealing those unequal treaties made by the late Qing Dynasty, to which the ROC government succeeded. From the Chinese perspective, the national treatment was not voluntarily accepted – rather it was imposed. And it was the lesser of two evils. Indeed, compared with foreigners' prerogatives, such as consular jurisdiction, the national treatment of foreigners represented progress in the history of relations between China and foreign countries. Chinese suspicion of national treatment, however, continued from the establishment of the ROC to the end of the 1940s due to historical reasons. This attitude was not altered by the change of the Chinese government in 1949. It was to be expected that the PRC government, led by the CCP, which considered itself the liberator that emancipated China from oppression of imperialism and feudalism, would not grant the Western powers national treatment embodied in those "traitorous treaties" [*maiguo tiaoyue*]. The long-hostile and suspicious attitude towards national treatment in China's modern history was not because China was unwilling to give equal treatment to foreign countries, but because national treatment, as well as MFN treatment, was closely connected with the dark age of Chinese history in which Chinese people were humiliated by the Western powers through a series of wars, including, the First Opium War (1840–1842), the Second Opium War (1856–1860), the Sino-French War (1884–1885), the Sino-Japanese *Jiawu* War (1894–1895), the war triggered by the Boxer Movement [*Yihetuan Yundong*] (1900). China suffered serious defeats in those wars and was forced to cede territory (e.g., Hong Kong Island to Britain in 1842 and Taiwan Island to Japan in 1895), pay indemnities, and lease land. Therefore, it is not difficult to understand Chinese xenophobia during that

---

232 See, e.g., Montreux Convention 1937, supra note 122. For Western Powers' willingness to repeal prerogative rights in China, see the Reply from the Secretary of State of the United States to the Foreign Minister of the Republic of China (May 1941), and the Note from the British Ambassador in the Republic of China to the Foreign Minister of the Republic of China (July 1941), in 5 (2) COMPILATION OF ARCHIVES OF THE HISTORY OF THE REPUBLIC OF CHINA, "Diplomacy", at 429–30, 532 (The Second Historical Archives of China (ed.), Jiangsu Ancient Books Publishing House 1997); see also Wang Jianlang, *Beijing Zhengfu Xiuyue Yundong Jianlun* [The Abolition of Unequal Treaties in the 1920s and Wellington Koo], in WELLINGTON KOO AND CHINESE DIPLOMACY 132, 143–44 (Jin Guangyao (ed.), Shanghai Classics Publishing House 2001).

233 NUSSBAUM, supra note 1, at 204, 206, 263.

period. Unfortunately, national treatment was introduced in China against this background, which doomed it to a rough road in China. When national treatment started to be gradually accepted under the principle of reciprocity and equality in the 1940s, it was adversely influenced by the change of China's political situation as the CCP came to power in mainland China. The concept of national treatment disappeared from the scene for more than three decades. Only after the CCP adopted the "reform and open" policy at the end of the 1970s did it receive a new life. With the development of China's economy and frequent contacts with people of other countries, the Chinese people's psychological response to national treatment had been fundamentally changed. National treatment is no longer seen as a big stick wielded by the Western powers to infringe upon China, but rather as a tool that can be used by all parties to create a level playing field for international trade.

Foreign banks and their treatment in China can also be divided into several stages. From the birth of the first foreign bank in China (1847) to the end of the Second World War, foreign banks enjoyed prerogative rights in China beyond Chinese banking law. From 1949 to 1978, their treatment in China took a sudden turn so that most foreign banks had to leave China. Only after 1978 was it feasible for foreign banks to open business in China again. However, the development of national treatment for foreign banks was much slower than that to general foreigners and foreign enterprises. Both the ROC government and the PRC government were cautious in according national treatment to foreign banks. The concept of national treatment was not introduced into the area of PRC's banking services until the PRC got access to the WTO in 2001.

CHAPTER 2
WTO National Treatment and China's Banking Commitments

From the wording of national treatment in China's Foreign Trade Law, China grants national treatment to other parties based on China's treaties.[1] Therefore, in order to fully comprehend what national treatment is in China and what national treatment means to foreign banks in China, it is essential to look to national treatment obligations in China's treaties, among which the WTO agreements are the most important. Indeed, China's accession to the WTO means that national treatment obligations in the WTO are applicable to China, which has brought about a great advance of national treatment in China and a great impact on China's banking law.

I. Overview of National Treatment under the GATT and the GATS

A. Significance of National Treatment in the GATT for the GATS

In the context of the GATT, national treatment is a basic principle against trade protectionism.[2] The fundamental purpose of GATT Article III is to "ensure equality of competitive conditions between imported and like domestic products".[3] Obviously, GATT Article III is within the scope of trade in goods. However, it

---

1 PRC Foreign Trade Law (amended 2004), art. 6, adopted at the Eighth Meeting of the Standing Committee of the Tenth NPC, April 6, 2004, effective July 1, 2004, GAZETTE OF THE NPC 247–53 (2004, no. 4).

2 OLIVIER LONG, LAW AND ITS LIMITATIONS IN THE GATT MULTILATERAL TRADE SYSTEM 9 (Graham and Trotman/Martinus Nijhoff 1987).

3 Appellate Body Report, *Canada – Certain Measures Concerning Periodicals* [hereinafter *Canada – Periodicals*], WT/DS31/AB/R, adopted July 30, 1997, Chapter IV, n.26; see also Panel Report, *Italian Discrimination against Imported Agricultural Machinery*, adopted October 23, 1958, BISD 7S/60, ¶ 13 (stating that "the intent of the drafters [of the GATT Article III] was to provide equal conditions of competition once goods had been cleared through customs"); Panel Report, *U.S. – Taxes on Petroleum and Certain Imported Substances*, adopted June 17, 1987, BISD 34S/136, ¶ 5.1.9 (stating that GATT Article III:2 "protects expectations on the competitive relationship between imported and domestic products"), and ¶ 5.2.2 (stating that the rationale of the national treatment obligation GATT Article III is "to protect expectations of the contracting parties as to the competitive relationship between their products and those of the other contracting parties").

is necessary to understand GATT Article III before probing into GATS national treatment because the GATT is the best background of the GATS, and "the GATS is broadly modelled on the GATT".[4] In the very beginning of the Uruguay Round negotiations, some countries were of the opinion that national treatment under the GATT could provide "a useful starting point" for the incorporation of the concept of national treatment in the agreement on services.[5] Even if GATS national treatment framework is not modelled on that of the GATT, as regarded by Brazil in the Uruguay Round negotiations,[6] it is still constructive to compare GATT national treatment and GATS national treatment. The significance of GATT national treatment for GATS national treatment is demonstrated by some WTO cases. For example, in the case of *EC-Bananas III*,[7] the Panel stated that "the drafters of the GATS have been guided by GATT concepts, provisions and past practice ..., they have chosen to use identical operative language of 'treatment no less favourable'...".[8] The Panel further pointed out that the formulation of GATS Article XVII derived from the "treatment no less favourable" standard of the GATT national treatment provisions in GATT Article III.[9]

B. Analysis of GATT Article III

GATT Article III contains 10 paragraphs, among which paragraphs 1, 2 and 4 are the most significant and relevant.

Paragraph 1 of GATT Article III
GATT Article III:1 reads:

> The contracting parties recognize that internal taxes and other internal charges, and laws, regulations and requirements affecting the internal sale, offering for sale, purchase, transportation, distribution or use of products, and internal quantitative regulations requiring the mixture, processing or use of products in specified amounts or proportions, should not be applied to imported or domestic products so as to afford protection to domestic production. (footnote omitted)

---

[4] Philip Ruttley, *Financial Service and the General Agreement on Trade in Services*, in LIBERALISATION AND PROTECTIONISM IN THE WORLD TRADING SYSTEM 184 (Philip Ruttley and Iain MacVay et al. (eds), Cameron May 1999); see also ERNST-ULRICH PETERSMANN, THE GATT/WTO DISPUTE SETTLEMENT SYSTEM: INTERNATIONAL LAW, INTERNATIONAL ORGANIZATIONS AND DISPUTE SETTLEMENT 210 (Kluwer Law International 1997).

[5] Note on the Meeting of 15–17 September, 1987, ¶ 17, MTN.GNS/10 (October 15, 1987).

[6] Note on the Meeting of 17–21 July, 1989, ¶ 214, MTN.GNS/24 (August, 1989).

[7] Panel Report, *European Communities – Regime for the Importation, Sale and Distribution of Bananas* [hereinafter *EC – Bananas III*], WT/DS27/R, adopted September 25, 1997.

[8] Id. ¶ 7.302.

[9] Id.

Paragraph 1 of GATT Article III is a general national treatment rule on trade in goods. It is to prevent any contracting party from protecting domestic products by applying discriminatory internal taxes, other internal charges, laws, regulations and other relevant requirements to imported products. In *Japan – Alcoholic Beverages II*,[10] the Appellate Body stated that GATT Article III:1 articulates a general principle which "informs the rest of Article III".[11]

Paragraph 2 of GATT Article III

GATT Article III:2 states:

> The products of the territory of any contracting party imported into the territory of any other contracting party shall not be subject, directly or indirectly, to internal taxes or other internal charges of any kind in excess of those applied, directly or indirectly, to like domestic products. Moreover, no contracting party shall otherwise apply internal taxes or other internal charges to imported or domestic products in a manner contrary to the principles set forth in paragraph 1. (footnote omitted)

GATT Article III:2 provides the detailed rules about internal taxes or other internal charges. The first sentence of GATT Article III:2 contains a very important definition – *like products* – which determines the scope of GATT Article III. The notion of *likeness* is a hard question in the history of the GATT 1947. In the 1970 *Working Party Report on Border Tax Adjustments*,[12] the Panel found:

> With regard to the interpretation of the term "like or similar products"... [t]he Working Party concluded that problems arising from the interpretation of the terms should be examined on a case-by-case basis. This would allow a fair assessment in each case of the different elements that constitute a "similar" product. Some criteria were suggested for determining, on a case-by-case basis, whether a product is "similar": the product's end-uses in a given market; consumers' tastes and habits, which change from country to country; the product's properties, nature and quality.[13]

Indeed, according to the GATT 1947 practice, the relevant factors for a determination of *like products* include the products' end-uses, consumers' status

---

[10] Appellate Body Report, *Japan – Taxes on Alcoholic Beverages* [hereinafter *Japan – Alcoholic Beverages II*], WT/DS8/AB/R, WT/DS10/AB/R, WT/DS11/AB/R, adopted November 1, 1996.

[11] Id. Section G.

[12] Report of the Working Party on Border Tax Adjustments, adopted by the Council on December 2, 1970, L/3464, BISD, 18S/97.

[13] Id. ¶ 18.

and habits, and the products' properties, nature and quality.[14] The GATT 1947 practice has been followed by the WTO dispute settlement practice.[15]

With regard to the second sentence of GATT Article III:2, there is a special note in Annex I of the GATT 1947 with the term of *directly competitive or substitutable products*.[16] From the early history of the GATT 1947, the scope of *directly competitive or substitutable products* is broad enough to encompass even distinctly different kinds of goods.[17] In *Japan – Alcoholic Beverages II*, the Panel and the Appellate Body provided another case-by-case approach for the determination of the range of *directly competitive or substitutable products*, and some ambiguous elements, such as physical characteristics, common end-uses and tariff classifications.[18]

Paragraph 4 of GATT Article III

GATT Article III:4 reads:

> The products of the territory of any contracting party imported into the territory of any other contracting party shall be accorded treatment no less favourable than that accorded to like products of national origin in respect of all laws, regulations and requirements affecting their internal sale, offering for sale, purchase, transportation, distribution or use. The provisions of this paragraph shall not prevent the application of differential internal transportation charges which are based exclusively on the economic operation of the means of transport and not on the nationality of the product.

Paragraph 4 is more important than other paragraphs of GATT Article III for the purpose of digging the background and terminology of GATS national

---

14 Id. Appellate Body Report, *Japan – Alcoholic Beverages II*, supra note 10, Section H:1(a); Appellate Body Report, *Canada – Periodicals*, WT/DS31/AB/R, Section V:A.

15 See Appellate Body Report, *Japan – Alcoholic Beverages II*, id, Section H:1(a). For detailed analysis of "like products", see Won-Mog Choi, 'Like Products' In International Trade Law: Towards a Consistent GATT/WTO Jurisprudence (Oxford Univ. Press 2003).

16 Ad Article III:2 in Annex I (Notes and Supplementary Provisions) of the GATT reads:

"A tax conforming to the requirements of the first sentence of paragraph 2 would be considered to be inconsistent with the provisions of the second sentence only in cases where competition was involved between, on the one hand, the taxed product and, on the other hand, a directly competitive or substitutable product which was not similarly taxed."

17 Won-Mog Choi, supra note 15, at 109.

18 Panel Report, *Japan – Alcoholic Beverages II*, WT/DS8/R, WT/DS/S10/R, WT/DS/S11/R, adopted November 1, 1996, ¶ 6.22 (stating that the decisive criterion in order to determine whether two products are directly competitive or substitutable is whether they have common end-uses, inter alia, as shown by elasticity of substitution); see also Appellate Body Report, *Japan – Alcoholic Beverages II*, supra note 10, Section H:2(a).

treatment.[19] It stipulates that the products imported shall be accorded treatment no less favourable than that accorded to like products in respect of all laws, regulations and requirements. Comparing with GATS Article XVII:1, one can easily find that the two paragraphs are similar to each other in the structure.[20] Both of them use the wording *treatment no less favourable*. In *U.S. – Section 337 of the Tariff Act of 1930*,[21] the GATT panel took account of *effective equality of opportunities* in respect of the application of laws, regulations and requirements, as a key test to analyse *treatment no less favourable*.[22] Moreover, this test was also adopted by a WTO panel in the report of *U.S. – Gasoline*,[23] the first panel report under WTO dispute settlement mechanism, indicating that the WTO practice has confirmed the test of *effective equality of opportunities*,[24] in spite of lacking details.

C. Negotiating History of National Treatment for Trade in Services

Early History

The history of national treatment dates back to earlier centuries.[25] However, in the field of trade in services, national treatment is still a new topic. In the middle of the 1980s, the United States called for negotiation of a framework of rules for trade in services comparable to GATT rules for the trade in goods, including, inter alia, the national treatment principle.[26] In 1986, an agreement was reached to negotiate services at Punta de Este,[27] and service negotiations became part of the job of the Trade Negotiations Committee, which was responsible for conducting the negotiations in the Uruguay Round. During the whole Uruguay Round negotiations, the goods negotiations and services negotiations were separated. The goods negotiations were guided by Group of Negotiations on Goods (GNG), and the

---

[19] Id. at 113.

[20] GATS article XVII:1 provides that "each Member shall accord to services and service suppliers of any other Member … treatment no less favourable than that it accords to its own like services and service suppliers".

[21] Panel Report, *U.S. – Section 337 of the Tariff Act of 1930*, adopted November 7, 1986, BISD 36S/345, L/6439.

[22] Id. ¶ 5.11.

[23] Panel Report, *U.S. – Standards for Reformulated and Conventional Gasoline* [hereinafter *U.S. — Gasoline*], WT/DS2/R, adopted May 20, 1996.

[24] Id. ¶ 6.10.

[25] John H. Jackson, The World Trading System: Law and Policy of International Economic Relations 213 (MIT Press 2nd edn, 1997).

[26] See Jack W. Flader, JR, *A Call For a General Agreement on Trade in Services*, 3 Transnat'l Law 661, 663 (1990).

[27] Ministerial Declaration on the Uruguay Round: Declaration of September 20, 1986, Part II: Negotiations on Trade in Services, BISD, 33rd Supplement, Geneva, June 1987, at 28.

service negotiations were guided by Group of Negotiations on Services (GNS).[28] Negotiating countries in the Uruguay Round knew that "it was worth trying to examine how far these principles [including national treatment] could be applied also to services",[29] and many countries were of the view that national treatment was at the heart of the service negotiations.[30] Nonetheless, the negotiations on national treatment for trade in services, like other services issues, were not smooth. Some countries recognized that national treatment might be "more difficult to apply to services than to goods".[31] One country even thought that the concept of national treatment was the most complex in the negotiations.[32] It was also the United States that made a first proposal to include national treatment as a fundamental element for a framework agreement on trade in services in October 1987.[33]

Montreal Agreement

As the United States desired, the Montreal agreement made at the mid-term review meeting of the Uruguay Round in December 1988 included a list of principles applicable to trade in services, such as transparency, market access, national treatment, etc.[34] In the Montreal Declaration,[35] there was a preliminary definition of national treatment for trade in services:

> When accorded in conformity with other provisions of the multilateral framework, it is understood that national treatment means that the services exports and/or exporters of any signatory are accorded in the market of any other signatory, in respect of all laws, regulations and administrative practices, treatment "no less favourable" than that accorded domestic services or services providers in the same market.[36]

---

[28] Id, at 27–28; see also JOHN CROOME, RESHAPING THE WORLD TRADING SYSTEM: A HISTORY OF THE URUGUAY ROUND 25 (Kluwer Law Int'l. 2nd edn, 1999); WENDY DOBSON AND PIERRE JACQUET, FINANCIAL SERVICES LIBERALIZATION IN THE WTO 72 (Institute for International Economics, 1998) (stating that one of the purposes of such a separation was to ease developing countries).

[29] Note on the Meeting of 23–25 February 1987, MTN.GNS/7, ¶ 29 (March 20, 1987).

[30] Note on the Meeting of 17 May 1988, MTN.GNS/15, ¶¶ 28, 40 (June 14, 1988).

[31] CROOME, supra note 28, at 105.

[32] See the opinion of the representative of India, in the Note on the Meeting of 17–21 July 1989, ¶ 212, MTN.GNS/24 (August, 1989).

[33] CROOME, supra note 28, at 107.

[34] Fred Lazar, *Services and the GATT: U.S. Motives and a Blueprint for Negotiation*, 24 J. WORLD TRADE 135, 135 (1990).

[35] Ministerial Declaration, MTN.TNC/8, in 3 THE GATT URUGUAY ROUND, A NEGOTIATING HISTORY (1986–1992), "DOCUMENT", at 62 (Terence P. Stewart (ed.), Kluwer Law and Taxation Publishers 1993).

[36] Id. Part II:7(c).

Chairman's July Text

In July 1990, the Chairman of the GNS issued the Draft Multilateral Framework for Trade in Services (Chairman's July Text),[37] under which the national treatment article was numbered XVII. It stated as follows:

> (1) In conformity with other relevant provisions of the framework, and as set out in their appropriate schedules, parties shall grant to services and service providers of other parties, in the application of all laws, regulations, administrative practices, and decisions of general application, treatment no less favourable than that accorded to like domestic services or service providers in like circumstances.
> (2) When necessary, the treatment a signatory accords to services or service providers of another signatory may be different from the treatment accorded to like domestic services or domestic providers of like services, as long as the treatment is equivalent in effect to the treatment accorded by the signatory to domestic providers in like circumstances.
> (3) The provisions of the framework on national treatment shall not apply to laws, regulations or requirements governing the procurement by governmental agencies of services purchased for governmental purposes and not with a view to use in production of services for commercial sale.
> (4) The provisions of the framework on national treatment shall not prevent the payment of subsidies or granting of incentives exclusively to domestic service providers.

Chairman's December Text

The Chairman's July text failed to provide a complete agreement acceptable to contracting parties.[38] In December 1990, the GNS Chairman released another draft text at Brussels, entitled the Draft Final Act Embodying the Result of the Uruguay Round of Multilateral Trade Negotiations (Chairman's December Text).[39] In this text, the article of national treatment, still numbered Article XVII, reads as follows:

> (1) Conformity with other relevant provisions of this Agreement, and in accordance with the conditions and qualifications set out in its schedule, each Party shall accord to services and service providers of other Parties, in respect of all measures affecting the supply of services, treatment no less favourable than that accorded to like domestic services or providers of like services.
> (2) Treatment a Party accords to services and service providers of other Parties shall be considered to be no less favourable within the meaning of paragraph 1 if it accords to the services or service providers of other Parties opportunities

37 GATT, MTN.GNS/35 (July 23, 1990).

38 2 The GATT Uruguay Round, A Negotiating History (1986–1992), "Commentary", at 2388 (Terence P. Stewart (ed.), Kluwer Law and Taxation Publishers 1993).

39 GATT, MTN/TNC/W/35/Rev.1, Annex II (December 3, 1990).

> to [compete] [supply services] that are no less favourable than those accorded to like domestic services or providers of like services. (footnote omitted, the bracket indicated that portion was especially controversial)

However, due to the deadlock over other issues, the negotiations in December 1990 failed and so did the Chairman's December text.[40]

Dunkel Draft

On December 20, 1991, Arthur Dunkel, Secretary-General of GATT of the time, released a "final draft act", the so-called Dunkel Draft.[41] In the Dunkel Draft, the GATS contained an article, specifically on national treatment, which constituted a blueprint for the final national treatment article, i.e. GATS Article XVII. The differences between GATS Article XVII in the Dunkel Draft and the final and official GATS Article XVII are very subtle. In the Dunkel Draft, GATS Article XVII reads:

> (1) In the sectors or sub-sectors inscribed in its Schedule of Commitment, and subject to any conditions and qualifications set out therein, each Party shall accord to services and service providers of any other Party, in respect of all measures affecting the supply of services, treatment no less favourable than that it accords to its own like services and service providers.* (* Commitments assumed under this Article shall not be construed to require any Party to compensate for any inherent competitive disadvantages which result from the foreign character of the relevant services or service providers) (bracket in original)
> (2) Party may meet the requirement of paragraph 1 by according to services and service providers of other Parties, either formally identical treatment or formally different treatment to that it accords to its own like services and service providers.
> (3) Formally identical or formally different treatment shall be considered to be less favourable if it modifies the conditions of competition in favour of services or service providers of the Party compared to like services or service providers of another Party.

In December 1993, the Uruguay Round ended with a series of agreements contained in the Final Act Embodying the Results of the Uruguay Round of

[40] See 2 THE GATT URUGUAY ROUND, A NEGOTIATING HISTORY (1986–1992), "COMMENTARY", supra note 38, at 2395.

[41] The Dunkel Draft is also called the Dunkel Text. JOHN H. JACKSON, THE WORLD TRADE ORGANIZATION: CONSTITUTION AND JURISPRUDENCE, § 2.4, at 28 (The Royal Institute of International Affairs 1998). For the official document of the Dunkel Draft, see MTN. TNC/W/FA, "Dunkel Draft" from the GATT Secretariat, collected and edited by the Institute for International Legal Information (William S. Hein 1992).

Multilateral Trade Negotiations (Final Act),[42] including, inter alia, the GATS. In January 1995, the GATS and other WTO multilateral trade agreements entered into force. From then on, the notion of national treatment began to apply to the trade in services.

D. Descriptive Analysis of GATS Article XVII

The GATS is composed of three pillars. The first pillar is the main text of the GATS agreement, including six Parts with twenty-nine articles and three *bis* articles.

1. Part I Scope and Definition
2. Part II General Obligations and Disciplines
3. Part III Specific Commitments
4. Part IV Progressive Liberalization
5. Part V Institutional Provisions
6. Part VI Final Provisions

The second pillar of the GATS contains eight Annexes.[43]

1. Annex on Article II Exemptions
2. Annex on Movement of Natural Persons Supplying Services under the Agreement
3. Annex on Air Transport Services
4. Annex on Financial Services
5. Second Annex on Financial Services
6. Annex on Negotiations on Maritime Transport Services
7. Annex on Telecommunications
8. Annex on Negotiations on Basic Telecommunications.

The third pillar of the GATS contains Schedules of Specific Commitments and Lists of Article II Exemptions of WTO Members. Schedules of Specific Commitments include WTO Members' market access commitments, national treatment commitments, and additional commitments, which are also annexed to the GATS.[44] Lists of Article II Exemptions (MFN exemptions) are part of the Annex on Article II Exemptions, an integral part of the GATS.[45] In addition, there

---

[42] Final Act, in THE LEGAL TEXTS: THE RESULTS OF THE URUGUAY ROUND OF MULTILATERAL TRADE NEGOTIATIONS (Cambridge Univ. Press 1999).

[43] GATS, art. XXIX (providing that the Annexes to the GATS are an integral part of it).

[44] Id. art. XX:3; see also Kevin C. Kennedy, *A WTO Agreement on Investment: A Solution in Search of a Problem*? 24 U. PA. J. INT'L. ECON. L. 110 (2003).

[45] See id. Annex on Article II Exemptions.

are eight Ministerial Decisions concerning the GATS, and one Understanding.[46] However, none of them is an integral part of the GATS.[47]

GATS Article XVII:1 reads:

> In the sectors inscribed in its Schedule, and subject to any conditions and qualifications set out therein, each Member shall accord to services and service suppliers of any other Member, in respect of all measures affecting the supply of services, treatment no less favourable than that it accords to its own like services and service suppliers. (footnote omitted)

GATS Article XVII:1 is the key rule of national treatment in service trade. The purpose of this paragraph is to prohibit discrimination against foreign services and service suppliers to the advantage of like services and service suppliers of national origin.[48]

Firstly, the scope of national treatment is limited in the sectors and subsectors inscribed in each Member's service schedule. This means that national treatment is not applicable to the service sectors or subsectors not covered by a Member's service schedule,[49] so one Member of the WTO may take discriminatory measures against services and service suppliers of any other Member in those reserved sectors or subsectors, without violating GATS Article XVII.

This reservation on national treatment came from the Uruguay Round negotiations on trade in services, particularly from the insistence of developing countries. In this regard, Peru's view could be the representative view of developing countries: "National treatment can be interpreted as an objective to be attained in the short, medium and long term, sector by sector, activity by activity, depending on the coverage and the commitments deriving from the final

---

46 Understanding on Commitments in Financial Services [hereinafter the Understanding], in THE LEGAL TEXTS: THE RESULTS OF THE URUGUAY ROUND OF MULTILATERAL TRADE NEGOTIATIONS, supra note 42, at 418–21.

47 Compared to the unclear status of the Ministerial Decisions under the GATS, the Ministerial Decisions under that GATT have legal effect. WTO Agreement Article XVI reads: "… the WTO shall be guided by the decisions, procedures and customary practices followed by the CONTRACTING PARTIES to GATT 1947 and the bodies established in the framework of GATT 1947". Article II: 2 of the WTO Agreement does not mention the Ministerial Decisions relating to the GATS or their legal status.

48 Panel Report, *EC – Bananas III*, supra note 7, ¶ 7.302.

49 In *China – Publications and Audiovisual Product*, the panel found: "A description of a service sector in a GATS schedule does not need to enumerate every activity that is included within the scope of that service, and is not meant to do so. A service sector or subsector in a GATS schedule thus includes not only every service activity specifically named within it, but also any service activity that falls within the scope of the definition of that sector or subsector referred to in the schedule." Panel Report, *China – Publications and Audiovisual Products*, WT/DS363/R, adopted January 19, 2010, ¶ 7.1014.

framework agreement."[50] Mexico held the same view.[51] This bottom-up approach provides more flexibility for WTO Members, especially for developing countries, to protect specific domestic services and service suppliers.

Secondly, even for those sectors or subsectors inscribed in each Member's service schedule, national treatment is not necessarily or fully applicable because national treatment may be limited through "any conditions and qualifications" set out in the Member's service schedule.

Thirdly, the beneficiaries of national treatment are both *services* and *service suppliers*. Service is defined by Article I (1)(3)(b) as any service in any sector except services supplied in the exercise of government authority.[52] Service supplier means any *person* that supplies a service,[53] while *person* is a legal term that is defined as either a natural person or a juridical person.[54] Moreover, branches and representative offices of service suppliers can also be accorded national treatment.[55]

Fourthly, the measures relating to national treatment are "all measures affecting the supply of services". *Measure* means any measure by a Member, whether in the form of a law, regulation, rule, procedure, decision, administrative action, or any other form.[56] *Supply of services* can be defined by the definition of *supply of a service*, which includes the production, distribution, marketing, sale and delivery of a service.[57]

Fifthly, the comparable domestic counterparts of beneficiaries of national treatment are a Member's own *like services* and *service suppliers*. However, the GATS articles do not provide any clear standard of likeness between services and service suppliers of one Member and those of another. In a note by the WTO Secretariat, it seems that *likeness* in the national treatment context depends "in principle on attributes of the product or supplier per se rather than on the means

---

50 Note on the Meeting of 17–21 July, 1989, ¶ 205, MTN.GNS/24 (August, 1989).

51 Id. ¶ 202.

52 GATS, art I:1(3) (c) (stateing that "a service supplied in the exercise of governmental authority" means any service which is supplied neither on a commercial basis nor in competition with one or more service supplies).

53 Id. art. XXVIII (g).

54 Id. art. XXVIII (j).

55 Footnote 12 of the GATS states: "Where the service is not supplied directly by a juridical person but through other forms of commercial presence such as a branch or a representative office, the service supplier (i.e. the juridical person) shall, nonetheless, through such presence be accorded the treatment provided for service suppliers under the Agreement. Such treatment shall be extended to the presence through which the service is supplied and need not be extended to any other parts of the supplier located outside the territory where the service is supplied." For the history of the interpretative note, see MTN. GNS/W/176 (October 26, 1993).

56 GATS, art. XXVIII (a).

57 Id. art. XXVIII (b).

by which the product is delivered".[58] It is argued by some people that like services and services suppliers cover "directly competitive or substitutable" services and services suppliers.[59] In *China – Electronic Payment Services*, the panel found that, for services to be considered "like", they need not necessarily be exactly the same, and services could qualify as "like" if they are "essentially or generally the same".[60] The panel further found:

> [L]ike services are services that are in a competitive relationship with each other (or would be if they were allowed to be supplied in a particular market). Indeed, only if the foreign and domestic services in question are in such a relationship can a measure of a Member modify the conditions of competition in favour of one or other of these services.[61]

It is also difficult to understand the relationships between like services and like service suppliers. In *EC – Bananas III*, the Panel's view is that, "to the extent that entities provide these like services, they are like service suppliers".[62] This view almost equates services and service suppliers, so it was criticized as "an exceedingly broad notion".[63] In fact, *like services and service supplier* is not a pure legal issue, but an issue of mixed laws and facts. In *Canada – Periodicals*, the Appellate Body stated that the determination of whether imported and domestic products are "like products" is a process by which legal rules have to be applied to facts.[64] If this conclusion is also applicable to the GATS, then the *likeness* issue (including like services and like service suppliers) in the GATS must be construed on a case-by-case basis. The case-by-case basis is supported by the panel report of China-Electronic Payment Services.[65]

---

58 The Work Programme on Electronic Commerce, Note by the Secretariat, S/C/W/68, ¶ 33 (November 16, 1998).

59 Patros C. Mavroidis, *Like Products: Some Thoughts at the Positive and Normative Level*, in REGULATORY BARRIERS AND THE PRINCIPLE OF NON-DISCRIMINATION IN WORLD TRADE LAW 125, 126–27 (Thomas Cottier and Petros C. Mavroidis (eds), Univ. of Michigan Press 2000).

60 Panel Report, *China-Electronic Payment Services*, WT/DS413/R, ¶ 7.305 (The panel considered the ordinary meaning of "like" by referring to its definition in the Shorter Oxford English Dictionary, i.e., "having the same characteristics or qualities as some other person or thing; of approximately identical shape, size, etc., with something else; similar")..

61 Panel Report, *China-Electronic Payment Services*, WT/DS413/R, ¶ 7.306.

62 Panel Report, *EC – Bananas III,* WT/DS27/R, ¶ 7.322.

63 Werner Zdouc, *WTO Dispute Settlement Practice Relationg to the GATS*, 2(2) J. INT'L ECON. L. 295, 332 (1999).

64 Appellate Body Report, *Canada – Periodicals*, WT/DS31/AB/R, Section V (A).

65 Panel Report, *China-Electronic Payment Services*, WT/DS413/R, ¶¶ 7.307, 7.311. In this case, the panel found that the Electronic Payment Services (EPS) supplied by China

E. Relationship between GATT and GATS National Treatment

Coexistence or Exclusiveness

After the establishment of the WTO, the issue of the relationship between GATT and GATS first appeared in the case of *Canada – Periodicals*.[66] Canada claimed that GATT Article III did not apply to its disputed Excise Tax Act because this Act was a measure pertaining to advertising services, which was within the purview of the GATS,[67] not the GATT. Canada further argued that, because Canada did not make commitment on advertising service sector, even though the measure was discriminatory, it was not a violation of the GATS obligations.

In terms of the structure of the WTO Agreement, including its annexes, and based on the general rule of interpretation of the Vienna Convention,[68] the Panel stated:

> The ordinary meaning of the texts of GATT 1994 and GATS as well as Article II:2 of the WTO Agreement, taken together, indicates that obligations under GATT 1994 and GATS can coexist and that one does not override the other ... . GATT 1994 and GATS are standing on the same plain in the WTO Agreement, without any hierarchical order between the two.[69]

Canada also argued that overlaps between GATT 1994 and GATS should be avoided.[70] With respect to this issue, the Panel stated: "Overlaps between the subject matter of disciplines in GATT 1994 and in GATS are inevitable, and will further increase with the progress of technology and the globalization of economic activities. We do not consider that such overlaps will undermine the coherence of the WTO system."[71]

The Appellate Body agreed with the Panel in this respect,[72] and further pointed out that the GATS does not diminish the scope of application of the GATT 1994.[73] Accordingly, the Appellate Body analysed the Canadian measure (Excise Tax Act) under GATT Article III, and found that relevant articles in the Excise Tax Act were inconsistent with the national treatment principle under GATT Article III.

UnionPay (CUP) are like EPS supplied by EPS suppliers of other Members, and that CUP and EPS suppliers of other Members are like suppliers of EPS. WT/DS413/R, ¶ 7.327.

66 Panel Report, *Canada – Periodicals*, WT/DS31/R.

67 Id. ¶ 5.13.

68 The Vienna Convention on the Law of Treaties of 1969, available at http://untreaty.un.org/ilc/texts/instruments/English/conventions/1_1_1969.pdf.

69 Panel Report, *Canada – Periodicals*, WT/DS31/R, ¶ 5.17.

70 Id. ¶ 5.18.

71 Id.

72 Appellate Body Report, *Canada – Periodicals*, WT/DS31/AB/R, at 20.

73 Id.

Almost at the same time with *Canada – Periodicals*, *EC – Bananas III* also faced the issue of relationship between GATT and GATS. In *EC – Bananas III*, the EC argued that the GATT and the GATS are mutually exclusive, and the GATS should not apply to the EC Import Licensing procedures because they were not measures "affecting trade in services" within the meaning of the GATS, so they were subject only to the GATT, not the GATS. With respect to this issue, the Panel found:

> [I]t is our view that if we were to find the scope of the GATS and that of GATT to be mutually exclusive, in other words, if we were to find that a measure considered to fall within the scope of one agreement could not at the same time fall within the scope of the other, the value of Members' obligations and commitments would be undermined and the object and purpose of both agreements would be frustrated. Obligations could be circumvented by the adoption of measures under one agreement with indirect effects on trade covered by the other without the possibility of any legal recourse … . If the scope of GATT and the GATS were interpreted to be mutually exclusive, that Member could escape its national treatment obligation and the Members whose products have been discriminated against would have no possibility of legal recourse on account that the measure regulates "services" and not goods.[74]

The Panel further found:

> [I]n principle, no measures are excluded a *priori* from the scope of the GATS as defined by its provisions. The scope of the GATS encompasses any measure of a Member to the extent it affects the supply of a service regardless of whether such measure directly governs the supply of a service or whether it regulates other matters but nevertheless affects trade in services.[75]

Therefore, the Panel concluded that the EC's argument had no legal basis.[76] As to this issue, the Appellate Body stated:

> Given the respective scope of application of the two agreements [the GATT 1994 and the GATS], they may or may not overlap, depending on the nature of the measures at issue. Certain measures could be found to fall exclusively within the scope of the GATT 1994, when they affect trade in goods as goods. Certain measures could be found to fall exclusively within the scope of the GATS, when they affect the supply of services as services. There is yet a third category of measures that could be found to fall within the scope of both the GATT 1994 and the GATS. These are measures that involve a service relating to a particular good or a service supplied in conjunction with a particular good. In all such cases in

---

74 Panel Report, *EC – Bananas III*, WT/DS27/R, ¶ 7.283.

75 Id. ¶ 7.285.

76 Id. ¶¶ 7.283, 7.286.

this third category, the measure in question could be scrutinized under both the GATT 1994 and the GATS.[77]

In a word, measures could be divided into three categories based on their position within the GATT and/or the GATS. The first two categories are exclusive. But the third category is within the scope of both the GATT and the GATS. If a measure constitutes discrimination against both foreign products and services or service suppliers, it could be in violation of national treatment obligations under both GATT Article III and GATS Article XVII.

From the above cases, two conclusions concerning the relationship between GATT national treatment and GATS national treatment could be reached. The first conclusion is that GATT national treatment and GATS national treatment may overlap. The second conclusion is whether a measure is in violation of both GATT Article III and GATS Article XVII should be based on a case-by-case approach. Unfortunately, neither of the cases provides clues to the case-by-case approach.

Differences between GATT and GATS National Treatment

In the beginning of the Uruguay Round negotiations, it was recognized that the extension to services of the basic principles (e.g. MFN and national treatment) laid down by the GATT was inadequate in ensuring effective and progressive liberalization of services.[78] In January 1987, the GNS pointed out that, "[t]he basic GATT concepts of transparency, non-discrimination and national treatment, can have a different meaning and relevance when applied to trade in services".[79] Some scholars also noted the differences. For example, in an article published in 1988, Jackson stated: "The most difficult and threatening GATT obligation [when applied to trade in services] is that of national treatment".[80] The Uruguay Round and its subsequent developments have proved that there indeed exist many differences between GATT and GATS national treatment.[81]

All products under the GATT are subject to national treatment in accordance with GATT Article III because national treatment is a general principle throughout

---

[77] Appellate Body Report, *EC – Bananas III*, WT/DS27/AB/R, adopted September 25, 1997, ¶ 221.

[78] Giorgio Sacerdoti, *The International Regulation of Services: Basic Concepts and Standards of Treatment*, in LIBERALIZATION OF SERVICES AND INTELLECTUAL PROPERTY IN THE URUGUAY ROUND OF GATT 27 (Giorgio Sacerdoti (ed.), University Press Fribourg, Switzerland 1990).

[79] Christoph Bail, *Conceptual Problems and Possible Elements of a Multilateral Framework for International Trade in Services*, in LIBERALIZATION OF SERVICES AND INTELLECTUAL PROPERTY IN THE URUGUAY ROUND OF GATT 44 (Giorgio Sacerdoti (ed.), University Press Fribourg, Switzerland 1990).

[80] John H. Jackson, *Constructing a Constitution for Trade in Services*, 11 THE WORLD ECON. 187, 190 (1988).

[81] See generally JACKSON, THE WORLD TRADING SYSTEM, supra note 25, ch. 8.

the GATT. However, under the GATS, national treatment is applicable merely to the sectors or sub-sectors[82] which are inscribed in a Member's Schedule of Specific Commitments on Services. It is not required by the GATS for a Member to open all service sectors and sub-sectors because trade in services is a progressive liberalization process. To date, there has been no WTO Member which has opened all service sectors and sub-sectors. For example, China has made commitments on nine sectors, excluding "Health related and social services", "Recreational, cultural and sporting services".[83] This way for scheduling specific commitments is often referred to as a *positive* list, meaning that only those sectors or sub-sectors listed in a Member's service schedule are subject to market access and national treatment obligations under the GATS. However, with regard to limitation measures on market access and national treatment for each opened service sector or sub-sector, they are inscribed in the Schedule through a *negative* list, meaning that any limitation measures *not* listed in a Schedule may be regarded as inconsistent with market access or national treatment obligations under the GATS. In a word, the GATS adopts a *hybrid positive-negative* list for scheduling specific commitments.[84]

Why did the drafters of the GATS make such an arrangement? The answer could be found from the negotiating history of the GATS Article XVII. According to the initial intention of the United States, national treatment would have to be a general obligation.[85] Even in the period of Montreal mid-term review, the USTR still insisted that national treatment be one of the four basic principles governing trade in services.[86] With the development of negotiations, however, there was a difference between the United States and the European Communities

---

[82] The classification of sectors and sub-sectors is based on the WTO Secretariat's Services Sectoral Classification List, and each sector contained in the Secretariat list is identified by the corresponding *Central Product Classification* (CPC) number. According to the Services Sectoral Classification List, there are 12 services sectors: (1) Business services; (2) Communication services; (3) Construction and related engineering services; (4) Distribution services; (5) Education services; (6) Environmental Services; (7) Financial services; (8) Health related and social services; (9) Tourism and travel-related services; (10) Recreational, cultural and sporting services; (11) Transport services; (12) Other services not included elsewhere. See MTN.GNS/W/120 (July 10, 1991); The Guidelines for the Scheduling of Specific Commitments under the GATS: Explanatory Note [hereinafter 2001 Scheduling Guidelines], S/L/92, ¶ 23 (March 28, 2001).

[83] The Schedule of Specific Commitments on Services of the People's Republic of China [hereinafter the China Schedule], WT/ACC/CHN/49/Add.2 (October 1, 2001), in COMPILATION OF THE LEGAL INSTRUMENTS ON CHINA'S ACCESSION TO THE WORLD TRADE ORGANIZATION 700–46 (Law Press China 2002).

[84] Bernard Hoekman, *Assessing the General Agreement on Trade in Services*, in THE URUGUAY ROUND AND THE DEVELOPING COUNTRIES 98 (Will Martin and L. Alan Winters (eds), Cambridge Univ. Press, 1996).

[85] Mary E. Footer, *The International Regulation of Trade in Services Following Completion of the Uruguay Round*, 29 INT'L LAW 453, 456 (1995).

[86] Id.

(EC) regarding national treatment obligations. The EC tended to regard national treatment in services as a soft obligation, instead of a binding general obligation as insisted by the United States.[87] For developing countries, a general obligation of national treatment in service trade was unacceptable.[88] For example, Brazil directly pointed out that "developing countries should not be expected to undertake the same level of market access or national treatment commitments as developed countries".[89] In the Indian view, the negotiation on national treatment should consider the different levels of economic development of different countries.[90] In the end, the view of the EC and the developing countries prevailed. As a result, the national treatment in the final service trade agreement was not designed to be a general principle,[91] which was regarded by some scholars as a defect for reducing the value of the GATS.[92]

According to the interpretation of the WTO Secretariat, the reason for the difference between GATT and GATS national treatment also lies in the nature of trade in services.[93] The entry of foreign goods can be controlled by import duties or other border measures. However, cross-border service is only one of the four modes of supply of services. There are other modes of supply of services,

---

[87] For example, at a WTO meeting in 1989, the representative of the EC stated: "National treatment could apply progressively in some cases and this application could vary from sector to sector and from country to country, depending on the regulatory structure." Note on the Meeting of 17–21 July, 1989, supra note 6, ¶ 210; see also Footer, supra note 85, at 458; Jack W. Flader, JR, *A Call For a General Agreement on Trade in Services*, 3 Transnat'l Law 661, 675 (1990).

[88] Bernard Hoekman, Developing Countries and the Uruguay Round: Negotiating on Services 5 (World Bank Policy Research Working Paper No.1220, 1993); Footer, supra note 85, at 460; Dilip K. Das, *Trade in Financial Services and the Role of the GATS: Against the Backdrop of the Asian Financial Crises*, 32 J. World Trade 79, 101 (1998).

[89] Note on the Meeting of 17-21 July, 1989, MTN.GNS/24, ¶ 214.

[90] Id. ¶ 212.

[91] It is worth noting that not everyone takes this view. For example, in Philip Ruttley's opinion, national treatment obligation is a general obligation set out by the GATS, as well as MFN treatment, transparency, mutual recognition, rules governing monopolies and other business practices restraining competition. See Ruttley, supra note 4, at 186. In China, some scholars also think that national treatment is one of the basic principles in the GATS. See Chen Xianmin, *Jiedu Fuwu Maoyi Zhongxieding de Jiben Yuanze* [Understanding the basic Principles of GATS], Faxue [Law Science] 98 (2003, no. 7); see also Zhou Qing, *Jiaru WTO dui Zhongguo Shangye Yinhang de Yingxiang he Duice* [The Impact and Countermeasures of China's Commercial Banks after Entry to the WTO], Jinrong Yu Baoxian [Finance and Insurance] 42 (2000, no. 10).

[92] See Das, supra note 88, at 100; see also Pierre Sauve, *Assessing the General Agreement on Trade in Services, Half-Full or Half-Empty*? 29 (4) J. World Trade 125, 138 (1995).

[93] WTO Secretariat, Trade in Services Division, *An Introduction to the GATS*, at 8 (October 1999), http://www.wto.org/english/tratop_e/serv_e/gsintr_e.doc.

such as commercial presence or presence of natural persons within a Member's territory, which are impossible to be controlled by border measures. In fact, for trade in services, there are few measures that are applied at the border, and "most restrictions arise from internal measures".[94] Under the background of progressive liberalization of trade in services, no WTO Member is willing to open totally its service markets. Although the negative approach supported by the United States was helpful for services liberalization, it was opposed by developing countries in the Uruguay Round. In the autumn of 1990, the United States agreed to the positive approach with respect to the liberalization of service sectors or sub-sectors, with the negative approach with respect to the limitations of the sectors and sub-sectors committed to open. Finally, the Uruguay Round negotiations adopted the *hybrid positive-negative* approach, a compromised approach.[95]

Although the GATT national treatment is a general obligation, it is applicable only to products, not to manufacturers. On the contrary, although the GATS national treatment is not a general obligation, it applies to both services and service suppliers, which makes the GATS national treatment more complicated than the GATT national treatment. In accordance with 2001 Scheduling Guidelines,[96] a limitation measure on national treatment (or market access) must be entered for the relevant sector and each mode of supply of services.[97] Because there are four modes of supply of services,[98] there are four opportunities for a Member to limit the application of national treatment for each service sector.

Service supplier is a new concept in the GATS. It means any person who supplies a service.[99] If a service is not supplied directly by a juridical person but through other forms of commercial presence such as a branch or a representative office, the service supplier (i.e.the juridical person) shall, nonetheless, through such presence be accorded the treatment provided for service suppliers under the Agreement.[100] The notion of commercial presence further complicates the definition of service supplier. To some extent, commercial presence and service supplier overlap,[101] because service suppliers may be involved in any of the four modes of supply.[102]

Commercial presence also enlarges the application scope of the GATS. For example, if a service company of a Member has established a branch in another

---

94 Aaditya Mattoo, *National Treatment in the GATS, Corner-stone or Pandora's Box*? 31 J. World Trade 107, 113 (1997).

95 Das, supra note 88, at 101; see also Anders Ahnlid, *Comparing GATT and GATS: Regime Creation under and after Hegemony*, 3 Rev. Int'l. Pol. Econ. 65, 81 (1996).

96 2001 Scheduling Guidelines, S/L/92.

97 Id. ¶ 39.

98 According to GATS Article I:2, the four modes of supply are: (1) cross-border supply; (2) consumption abroad; (3) commercial presence; (4) presence of natural persons.

99 GATS, art. XXVIII(g).

100 See id. art. XXVIII(g), footnote.

101 Zdouc, supra note 63, at 328.

102 Id. at 328–29.

Member and begun to provide services through the branch in the territory of another Member, both the service and the branch shall be accorded no less favourable treatment than that accorded to the like service or service suppliers in another Member, namely, the host country. In contrast, the GATT merely protects goods from other Members. In other words, if goods are produced in the host country through a legal entity established in this country (e.g. a joint venture), then neither the goods nor the manufacturer of the goods will be protected by the national treatment principle of the GATT.

The reason why services and service suppliers run parallel in the GATS also lies in the nature of the trade in services. Services are different from goods because the production and consumption of services must occur simultaneously at the time of production.[103] It is difficult for services to be supplied without the presence of service suppliers. However, goods or products can be transacted separately from manufacturers.

F. National Treatment in the Understanding

The Understanding on Commitments in Financial Services,[104] as part of the Final Act, stipulates higher requirements for financial liberalization. The Understanding is not applicable to all WTO Members, but only to the Members which have agreed to be bound by it. Part C of the Understanding, entitled "National Treatment", reads as follows:

> Under terms and conditions that accord national treatment, each Member shall grant to financial service suppliers of any other Member established in its territory access to payment and clearing systems operated by public entities, and to official funding and refinancing facilities available in the normal course of ordinary business. This paragraph is not intended to confer access to the Members' lender of last resort facilities.
>
> When membership or participation in, or access to, any self-regulatory body, securities or futures exchange or market, clearing agency, or any other organization or association, is required by a Member in order for financial service suppliers of any other Member to supply financial services on an equal basis with financial service suppliers of the Member, or when the Member provides directly or indirectly such entities, privileges or advantages in supplying financial services, the Member shall ensure that such entities accord national treatment to financial service supplier of an other Member resident in the territory of the Member.

---

[103] Tycho H.E. Stahl, *Liberalizing International Trade in Services: The Case for Sidestepping the GATT*, 19 Yale J. Int'l L. 405, 409 (1994).

[104] The Understanding, supra note 46.

That is to say, for a Member adhering to the Understanding, it shall provide additional national treatment to foreign financial service suppliers established or resident in the territory of the host Member, including at least the follows:

- access to public payment and clearing systems
- access to official funding and refinancing facilities
- access to self-regulatory bodies
- access to securities or future exchange or market
- access to clearing agency

Although these accession rights based on national treatment for foreign financial service suppliers are only written in the Understanding, not in the GATS or in the Annex on Financial Services, it does not mean that a Member not adhering to the Understanding cannot grant the rights to foreign financial service suppliers on a voluntary basis. For example, China has not acceded to the Understanding, but China commits in the Schedule of Specific Commitments on Services of the People's Republic of China (the China Schedule) that the representative offices of foreign securities institutions may become special members of Chinese stock exchanges.[105]

II. China's WTO National Treatment Commitments

The above section of Chapter 3 discusses national treatment obligations under GATS/WTO and its development in the financial sector, which definitely apply to China's banking services as basic WTO rules. However, they only deal with part of national treatment obligations under the GATS/WTO framework. In addition to national treatment obligations in the Multilateral Trade Agreements under the WTO, China needs to conform to the special "terms" concluded between China and the WTO,[106] i.e., China's specific national treatment commitments. Actually, the main obstacle for China's entry to the WTO was not whether China would implement the WTO agreements themselves, but whether China could satisfy some WTO Members' WTO-plus demands; or to put it another way, whether China could undertake more stringent obligations to liberalize its trade in goods and services pressed for by some WTO Members, especially the United States and the EC. It took fifteen years (1986–2001) for China to negotiate those special terms on a multilateral basis and a bilateral basis, during which national treatment was the focus of the negotiations.[107] To study the relationship between GATS/

---

[105] The China Schedule, 7B, WT/ACC/CHN/49/Add.2 (October 1, 2001), available in *Compilation of the Legal Instruments on China's Accession to the World Trade Organization* (Law Press China 2002), at 700–46.

[106] See the WTO Agreement, art. XII.

[107] Liu Jianwen and Xiong Wei, *Guomin Daiyu yu Waizi Shuishou Youhui Zhengce de Gaige* [National Treatment and the Reform of the Preferential Tax Policy for Foreign

WTO national treatment obligations and China's banking law, it is necessary to look to both GATS/WTO national treatment articles and China's specific national treatment commitments under the WTO.

A. China's WTO Accession Agreements

The significance of China's WTO accession agreements for analysing China's WTO obligations is that the commitments in China's WTO accession agreements are China's obligations enforceable within the WTO dispute settlement mechanism. GATS Article XXIII:1 provides that failure in carrying out specific commitments could be the reason of recourse to the DSU. The WTO jurisprudence has proved Pierre Sauve's prediction that GATS dispute settlement cases would involve interpreting Member's specific commitments.[108] For example, the first WTO case dealing solely with trade in services under the GATS, i.e., *Mexico – Telecoms*, clearly shows the significance of a Member's specific commitments.[109] In *U.S. – Gambling*, the focus of the case is whether the United States undertook a specific commitment on gambling and betting services.[110] Moreover, China's WTO accession agreements also partly change existing WTO rules, especially national treatment obligations under GATT 1994, GATS and other relevant Multilateral Trade Agreements,[111] which are addressed in the following sections of this chapter.

Legal Structure of China's WTO Accession Agreements

China's WTO accession agreements include mainly the China Accession Protocol,[112] the Working Party Report,[113] the China Schedule,[114] and the Schedule of Concessions and Commitments annexed to the GATT 1994.[115] From the perspective of trade in services, the China Accession Protocol, the Working Party Report and the China Schedule are the main accession legal instruments, all of which are interrelated and interconnected. The China Accession Protocol is the main pillar.

Investment], ZHONGGUO FAXUE [CHINESE LEGAL SCIENCE] 53, 54 (1998, no. 2).

108 See Sauve, supra note 92, at 140.

109 In *Mexico – Telecoms*, the US mainly claimed that Mexico's relevant telecommunication measures were inconsistent with its commitments inscribed in its Schedule. See Panel Report, *Mexico – Measures Affecting Telecommunications Services* [hereinafter *Mexico – Telecoms*], WT/DS204/R, adopted June 1, 2004, ¶ 3.1.

110 Panel Report, *U.S. – Gambling*, WT/DS285/R, adopted April 20, 2005, ¶¶ 3.30–3.70; See also Appellate Boday Report, WT/DS285/AB/R.

111 For the definition of the Multilateral Trade Agreements, see chapter 1 of this book, footnote 6.

112 China Accession Protocol, WT/L/432.

113 Working Party Report, WT/ACC/CHN/49.

114 The China Schedule, WT/ACC/CHN/49/Add.2.

115 Schedule of Concessions and Commitments annexed to the GATT 1994, WT/ACC/CHN/49/Add.1.

The China Schedule is annexed to the China Accession Protocol,[116] and parts of the Working Party Report, i.e., the commitments referred to in paragraph 342 of the Working Party Report, are also contained in the China Accession Protocol as an integral part.[117] The China Accession Protocol and relevant commitments embodied in the China Schedule and the Working Party Report constitute "an integral part of the WTO Agreement".[118] It must be noted that, besides the part specifically incorporated into the China Accession Protocol, other parts of the Working Party Report are not of no value. On the contrary, they may be part of the "context" for interpretation of the China Accession Protocol.[119]

Legal Status of China's WTO Accession Agreements

Both the Multilateral Trade Agreements and the China Accession Protocol are integral parts of the WTO Agreement.[120] Which one shall prevail in case of conflicts? From the WTO Agreement, there is not a clear-cut answer to this question. Article XVI:3 of the WTO Agreement states: "In the event of a conflict between a provision of this Agreement and a provision of any of the Multilateral Trade Agreements, the provision of this Agreement shall prevail to the extent of the conflict." Article XVI:3 of the WTO Agreement only deals with a potential conflict between a provision of the WTO Agreement and a provision of any of the Multilateral Trade Agreements, irrelevant to a potential conflict between a provision of a Member's accession protocol and a provision of any of the Multilateral Trade Agreements. In my view, if there is a conflict, the China Accession Protocol (including the binding paragraphs in the Working Party Report and the annexed schedules on trade in goods and services) would prevail over the GATT 1994, the GATS and other Multilateral Trade Agreements annexed to the WTO Agreement.

Firstly, the China Accession Protocol is the fundamental agreement between China and the WTO, which is the basis on which China performs its obligations in the GATT 1994, the GATS, the TRIPS, etc. According to the Vienna Convention,[121] a treaty is "an international agreement concluded *between States* in written form and governed by international law, whether embodied in a single instrument or in two or more related instruments and whatever its particular designation".[122] (emphasis added) However, the Vienna Convention does not preclude non-state

116 China Accession Protocol, WT/L/432, Part II:1.

117 Id. Part I:1(2).

118 Id.

119 See Michael Lennard, *Navigating by the Stars: Interpreting the WTO Agreements*, 5(1) J. INT'L ECON. L. 17, 26 (2002).

120 The WTO Agreement, Art. II:2.

121 The Vienna Convention, supra note 68.

122 Id. art. 2:1(a).

subjects from concluding a treaty.[123] It is generally acknowledged that the subjects of treaties are states and international organizations.[124]

According to the PRC Constitution,[125] the Standing Committee of the NPC shall ratify treaties and important agreements concluded with "foreign states".[126] Thus, the PRC Constitution does not contain "international organizations" as treaty-making subjects.[127] Nevertheless, to some extent, this constitutional weakness has been offset by a special provision in the Law of the PRC on the Procedure of the Conclusion of Treaties,[128] which states: "The procedures for the conclusion of treaties or agreements with international organizations by the People's Republic of China shall follow this Law and the constitution of the relevant international organization."[129] Therefore, the China Accession Protocol, as a treaty between the PRC and the WTO, has both an international law basis[130] and a municipal law basis.

---

123 Article 3 of the Vienna Convention states: "The fact that the present Convention does not apply to international agreements concluded between States and other subjects of international law or between such other subjects of international law, or to international agreements not in written form, shall not affect: (a) the legal force of such agreements . . . . "

124 See Malgosia Fitzmaurice, *The Identification and Character of Treaties and Treaty Obligations between States in International Law*, 2002 Brit. Y.B. Int'l L. 141, 157; Jan Klabbers, The Concept of Treaty in International Law 48 (Kluwer Law International, 1996); Gerhard Von Glahn, Law Among Nations: an Introduction to Public International Law 507 (Macmillan Publishing Company 5th edn, 1986); Paul Reuter, Introduction to the Law of Treaties ¶ 77, at 27 (Jose Mico et al. (trans.), Printer Publishers 1989); I.A. Shearer, Starke's International Law 404 (Butterworths 11th edn, 1994) [hereinafter STARKE'S INTERNATIONAL LAW]; see also the 1986 Vienna Convention on the Law of the Treaties between States and International Organizations or between International Organizations (not effective yet), in P.K. Menon, The Law of Treaties Between States and International Organizations 159–245 (The Edwin Mellen Press 1992); also available in http://www.un.org/law/ilc/texts/trbtstat.htm.

125 PRC Constitution 1982, adopted at the Fifth Session of the Fifth NPC on December 4, 1982, effective December 4, 1982, amended in 1988, 1993, 1999, 2004, in Falü Huibian 2004, at 1–34 (People's Publishing House 2005).

126 Id. art. 67 (14);

127 See Zhang Naigen, *Lun Tiaoyu Pizhun de Xianfa Chengxu Xiugai* [On the Constitution Amendment in Treaty Ratification Process], Zhengzhi Yu Falü [Pol. Sci. & L.] 17, 19 (2004, no. 1).

128 Law of the PRC on the Procedure of the Conclusion of Treaties [*Zhonghua Renmin Gongheguo Dijie Tiaoyue Chengxufa*, hereinafter Treaty Procedure Law], adopted at the 17th meeting of the Standing Committee of the 7th NPC on December 28, 1990, entered into force at the same date, Gazette of the NPC (1990, no. 6).

129 Id. art. 18.

130 1 Oppenheim's International Law, Peace, Part 2 to 4, § 596, at 1220 (Robert Jennings and Arthur Watts (eds), Longman, 9th edn, 1992) [hereinafter Oppenheim's International Law] (stating that the Vienna Convention which only deals with treaties between states does not affect the legal force of agreements between states and international organizations).

However, it seems there is a problem concerning ratification or acceptance. Unlike normal ratification which takes place after the conclusion of a treaty, China's "ratification" of the China Accession Protocol was prior to the conclusion of the instrument. On August 25, 2000, one year before the signature of the China Accession Protocol, the Standing Committee of the NPC passed a special decision authorizing the highest administrative institution of the PRC, i.e. the State Council, to negotiate and accept the WTO accession protocol, and the PRC President to ratify it. On November 11, 2001, one day after the signature of the China Accession Protocol, China's President of the time, Jiang Zemin, accepted the China Accession Protocol without seeking approval from the Standing Committee of the NPC. Zhang Naigen argues that the authorization of the Standing Committee of the NPC is in violation of the PRC Constitution because the PRC Constitution does not confer on the Standing Committee the power of prior ratification (or prior acceptance) of a treaty or an important agreement.[131] According to the authoritative view of international law, ratification is "only the confirmation of an already existing treaty".[132] Although the China Accession Protocol uses the term "acceptance", not "ratification", in Brownlie's view the expression of "subject to acceptance" is equivalent to "subject to ratification".[133] In my view, although the PRC Constitution does not confer the NPC Standing Committee a prior-approval right to accept a treaty, the Treaty Procedure Law does provide that the NPC Standing Committee may make a decision to accede to multilateral treaties, [134] and this law does not limit the time of making such a decision. Thus, it seems that the NPC Standing Committee's prior decision to authorize the State Council to accept the WTO accession documents is not in violation of the concrete treaty-making law in China, notwithstanding a lack of constitutional basis. In fact, the Treaty Procedure Law has partly filled the vacuum of the PRC Constitution regarding acceptance of treaties. The minor problem on ratification process does not affect the validity of the China Accession Protocol as a treaty.

Indeed, the WTO Agreement is a treaty.[135] The China Accession Protocol as an integral part of the WTO Agreement is part of the treaty. In essence, The China Accession Protocol is equal to a trade agreement.[136] In public international law, "protocol" is generally recognized as a term for a treaty.[137] The China Accession

---

131 Zhang, supra note 127, at 18.

132 1 OPPENHEIM'S INTERNATIONAL LAW, supra note 130, § 606, at 1231.

133 IAN BROWNLIE, PRINCIPLES OF PUBLIC INTERNATIONAL LAW 612 (Oxford Univ. Press 5th edn, 1998).

134 See Treaty Procedure Law, supra note 128, art. 11(1).

135 Appellate Body Report, *Japan – Alcoholic Beverages II*, WT/DS8/AB/R, WT/DS10/AB/R, WT/DS11/AB/R, Section F.

136 For the legal status of GATT accession protocols, see LONG, supra note 2, at 37 (discussing that an accession protocol is tantamount to a trade agreement).

137 See STARKE'S INTERNATIONAL LAW, supra note 124, at 401–02; see also 1 OPPENHEIM'S INTERNATIONAL LAW, supra note 130, § 586, at 1209, n.2 (discussing that a protocol may be

Protocol is the origin of the application of covered agreements of the WTO Agreement to China. In other words, the performance of the obligations in the China Accession Protocol is a precondition for the performance of obligations in the GATT 1994, the GATS, the TRIPS, etc.

Furthermore, Part I:1(3) of the China Accession Protocol states: "*Except as otherwise provided for in this Protocol*, those obligations in the Multilateral Trade Agreements annexed to the WTO Agreement ... shall be implemented by China ...." This sentence implies that special provisions in the China Accession Protocol should prevail over those obligations in the Multilateral Trade Agreements. In other words, the China Accession Protocol should prevail over the GATS or other agreements under the WTO.

Moreover, according to some WTO rules, special terms prevail over general terms.[138] For example, there is a general interpretative note to Annex 1A (Multilateral Agreements on Trade in Goods) of the WTO Agreement, which reads as follows:

> In the event of conflict between a provision of the General Agreement on Tariffs and Trade 1994 and a provision of another agreement in Annex 1A to the Agreement Establishing the World Trade Organization (referred to in the agreements in Annex 1A as the "WTO Agreement"), *the provision of the other agreement shall prevail* to the extent of the conflict.. (emphasis added)

Additionally, Article 1.2 of the DSU reads as follows:

> The rules and procedures of this Understanding shall apply subject to such special or additional rules and procedures on dispute settlement contained in the covered agreements as are identified in Appendix 2 to this Understanding. To the extent that there is a difference between the rules and procedures of this Understanding and the special or additional rules and procedures set forth in Appendix 2, *the special or additional rules and procedures* in Appendix 2 *shall prevail*. (emphasis added)

The above interpretative rules reflect a rooted legal maxim that a special rule overrules a general one, i.e., *lex specialis derogat generali*.[139] The prevailing status of a specific agreement over a general one is also accepted by many international

---

concluded as a treaty, or an integral part of a treaty).

[138] See Ravi P. Kewalram, *WTO Dispute Settlement and Sub-National Entities in China*, in CHINA AND THE WORLD TRADING SYSTEM: ENTERING THE NEW MILLENNIUM 413, 415 (Deborah Z. Cass and Brett G. Williams et al. (eds), Cambridge Univ. Press 2003).

[139] See DICTIONARY OF INTERNATIONAL AND COMPARATIVE LAW 198 (James R. Fox (ed.), Oceana Publications 3rd edn, 2003); 2 JOWITT'S DICTIONARY OF ENGLISH LAW, L–Z, at 1090 (Sweet & Maxwell 2nd edn, 1977); DICTIONARY OF CANADIAN LAW 677 (Carswell 2nd edn, 1995).

law scholars.[140] Compared with the GATT, the GATS, and the TRIPS, the China Accession Protocol is *lex specialis*. Therefore, the China Accession Protocol takes precedence over the three *generali* treaties.[141]

The consequence of precedence of China's special WTO commitments over general rules and obligations in the Multilateral Trade Agreements is that China must first implement its obligations reflected in its WTO commitments. Then, China shall implement those obligations in the GATT 1994, the GATS and the TRIPS. This is not a time order for implementation, but a precedence order for implementation. China needs to simultaneously implement national treatment obligations under the China Accession Protocol, the GATT 1994, the GATS, and the TRIPS, but the order of implementing relevant rules of national treatment is as follows: firstly, the special national treatment obligations in the China Accession Protocol, secondly, national treatment articles in the Multilateral Trade Agreements.

B. National Treatment Commitments in the China Accession Protocol

When analysing China's WTO commitments, especially with respect to services, people often focus merely on China's specific commitments in the China Schedule, neglecting other relevant commitments in the China Accession Protocol and the Working Party Report. In fact, China's national treatment commitments relating to banking services, as well as other services, are scattered among all of the three instruments. The general national treatment commitments in the China Accession Protocol and the Working Party Report also apply to banking services. Therefore, it is necessary to regard the three instruments as a whole in order to fully comprehend China's national treatment commitments. I firstly look at the China Accession Protocol. There are many paragraphs and sub-paragraphs relating to national treatment in this Protocol.

Non-discrimination Commitments

Part I:3 of the China Accession Protocol reads as follows:

> Except as otherwise provided for in this Protocol, *foreign individuals and enterprises and foreign-funded enterprises* shall be accorded treatment no less favourable than that accorded to *other individuals and enterprises* in respect of:

---

[140] See, e.g., Antonio Cassese, International Law § 8.3.2, at 170 (Oxford Univ. Press 2001) (discussing *lex specialis derogat generali* as one of the general principles governing relationships between rules having the same rank); Anthony Aust, Modern Treaty Law and Practice 201 (Cambridge Univ. Press 2000) (arguing that *lex specialis derogat generali* is a supplementary means of interpretation which should not be followed "slavishly"); John H. Jackson, William J. Davey, Alan O. Sykes, Jr, Legal Problems of International Economic Regulations: Cases, Materials and Text 313 (West Group 4th edn, 2002).

[141] For the treaty nature of the GATT, the GATS and the TRIPS, see Jackson, The World Trade Organization: Constitution and Jurisprudence, supra note 41, at 22.

(a) the procurement of inputs and goods and *services* necessary for production and the conditions under which their goods are produced, marketed or sold, in the domestic market and for export; and
(b) the prices and availability of goods and *services* supplied by national and sub-national authorities and public or state enterprises, in areas including transportation, energy, basic telecommunications, other utilities and factors of production. (emphasis added)

From the text of the paragraph, the comparison of treatment is between "foreign individuals and enterprises and foreign-funded enterprises" and "other individuals and enterprises". What does other individuals and enterprises refer to? Does it refer to domestic individuals and enterprises? If so, this non-discrimination paragraph is a national treatment paragraph. Or, does it refer to individuals and enterprises of other WTO Members? If so, this non-discrimination paragraph is a MFN paragraph. Or, does it refer to domestic individuals and enterprises, and individuals and enterprises of other WTO Members? If so, this non-discrimination paragraph covers both national treatment and MFN treatment.

I take the view of the last interpretation. Part I:3 of the China Accession Protocol is entitled "non-discrimination", not "national treatment", or "MFN treatment", which implies that this paragraph is applicable to both national treatment and MFN treatment because non-discrimination includes national treatment and MFN treatment.[142] From the practice of the WTO dispute settlement, the Appellate Body of the WTO has attached the greatest weight to the interpretation criterion of "the ordinary meaning of the terms" adopted by the Vienna Convention.[143] In *Mexico – Telecoms*,[144] the Panel also applied the general rule of interpretation of the Vienna Convention in interpreting the meaning of a Member's commitment.[145] It is obvious that the ordinary meaning of non-discrimination includes both national treatment and MFN treatment.[146] However, this conclusion should be given some reservation because Part I:3 of the China Accession Protocol uses the word *foreign*, which is naturally associated with its antonym *domestic* in people's mind. In any event, Part I:3 will be related to national treatment, no matter whether it also covers MFN treatment. This conclusion is further supported by the title of Part II:1 of the Working Party Report, i.e. "Non-Discrimination (including national treatment)".

---

[142] See Non-Discrimination: Most-Favoured-Nation Treatment and National Treatment, Note by the Secretariat, ¶ 1, WT/WGTI/W/118 (June 4, 2002).

[143] Claus-Dieter Ehlermann, *Reflections on the Appellate Body of the WTO*, 6(3) J. Int'l Econ. L. 695, 699 (2003).

[144] Panel Report, *Mexico – Telecoms*, WT/DS285/R.

[145] Id. ¶ 7.15.

[146] Kalypso Nicolaidis, *Non-Discriminatory Mutual Recognition: An Oxymoron in the New WTO Lexicon?* in Regulatory Barriers and the Principle of Non-Discrimination in World Trade Law, supra note 59, at 267.

As a matter of fact, Part II:1 of the Working Party Report, especially paragraph 15, provides the background of Part I:3 of the China Accession Protocol.[147]

National Treatment in Right to Trade

In the China Accession Protocol, right to trade is the right to import and export goods.[148] Thus, the national treatment commitments in trading rights are applicable merely to trade in goods, not to trade in services. Part I:5(2) of the China Accession Protocol reads: "Except as otherwise provided for in this Protocol, all *foreign individuals and enterprises*, including those not invested or registered in China, shall be accorded treatment no less favourable than that accorded to *enterprises in China* with respect to the right to trade." (emphasis added)

This subparagraph also has the problem of a mixture of national treatment and MFN because of the ambiguous concept of *enterprises in China*. If *enterprises in China* include both domestic enterprises and foreign enterprises in the territory of China, then the subparagraph on right to trade is applicable to both national treatment and MFN treatment. However, in accordance with the same logic used in the discussion of Part I:3 of the China Accession Protocol in the preceding section, it could be inferred that Part I:5(2) is related to national treatment at least.

National Treatment in Import and Export Licences and Quotas

Part I:8(2) of the China Accession Protocol states: "Except as otherwise provided for in this Protocol, *foreign individuals and enterprises and foreign-funded enterprises* shall be accorded treatment no less favourable than that accorded to *other individuals and enterprises* in respect of the distribution of import and export licences and quotas." (emphasis added)

If *other individuals and enterprises* include both foreign individuals and enterprises in or out of the territory of China on the one hand, and China's domestic individuals and enterprises on the other hand, Part I:8(2) of the China Accession

---

[147] Paragraph 15 of Part II:1 of the Working Party Report reads as follows:

Some members expressd concern regarding the application of the principle of non-discrimination in relation to foreign individuals and enterprises (whether wholly or partly foreign funded). Those members stated that China should enter a commitment to accord non-discriminatory treatment to all foreign individuals and enterprises and foreign-funded enterprises in respect of the procurement of inputs and goods and services necessary for production of goods and the conditions under which their goods were produced, marketed or sold, in the domestic market and for export. In addition, those members said that China should also enter a commitment to guarantee non-discriminatory treatment in respect of the prices and availability of goods and services supplied by national and sub-national authorities and public or state enterprises, in areas including transportation, energy, basic telecommunications, other utilities and factors of production.

[148] Part I:5(1) of the China Accession Protocol states: "... All such goods shall be accorded national treatment under Article III of the GATT 1994, especially paragraph 4 thereof, in respect of their internal sale, offering for sale, purchase, transportation, distribution or use, including their direct access to end-users."

Protocol is another provision of non-discrimination, like Part I:3 and Part I:5(2). It it noteworthy that Part I:8(2) of the China Accession Protocol is the commitment under the framework of trade in goods because the distribution of import and export licences and quotas is only relevant to trade in goods. Thus, Part I:8(2) of the China Accession Protocol is not in the scope of trade in services.

National Treatment in Border Tax Adjustments
Part I:11(4) of the China Accession Protocol states: "Foreign individuals and enterprises and foreign-funded enterprises shall, upon accession, be accorded treatment no less favourable than that accorded to other individuals and enterprises in respect of the provision of border tax adjustments."

Part I:11(4) adopts the same model as Part I:3 and Part I:8(2), which is another commitment relating to national treatment. However, because border tax is one of the special characteristics of trade in goods, this paragraph applies only to trade in goods under GATT 1994.

In addition to the above paragraphs or subparagraphs in the text of the China Accession Protocol, there is an important provision in Annex 1A of the China Accession Protocol, stating that China should provide information on "the repeal and cessation of all WTO inconsistent laws, regulations and other measures on national treatment" to the WTO under the transitional review mechanism.[149] This paragraph drops a hint that China must repeal all WTO national treatment inconsistent laws, regulations and other measures. Actually, in paragraph 68 of the Working Party Report, China promised to revise or annul administrative regulations or departmental rules inconsistent with China's obligations under the WTO agreements and the China Accession Protocol.

C. National Treatment Commitments in the Working Party Report

The Working Party Report includes three hundred and thirty-three paragraphs, in which nine paragraphs (paragraphs 15 to 23) are under the title "Non-Discrimination (including national treatment)". Among the nine paragraphs, four paragraphs (paragraphs 18–19, paragraphs 22–23) have binding force, and six paragraphs (paragraphs 15–19, 22) address both goods and services, and three paragraphs (paragraphs 20–21, 23) only deal with trade in goods under GATT 1994.

In addition to the nine non-discrimination paragraphs, there are other paragraphs relating to national treatment in the Working Party Report, including paragraphs 33 (national treatment in foreign exchange), 52, 53 (national treatment in government pricing, including products and services), 79 (national treatment subject to judicial review), 81, 83, 170, 189, 190, 191, 195, 196, 213, 215, 222 (Trade in goods), 255, 256, 261 (Intellectual property rights).

---

[149] China Accession Protocol, WT/L/432, Annex 1A, ¶ II:1(a). It must be noted that this paragraph applies only to trade in goods because its subtitle is "Non-discrimination (to be notified to the Council for Trade in Goods)".

Non-Discrimination Commitments

The Working Party Report provides the rationales and backgrounds for some provisions in the China Accession Protocol. Paragraph 15 of the Working Party Report indicates that the non-discrimination commitments reflected in Part I:3 of the China Accession Protocol come from special requirements of some WTO Members in order to guarantee non-discrimination treatment.

Paragraph 19 of the Working Party Report, which has binding force,[150] states: "The representative of China confirmed that, consistent with China's rights and obligations under the WTO Agreement and the Draft Protocol, China would provide *non-discriminatory treatment to all WTO Members*, including Members of the WTO that were separate customs territories … ." (emphasis added) This paragraph is not the repetition of Part I:3 of the China Accession Protocol. It is aimed at *all WTO Members*, while Part I:3 of the China Accession Protocol is aimed at *foreign individuals and enterprises and foreign-funded enterprises*.

Paragraph 46 of the Working Party Report provides that the enterprises of other WTO Members have an adequate opportunity to compete for sales to and purchases from Chinese state-owned and state-invested enterprises on non-discriminatory terms and conditions. It is clear that non-discrimination treatment in paragraph 46 of the Working Party Report refers only to national treatment because it compares the treatment of Chinese state-owned and state-invested enterprises with that of foreign enterprises.

Repeal of Law Inconsistent with National Treatment

Although there is a general commitment to revise or annul administrative regulations or departmental rules if they are inconsistent with China's obligations under the WTO Agreement and the China Accession Protocol and the Working Party Report,[151] there is also a special paragraph to emphasize the necessity to repeal laws inconsistent with national treatment obligations. Paragraph 22 of the Working Party Report, which is legally binding on China,[152] states:

> China would repeal and cease to apply all such existing laws, regulations and other measures whose effect was inconsistent with WTO rules on national treatment. This commitment was made in relation to final or interim laws, administrative measures, rules and notices, or any other form of stipulation or guideline … .

Paragraph 22 of the Working Party Report echoes the provision in Annex 1A of the China Accession Protocol which requires China to provide the information on the repeal and cessation of all WTO inconsistent laws, regulations and other

150 Working Party Report, WT/ACC/CHN/49, ¶ 342.

151 See Working Party Report, WT/ACC/CHN/49, ¶ 68.

152 Id. ¶ 342.

measures on national treatment.[153] However, paragraph 22 of the Working Party Report is broader than paragraph II.1(a) of the Annex 1(A) of the China Accession Protocol because it seems that the latter is limited to trade in goods, while the former covers both trade in goods and trade in services.

D. China's Specific National Treatment Commitments in Banking Services

While the China Accession Protocol is a treaty between China and the WTO, the China Schedule can also be regarded as a common agreement among all WTO Members.[154] Actually, the China Schedule is not only an integral part of the China Accession Protocol, but also an integral part of the GATS.[155] In addition to the national treatment commitments in the China Accession Protocol and the Working Party Report, which generally apply to all service sectors in the China Schedule, the specific national treatment commitments relating to banking services in the China Schedule apply to banking services in China.

China's national treatment limitations on banking services seem to be very simple. For mode 1 (cross-border supply), there is no limitation listed in the national treatment column because it uses the word "none", i.e. a full commitment. For mode 2 (consumption abroad), there is not any national treatment limitation, i.e. "none", as in mode 1.

For mode 3 (commercial presence), the commitments made by China read: "Except for geographic restrictions and client limitations on local currency business (listed in the market access column), foreign financial institution may do business, without restrictions or need for case-by-case approval, with *foreign invested enterprises, non-Chinese natural persons, Chinese natural persons and Chinese enterprises*. Otherwise, none." (emphasis added) From the commitments, China made merely two national treatment limitations for mode 3 of banking services – geographic restrictions and client limitations. Since the two kinds of limitation had been eliminated by the end of 2006, there should be no national treatment limitation for commercial presence in China's banking services market after December 2006. These national treatment commitments on banking services originally appeared in the US-China Bilateral WTO Agreement,[156] and spread to all other WTO Members by MFN treatment after being consolidated into the China Schedule.

---

153 China Accession Protocol, WT/L/432, Annex 1A, ¶ II:1(a).

154 See Appellate Body Report, *U.S. – Gambling*, WT/DS285/AB/R, adopted April 20, 2005, ¶ 159; Appellate Body Report, *EC – Computer Equipment*, WT/DS62/AB/R, adopted June 22, 1998, ¶ 109.

155 GATS, art. XX:3 (stating that "[s]chedules of specific commitments shall be annexed to this Agreement [GATS] and shall form an integral part thereof").

156 See Summary of US–China Bilateral WTO Agreement, http://www.uschina.org/public/991115a.html.

For mode 4 (Presence of natural persons), China does not make a national treatment commitment except as indicated in the horizontal commitments. The horizontal commitments with respect to mode 4 states: "Unbound except for the measures concerning the entry and temporary stay of natural persons who fall into the categories referred to in the market access column."[157] This is another example that national treatment commitments are connected to market access commitments in the China Schedule.

China's national treatment commitments in banking services also provide some clues for the clarification of the ambiguous concept in Part I:3 of the China Accession Protocol, i.e. *other individuals and enterprises*. From the wording of China's banking commitments, in the context of national treatment, it could be deduced that *individuals* include *non-Chinese natural persons* and *Chinese natural persons*, and *enterprises* include *foreign invested enterprises* and *Chinese enterprises*.

From the analysis of China's banking commitments, one may find that China's specific commitments on banking services focus on commercial presence because commercial presence is the mode of supply favoured by most banking service suppliers. It is generally acknowledged that consumption abroad and the presence of natural persons are of lesser importance for financial services.[158] As to cross-border supply, most countries are unbound due to the high risks of capital movement. In China's banking commitments, there is no limitation on the number of foreign banks, no limitation on the total value of banking service transactions, no economic needs test, no requirement of specific types of legal entity or joint venture for foreign banks. Foreign banks can enter China in the form of branches, subsidiaries, joint ventures, or representative offices.[159] Since the geographic restraints and client limitations were eliminated by the end of 2006, the banking service part of China's Schedule has become shorter, while the national treatment enjoyed by foreign banks has become broader.

---

157 See the China Schedule, WT/ACC/CHN/49/Add.2, Horizontal Commitments.

158 Constance Z. Wagner, *The New WTO Agreement on Financial Services and Chapter 14 of NAFTA: Has Free Trade in Banking Finally Arrived?* 5 NAFTA: L. & BUS. REV. AM. 5, 15 (1999).

159 The main difference between a representative office and the other three types of commercial presence is that a representative office cannot engage in any profit-making activities except some professional services. See the China Schedule, WT/ACC/CHN/49/Add.2, horizontal commitments.

III. Changes of GATS/WTO National Treatment in China

From 1995 to August 2012, twenty-nine new Members entered the WTO.[160] Consequently, there are twenty-nine new protocols of accession,[161] among which only the China Accession Protocol has a non-discrimination article and many national treatment provisions. Indeed, China's national treatment commitments are broader than those of the new WTO Members due to the fact that China's national treatment commitments are different from the existing national treatment obligations under the GATS/WTO. In fact, China's national treatment commitments, as well as its other WTO commitments, go beyond the requirements of the GATS/WTO, and constitute GATS/WTO-plus obligations. As a result, China has to undertake deeper and broader national treatment obligations than the WTO agreements demand.

A. GATS/WTO-plus – Minority Shareholder Rights

GATS: Majority Shareholder Rights

Under the GATS, in the case of supply of a service through commercial presence, an enterprise with foreign minority ownership is not deemed a *juridical person of another Member*, because it is not *owned* or *controlled* by foreign natural persons or foreign juridical persons.[162] Therefore, in general, with respect to treatment of a Sino-foreign equity joint venture with foreign minority shares, foreign countries cannot complain against China based on GATS national treatment obligations because such a joint venture is not regarded as a *juridical person of another Member*, but regarded as a domestic juridical person, whose treatment, whether favourable or less favourable compared with other domestic juridical persons, is outside the area of the GATS/WTO. In fact, GATS only protects rights of foreign individuals and enterprises, including foreign enterprises, the subsidiaries of

---

160 They are Albania, Armenia, Bulgaria, Cambodia, China, Cape Verde, Croatia, Ecuador, Estonia, FYR Macedonia, Georgia, Jordan, Kyrgyz Republic, Lithuania, Latvia, Moldova, Mongolia, Montenegro, Nepal, Oman, Panama, Russia, Samoa, Saudi Arabia, Chinese Taipei, Tonga, Ukraine, Vanuatu, and Viet Nam, http://www.wto.org/english/thewto_e/acc_e/completeacc_e.htm (August 24, 2012).

161 See *Protocols of Accession for New Members since 1995, Including Commitments in Goods and Services*, http://www.wto.org/english/thewto_e/acc_e/completeacc_e.htm (August 24, 2012).

162 GATS Article XXVIII (n) states: a juridical person is:

(i) "owned" by persons of a Member if more than 50 percent of the equity interests in it is beneficially owned by persons of that Member;

(ii) "controlled" by persons of a Member if such persons have the power to name a majority of its directors or otherwise to legally direct its actions;

(iii) "affiliated" with another person when it controls, or is controlled by, that other person; or when it and the other person are both controlled by the same person.

foreign enterprises, the branches of foreign enterprises, and joint ventures with foreign majority ownership.[163] Most WTO Members follow the GATS rule and take advantage of the exclusion of foreign minority ownership from the GATS. For example, according to the Report of the Working Party on the Accession of the Kyrgyz Republic,[164] national treatment is granted to *foreign-owned* domestic suppliers.[165]

Minority Shareholder Rights

During the Uruguay Round negotiations, the OECD countries were not satisfied with the exclusion of minority shareholder rights from the scope of GATS obligations, especially with respect to financial services. They reached a special agreement, i.e. the Understanding,[166] which has a higher degree of liberalization than the GATS.[167] According to the Understanding, commercial presence includes, inter alia, *wholly- or partly-owned* subsidiaries, joint ventures.[168] Through the Understanding, the scope of national treatment obligations in financial services is extended to all joint ventures. The adoption of the Understanding is on a voluntary basis,[169] but it does not mean that a WTO Member not adhering to it cannot accord similar rights to joint ventures with foreign minority shares.

In fact, one of the important characteristics of China's WTO commitments is that all foreign-funded enterprises established in China are in the scope of the WTO framework and enjoy WTO rights, such as national treatment, regardless of foreign investors' ownership percentage. Therefore, national treatment equally applies to all foreign-funded enterprises in China, no matter whether foreign investors are minority shareholders, or majority shareholders or 100 per cent shareholders. In this regard, the breadth of China's commitments exceeds the scope of national treatment obligations in the GATS that only cover those foreign-funded enterprises with foreigner control or ownership with equity interests more than 50 percent. However, some Chinese scholars misunderstand the scope of WTO national treatment so as to exclude foreign-funded enterprises from the scope of national treatment.[170]

---

163 Some are of the view that the GATS legitimizes the differentiation between "national" and "foreign" firms. See Mina Mashayekhi and Murray Gibbs, *Lessons from the Uruguay Round Negotiations on Investment*, 33(6) J. World Trade 1, 20 (1999).

164 Report of the Working Party on the Accession of the Kyrgyz Republic, WT/ACC/KGZ/26 (July 31, 1998).

165 Id. ¶ 166.

166 The Understanding, supra note 46.

167 Yi Wang, *Most-Favoured-Nation Treatment under the General Agreement on Trade in Services And Its Application in Financial Services*, 30 J. World Trade 91, 110 (1996).

168 The Understanding, supra note 46, ¶ D (2).

169 Id. preamble.

170 See, e.g., Li Lian, *Woguo Waizi Guomin Daiyu Ruogan Falü Wenti TanTao* [Discussing Relevant Legal Issues Relating to National Treatment for Foreign Investment

Furthermore, China, through its WTO accession instruments, extends national treatment not only to joint ventures with foreign minority shares in the financial service sector, which is what OECD countries do through the Understanding,[171] but also to all joint ventures with foreign minority shares in all other service sectors inscribed in the China Schedule. It is no exaggeration to say that, although China is not an OECD member, China's WTO commitments on national treatment are deeper and wider than all other country groups.[172]

Significance of Minority Shareholder Rights

The significance of adding minority shareholder rights to China's WTO commitments could be finally decided in the WTO dispute settlement mechanism. Under the general GATS/WTO framework, a WTO Member cannot claim before the WTO Dispute Settlement Body the rights of its persons who make service investment in China as minority shareholders. On the contrary, according to China's WTO commitments, a WTO Member may have recourse to the WTO dispute settlement mechanism to ensure implementation of all commitments in the China Schedule, including minority shareholder rights.[173] Without the special rule on protection of minority shareholder rights in China's WTO commitments, all disputes relating to Sino-foreign equity joint ventures with foreigners as minority shareholders would be outside the jurisdiction of the WTO dispute settlement mechanism. With the introduction of minority shareholder rights in the China-WTO framework, China has further yielded part of its jurisdiction power to the WTO dispute settlement system, reflecting the implications of WTO accession for China's sovereignty. As pointed out by Jackson, national treatment obligations have enormous implications for sovereignty.[174]

---

in China], 4 Guoji Jingjifa Luncong [Chinese J. Int'l. Econ. L.] 422, 439 (Law Press China 2001) (arguing that WTO national treatment obligations do not apply to foreign-funded enterprises located in China because the foreign-funded enterprises are not foreign enterprises, but China's domestic enterprises registered in China).

171 It is noteworthy that national treatment concerning investment and multinational enterprises in the OECD members applies only to "foreign-controlled enterprises". See OECD Declaration on International Investment and Multinational Enterprises, III.1, June 27, 2000, http://www.ausncp.gov.au/content/docs/158_171_20000627_oecd.pdf.

172 Aaditya Mattoo, *China's Accession to the WTO: The Services Dimension*, 6(2) J. Int'l Econ. L. 299, 304 (2003).

173 See Working Party Report, WT/ACC/CHN/49, ¶ 320. It is noteworthy that paragraph 320 of the Working Party Report is legally binding according to paragraph 342 of the Working Party Report.

174 John H. Jackson, *The WTO 'Constitution' and Proposed Reforms: Seven 'Mantras' Revisited*, 4(1) J. Int'l Econ. L. 67, 70 (2001).

B. Beneficiaries of National Treatment

Three Beneficiaries

From Part I:3, I:5(2), I:8(2) and I:11(4) of the China Accession Protocol, and paragraphs 18 and 53 of the Working Party Report, one can find that China's WTO commitments on national treatment focus on foreign individuals and enterprises and foreign-funded enterprises. By comparison, GATS Article XVII looks upon services and service suppliers, and GATT 1994 Article III deals with products of other WTO Members. That is to say, China grants national treatment directly to three types of beneficiaries: foreign individuals, foreign enterprises and foreign-funded enterprises.[175] However, there are no clear definitions of the three beneficiaries under China's laws. What is a foreign individual? What is a foreign enterprise? What is the main factor of being "foreign"? It is well known that foreign-funded enterprises include three types of organization, i.e. Sino-foreign equity joint venture, Sino-foreign contractual joint venture, and wholly-foreign-funded enterprise,[176] all of which may obtain the status of Chinese legal persons upon satisfying legal requirements of establishment in China. However, there are no clear definitions of the three types of foreign-funded enterprises in China's laws and China's WTO commitments, especially for the elusive concept of contractual joint venture.

Differences and Relationships with Relevant Concepts in the GATS

The adoption of three beneficiaries does not mean that China has a set of separate standards of national treatment, or that China does not apply the national treatment rules in the GATS and GATT 1994. In fact, traditional concepts in the WTO national treatment rules, such as like products and like services, also appear in China's WTO commitments. For example, Part I:5(1) of the China Accession Protocol states that such goods shall be accorded national treatment under Article III of the GATT 1994. In my view, China's emphasis on beneficiaries, other than products and services, is meaningful mainly to foreign direct investment in China. China's WTO national treatment commitments are not only commitments in trade, but also commitments in investment through the introduction of the three types of beneficiaries. Moreover, in terms of the GATS, *foreign individuals and enterprises and foreign-funded enterprises* or *other individuals and enterprises* are in essence service suppliers when they supply services.[177] *Service supplier* is a new concept

[175] The China Accession Protocol and the Working Party Report use the wording of "foreign-funded enterprises", while the China Schedule uses the wording of "foreign invested enterprises", both of which have the same meaning, and are interchangeable.

[176] It must be noted that "wholly-foreign-funded enterprises" are equal to "foreign capital enterprises". See the China Schedule, WT/ACC/CHN/49/Add.2, Horizontal Commitments, column of Limitation on Market Access.

[177] See GATS, art. XXVIII (g).

in the GATS.[178] It means any person that supplies a service.[179] If a service is not supplied directly by a juridical person but through other forms of commercial presence such as a branch or a representative office, the service supplier (i.e. the juridical person) shall, through such presence, be accorded the treatment provided for service suppliers under the Agreement.[180]

From the perspective of mode 3 of service supply, *foreign individuals and enterprises and foreign-funded enterprises* may also constitute commercial presence. The notion of commercial presence complicates the definition of service suppliers. To some extent, commercial presence and service suppliers are overlapping but not identical,[181] because service suppliers may be involved in any of the four modes of supply.[182] In any case, whether they are service suppliers or have commercial presence, the three types of beneficiaries in China's WTO commitments are still in the domain of the GATS framework. If there is a difference, the difference could be that the GATS compares treatment between domestic and foreign services and service suppliers, while China's WTO national treatment commitments primarily compare treatment between domestic and foreign service suppliers.

Another difference between China's WTO national treatment commitments and WTO national treatment articles is that China's national treatment commitments lack the word *like* before *other individuals and enterprises*, while both GATT 1994 (Article III) and GATS (Article XVII) use *like* products and *like* services and service suppliers. In my view, although China's WTO accession instruments do not provide any reason for the omission of the word *like*, it does not necessarily imply that China has abandoned the basic rule of comparison between treatment of foreign and domestic like service suppliers. If China permitted foreign individuals and enterprises and foreign-funded enterprises to get treatment no less favourable than that accorded to any kind of domestic individuals and enterprises, like or unlike, that would cause utter chaos in applying WTO national treatment obligations. Consequently, China's rights under the WTO would be seriously prejudiced. China's intention of avoiding such a disastrous implication is clearly expressed in the Working Party Report.[183] It goes without saying that there is a

---

178 In Dunkel Draft, it was named "service provider".

179 GATS, art. XXVIII(g).

180 See id. art. XXVII(g), footnote.

181 Zdouc, supra note 63, at 328.

182 Id. at 328–29.

183 Working Party Report, WT/ACC/CHN/49, ¶ 17 (stating that "... any commitment to provide non-discriminatory treatment to Chinese enterprises, including foreign-funded enterprises, and foreign enterprises and individuals in China, would be subject to other provisions of the Draft Protocol and, in particular, would not prejudice China's rights under the GATS, China's Schedule of Specific Commitments or commitments undertaken in relation to trade-related investment measures").

latent *like* before *other individuals and enterprises* in China's non-discriminatory commitments, especially in Part I:3 of the China Accession Protocol.

A GATS/WTO-Plus Obligation

From the Working Party Report, one can find the origin of China's special WTO commitments for the three types of beneficiaries. During China's WTO accession negotiations, some WTO Members asked China to accord non-discriminatory treatment to all foreign individuals, enterprises and foreign-funded enterprises.[184] It indicates that the emphasis on the three types of beneficiaries is not the result of China's offer, but the *quid pro quo* for China's accession to the WTO.[185] Indeed, China's broader and deeper national treatment commitments are part of the entrance fees that China must pay to other WTO Members in exchange for benefits that it can get from them, for example most-favoured-nation treatment.[186] This exchange is not an equal bargain, but an unequal *quid pro quo*. In the history of the GATT, the accession negotiations were "in favour of newcomers".[187] However, China's WTO accession history indicates that current WTO accession negotiations are less favourable to newcomers, especially to such a big country like China.

It is notable that China's WTO commitments of granting national treatment to foreign individuals, enterprises and foreign-funded enterprises are not commitments of binding the *status quo*,[188] or below the *status quo*,[189] but beyond

---

[184] See id. ¶ 15.

[185] Cf. Zhao Weitian, *New Development on the Rule of Non-discrimination of WTO: Discussion on the Provisions about Non-discrimination in the Protocol on the Accession of the PRC*, 20 ZHENGFA LUNTAN [TRIBUNE OF POLITICAL SCIENCE & LAW/JOURNAL OF CHINA UNIV. OF POLITICAL SCIENCE & LAW) 23, 30 (2002, no. 4) (stating that granting national treatment to foreign individuals, enterprises and foreign-funded enterprises is the necessity of historical development and consistent with the requirement of the times).

[186] See LONG, supra note 2, at 36 (discussing the reasons for "contribution" made by new members for their accession to the GATT); see also JOHN H. JACKSON, RESTRUCTURING THE GATT SYSTEM 18 (Royal Institute of International Affairs, Printer Publisher, 1990) (stating that the GATT accession process is to negotiate ticket of admission).

[187] GERARD CURZON, MULTILATERAL COMMERCIAL DIPLOMACY: THE GENERAL AGREEMENT ON TARIFFS AND TRADE AND ITS IMPACT ON NATIONAL COMMERCIAL POLICIES AND TECHNIQUES 35–36 (Michael Joseph 1965); see also KENNETH W. DAM, THE GATT: LAW AND INTERNATIONAL ECONOMIC ORGANIZATION 110 (Univ. of Chicago Press 1970) (stating that the accession negotiations were "ritualistic" rather than "substantive" for less-developed countries).

[188] The service commitments made by the OECD countries are commitments of binding the status quo, rather than the commitments to decrease existing restrictions. See Sauve, supra note 92, at 142. In addition, most developing countries, as pointed out by Pierre Sauve, also committed to bind the status quo. See Pierre Sauve, *Financial Services and the WTO: What Next*? in TRADE RULES BEHIND BORDERS: ESSAYS ON SERVICES, INVESTMENT AND THE NEW TRADE AGENDA 131, 160 (Cameron May 2003).

[189] According to Pierre Sauve's statistic based on US Department of Treasury's *National Treatment Study Report 1998*, with respect to banking services, five WTO

the *status quo*. Chinese foreign-funded enterprises laws have no national treatment or non-discriminatory treatment article. Although China's Foreign Trade Law stipulates that China grants national treatment and MFN to other contracting parties, acceding parties based on international treaties or agreements, or to other parties based on mutual benefit and reciprocity principles,[190] it fails to grant national treatment to foreign individuals, enterprises and foreign-funded enterprises. In fact, China's special commitments of granting national treatment to the three types of beneficiaries exceed the treatment granted by China's laws and the WTO agreements. It is not only a WTO-plus obligation,[191] but also a China's

---

Members' commitments are below the status quo, i.e. Hong Kong, India, Indonesia, Korea and Philippines. See Sauve, *Financial Services and the WTO: What Next*? id, at 161. *National Treatment Study Report 1998* is available at http://www.treas.gov/offices/international-affairs/nts/.

[190] See Article 6 of the PRC Foreign Trade Law (amended 2004), supra note 1. Another shortcoming of China's Foreign Trade Law is that the national treatment obligation in this law does not apply to Hong Kong, Macao and Taiwan because they are separate customs territories that are outside the scope of this law. See Article 43 of the PRC Foreign Trade Law. China's WTO commitments, however, apply not only to country members, but also to separate customs territories with WTO membership, like Hong Kong, Macao and Taiwan.

[191] Article XII of the WTO Agreement does not restrain the scope of terms to be negotiated between a WTO applicant and interested WTO Members, and neither does GATT Article XXXIII. GATT Article XXXIII provides that an applicant may access to GATT 1994 "on terms to be agreed between such government and the CONTRACTING PARTIES". Therefore, some WTO Members demand a WTO acceding party to undertake obligations more than what WTO requires, which is the so-called WTO-plus. For the concept of WTO-plus, see Andreas R. Ziegler, *Lessons from the WTO from Recent EFTA Bilateral Free Trade Agreements*, in THE WTO AND THE DOHA ROUND: THE CHANGING FACE OF WORLD TRADE 229, footnote 65, at 241 (Ross P. Buckley (ed.), Kluwer Law International 2003); see also Julia Ya Qin, *"WTO-Plus" Obligations and Their Implications for the WTO Legal System – An Appraisal of the China Accession Protocol*, 37 (3) J. WORLD TRADE 483–522 (2003) (arguing that WTO-plus obligations should not be imposed on any particular acceding Member because the imposition of WTO-plus rules on a single Member undermines the WTO rule of law); see also Technical Note on the Accession Process, Note by the Secretariat, WT/ACC/7/Rev.2, November 1, 2000, at 6 (indicating that some WTO Members objected to the imposition of WTO-plus obligations). Historically the concept of WTO-plus is modelled on the concept of GATT-plus, see ATLANTIC COUNCIL OF THE UNITED STATES, GATT PLUS – A PROPOSAL FOR TRADE REFORM, REPORT OF THE SPECIAL ADVISORY PANEL TO THE TRADE COMMITTEE OF THE ATLANTIC COUNCIL (Praeger Publishers 1975); see also LONG, supra note 2, at 39. In GATT history, Poland's GATT accession protocol which entered into force on October 18, 1967 includes a GATT-plus clause, i.e. the special safeguard clause, see Part I:4 of the Protocol for the Accession of Poland, BISD 15S/46, 48; This is also the case of Romania's GATT accession, see Part I:4 of the Protocol for the Accession of Romania to the GATT, October 15, 1971, BISD 18S/5, 7. Hungary's GATT accession protocol also contains a similar special safeguard clause, see Part I:5 of the Protocol for the Accession of Hungary to the GATT, August 8, 1973, BISD 20S/3, 4–5.

national law-plus obligation. The trade liberalization in China will be driven by the special commitment in relation to beneficiaries of national treatment, which has *de facto* amended China's foreign-funded laws and foreign trade law, and provided national treatment of the broadest scope, far beyond that required by the WTO.

C. Mixture of National Treatment and MFN Treatment

Both the China Accession Protocol (Part I:3) and the Working Party Report (Part II:1, including paragraphs 15–23) use the title of non-discrimination, rather than MFN treatment or national treatment, and the non-discrimination treatment granted to *foreign individuals and enterprises and foreign funded enterprises* shall be no less favourable than that accorded to *other individuals and enterprises*. Since there is no definition of *other individuals and enterprises*, an ordinary reading of the text will lead to a conclusion that *other individuals and enterprises* include both other domestic individuals and enterprises and other foreign individuals and enterprises. The comparison of treatment between foreign and domestic subjects is related to national treatment, while the comparison of treatment between some foreign subjects and other foreign subjects is related to MFN treatment. Thus, national treatment and MFN treatment are intertwined in China's WTO commitments entitled "non-discrimination".

The mixture of national treatment and MFN treatment may change the reasoning with future WTO disputes on China's measures claimed to be inconsistent with MFN treatment or national treatment obligations. In *EC – Banana III*, the Panel interpreted the *treatment no less favourable* standard in Article II of the GATS (MFN) by reference to paragraphs 2 and 3 of Article XVII of the GATS (national treatment).[192] In the Panel's view, the same wording, i.e. *treatment no less favourable*, no matter whether it is with respect to national treatment or MFN treatment, should be used as the basis of interpreting each. However, the Appellate Body disagreed to the Panel's reasoning on this issue. The Appellate Body separated national treatment and MFN articles in the interpretation of either of them. The Appellate Body pointed out that "[t]he Panel would have been on safer ground had it compared the MFN obligation in Article II of the GATS with the MFN and MFN-type obligations in the GATT 1994",[193] other than with Article XVII of the GATS.

It is predictable that the tendency to separate MFN and national treatment articles when interpreting a concept with the same wording, like *treatment no less favourable*, may disappear in future WTO cases on China MFN-inconsistent or national treatment-inconsistent measures, because China has combined the two types of treatment into a single non-discrimination treatment. The mixture of MFN treatment and national treatment in China's WTO commitments does not

192 Panel Report, *EC – Banana III*, WT/DS27/R, adopted September 25, 1997, ¶ 7.301.

193 Appellate Body Report, *EC – Banana III*, WT/DS27/AB/R, adopted September 25, 1997, ¶ 231.

fundamentally change the current separated status of MFN articles and national treatment articles under the WTO framework, as most WTO Members still use the traditional expressions. For example, in the commitments of the Separate Customs Territory of Taiwan, Penghu, Kinmen and Matsu, the principles of MFN and national treatment are expressed in parallel, instead of being in a single non-discrimination clause.[194] Kyrgyz and Estonia's national treatment commitments are also expressed in independent paragraphs.[195] Furthermore, there is no mixture of national treatment and MFN in the WTO commitments of Lithuania, Croatia, and Macedonia.[196] However, with respect to China, the mixture of national treatment and MFN treatment will have far-reaching implications for interpretation and implementation of China's WTO commitments on MFN treatment and national treatment.

IV. Concluding Remarks

China's specific national treatment commitments under the WTO, which are scattered among China's WTO accession instruments, prevail over GATT Article III and GATS Article XVII. From the perspective of national treatment, China's banking services are primarily covered by the national treatment commitments in the China Accession Protocol and the Working Party Report, as well as the specific national treatment commitments relating to banking services in the China Schedule.

Moreover, China's national treatment commitments go beyond the requirements of the GATS/WTO and constitute GATS/WTO-plus obligations. In China, all kinds of foreign-funded enterprises with different percentages of foreign shares are covered by the WTO, no matter whether foreign shareholders are majority shareholders or minority shareholders. As a result, all foreign-funded enterprises in China enjoy national treatment under the WTO. This far exceeds what the GATS/WTO provides. In addition, China's specific commitments of granting national treatment to the three types of beneficiaries also exceed the scope of the WTO agreements.

In a word, China's specific national treatment commitments constitute a significant part of China's GATS/WTO national treatment obligations, which have a great impact on China's domestic law, especially on China's banking law.

---

[194] See Report of the Working Party on the Accession of the Separate Customs Territory of Taiwan, Penghu, Kinmen and Matsu, WT/ACC/TPKM/18, ¶ 8 (October 5, 2001).

[195] See Report of the Working Party on the Accession of the Kyrgyz Republic, WT/ACC/KGZ/26, 166 (July 31, 1998); Report of the Working Party on the Accession of Estonia to the WTO, WT/ACC/EST/28, ¶ 15 (April 9, 1999).

[196] See WT/ACC/LTU/52 (November 7, 2000); WT/ACC/HRV/59 (June 29, 2000); WT/ACC/807/27 (September 26, 2002).

CHAPTER 3
Market Access, Forms, and Legal Status of Foreign-Funded Banks in China

In 1983, the PBC issued its first foreign banking rule, i.e., the Measures for Administration of Establishing Permanent Representative Offices of Overseas Chinese-Funded and Foreign-Funded Financial Institutions in China.[1] This was the PRC's first step to allow market access of foreign banks to China. In 1985, the PRC issued the Regulation on Administration of Wholly-Foreign-Funded Banks and Sino-Foreign Equity Joint Venture Banks in the Special Economic Zones,[2] allowing foreign-funded banks to enter four Special Economic Zones, Shenzhen, Xiamen, Zhuhai and Shantou. In 1987, the State Council published the Relevant Interim Provisions on Administration of Business of Wholly-Foreign-Funded Banks and Sino-Foreign Equity Joint Venture Banks in the Special Economic Zones.[3] In 1990, the PRC issued the Regulation on Administration of Wholly-Foreign-Funded Financial Institutions and Sino-Foreign Equity Joint Venture Financial Institutions in Shanghai,[4] regulating foreign financial institutions in

[1] Measures for Administration of Establishing Permanent Representative Offices of Overseas Chinese-Funded and Foreign-Funded Financial Institutions in China [*Guanyu Qiaozi Waizi Jinrong Jigou zai Zhongguo Sheli Changzhu Daibiao Jigou de Guanli Banfa*], issued by the PBC on February 1, 1983, effective February 1, 1983, void June 11, 1991, GAZETTE OF THE STATE COUNCIL 76–78 (1983, no. 2).

[2] Regulation on Administration of Wholly-Foreign-Funded Banks and Sino-Foreign Equity Joint Venture Banks in the Special Economic Zones [*Jingji Tequ Waizi Yinhang Zhongwai Hezi Yinhang Guanli Tiaoli*], State Council Decree [*Guofa*] No. 48, issued on April 2, 1985, effective April 2, 1985, void April 1, 1994, GAZETTE OF THE STATE COUNCIL 349–53 (1985, no. 12).

[3] Relevant Interim Provisions on Administration of Business of Wholly-Foreign-Funded Banks and Sino-Foreign Equity Joint Venture Banks in the Special Economic Zones [*Guanyu Jingji Tequ Waizi Yinhang, Zhongwai Hezi Yinhang Yewu Guanli de Ruogan Zanxing Guiding*], June 17, 1987, void April 1,1994, in ZHONGHUA RENMIN GONGHEGUO JINRONG FAGUI HUIBIAN [COMPILATION OF FINANCIAL REGULATIONS OF THE PRC] 202 (Regulation Compilation Office of the Legal Affairs Bureau of the State Council (ed.), Law Press China 1992).

[4] Regulation on Administration of Wholly-Foreign-Funded Financial Institutions and Sino-Foreign Equity Joint Venture Financial Institutions in Shanghai [*Shanghai Waizi Jinrong Jigou Zhongwai Hezi Jinrong Jigou Guanli Tiaoli*], PBC Decree [1990] No. 2, State Council Reply [1990] No. 76, approved by the State Council on September 7, 1990, effective September 8, 1990, void April 1, 1994, GAZETTE OF THE STATE COUNCIL 799–807 (1990, no. 21).

Shanghai. Based on the experience of the above foreign banking regulations and rules, the PRC issued the Regulation on Administration of Foreign-Funded Financial Institutions in 1994 (FFFI Regulation 1994),[5] regulating foreign-funded banks in the whole territory of China, except Hong Kong, Macao and Taiwan. Foreign-funded banks were allowed to enter China's financial market in accordance with the above regulations, despite many limitations on the establishment and business of foreign-funded banks.

Since China entered the WTO, the market access of foreign banks to China has been greatly enlarged. By September 2011, 207 representative offices had been set up by foreign banks, and 39 wholly-foreign-funded banks (with 247 branches and subsidiaries) had been established by financial investors from more than a dozen states and regions. There was one wholly-foreign-funded finance company, and 93 foreign bank branches had been set up by foreign banks from dozens of states and regions.[6] By September 2011, the total assets of foreign-funded banks in China were RMB 2.06 trillion.[7]

I. Market Access of Foreign-Funded Banks

A. Market Access under the GATS

GATS Article XVI

Market access obligations are identified by the GATS, though they cannot be found in the GATT.[8] They are set forth in Article XVI of GATS. The provision reads as follows:

> 1. With respect to market access through the modes of supply identified in Article I, each Member shall accord services and service suppliers of any other Member treatment no less favourable than that provided for under the terms, limitations and conditions agreed and specified in its Schedule. (original footnote omitted)

---

[5] FFFI Regulation 1994 [*Waizi Jinrong Jigou Guanli Tiaoli*], State Council Decree No. 148, promulgated on February 25, 1994, effective April 1, 1994, void February 1, 2002, GAZETTE OF THE STATE COUNCIL 76–83 (1994, no. 3). This FFFI Regulation 1994 replaced the two foreign banking regulations, i.e., Regulation on Administration of Wholly-Foreign-Funded Banks and Sino-Foreign Equity Joint Venture Banks in the Special Economic Zones (1985), and Regulation on Administration of Wholly-Foreign-Funded Financial Institutions and Sino-Foreign Equity Joint Venture Financial Institutions in Shanghai (1990).

[6] S/FIN/M/71, para.17.

[7] The Opening of Chinese Banking Industry and Regulation of Foreign-Funded Banks in China After 10 Years of WTO Accession, http://www.cbrc.gov.cn/chinese/home/docView/F66A0967E8A74157AD58642D5A1BEF76.html (published December 16, 2011).

[8] Bernard Hoekman, *Assessing the General Agreement on Trade in Services*, in THE URUGUAY ROUND AND THE DEVELOPING COUNTRIES 93 (Will Martin and L. Alan Winters (eds), Cambridge Univ. Press, 1996).

2. In sectors where market-access commitments are undertaken, the measures which a Member shall not maintain or adopt either on the basis of a regional subdivision or on the basis of its entire territory, unless otherwise specified in its Schedule, are defined as:

(a) limitations on the number of service suppliers whether in the form of numerical quotas, monopolies, exclusive service suppliers or the requirements of an economic needs test;
(b) limitations on the total value of service transactions or assets in the form of numerical quotas or the requirement of an economic needs test;
(c) limitations on the total number of service operations or on the total quantity of service output expressed in terms of designated numerical units in the form of quotas or the requirement of an economic needs test; (original footnote omitted)
(d) limitations on the total number of natural persons that may be employed in a particular service sector or that a service supplier may employ and who are necessary for, and directly related to, the supply of a specific service in the form of numerical quotas or the requirement of an economic needs test;
(e) measures which restrict or require specific types of legal entity or joint venture through which a service supplier may supply a service; and
(f) limitations on the participation of foreign capital in terms of maximum percentage limit on foreign shareholding or the total value of individual or aggregate foreign investment.

Among the six types of limitation measures, the first four concern quantitative limitations on market access, the fifth concerns legal entity or joint venture limitations, and the sixth covers foreign capital limitations.[9] According to a statement in the 2001 Scheduling Guidelines, the list is exhaustive.[10] There is a similar statement in the Guidelines for the Scheduling of Initial Commitments in Trade in Services: Explanatory Note (1993 Scheduling Guidelines) circulated during the Uruguay Round negotiations.[11] Usually a Member only inscribes some of the six types of limitation measures in its market access column in its service schedule.

---

[9] For further discussion of GATS Article XVI, see Appellate Body Report, *US – Measures Affecting the Cross-Border Supply of Gambling and Betting Services* [hereinafter *US – Gambling*], WT/DS285/AB/R, adopted April 20, 2005, ¶¶ 214–65.

[10] 2001 Scheduling Guidelines, S/L/92, ¶ 8 (March 28, 2001). In Hoekman's view, the exhaustive list weakens the scope of market access obligation because it does not cover other measures that have similar effects like the six kinds of measures. See Hoekman, supra note 8, at 112.

[11] 1993 Scheduling Guidelines, MTN.GNS/W/164, ¶ 4 (September 3, 1993). In *US – Gambling*, the US argued that the 1993 Scheduling Guidelines were only "preparatory work", not "context" for the interpretation of US GATS Schedule under the Vienna Convention on the Law of Treaties, while the view of Antigua was to the contrary (WT/DS285/AB/R, ¶¶

GATS Article XVI:1 obliges a Member to accord market access based on its service schedule. GATS Article XVI:2 gives a list of limitation measures on market access which a Member should not take unless otherwise specified in its service schedule. From the structure of the GATS, market access and national treatment are in the same part, i.e. Part III (specific commitments), which means that market access is not a general obligation under the GATS.

GATS Article XX:2

GATS Article XX:2 provides: "Measures inconsistent with both Articles XVI and XVII shall be inscribed in the column relating to Article XVI. In this case the inscription will be considered to provide a condition or qualification to Article XVII as well." This means that, at least sometimes, some limitation measures inscribed in the market access column of China's Service Schedule are also limitation measures in the national treatment column. The reason for the overlap is that "market access restrictions in the form of limitations or conditions on modes of supply are likely to violate national treatment for these modes as well".[12] However, the GATS does not state which measures or what kinds of measures entered in the market access column of a service schedule are also regarded as limitation measures in the national treatment column.

Because GATS Article XX:2 connects market access and national treatment, any limitation measure taken at the stage of market access could be regarded as a limitation measure in the sense of national treatment provided that market access measure is also discriminatory. Consequently, it is necessary to look upon market access limitations in the China Schedule to explore the whole boundary of national treatment obligations for a sector or sub-sector.

2001 Scheduling Guidelines

The 2001 Scheduling Guidelines should not be considered as a legal interpretation of the GATS.[13] In *Mexico – Telecoms*,[14] the Panel found that "the source, content, and use by negotiators of the Explanatory Note, together with its later adoption by Members as the Scheduling Guidelines, provide an important element with which to interpret the provisions of the GATS".[15] It seems the Panel overestimated the

17, 49). In this regard, the EU agreed with the US WT/DS285/AB/R, ¶ 100). The Appellate Body found that "documents can be characterized as context only where there is sufficient evidence of their constituting an 'agreement relating to the treaty' between the parties or of their accept[ance by the parties] as an instrument related to the treaty," so the Appellate Body overruled the panel's finding categorizing the 1993 Scheduling Guidelines as context for the interpretation of the US GATS Schedules (WT/DS285/AB/R, ¶¶175, 178).

12 Bernard Hoekman, *Market Access through Multilateral Agreement: From Goods to Services*, 15 The World Econ. 707, 720 (1992).

13 2001 Scheduling Guidelines, S/L/92, *Introduction.*

14 Panel Report, *Mexico – Telecoms*, WT/DS204/R, adopted June 1, 2004.

15 Id. ¶ 7.43.

legal status of the Scheduling Guidelines. In *U.S. – Gambling*, the Panel found that the 1993 Scheduling Guidelines could be used as the context of GATS service schedules, within the meaning of Article 31 of the Vienna Convention on the Law of Treaties.[16] But this finding was overruled by the Appellate Body. The Appellate Body found that the 1993 Scheduling Guidelines were drafted by the GATT Secretariat rather than the parties to the negotiations, so they could not constitute "an agreement relating to the treaty", and could not be accepted "as an instrument related to the treaty".[17] As a result, the Appellate Body was of the view that the 1993 Scheduling Guidelines could not be regarded as the context in interpreting GATS service schedules.[18] Certainly, the Appellate Body's understanding of the legal status of the 1993 Scheduling Guidelines applies to the 2001 Scheduling Guidelines likewise. Moreover, the Appellate Body also found that the 2001 Scheduling Guidelines could not constitute *subsequent practice* within the meaning of Article 31(3)(b) of the Vienna Convention on the Law of Treaties.[19]

In spite of the limitation on the legal status of the 2001 Scheduling Guidelines, it cannot be denied that the 2001 Scheduling Guidelines are helpful in understanding GATS service schedules. In the *U.S. – Gambling*, although the Appellate Body did not consider the 1993 Scheduling Guidelines as *context* or *subsequent practice* in interpreting GATS service schedules, it did recognize that the 1993 Scheduling Guidelines could be *preparatory work of the treaty*,[20] and used as supplemental means of interpretation identified in Article 32 of the Vienna Convention on the Law of Treaties.[21] For the same reason, the 2001 Scheduling Guidelines can also be used as supplemental means of interpreting GATS service schedules.

The 2001 Scheduling Guidelines provide: "[I]n accordance with Article XX:2, any discriminatory measure scheduled in the market access column is also to be regarded as scheduled under Article XVII and subject to the provisions of that Article."[22] This sentence is almost the same as that of the 1993 Scheduling Guidelines.[23] The word *any* implies that all six limitation measures listed in Article XVI:2 may be regarded as national treatment limitation measures, provided that they are discriminatory. If a measure scheduled in the market access column

16 Panel Report, *US – Gambling*, WT/DS285/R, ¶ 6.82, adopted April 20, 2005.

17 Appellate Body Report, *US – Gambling*, WT/DS285/AB/R, adopted April 20, 2005, ¶ 175.

18 Id. ¶ 178.

19 Id. ¶ 193.

20 Id. ¶ 196.

21 Id. ¶ 197.

22 2001 Scheduling Guidelines, S/L/92, ¶ 18.

23 1993 Scheduling Guidelines, MTN.GNS/W/164, ¶ 11 (September 3, 1993) (stating that "in accordance with the footnotes to Article XVI:2 and Article XX:2, any discriminatory measure scheduled in the market access column is also to be regarded as scheduled under Article XVII and subject to the provisions of that Article").

is non-discriminatory, then it is only a pure market access limitation measure, without any relationship with national treatment.

In comparison with the 1993 Scheduling Guidelines, the 2001 Scheduling Guidelines make a piece of advice; that is, when measures inconsistent with both Articles XVI and XVII are inscribed in the column relating to Article XVI, Members could indicate that this is the case for national treatment, e.g. by adding the wording *also limits national treatment* to the market access column.[24] However, the effect of this advice is restrained by the fact that the 2001 Scheduling Guidelines apply only to the service schedules after the adoption of the 2001 Scheduling Guidelines, and the service schedules prior to the adoption of the 2001 Scheduling Guidelines should be understood to be drafted based on the 1993 Scheduling Guidelines.[25] Consequently, the 2001 Scheduling Guidelines have no retroactive effect, so the issue of overlap between GATS Article XVI and XVII still remains, especially for those pre-2001 schedules. Even for post-2001 schedules, if some Members fail to indicate the above magic words in the market access column,[26] the overlap issue still remains.

Pre-entry and Post-entry Measures

The overlap issue between market access and national treatment can also be described as the issue of pre-entry and post-entry. If a Member takes a pre-entry measure not inscribed in either the market access column or the national treatment column but affecting the supply of services, is it in violation of national treatment obligations under GATS Article XVII? In other words, are GATS national treatment obligations binding on post-entry measures only, or on both post-entry and pre-entry measures?

In this connection, the GATT national treatment and its long-term practice provide no clue. According to GATT Article III:1, national treatment obligations are on "*internal* taxes, and other *internal* charges, and laws, regulations and requirements affecting the *internal* sale, offering for sale, purchase, transportation, distribution or use of products, and *internal* quantitative regulations requiring the mixture, processing or use of products …", therefore, limitation measures on national treatment in the context of the GATT are all post-entry measures. The pre-entry measures are mainly subject to GATT Article II, "Schedules of Concessions", and GATT Article XI, "General Elimination of Quantitative Restrictions".[27] There is no overlap between GATT Article III and GATT Article II or Article XI. They are separated by a pre-entry or a post-entry standard. Only after crossing the border of a Member is a product entitled to national treatment. So the GATT experience

[24] 2001 Scheduling Guidelines, S/L/92, ¶ 18.

[25] Id. N 1.

[26] It is noteworthy that the 2001 Scheduling Guidelines is not an inherent part of the WTO Agreement. Therefore, it is not legally binding on WTO Members.

[27] Aaditya Mattoo, *National Treatment in the GATS, Corner-stone or Pandora's Box*? 31 J. World Trade 107, 112 (1997).

cannot provide a clue to the overlap issue between market access limitations and national treatment limitations under the GATS.

GATS Article XVII:1 states: "[E]ach Member shall accord to services and service suppliers of any other Member, in respect of all measures affecting the supply of services, treatment no less favourable than that it accords to its own like services and service suppliers." From the text of GATS Article XVII:1, it is unclear whether or not *all measures* include pre-entry and post-entry measures or just post-entry measures. The key to determine the scope of GATS national treatment is to interpret the ordinary meaning of *all measures affecting the supply of services*.

In *EC – Bananas III*, the Panel pointed out:

> [T]he drafters [of the GATS] consciously adopted the terms "affecting" and "supply of a service" to ensure that the disciplines of the GATS would cover any measure bearing upon conditions of competition in supply of a service, regardless of whether the measure directly governs or indirectly affects the supply of the service.[28]

The Appellate Body in the case supported the Panel's opinion and further held:

> In our view, the use of the term "affecting" reflects the intent of the drafters to *give a broad reach to the GATS*. The ordinary meaning of the word "affecting" implies a measure that has "an effect on", which indicates *a broad scope of application*. This interpretation is further reinforced by the conclusions of previous Panels that the term "affecting" in the context of Article III of the GATT is wider in scope than such terms as "regulating" or "governing".[29] (emphasis added)

In addition, the Appellate Body also agreed with the Panel on the point that GATS Article XXVIII (c)[30] does not "narrow the meaning of the term 'affecting' to 'in respect of'".[31] In *Canada – Automotive*,[32] the Panel reiterated that GATS

---

[28] Panel Report, *EC – Bananas III*, WT/DS27/R, adopted September 25, 1997, ¶ 7.281.

[29] Appellate Body Report, *EC – Bananas III*, WT/DS27/AB/R, adopted September 25, 1997, ¶ 220.

[30] GATS Article XXVIII (c) states:
"[For the purpose of this Agreement] 'measures by Members affecting trade in services' include measures in respect of (i) the purchase, payment or use of a service; (ii) the access to and use of, in connection with the supply of a service, services which are required by those Members to be offered to the public generally; (iii) the presence, including commercial presence, of persons of a Member for the supply of a service in the territory of another Member."

[31] Appellate Body Report, *EC – Bananas III*, WT/DS27/AB/R, ¶ 220.

[32] Panel Report, *Canada – Certain Measures Affecting the Automotive Industry* [hereinafter *Canada – Automotive*], WT/DS139/R, WT/DS142/R, adopted June 19, 2000.

Article I does not a priori exclude any measure from the scope of application of the GATS.[33]

Summing up, the above cases about the scope of measures in the GATS are all in support of a conclusion that the notion of measures in the GATS is not a narrow one, but a broad one.[34] Therefore, the ordinary meaning of Article XVII, *all measures affecting the supply of services*, could include any measure that may affect the supply of services, no matter how the service is supplied, or when the services is supplied. Moreover, as acknowledged by the WTO Committee on Specific Commitments, in the six exhaustive categories of market access limitations, there are some restrictions with post-entry effect, such as XVI:2 (b), "limitations on the total value of service transactions or asset", and XVI:2 (c), "limitations on the total number of service operations or the quantity of service output".[35] Thus, GATS national treatment obligations could be binding on both pre-entry and post-entry measures. The extension of national treatment from post-entry to pre-entry is regarded as a revolution by many countries.[36]

One argument against the broad interpretation of GATS national treatment obligations is that it would reduce the meaning or effect of GATS Article XVI, and make this Article "address primarily non-discriminatory market access restrictions".[37] Actually, a broad national treatment interpretation is not incompatible with discriminatory market access restrictions. If market access restrictions can be divided into discriminatory and non-discriminatory measures, then the discriminatory measures are national treatment limitations, as well as market access limitations. It is possible that some market access measures are discriminatory by their nature, for example limitations on the participation of foreign capital, but it does not mean that they are not in violation of market access obligations just because they are in violation of national treatment obligations under GATS Article XVII. The presumption of GATS Article XX:2 is that a limitation measure may be inconsistent with both GATS Article XVI and GATS Article XVII, and it does not mean that, if a limitation measure is inconsistent with GATS Article XVII, it will not fall into GATS Article XVI as well. Indeed, a broad national treatment interpretation could increase the applicable scope of GATS Article XVII, but simultaneously, it does not decrease the scope of GATS Article XVI. If a Member's measure is not inconsistent

---

33 Id. ¶ 10.234.

34 In accordance with Article 31:3(b) of the Vienna Convention on the Law of Treaties of 1969 (stating that treaty interpretation shall take into account any subsequent practice in the application of the treaty which establishes the agreement of the parties), WTO practice, by way of the WTO dispute settlement mechanism, could be the resource of interpretation of the WTO agreements.

35 Revision of Scheduling Guidelines, Note by Secretariat, Committee on Specific Commitments, MTN.GNS/W/164 and 164/Add.1, S/CSC/W/19 (March 5, 1999).

36 National Treatment, UNCTAD Series, UNCTAD/ITE/IIT/11 (Vol. IV), at 4, United Nations, New York and Geneva, 1999.

37 Mattoo, supra note 27, at 116.

with both market access commitments and national treatment commitments, another Member may complain against it based on both GATS Article XVII and XVI.

Debate on the Issue of Unbound/None or None/Unbound

The relationship of GATS Article XVI and XVII, together with Article XX:2, is especially unclear under two extreme circumstances. The first circumstance is an "Unbound" entry in the market access column, with a "None" entry in the national treatment column. The second circumstance is a "None" entry in the market access column and an "Unbound" entry in the national treatment column. In fact, the two circumstances are two sides of a coin. I only focus on the first example for the purpose of convenience and conciseness. If the first issue were resolved, the second issue would be readily solved. Thus, the two questions can be simplified as the following one: If a Member entered "Unbound" in the market access column and "None" in the national treatment column, could the Member maintain any discriminatory measure of market access? In other words, if there is a conflict between a market access limitation and a national treatment requirement, which one shall prevail? Shall "Unbound" override "None" or "None" override "Unbound"? This question was highly debated in the meetings of the Council for Trade in Services.[38]

In one view, if a Member enters "Unbound" in the market access column, then the Member has the right to introduce any market access limitations, discriminatory or non-discriminatory, although there is a "None" entry in the national treatment column.[39] Based on this view, "Unbound" overrides "None". The representative country holding this view is Brazil.[40]

On the contrary, according to another view, "Unbound" under the market access column and "None" under the national treatment column mean that the Member could not introduce any discriminatory measure falling under Article XVI.[41] Based on this view, "None" overrides "Unbound". Switzerland prefers this view.[42]

In order to address the issue of conflict between "Unbound" and "None", it is necessary to first determine whether GATS Article XX:2 applies to such situation. Switzerland used the literal reading method, arguing that "Unbound" in a service schedule neither constituted an "inscribed" "measure", nor a condition or qualification,[43] so this issue could not be resolved through GATS Article XX:2.

---

38 Report of the Meeting Held on June 5, 2002, Note by the Secretariat, S/C/M/60, ¶ 19 (July 10, 2002); see also S/C/M/61, S/C/M/63, S/C/M/65, S/C/M/66.

39 Report of the Meeting Held on February 28, 2003, Note by the Secretariat, S/C/M/65, ¶ 8 (March 21, 2003).

40 Id.

41 Id. ¶ 9.

42 Id.; see also Communication from Switzerland, Consideration of Issues Relating to Article XX:2 of the GATS, JOB(03)/214, ¶ 19 (November 27, 2003) (arguing that this approach is the only one that never shows any internal inconsistency).

43 Report of the Meeting Held on May 14, 2003, Note by the Secretariat, S/C/M/66, ¶ 22 (June 18, 2003).

This non-application of Article XX:2 to an "Unbound"/"None" situation is also supported by Australia and the EC.[44] Brazil also agreed that Article XX:2 did not apply to the situation, but it pointed out that the non-application of XX:2 itself could not resolve the "Unbound"/"None" issue.[45]

China-Electronic Payment Services

In *China – Electronic Payment Services*, one of the issues focused on the overlap between market access and national treatment. China has inscribed the term "Unbound" in the market access column, and "None" in the column entitled "Limitations on National Treatment". The United States argues that China's full national treatment commitment implies that measures inconsistent with both Articles XVI and XVII are subject to China's obligations under Article XVII. China, on the other hand, argues that its absence of market access commitment means that such measures are not subject to any obligations it may have under Article XVII.

China argued that the measures described in Article XVI:2 cannot simultaneously be subject to Article XVII, without wholly disregarding the basis upon which market access and national treatment commitments were scheduled. In the Chinese view, Article XX:2 establishes the "order of precedence" in favour of Article XVI, as well as the principle of effectiveness of treaty interpretation (*effet utile*), and Article XVI governs "all aspects" of the measures described in Article XVI:2(a) – (f), including any respect in which such a measure is potentially discriminatory. Articles XVI and XVII are thus "mutually exclusive" in their respective spheres of application.[46] Obviously, China supports the approach 1.1. The European Union, Japan, Australia and Ecuador are on China's side.[47]

On the contrary, in the US view, the inscription of "Unbound" for market access affects the scope of its national treatment commitment, and Article XVI:2, for the United States, does not extend to restrictions that are discriminatory. For the United States, Article XX:2 does not make Articles XVI and XVII "mutually exclusive" in their respective spheres of application, so an "Unbound" inscription for market access, combined with a "None" for national treatment, "carves out" only overall quantitative limitations, not limitations that discriminate against foreign suppliers.[48] Obviously, the US supports approach 2.2. Guatemala is on the American side.[49]

The panel stated that the ordinary meaning of the term "None" is clear when read in conjunction with the title of the column in which the term appears, and the entry of "None" in the national treatment column suggests that China would

44 Id. ¶¶ 23, 24.
45 Id. ¶ 25.
46 WT/DS413/R, ¶ 7.642.
47 WT/DS413/R, ¶ 7.644.
48 WT/DS413/R, ¶ 7.643.
49 WT/DS413/R, ¶ 7.644.

be committed to providing full national treatment.[50] Because the term "unbound" indicates an absence of constraint or obligation, China is under no constraint or obligation to grant market access within the terms of Article XVI:2. The panel regarded Article XX:2 as a further indication that measures within the scope of any of the subparagraphs of Article XVI:2 can have discriminatory aspects.

In the panel's view, the scope of Article XVI and the scope of Article XVII are not mutually exclusive. Both provisions can apply to a single measure. The special rule in Article XX:2 provides a simpler requirement: a Member need only make a single inscription of the measure under the market access column, which then provides an implicit limitation under national treatment.[51] The wording of Article XX:2 indicates that what is inscribed in the market access column is a "measure" which, in the situation of conflict contemplated by Article XX:2, must encompass aspects that are inconsistent with both Articles XVI and XVII. In this way, a single inscription under Article XVI of a "measure" will provide a limitation as well under Article XVII.[52] The panel said as follows:

> In our view, it would be incongruous if an inscription of "Unbound" had an effect different from that of inscribing individually all possible measures within the six categories foreseen under Article XVI:2. To take a different interpretation would be to elevate form over substance. In our assessment, therefore, an inscription of the term "Unbound" in the market access column should be viewed as an inscription of "measures", specifically of all those defined in Article XVI:2, which a Member may not maintain or adopt, unless otherwise specified in its schedule. For this reason, we find that Article XX:2 does apply to situations where a Member has inscribed "Unbound" in the market access column of its schedule. In the Panel's view, the inscription of "Unbound" in the market access column of China's Schedule has the equivalent effect of an inscription of all possible measures falling within Article XVI:2.[53]
>
> ... [A]n "Unbound" inscription in the market access column encompasses inconsistencies with Article XVII as well as those arising from Article XVI. The inscription of "Unbound" will therefore, in the terms of Article XX:2, "provide a condition or qualification to Article XVII as well", thus permitting China to maintain measures that are inconsistent with both Articles XVI and XVII. With an inscription of "Unbound" for subsector (d) in mode 1 under Article XVI, and a corresponding "None" for Article XVII, China has indicated that it is free to maintain the full range of limitations expressed in the six categories of XVI:2, whether discriminatory or not.[54]

50 WT/DS413/R, ¶ 7.647.
51 WT/DS413/R, ¶ 7.654.
52 WT/DS413/R, ¶ 7.655.
53 WT/DS413/R, ¶ 7.656.
54 WT/DS413/R, ¶ 7.657.

The Panel finds that the obligations in Article XVI:2 can extend to measures that are also within the scope of Article XVII, so China may introduce or maintain any measures falling within Article XVI:2, including those that may be discriminatory within the meaning of Article XVII.[55]

> By inscribing "Unbound" under market access, China reserves the right to maintain any type of measure within the six categories falling under Article XVI:2, regardless of its inscription in the national treatment column.[56]

The panel finds that China's market access entry allows it to maintain any measures that are inconsistent with both Articles XVI and XVII.[57]

As to China's view of "order of precedence", the panel disagreed:

> ...[W]e [The panel] do not find that either of Articles XVI or XVII is substantively subordinate to the other. We find simply that Article XX:2 establishes a certain scheduling primacy for entries in the market access column, in that a WTO Member not wishing to make any commitment under Article XVI, discriminatory or non-discriminatory, may do so by inscribing the term "Unbound" in the market access column of its schedule.[58]

Although the panel in *China – Electronic Payment Services* supported China's view on the relationship between "unbound" market access and "none" national treatment, the panel's approach is different from China's approach. China chose the "mutually exclusive" approach, while the panel said Article XVI and Article XVII were not "mutually exclusive". China's view of the "order of precedence" in favour of Article XVI was also rejected by the panel. The panel denied a hierarchy between Article XVI and Article XVII, but the panel created a "scheduling primacy" for entries in the market access column based on Article XX:2.

B. China's WTO Market Access Commitments in Banking

Scope of Banking Services

In the China Schedule, China committed to open six types of banking services:

a. Acceptance of deposits and other repayable funds from the public;
b. Lending of all types, including consumer credit, mortgage credit, factoring and financing of commercial transaction;
c. Financial leasing;

---

55 WT/DS413/R, ¶ 7.650.
56 WT/DS413/R, ¶ 7.663.
57 WT/DS413/R, ¶ 7.661.
58 WT/DS413/R, ¶ 7.660.

d. All payment and money transmission services, including credit, charge and debit cards, travellers cheques and bankers drafts (including import and export settlement);
e. Guarantees and commitments;
f. Trading for own account or for account of customers of foreign exchange.

The above six types of banking services are the scope within which China is bound by the GATS/WTO obligations, including, inter alia, market access and national treatment obligations.[59] Any other banking services, which are not inscribed in the China Schedule, are outside the scope of China's market access and national treatment commitments.

The scope of "banking services" was one of the preliminary issues in *China – Electronic Payment Services*.[60] China argued that the ordinary meaning of "banking services" was services provided by banks,[61] but the United States argued that "banking services" did not have the effect of narrowing the scope of the commitments to "banks".[62] The panel found that "banking services" in the China Schedule should include services supplied by banks and *non*-banks.[63]

Limitations on Market Access in Banking

In banking services, China's market access commitments are expressed in four modes.

For mode 1 (cross-border supply), China did not make any commitment, except for (a) the provision and transfer of financial information, and financial data processing and related software by suppliers of other financial services; (b) advisory, intermediation and other auxiliary financial services on all activities, including credit reference and analysis, investment and portfolio research and advice, advice on acquisitions and on corporate restructuring and strategy.

For mode 2 (consumption abroad), China made a full commitment, indicating there is no market access limitation for Chinese individuals and enterprises to seek banking services abroad. The full commitment creates legitimate trade expectations and obligations with respect to the banking sector.[64]

---

[59] Additionally, in the China Schedule, banks can also engage in "other financial services" including: Provision and transfer of financial information, and financial data processing and related software by supplier of other financial services; Advisory, intermediation and other auxiliary financial services on all activities listed in subparagraphs (a) through (k), including credit reference and analysis, investment and portfolio research and advice, advice on acquisitions and on corporate restructuring and strategy.

[60] WT/DS/413/R, adopted August 31, 2012.

[61] WT/DS/413/R, ¶ 7.121.

[62] WT/DS/413/R, ¶ 7.122.

[63] WT/DS/413/R, ¶ 7.127.

[64] For the effect of a full market access commitment in a Member's schedule, see Panel Report, *US —Gambling*, WT/DS285/R, ¶ 6.527.

For mode 3 (commercial presence), China made a non-full commitment. The first limitation is geographic limitation. Within five years after accession, all geographic restrictions should be removed. The second limitation is limitation on clients. Within five years after accession, foreign financial institutions should be permitted to provide services to all Chinese clients. The third limitation is on licensing. Criteria for authorization to deal in China's financial services sector are to be solely prudential (i.e., contain no economic needs test or quantitative limits on licences). Within five years after accession, any existing non-prudential measures restricting ownership, operation, and juridical form of foreign financial institutions, including on internal branching and licences, shall be eliminated. The condition to establish a subsidiary of a foreign bank is that the total assets shall be more than USD 10 billion at the end of the year prior to filing the application. The condition to establish a branch of a foreign bank is that the total assets shall be more than USD 20 billion at the end of the year prior to filing the application. The condition to establish a joint venture bank is that the total assets shall be more than USD 10 billion at the end of the year prior to filing the application. The conditions to engage in local currency business include three years' business operation in China and being profitable for two consecutive years prior to the application.

For mode 4 (presence of natural persons), China did not make any commitment, except as indicated in the horizontal commitments.[65]

In the above market accession commitments, geographic restrictions and client limitations on local currency business (listed in the market access column) are also restrictions and limitations on national treatment obligations.[66] In December 2006, all geographic restrictions and client limitations on local currency business were eliminated. Other limitations in the market accession column, i.e. licensing

[65] According to the horizontal commitments in the China Schedule, China permits the entry and temporary stay of natural persons who fall into one of the following categories:

Managers, executives and specialists defined as senior employees of a corporation of a WTO Member that has established a representative office, branch or subsidiary in the territory of the People's Republic of China, temporarily moving as intra-corporate transferees, shall be permitted entry for an initial stay of three years;

Managers, executives and specialists defined as senior employees of a corporation of WTO Members, being engaged in the foreign invested enterprises in the territory of the People's Republic of China for conducting business, shall be granted a long-term stay permit as stipulated in the terms of contracts concerned or an initial stay of three years, whichever is shorter;

Service salespersons – persons not based in the territory of the People's Republic of China and receiving no remuneration from a source located within China, and who are engaged in activities related to representing a service supplier for the purpose of negotiation for the sale of services of that supplier where such sales are not directly made to the general public and the salesperson is not engaged in supplying the service: entry for salespersons is limited to a 90-day period.

[66] See the China Schedule, WT/ACC/CHN/49/Add.2 (October 1, 2001), 7B, Column of Limitation on National Treatment, mode 3.

requirements, remain unless replaced by a new schedule as a result of a new round of service trade negotiations.

II. Forms and Market Access Conditions of Foreign-Funded Banks in China

Before the end of 2006, the definition of *foreign-funded banks* [*waizi yinhang*] mainly appeared in some junior banking rules issued by the People's Bank of China or the CBRC, referring to three kinds of foreign-related banks, i.e. wholly-foreign-funded banks [*waishang duzi yinhang*], Sino-foreign equity joint-venture banks [*zhongwai hezi yinhang*], and foreign bank branches [*waiguo yinhang fenhang*].[67]

The definition of foreign-funded banks was officially adopted by the State Council in the Regulation on Administration of Foreign-Funded Banks (FFB Regulation 2006),[68] which replaced the FFFI Regulation 2001.[69] Different from the old definition of foreign-funded banks, according to Article 2 of the FFB Regulation 2006, foreign-funded banks refer to four kinds of institutions in the territory of the People's Republic of China, including wholly-foreign-funded banks, Sino-foreign equity joint venture banks, foreign bank branches, and representative offices of foreign banks [*waiguo yinhang daibiaochu*].

According to Article 9 of the FFB Regulation 2006, the following conditions must be met for establishing a wholly-foreign-funded bank, a Sino-foreign equity joint venture bank, a foreign bank branch, or a representative office of a foreign bank:

1. Ability of making continuous profits, good reputation;
2. Experience of international financial activities;
3. Effective anti-money laundering system;
4. Effective supervision by the financial regulator of its home country, approval by the financial regulator of its home country.
5. Other prudential conditions of the CBRC.

---

[67] See the Measures for Administration of Foreign Debt of Foreign-Funded Banks in Chinese Territory, art. 2, issued by the CBRC on May 27, 2004, effective as of June 27, 2004, NDRC, PBC & CBRC [2004] Decree No. 9, http://www.safe.gov.cn/model_safe/laws/law_detail.jsp?ID=80800000000000000,29&id=4.

[68] FFB Regulation 2006, State Council Decree 478, promulgated on November 11, 2006, effective on December 11, 2006, art. 73, GAZETTE OF THE STATE COUNCIL 13–19 (2007, no. 1).

[69] FFFI Regulation 2001, State Council Decree 340, promulgated on December 20, 2001, effective February 1, 2002, void on December 11, 2006, GAZETTE OF THE STATE COUNCIL 18–22 (2002, no. 3).

The above conditions are only general conditions for establishment of any kind of foreign-funded banks in China. For each special kind (e.g., wholly-foreign-funded bank), there are some extra conditions which will be discussed in the following sections.

It must be noted that the definition of *foreign-funded commercial banks* [*waizi shangye yinhang*] in the Commercial Banking Law 1995 and Commercial Banking Law 2003,[70] which refers only to wholly-foreign-funded commercial banks, is narrower than the definition of foreign-funded banks in the FFB Regulation 2006.

A. Wholly-Foreign-Funded Banks

A wholly-foreign-funded bank is funded by a foreign bank, or co-funded by a foreign bank and other foreign financial institutions.[71] There is no Chinese fund in a wholly-foreign-funded bank.

A wholly-foreign-funded bank is a bank registered in China with Chinese legal personality. As a bank, it is governed by Chinese banking law, mainly the PRC Commercial Banking Law and the FFB Regulation. As a corporation, it is governed by the PRC Corporation Law.[72] Furthermore, as a foreign-funded enterprise, it is governed by the PRC Wholly-Foreign-Funded Enterprise Law.[73] In a word, a wholly-foreign-funded bank is regulated and protected by three kinds of laws with different natures, i.e., banking law, corporation law and investment law.

According to Article 1 of the Wholly-Foreign-Funded Enterprise Law 2000, the PRC protects the lawful rights and interests of a wholly-foreign-funded enterprise in the territory of China. The promise to protect the lawful rights and interests of foreign investors is reaffirmed by Article 4 of the FFB Regulation 2006 and Article 2 of the Sino-Foreign Equity Joint Venture Law, which provide that the lawful rights and interests of a foreign-funded bank are protected by Chinese law. Nationalization and expropriation of a wholly-foreign-funded enterprise in China are not allowed by the Wholly-Foreign-Funded Enterprise Law. Only under special circumstances, when public interest requires, may a wholly-foreign-funded

---

[70] Commercial Banking Law 1995 [*Shangye Yinhangfa*], art. 88, adopted at the Thirteenth Meeting of the Standing Committee of the Eighth NPC on May 10, 1995, effective July 1, 1995, Falü Huibian 1995, 152–170 (People's Publishing House 1996); Commercial Banking Law 2003, art. 92, GAZETTE OF THE NPC 36–44 (2004, no. 1).

[71] FFB Regulation 2006, art. 2(1).

[72] PRC Corporation Law [*Gongsifa*], adopted at the Fifth Meeting of the Standing Committee of the Eighth NPC on December 29, 1993, effective July 1, 1994, first amended in 1999; secondly amended in 2004, GAZETTE OF THE NPC 485–506 (2004, no. 6); thirdly amended in 2005, GAZETTE OF THE NPC 548–570 (2005, no. 7).

[73] Wholly-Foreign-Funded Enterprise Law [*Waizi Qiyefa*], adopted at the Fourth Session of the Sixth NPC on April 12, 1986, effective April 12, 1986, Falü Huibian 1986, at 63–66 (People's Publishing House 1987); Amended in 2000, Falü Huibian 2000, at 206–09 (People's Publishing House 2001).

enterprise be expropriated by legal procedures and appropriate compensation shall be made.[74]

Although the Wholly-Foreign-Funded Enterprise Law 2000 does not provide that a wholly-foreign-funded bank should be a limited liability company, which means that it may be a limited liability company or a joint-stock company, Article 8 of the Wholly-Foreign-Funded Enterprise Law 2000 does provide that a wholly-foreign-funded enterprise has the status of a Chinese legal person. In PRC Corporation Law, there is not a special chapter or section designed for wholly-foreign-funded corporations or Sino-foreign equity joint ventures. No matter whether a wholly-foreign-funded bank takes the form of a limited liability company or a joint-stock company, it is covered by PRC Corporation Law unless otherwise provided by the special wholly-foreign-funded enterprise law.[75]

According to Article 10 of the FFB Regulation 2006, the sole shareholder or the shareholder with majority shares of a wholly-foreign-funded bank in China must meet the following conditions:

1. The shareholder must be a commercial bank;
2. The shareholder should have set up a representative office in China for at least two years;
3. The total assets of the shareholder at the end of the year prior to filing the application should be not less than USD 10 billion;
4. Its capital adequacy ratio shall satisfy the requirements of its home country and the CBRC.

B. Sino-Foreign Equity Joint Venture Banks

A Sino-foreign equity joint venture bank is jointly funded by one or more foreign financial institutions and Chinese companies or enterprises.[76] A Sino-foreign equity joint venture bank is also a bank registered in China with Chinese legal personality. It is also governed simultaneously by the the PRC Commercial Banking Law, FFB Regulation, the PRC Corporation Law and the Sino-Foreign Equity Joint Venture Law.[77] In a word, like a wholly-funded bank, a Sino-foreign equity joint venture bank is regulated and protected by three kinds of laws with different nature, i.e., banking law, corporation law and investment law.

Article 2 of the Sino-Foreign Equity Joint Venture Law 2001 stipulates that the PRC government protects the lawful rights and interests of foreign investors

---

[74] Wholly-Foreign-Funded Enterprise Law 2000, art. 5.

[75] See PRC Corporation Law 2005, art. 218.

[76] FFB Regulation 2006, art. 2(2).

[77] Sino-Foreign Equity Joint Venture Law [*Zhongwai Hezuo Jingying Qiyefa*], adopted at the Second Session of the Fifth NPC on July 1, 1979, effective July 1, 1979, Falü Huibian 1979–1984, at 168–71 (People's Publishing House 1985); Amended in 1990 and 2001, Falü Huibian 2001, at 58–62 (People's Publishing House 2002).

in Sino-foreign equity joint ventures. Nationalization and expropriation of Sino-Foreign equity joint venture banks in China are not allowed by the Sino-Foreign Equity Joint Venture Law. Only under special circumstances, when public interest requires, may Sino-foreign equity joint ventures be expropriated by legal procedures and appropriate compensation shall be made.[78]

Different from a wholly-foreign-funded enterprise, which may take either the form of a limited liability company or the form of a joint stock company, a Sino-foreign equity joint venture should take the form of a limited liability company.[79] Accordingly, a Sino-foreign equity joint venture bank should be a limited liability company.

According to Article 11 of the FFB Regulation 2006, the sole shareholder or the shareholder with majority shares of a Sino-foreign equity joint venture bank in China must meet the following conditions:

1. The shareholder must be a commercial bank;
2. The shareholder should have set up a representative office in China;
3. The total assets of the shareholder at the end of the year before application should be not less than USD 10 billion;
4. Its capital adequacy ratio shall satisfy the requirements of its home country and the CBRC.

According to Article 29 of FFB Regulation 2006, the business scope of wholly-foreign-funded banks and Sino-foreign equity joint venture banks is the same, including the following:

1. Taking in public deposits;
2. Offering short-term, medium-term and long term loans;
3. Handling acceptance and discount of negotiable instruments;
4. Buying and selling government bonds or financial bonds, and foreign currency securities except stocks;
5. Providing letter of credit services and guaranty services;
6. Handling domestic and foreign settlements;
7. Buying and selling foreign exchange by itself or as an agent;
8. Insurance agency;
9. Undertaking inter-bank loans;
10. Engaging in bank card business;
11. Providing safe box services;
12. Credit investigation and consulting services;
13. Other businesses approved by the banking regulatory institution of the State Council.

---

78 Sino-Foreign Equity Joint Venture Law 2001, art. 2.

79 Sino-Foreign Equity Joint Venture Law 2001, art. 4.

C. Foreign Bank Branches and Sub-branches

In China, a foreign bank branch is a branch set up by a foreign bank, so a foreign bank branch does not have independent legal personality and its mother bank located in a foreign country should be responsible for the branch.[80] In fact, any branch of a foreign company in China cannot be regarded as a Chinese legal person, and its civil liability must be borne by the foreign company.[81] Although a foreign company branch does not have independent legal personality in China, after completing application and approval procedure and obtaining a business licence, it is allowed to engage in business and its lawful rights and interests are protected by Chinese law.[82] In the PRC Corporation Law 2005, there is a special chapter concerning branches of foreign companies. Therefore, the lawful rights and interests of a foreign bank branch in China are protected and regulated by Chinese banking law and corporation law.

However, not every foreign bank is allowed to set up a branch in China. According to Article 12 of the FFB Regulation 2006, in order to set up a branch in China, a foreign bank must meet following conditions:

1. The total assets of the foreign bank shall not be less than USD 20 billion;
2. The capital adequacy ratio shall satisfy the requirements of its home country and the CBRC;
3. The foreign bank should have had a representative office in China for more than two years.

Moreover, Article 8 of the FFB Regulation 2006 provides that the home office of the foreign bank shall allocate working capital to its Chinese branch not less than RMB 200 million.

According to Article 25 of the Detailed Rules for Implementation of the Regulation on Administration of Foreign-Funded Banks of 2006 (DRI 2006), the legal status of a foreign bank branch can be changed into that of a wholly-foreign-funded bank after meeting conditions for establishing a wholly-foreign-funded bank,[83] and the newly-established wholly-foreign-funded bank may succeed to all

80 FFB Regulation 2006, art. 32.

81 PRC Corporation Law 2005, art. 196.

82 PRC Corporation Law 2005, art. 197.

83 FFB Regulation 2006, art. 24; see also DRI 2006, art. 25 (providing that a foreign bank applying to convert its existing branch in China into a wholly-foreign-funded bank solely funded by the foreign bank shall satisfy the requirements for the establishment of a wholly-foreign-funded bank prescribed in the FFB Regulation and this DRI, and shall have the capacity for long-term persistent operation in China and for effective management of the proposed bank).

business of the former foreign bank branch.[84] In fact, The Chinese government encourages a foreign bank branch to be transformed into a wholly-foreign-funded bank with Chinese legal personality so that Chinese banking regulators can impose sufficient, effective, and prompt supervision on the foreign-funded bank and reduce risks of Chinese depositors,[85] which is called the policy of legal personality orientation [*faren daoxiang zhengce*].

A foreign bank may set up several branches in China. Under such circumstance, the CBRC conducts consolidated supervision and regulation [*bingbiao jianguan*] over those branches. If there are two or more branches of a foreign bank, the head office of the foreign bank or the regional office of the foreign bank shall designate one of its Chinese branches as the managing bank responsible for uniform management in China, as well as consolidating and reporting financial and comprehensive information of all branches within the Chinese territory.[86] A foreign bank branch in China may set up a sub-branch [*zhihang*]. The sub-branch may engage in banking business authorized by the foreign bank branch.[87]

According to Article 31 of the FFB Regulation 2006, the business scope of a foreign bank branch is as follows:

1. Taking in public deposits;
2. Offering short-term, medium-term and long-term loans;
3. Handling acceptance and discount of negotiable instruments;
4. Buying and selling government bonds or financial bonds, and foreign currency securities except stocks;
5. Providing letter of credit services and guaranty services;
6. Handling domestic and foreign settlements;
7. Buying and selling foreign exchange by itself or as an agent;
8. Insurance agency;
9. Undertaking inter-bank loans;
10. Providing safe box services;
11. Credit investigation and consulting services;
12. Other businesses approved by the banking regulatory institution of the State Council.

Compared with the business scope of wholly-foreign-funded banks and Sino-foreign equity joint venture banks, the business scope of foreign bank branches lacks bank card business.

---

84 DRI 2006, art. 51, issued by the CBRC on Novemeber 24, 2006, effective December 11, 2006, CBRC Decree [2006] No. 6.

85 Wang Zhaoxing, Records of Inverviews of Wang Zhaoxing by the Chinese Government Web, December 11, 2006, http://zhuanti.cbrc.gov.cn/subject/subject/duiwai/main.do?newsclass=8a8183d60f529195010f5648c28b0009&levelnum=2 (Dec. 31, 2006).

86 DRI 2006, art. 90.

87 DRI 2006, art. 52, para.2.

D. Branches and Sub-branches of Wholly-Foreign-Funded Banks or Sino-Foreign Equity Joint Venture Banks

To set up a branch, a wholly-foreign-funded bank or a Sino-foreign equity joint venture bank should allocate working capital of no less than RMB 100 million or other freely convertible currencies with the equivalent value. The total amount of working capital allocated to all branches and sub-branches by a wholly-foreign-funded bank or a Sino-foreign equity joint venture bank shall be not higher than 60 per cent of the total capital of the bank.[88]

Branches and sub-branches of wholly-foreign-funded banks or Sino-foreign equity joint venture banks are able to engage in banking business authorized by their head offices.[89]

E. Representative Offices of Foreign Banks

Foreign banks may set up representative offices in China. Different from branches or sub-branches of foreign banks, they are forbidden to do operational business.[90] Representative offices can only engage in non-operational activities, such as liaison, market investigation, advice, and their civil liability should be borne by foreign banks.[91] One meaning of setting up a representative office is that a representative office is one of the conditions for a foreign bank to establish a wholly-foreign-funded bank or a Sino-foreign equity joint venture bank in China.

Since representative offices cannot do operational business, they are excluded from the definition of "operational institutions of foreign-funded banks" [*waizi yinhang yingyexing jigou*], a general term referring to wholly-foreign-funded banks, Sino-foreign equity joint venture banks, and foreign bank branches as a whole.[92]

Although foreign banks may set up representative offices in China, according to Paragraph 7 of the Announcement of the CBRC on Related Issues after Promulgation of the DRI 2006, wholly-foreign-funded banks and Sino-foreign equity joint venture banks, after December 11, 2006, cannot set up representative offices in China.

F. Foreign Banks and Foreign Financial Institutions

According Article 3 of the FFB Regulation 2006, foreign banks [*waiguo yinhang*] refer to commercial banks registered outside the territory of China and approved or licensed by their home country financial regulators. Foreign financial institutions [*waiguo jinrong jigou*] refer to financial institutions registered outside the territory

---

88 FFB Regulation 2006, art. 8.

89 DRI 2006, art. 52, para. 1.

90 FFB Regulation 2006, art. 57.

91 FFB Regulation 2006, art. 33.

92 FFB Regulation 2006, art. 2, last paragraph.

of China and approved or licensed by their home country financial regulators. They are not Chinese legal person, but when they enter the Chinese financial market as banking investors, they can get the protection of Chinese law. For example, Article 4 of the Wholly-Foreign-Funded Enterprise Law 2000 provides that the investment, profits and other lawful rights and interests of foreign investors are protected by Chinese law. To gurantee the protection of foreign enterprises, Article 5 of the PRC Civil Procedure Law accords foreign enterprises procedural rights as favourable as those of Chinese domestic enterprises.

It must be noted that the definition of "foreign-funded financial institutions" is different from that of "foreign financial institutions". The former referred to foreign-funded banks and foreign-funded financial companies, which was adopted in the FFFI Regulation 1994 and the FFFI Regulation 2001. The definition of "foreign-funded financial institutions" has become an historical definition after being replaced by the definition of "foreign-funded banks" in the FFB Regulation 2006, excluding foreign-funded financial companies from the regulation.

G. Foreign-Funded Financial Holding Companies

According to Article 43 of the Commercial Banking Law 2003, commercial banks in China are prohibited from making trust investment and securities business, unless otherwise provided by the state. According to Article 6 of the Securities Law 2005, the operation and regulation of securities are separated from those of banking, trust and insurance, unless otherwise provided by the state.[93] In order to break the limitation of separate operation, some steps have been taken to do indirect mixed operations by way of setting up financial holding companies.

In 2002, the State Council approved the CITIC Group Corporation to be China's first financial holding company;[94] In 2007, the State Council approved the reform and reorganization plan of China Everbright Group (China Everbright Group Ltd.) to become a financial holding company.[95] The financial holding companies

---

93 "Unless otherwise provided by the State" is different to "unless otherwise provided by the State Council". "State" is not "State Council". Strictly speaking, "state" means the NPC or the NPC Standing Committee. When looking at the drafts of the Commercial Banking Law 2003, we can find that the condition for a bank to invest in a non-banking financial institution or enterprises was "otherwise provided by the State Council" (Jiang Qiangui, The Report of the review on the draft of Chinese Banking Supervision Law and on Two Drafts of Amendment of PBC Law and Commercial Banking Law, PRC Law Commission, the Six Session of the NPC Standing Committee, Dec. 22, 2003). In the official text of the Commercial Banking Law 2003, the condition to do mixed operations and non-banking financial investment is "otherwise provided by the State". This change shows that "the State" is different from "the State Council". Therefore, the State Council has no power to approve a bank to do securities business "unless otherwise provided by the State".

94 The History of CITIC Group, http://www.citicgroup.com.cn/wps/portal/encitic/gyzx/jtls2?lctn=6 (last visited September 22, 2012).

95 http://www.cebbank.com/Info/5806263 (published September 6, 2007).

can do mixed operations including banking, securities, and insurance through its different and separate subsidiaries. The PBC started to draft the Regulation on Supervision of Financial Holding Companies in 2005.[96] The Ministry of Finance of PRC even issued a rule on financial holding companies in 2009.[97] However, mixed operations and practice of financial holding companies are still in a pilot stage. There is no law or regulation to allow foreigners to establish a foreign-funded financial holding company, so there is not any foreign-funded financial holding company in China.

H. Foreign Minority Shareholders

As discussed in chapter 2, either a Sino-foreign equity joint venture with foreign majority shares or a Sino-foreign equity joint venture with foreign minority shares is within the scope of China's WTO commitments. Thus, all Sino-foreign equity joint venture banks in China, no matter whether their foreign investors are minority shareholders or majority shareholders, enjoy the rights granted by the GATS/WTO.

However, not all minority shareholder rights in China are within the scope of the GATS/WTO. Only those foreign investors whose investment in China amounts to or exceeds 25 per cent of the registered capital of the joint venture may enjoy minority shareholder rights granted by China's WTO commitments. This is due to a market access limitation made by China when it entered the WTO. According to the China Schedule, the proportion of foreign investment in an equity joint venture shall not be less than 25 per cent of the registered capital of the joint venture.[98] It means that an enterprise with less than 25 per cent foreign investment is not regarded as a Sino-foreign equity joint venture, but a Chinese domestic enterprise with foreign minority shares. Thus, the Chinese domestic enterprise with foreign minority shares below 25 per cent cannot enjoy the treatment of a Sino-foreign joint venture, nor is it protected by the GATS/WTO. That is to say, only if the foreign investment in an enterprise is up to 25 per cent of the registered capital of the enterprise could the foreign investment be protected or regulated by the WTO and enjoy minority shareholder rights granted by China's WTO commitments.

The 25 per cent cap does not mean that the lawful interests of foreign shareholders with less than 25 per cent investment are not protected by Chinese law. As a matter of fact, foreign shareholders with less than 25 per cent investment may enjoy the minority shareholder rights provided by relevant BITs, China's Corporation Law or other relevant laws, regulations on cross-border merger and acquisition, such as the Measures for Administration of Equity Investment of Overseas Financial

---

96 Http://news.xinhuanet.com/fortune/2005-04/08/content_2802616.htm.

97 Relevant Measures for Financial Management of Financial Holding Companies[*Jinrong Konggu Gongsi Caiwu Guanli Ruogan Guiding*], Ministry of Finance, China, September 1, 2009, Caijin [2009] No. 89.

98 The China Schedule, WT/ACC/CHN/49/Add.2, Horizontal Commitments, column of Limitation on Market Access.

Institutions in Chinese-Funded Financial Institutions of 2003,[99] although they cannot enjoy the minority shareholder rights under the GATS/WTO. The merger and acquisition of Chinese-funded banks by foreign financial institutions are not covered by the FFB Regulation 2006.

In accordance with the Article 7 of the Measures for Administration of Equity Investment of Overseas Financial Institutions in Chinese-Funded Financial Institutions 2003, before making equity investment in a Chinese-funded financial institution, an overseas financial institution must meet the following conditions:

1. In order to invest in a Chinese-funded bank, the total assets of the overseas financial institution last year should not be less than USD 10 billion;
2. Long term credit rating by recognized international credit rating agency during the last two years must be good;
3. Being profitable for two consecutive years;
4. The capital adequacy ratio of the overseas commercial bank shall not be less than 8 per cent;
5. A sound internal control system;
6. A sound financial regulation system in its home (registration standard) country or region;
7. Good economic conditions in its home country or region;
8. Other prudential conditions required by the CBRC.

According to Article 8 of the Measures for Administration of Equity Investment of Overseas Financial Institutions in Chinese-Funded Financial Institutions 2003, the equity ratio invested by a single overseas financial institution in a Chinese-funded financial institution shall be no more than 20 per cent. Article 9 provides that if the aggregate percentage of equity investment of multiple overseas financial institutions in a non-listed Chinese-funded financial institution reaches or exceeds 25 per cent, such non-listed Chinese-funded financial institution shall be regarded as a foreign-funded financial institution.

III. Foreign-Funded Banks in Chinese People's Courts

According to Article 5 of PRC Civil Procedure Law, generally speaking, foreign-funded banks have the same procedural rights and obligations as Chinese-funded banks. This is also the case for Chinese Administrative Procedure Law.[100] Wholly-

[99] Measures for Administration of Equity Investment of Overseas Financial Institutions in Chinese-Funded Financial Institutions [*Jingwai Jinrong Jigou Touzi Rugu Zhongzi Jinrong Jigou Guanli Banfa*], CBRC decree [2003] no. 6, available at http://www.cbrc.gov.cn/upload/zwgk/ml3/2/2-1-1.doc.

[100] Paragraph 1 of Article 71 of the Administrative Procedure Law provides that foreigners and foreign institutes have the same litigation rights and obligations as Chinese

foreign-funded banks and Sino-foreign equity joint venture banks are legal persons registered in China. In other words, wholly-foreign-funded banks and Sino-foreign equity joint venture banks are Chinese legal persons, although foreign-funded.

The following two cases relating to two foreign-funded banks may illustrate whether foreign-funded banks can get legal protection from Chinese courts. The two cases are from the Gazette of the Supreme People's Court, the most authoritative source of Chinese cases and judicial interpretations.

A. The Case of Xiamen International Bank (1997)

Xiamen International Bank (XIB) is China's first Sino-foreign equity joint venture bank, based in Xiamen, Fujian Province. Its shareholders include Industrial and Commercial Bank of China, Fujian Investment & Enterprise Holdings Corporation, Xiamen C&D Corporation Limited, Min Xin Holdings Limited (Hong Kong listed), Asian Development Bank, Shinsei Bank Limited (from Japan) and Sino Finance Group Company Limited, USA.[101] In 1996, XIB filed a civil lawsuit in Siming District People's Court of Xiamen against two defendants, Jinjiang Houtai Shoes Ltd, and Jinjiang Xiaosheng Clothing Ltd, for breach of a loan agreement. XIB was the lender. The first defendant, Jinjiang Houtai Shoes Ltd, was the borrower. The second defendant, Jinjiang Xiaosheng Clothing Ltd, was the guarantor of the loan agreement. After hearing the case, Siming District People's Court made a judgement that Jinjiang Houtai Shoes Ltd should compensate for breach of the loan agreement, but the Jinjiang Xiaosheng Clothing Ltd. was relieved from its guaranty obligation because it had notified (in written form) the plaintiff to exercise its rights against the first defendant but the plaintiff failed to do so .According to a judicial interpretation effective at that time and applicable for all, plaintiff's ignorance of the notice for a certain period of time (in this case, more than one year) would make it lose the right as a guarantee. This judgement was supported by the appellate court, Xiamen Intermediate People's Court.[102]

B. The Case of US Citibank Shanghai Branch (2002)

In 2002, a Chinese citizen, Wu Weiming, filed a lawsuit against the Citibank Shanghai Branch for charging service fees on a savings account with daily average deposit lower than USD 5,000. The court of first instance, Shanghai Pudong New Area People's Court [*Shanghai Pudong Xinqu Renmin Fayuan*], stated in the judgement: "Charging service fees by foreign-funded financial institutions does not conflict with any law or regulation. There is no law or regulation to prohibit foreign-funded financial institutions from charging such fees. Therefore, it was

---

domestic citizens and institutions.

[101] Xiamen International Bank, Introduction, http://www.xib.com.cn/english/sub1-1.htm

[102] *Xiamen International Bank v. Jinjiang Houtai Shoes Ltd., and Jinjiang Xiaosheng Clothing Ltd.*, GAZETTE OF THE SUPREME PEOPLE'S COURT 71–72 (1998, no. 2).

not illegal."[103] The appellate court, Shanghai No. 1 Intermediate People's Court [*Shanghaishi Diyi Zhongji Renmin Fayuan*] supported the judgement.[104]

C. A Table of Cases relating to Foreign Banks in China

The Chinese legal system is a civil law system, rather than a common law system. The cases of Chinese people's courts do not have binding force for similar cases. In November 2010, the Supreme People's Court issued the Provisions on the Work of Guiding Cases. Article 2 of the Provisions states that a guiding case [*zhidaoxing anli*] shall satisfy the following conditions: (1) The case must have widespread social concerns; (2) The law has only rough principles; (3) The case must be typical; (4) The case must be difficult, sophisticated, or brand new; (5) Other cases which can play a guiding role. Article 7 of the Provisions clearly states that Chinese people's courts at different levels, when dealing with similar cases, must refer to the guiding case promulgated by the Supreme People's Court. Therefore, it is meaningful to analyse the cases relating to foreign-funded banks, from which one can find the practice of people's courts in dealing with such cases. The cases listed in table 3.1 are selected and digested mainly from the following sources:

- Gazette of the Supreme People's Court
- Selected Cases of the People's Courts [*Renmin Fayuan Anli Xuan*]
- Overview of Chinese Cases [*Zhongguo Shenpan Anli Yaolan*]

All of the cases published are in Chinese language.

After reviewing the cases, one can make three conclusions. Firstly, in China, foreign-funded banks have the right to access to Chinese courts. Secondly, the lawful rights and interests of foreign-funded banks can get protection from Chinese courts. Thirdly, foreign-funded banks should positively exercise their lawful rights according to Chinese law, otherwise, they will take the risk of losing the lawful rights. It is noteworthy that such a risk is not designed for foreign-funded banks. For example, the judicial interpretation related to the guarantee law in the Case of Xiamen International Bank applied equally to all parties, no matter whether they were foreigners or Chinese.

---

[103] *Wu Weiming v. Citibank Shanghai Branch*, Gazette of the Supreme People's Court 42–46 (2005, no. 9).

[104] *Wu Weiming v. Citibank Shanghai Branch*, id.

Table 3.1 Selected cases relating to foreign-funded banks in China

Judgement Year	Case Name	Status of Foreign-Funded Banks	Type of Foreign-Funded Banks	Cause of Action	Court of First Instance	Court of Appeal	Result – For or Against foreign party
1997	Hanli Company v. Chohung Bank of South Korea	Defendant	Foreign bank	Payment under a Letter of Credit	Yangzhou Intermediate People's Court, Jiangsu Province	None	Against
2001	Shanghai Shenda Joint-Stock Company v. HSBC Shanghai Branch	Defendant	Foreign bank branch	Trust and agency contract	Shanghai Pudong New Area People's Court	Shanghai No. 1 Intermediate People's Court	Against
2001	HSBC Xiamen Branch v. Xiamen Xiangyu Chongli Int'l Trade Company et al.	Plaintiff	Foreign bank branch	Loan agreement liability and guarantee liability	Xiamen Huli District People's Court, Fujian Province	None	For
2002	Fuxinda (Tianjin) International Trade Ltd v. Banque LCL Le Credit Lyonnais	Defendant	Foreign bank	Liability in notifying a Letter of Credit	Tianjin No. 1 Intermediate People's Court	Tianjin Higher People's Court	For
2002	Jiangsu Huaiyin Foreign Trade Company v. Nedbank of South Africa	Defendant	Foreign bank	Payment under a Letter of Credit/ Jurisdiction Dispute	Huaiyin Intermediate People's Court, Jiangsu Province	Jiangsu Higher People's Court	Against
2003	Bank of East Asia v. Shanghai Xinhongye Real Estate Ltd et al.	Plaintiff	Hong Kong Banks	Loan agreement liability and Guarantee Liability	Shanghai Higher People's Court	None	For
2006	Standard Chartered Bank (Hong Kong) v. Shandong Cereals & Oil Group Corporation, et al.	Plaintiff	Hong Kong bank	Loan agreement and guarantee	Jinan City Intermediate People's Court	Shandong Higher People's Court	Against

continued ...

Judgement Year	Case Name	Status of Foreign-Funded Banks	Type of Foreign-Funded Banks	Cause of Action	Court of First Instance	Court of Appeal	Result – For or Against foreign party
2009	Korea Exchange Bank v. Huaxia Bank (Qingdao Branch)	Plaintiff	Foreign bank	Letter of credit	Qingdao City Intermediate People's Court	Shandong Higher People's Court	Against
2010	Australia and New Zealand Banking Group (Shanghai Branch) v. Agricultural Bank of China (Ningbo Branch)	defendant	Foreign bank branch	Letter of Credit fraud	Ningbo City Intermediate People's Court	Zhejiang Higher People's Court	Against
2010	Daegu Bank South Korea v. Bank of Communication (Weihai Branch)	Plaintiff	Foreign bank branch	Draft Collection	Weihai City Intermediate People's Court	Shandong Higher People's Court	Against
2010	United Overseas Bank (UOB), HSBC v. Shanghai Golden Landmark Co. Ltd.	plaintiffs	Wholly-Foreign-Funded bank	loan	Shanghai Higher People's Court	None available	For
2011	Citibank N.A. v. Trade Mark Appeal Board of State Administration of Industry and Commerce (Citigroup Limited HK as Third Party)	Plaintiff	Foreign bank	Trade Mark (administrative case)	Beijing No. 1 Intermediate People's Court	None available	Against
2011	Citibank N.A. and Citigroup v. Trade Mark Appeal Board of State Administration of Industry and Commerce (CITIC Group as Third Party)	Plaintiff	Foreign bank	Trade Mark (administrative case)	Beijing No. 1 Intermediate People's Court	Beijing Higher People's Court	For

Note: compiled by the author.

IV. The Special Legal Status of Hong Kong/Macao/Taiwan Banks in Mainland China

Hong Kong and Macao returned to China at the end of 1990s. Under the framework of the "One Country, Two Systems",[105] most Chinese laws, including Chinese banking laws, do not apply to Hong Kong or Macao.[106] Theoretically, Hong Kong banks and Macao banks are not "foreign banks", but "Chinese banks" in the broadest sense of the words. Accordingly, HK-funded and Macao-funded banks in Mainland China are not "foreign-funded financial institutions", but "Chinese financial institutions". The Chinese nature comes from the concept of "One Country". But in practice, HK-funded and Macao-funded banks in China enjoy the same treatment as foreign banks, which indicates the impact of another concept, "Two Systems".

Article 72 of the FFB Regulation 2006 provides that the regulation applies *mutatis mutandis* to Hong Kong, Macao and Taiwan banks established in Mainland China, meaning that HK-funded banks, Macao-funded banks, and Taiwan-funded banks are granted the same rights and the same obligations as foreign-funded banks.

A. CEPA

Current Chinese foreign trade policy is a mixture of multilateralism and regionalism. After entry to the WTO in 2001, China began to pay close attention to regional trade integration so as to take advantage of regional trade agreements to maximize trade benefits. The Central Committee of the Chinese Communist Party and the State Council made a significant strategic decision to conclude regional trade agreements.[107] This policy change was compatible with the belief of Hong Kong, also a Member of the WTO,[108] that free trade agreements (FTAs) are helpful in expanding trade and investment.[109] This consensus led to the conclusion of the

---

105 The Basic Law of the Hong Kong Special Administrative Region of the People's Republic of China, preamble, promulgated on April 4, 1990, effective as of July 1, 1997, available at http://www.info.gov.hk/basic_law/fulltext/.

106 According to paragraph 2 of Article 18 of the HKSAR Basic Law, China's national laws [*quanguoxing falü*] shall not be applied to the HKSAR except for those listed in Annex III of the HKSAR Basic Law. There are six laws listed in Annex III of the HKSAR Basic Law, including the Resolution on the Capital, Calendar, National Anthem and National Flag, Resolution on the National Day of the PRC, Nationality Law of the PRC, etc.

107 See General Office of the State Council, The Notice on Relevant Works for Implementing the CEPA, *Guobanfa* [2003] No.95, para. 1(1).

108 Hong Kong became a WTO Member in January 1995, http://www.wto.org/english/thewto_e/whatis_e/tif_e/org6_e.htm.

109 See Trade Policy Review Body, Trade Policy Review, Hong Kong, China Report by the Government, WT/TPR/G/109, ¶¶ 41, 42 (November 18, 2002).

Closer Economic Partnership Arrangement (CEPA) in June 2003.[110] On October 27, 2004, the two sides reached an agreement to provide further liberalization measures on trade in goods and services for the second stage of the CEPA, i.e., the Supplement to the Mainland and Hong Kong Closer Economic Partnership Agreement (CEPA II).[111] On October 18, 2005, the Mainland and Hong Kong signed the Supplement II to the Mainland and Hong Kong Closer Economic Partnership Agreement (CEPA III).[112] On June 27, 2006, the two sides signed the Supplement III to the Mainland and Hong Kong Closer Economic Partnership Agreement.[113] On June 26, 2007, July 29, 2008, May 9, 2008, May 27, 2010, December 13, 2011, June 29, 2012, the Supplements IV, V, VI, VII, VIII and IX were signed respectively.[114] The characteristic of the CEPA is that the FTA is between two separate customs territories under one country,[115] which results in not only international law issues, but also domestic law issues.

Mainland China has made a number of banking commitments to Hong Kong under the CEPA which are more favourable than China's banking commitments to other countries. In order to analyse China's banking commitments in the CEPA, it is necessary to look at two important concepts: banking services and banking service suppliers.

Banking Services

China's CEPA Schedule includes thefollowing banking services:

a. Acceptance of deposits and other repayable funds from the public;
b. Lending of all types, including consumer credit, mortgage credit, factoring and financing of commercial transaction;
c. Financial leasing;
d. All payment and money transmission services, including credit, charge and debit cards, travellers cheques and bankers drafts (including import and export settlement);
e. Guarantees and commitments;
f. Trading for own account or for account of customers: foreign exchange.

---

[110] CEPA, Main Text, http://www.tid.gov.hk/sc_chi/cepa/legaltext/files/main_sc.doc (last updated May 17, 2012).

[111] CEPA II, Main Text, http://www.tid.gov.hk/sc_chi/cepa/files/sa_main_sc.doc (last updated May 16, 2012) .

[112] CEPA III, Main Text, http://www.tid.gov.hk/english/cepa/legaltext/files/sa2_main_e.doc (last updated May 16, 2012).

[113] CEPA IV, Main Text, http://www.tid.gov.hk/tc_chi/cepa/legaltext/files/sa3_main_c.doc (last updated May 16, 2012) .

[114] Http://www.tid.gov.hk/sc_chi/cepa/legaltext/cepa_legaltext.html (last updated June 29, 2012).

[115] Wei Wang, "CEPA: A Lawful Free Trade Agreement under 'One Country, Two Customs Territories'?" *Law and Business Review of Americas*, Vol. 10, No. 3 (2004), at 647–66.

By comparison with China's WTO banking service commitments in China's WTO Schedule,[116] the scope of banking services in China's CEPA Schedule is almost equal to that in China's WTO Schedule. The fact that China's CEPA Schedule does not include more categories of banking services indirectly shows that the scope of banking services in China's WTO Schedule is broad enough.[117]

Banking Service Suppliers

According to Article XXVIII (g) of the GATS, "service supplier" means any person that supplies a service. "Person" means either a natural person or a juridical person.[118] Because the concept of "natural person" is meaningless in supplying banking services, "juridical person" is the focus of analysis regarding banking services. GATS Article XXVIII (m)(i) stipulates that "juridical person" of another Member means a juridical person which is constituted or otherwise organized under the law of that other Member, and is engaged in substantive business operations in the territory of that Member or any other Member.[119] Under the WTO, no minimum operation time is required for being a "service supplier". However, according to CEPA Annex 5 "Definition of 'Service Supplier' and related Rules", the standards of a Hong Kong service supplier (HKSS) providing service by way of a juridical person include the following:

1. establishment or registration based on HKSAR Corporation Regulations or other regulations, with a valid business registration certificate or licence;
2. being engaged in substantive business operations in Hong Kong for at least three years. Thus, the tests to determine engagement in substantive business operations in Hong Kong include, inter alia, a minimum number of three years of registration and operations in Hong Kong.[120]

The conditions for becoming a Hong Kong banking service supplier are stricter than those for becoming an ordinary HKSS. To be a Hong Kong banking service supplier, a Hong Kong bank or a Hong Kong finance company should have engaged in substantive business operations for five years or more after it has been granted a licence by the Hong Kong Monetary Authority (HKMA) pursuant to the

---

[116] The China Schedule, WT/ACC/CHN/49/Add.2.

[117] It must be noted, in the CEPA II, the scope of banking services is broadened to include insurance agency business, which is not listed in China's WTO Schedule.

[118] See GATS, art. XXVIII(j).

[119] In the case of the supply of a service through commercial presence, owned or controlled by (1) natural persons of that Member; or (2) juridical persons of that other Member. See GATS, art. XXVIII (m)(ii).

[120] See CEPA, Annex 5, "Definition of 'Service Supplier' and related Rules", ¶¶ 3.1.1, 3.1.2(2), http://www.tid.gov.hk/sc_chi/cepa/files/annex5_sc.doc (last updated July 1, 2010). In addition to the operation year requirement, there are other requirements for being an HKSS, e.g. profit tax, business premises, employment of staff. See id, ¶¶ 3.1.2(3) (4) (5).

Hong Kong Banking Ordinance.[121] An applicant for the status of a Hong Kong banking service supplier should submit its applications for a Certificate of HKSS to the Trade and Industry Department (TID) of the HKSAR through the Banking Supervision Department of the HKMA.[122] After obtaining a Certificate of HKSS from the TID, the Hong Kong banking service supplier should apply to the CBRC to obtain the CEPA treatment.[123]

It is noteworthy that foreign banks and finance companies can get the benefits of the CEPA by way of investment in Hong Kong banks or finance companies. In accordance with Annex 5 of the CEPA, if more than 50 percent of the equity of a Hong Kong service supplier has been owned for at least one year after a merger or acquisition by a foreign service supplier, the service supplier which has been merged or acquired will be regarded as a Hong Kong service supplier.[124] Thus, foreign banks and finance companies may indirectly obtain the status of "Hong Kong banking service suppliers" so as to get the more favourable treatment from China. To some extent, the CEPA can stimulate foreign direct investment (FDI) to Hong Kong, which is a good example of China's support to Hong Kong's economy. Meanwhile, the draftsmen of the CEPA noted the possibility of foreign "shell companies" to benefit from CEPA's favourable treatment by only registering a company in Hong Kong, so they designed the five-year substantive business operation standard, more than 50 per cent equity requirement and one year requirement after merger or acquirement, all of which aim to prevent foreign "shell companies" from taking advantage of the CEPA benefits.

So far, for the purpose of gaining the benefits of the CEPA, a number of foreign bank branches in Hong Kong have changed their status to Hong Kong banks. For example, the Citibank Hong Kong Branch became the Citibank (Hong Kong) Ltd in 2004,[125] and the Standard Chartered Hong Kong Branch became a Hong Kong bank, i.e., the Standard Chartered (Hong Kong) Ltd, wholly-owned by the Standard Chartered Bank.[126]

---

121 Id. ¶ 3.1.2(2).

122 Notice to Service Suppliers No. 2/2003: Application Procedures for Certificate of Hong Kong Service Supplier, issued by the TID of the HKSAR Government, WT 324/9/5/7, ¶ 9 (November 14, 2003).

123 See CEPA, Annex 5, art. 7, and the Notice to Service Suppliers No. 2/2003: Application Procedures for Certificate of Hong Kong Service Supplier, issued by the TID of the HKSAR Government, WT 324/9/5/7, ¶ 14 (November 14, 2003).

124 CEPA, Annex 4, footnote 2.

125 Http://www.info.gov.hk/hkma/chi/press/2004/20041029c4.htm (October 29, 2004).

126 Http://www.standardchartered.com.hk/chi/news/2004/c_press_20040511.pdf (May 11, 2004).

Market Access Commitments in Banking Services

As to specific market access commitments, China provides more favourable treatment to Hong Kong banking service suppliers under the CEPA.[127] Firstly, the minimum total assets requirement for a Hong Kong bank to establish a branch or juridical person in China falls to USD 6 billion. This requirement reduces the threshold of market access by allowing medium-size Hong Kong banks to enter the Chinese market.[128] For example, a medium-size Hong Kong local bank, Wing Lung Bank, set up a branch in Shenzhen on March 29, 2004,[129] which became the first beneficiary of CEPA's reduction of the minimum total assets requirement. In June 2004, two other medium-size banks from Hong Kong, DahSing Bank and Shanghai Commercial Bank opened branches in Shenzhen.[130] Secondly, there is no precondition for a Hong Kong bank to set up a representative office before establishing an equity joint venture bank or equity joint venture finance company. Thirdly, the conditions for a branch of a Hong Kong bank located in China to apply for renminbi (RMB) business include: (1) two years' business operations in China; (2) comprehensive consideration of whole branches operations in order to determine whether it satisfies the profitable qualification, unlike individual consideration of a single branch operation applicable to non-HK foreign bank branches. Fourthly, according to the CEPA III Schedule, "the level of operating funds required of Mainland branches of Hong Kong banks for offering renminbi and foreign currency businesses to local customers will be assessed on the basis of all Mainland branches of the bank concerned rather than each branch individually, and on the condition that the average level of operating funds of all Mainland branches of the bank concerned is over RMB500 million, the requirement on the level of operating fund of an individual branch should not be less than RMB 300 million."[131]

In comparison, China's WTO commitments in banking services are stricter. For example, the minimum total assets requirement to establish a foreign bank subsidiary is USD 10 billion at the end of the year prior to filing the application, while the minimum total assets requirement to establish a foreign bank branch

---

127 See Specific Commitments on Opening Service Trade Area, Table 1 of Annex 4 of the CEPA, http://www.tid.gov.hk/sc_chi/cepa/files/annex4_sc.doc (Last updated June 29, 2012). The existing schedule of specific commitments under current CEPA is unilateral. There are only service commitments made by the Mainland China to the HKSAR. According to the arrangement, the Mainland China and the HKSAR will negotiate service commitments to be made by the HKSAR to the Mainland China, which will be contained in Table 2 of Annex 4 of the CEPA.

128 Prior to the CEPA, only four large banks in Hong Kong had set up branches in China, i.e. the HSBC, Hang Seng Bank, Bank of East Asia and Bank of China Hong Kong Limited. See http://www.southcn.com/news/hktwma/jingji/200307040705.htm (June 4, 2003).

129 Http://www.china.org.cn/chinese/zhuanti/qkjc/688897.htm (October 26, 2004).

130 Http://finance.sina.com.cn/b/20040604/1658797123.shtml (June 4, 2004); http://www.gd.xinhuanet.com/newscenter/2004-06/22/content_2358044.htm (June 22, 2004).

131 CEPA III, Annex 2.

is USD 20 billion at the end of the year prior to filing the application, and the minimum total assets requirement to establish a equity joint venture bank is USD 10 billion, while for a Hong Kong bank, the total assets requirement is reduced to USD 6 billion. Moreover, under the WTO, the conditions for foreign-funded banks to engage in local currency business are three years business operations in China and being profitable for two consecutive years prior to the application, rather than the CEPA's requirement of two years' operations.

National Treatment Commitments in Banking Services

In China's CEPA Schedule, it seems that the specific commitments are merely related to market access. There is not a special column of national treatment. Does that mean China's CEPA Schedule is irrelevant to national treatment? Or does that mean that China has not made national treatment commitments under the CEPA? This is a very confusing issue. Paragraph 3 of the Annex 4 of the CEPA states: "In respect of the service sectors, sub-sectors or relevant measures not covered by this Annex, the Mainland [China] will apply Annex 9 of the 'Schedule of Specific Commitments on Services List of Article II MFN Exemptions' of the 'Protocol on the Accession of the People's Republic of China'." This paragraph may connect China's CEPA Schedule with China's WTO Schedule so as to complicate the seemingly simple commitments under the CEPA. Because national treatment limitation measures are covered in China's WTO Schedule,[132] are they, as "relevant measures", also covered in China's CEPA Schedule according to paragraph 3 of the Annex 4 of the CEPA? If so, China's specific commitments concerning national treatment (as well as market access commitments and additional commitments) in the WTO Schedule are to be "incorporated" into the CEPA as part of China's commitments to Hong Kong under the CEPA framework.

It is highly possible that this is the intention of the draftsmen of the CEPA, otherwise why is China's WTO Schedule mentioned in the CEPA? It is China's WTO obligation to abide by its WTO specific commitments. It is unnecessary for the CEPA to confirm China's WTO obligations. According to the principle of effectiveness, *ut res magis valeat quam pereat*, which has been used in WTO cases on many occasions,[133] paragraph 3 of the Annex 4 of the CEPA must be

[132] See WT/ACC/CHN/49/Add.2.

[133] Panel Report on *Canada – Term of Patent Protection*, WT/DS170/R, ¶ 6.49, footnote 30 (stating that "the principle of effective interpretation ... reflects the general rule of interpretation which requires that a treaty be interpreted to give meaning and effect to all the terms of the treaty."); Appellate Body Report, in *Japan – Taxes on Alcoholic Beverages*, WT/DS8/AB/R, WT/DS10/AB/R, WT/DS11/AB/R, adopted November 1, 1996, section D (stating that "the principle of effectiveness" is a fundamental interpretation principle); Appellate Body Report, *United States – Import Prohibition of Certain Shrimp and Shrimp Products*, WT/DS58/AB/R, adopted November 21, 2001, ¶ 131 and footnote 116 (interpreting the concept of "exhaustible natural resources" in line with the principle of effectiveness); Appellate Body Report, *United States – Restrictions on Imports of Cotton*

interpreted so as to make this paragraph meaningful and effective. In the first WTO Appellate Body Report, the Appellate Body held that an interpretation could not result in reducing whole clauses or paragraphs of a treaty to "redundancy or inutility".[134] According to the principle of interpretation of effectiveness, it is highly probable[135] that paragraph 3 of the Annex 4 of the CEPA has incorporated China's WTO Schedule into the CEPA to supplement China's CEPA Schedule. If this interpretation is right, the two service schedules under two different trade regimes are closely related, especially with respect to national treatment commitments.

If China's specific national treatment commitments in China's WTO Schedule are incorporated into the CEPA based on paragraph 3 of the Annex 4 of the CEPA, China's national treatment commitments in banking services under the framework of the WTO can also be regarded as China's banking commitments under the framework of the CEPA. Therefore, the following banking commitments under the WTO are applicable to Hong Kong banking services and service suppliers under the CEPA:

---

and Man-Made Fibre Underwear, WT/DS24/AB/R, adopted February 25, 1997, section IV:1, DSR 1997:I, at 24 (invoking the principle of effectiveness in treaty interpretation); Panel Report, *Korea – Definitive Safeguard Measure on Imports of Certain Dairy Products*, WT/DS98/R, adopted January 12, 2000, ¶¶ 4.609, 7.37 (stating that all terms must be given full meaning and must be interpreted to avoid inconsistencies and inutility); Appellate Body Report, *Korea – Definitive Safeguard Measure on Imports of Certain Dairy Products*, WT/DS98/AB/R, adopted January 12, 2000, ¶ 81 (stating that it is the duty of any treaty interpreter to give meaning to all provisions of a treaty); Appellate Body Report, *Canada – Measures Affecting the Importation of Milk and the Exportation of Dairy Products*, WT/DS103/AB/R, WT/DS113/AB/R, adopted October 27, 1999, ¶ 133 (applying "the fundamental principle of *effet utile*" and stating that the treaty interpreter should give effect to a "legal operative meaning for the terms of the treaty"); Appellate Body Report, *Argentina – Safeguard Measures on Imports of Footwear*, WT/DS121/AB/R, adopted January 12, 2000, ¶ 88 (holding that "the Panel failed to give meaning and legal effect to *all* the relevant terms of the *WTO Agreemen*"); Appellate Body Report, *United States – Section 211 Omnibus Appropriations Act*, WT/DS176/AB/R, adopted February 1, 2002, ¶¶ 161, 338; Panel Report on EC – *Trade Description on Sardines*, WT/DS231/R, adopted October 23, 2002, ¶ 7.76 (stating the principle of effectiveness is "a corollary of the general rule of interpretation in the Vienna Convention"); Appellate Body Report, *United States – Continued Dumping and Subsidy Offset Act of 2000*, WT/DS217/AB/R, WT/DS234/AB/R, adopted January 27, 2003, ¶ 271 (stating that the interpretative principle of effectiveness should guide the interpretation of the WTO Agreement).

[134] Appellate Body Report, in *United States – Standards for Reformulated and Conventional Gasoline*, WT/DS2/AB/R, adopted May 20, 1996, section IV.

[135] Although the principle of effectiveness is a fundamental principle of interpretation, it should be treated with some caution. See Michael Lennard, *Navigating by the Stars: Interpreting the WTO Agreements*, 5(1) Journal of International Economic Law 59–60 (2002).

1. For mode one (cross-border supply), China makes full national treatment commitments;
2. For mode two (consumption abroad), China makes full national treatment commitments;
3. For mode three (commercial presence), China makes partial national treatment commitments;[136]
4. For mode four (presence of natural persons), China does not make national treatment commitment except as indicated in the horizontal commitments.[137]

Financial Cooperation Commitments

In order to strengthen banking cooperation and embody the support from China to Hong Kong, the draftsmen of the CEPA devised a special article, i.e. Article 13, providing financial cooperation between the two sides. According to CEPA Article 13, China shall adopt four supporting measures. Firstly, China supports wholly state-owned commercial banks [*guoyou shangye yinhang*] and certain joint-stock commercial banks [*gufenzhi shangye yinhang*] in relocating their international treasury and foreign exchange trading centres to Hong Kong.[138] Secondly, China supports its banks in developing network and business activities in Hong Kong through acquisition.[139] Thirdly, China supports the full utilization of financial intermediaries in Hong Kong during the process of reform, restructuring and development of the financial sector in China.[140] Fourthly, China supports eligible companies, including private enterprises, in listing in Hong Kong.[141] Besides the four supporting measures, the financial regulators of China and Hong Kong shall strengthen regulatory cooperation and information sharing.[142] The above supportive measures aim to strengthen Hong Kong's position as an international financial center in Asia.[143]

---

[136] China's WTO banking commitments relating to mode three is: "Except for geographic restrictions and client limitations on local currency business (listed in the market access column), foreign financial institution may do business, without restrictions or need for case-by-case approval, with foreign invested enterprises, non-Chinese natural persons, Chinese natural persons and Chinese enterprises. Otherwise, none."

[137] The horizontal commitments with respect to mode four states: "Unbound except for the measures concerning the entry and temporary stay of natural persons who fall into the categories referred to in the market access column." WT/ACC/CHN/49/Add.2.

[138] CEPA, art. 13(1).

[139] CEPA, art. 13(2).

[140] CEPA, art. 13(3).

[141] CEPA, art. 13(5).

[142] CEPA, art. 13(4).

[143] The HKSAR Basic Law provides that the Government of the HKSAR should provide an appropriate environment for the maintenance of the status of Hong Kong as an international financial centre. See the Basic Law of the Hong Kong Special Administrative

B. ECFA

FFB Regulation 2006 opened a possibility for Taiwan Banks to set up subsidiaries or branches in the Mainland. However, before 2010, there were only some Taiwan Bank representative offices in the Mainland. As representative offices, they could not do banking business in the Mainland.

On June 29, 2010, the Cross-Straits Economic Cooperation Framework Agreement (ECFA) was signed between the Mainland and Taiwan.[144] It became a history-marking event between the two parties' market access of banking services. Some favourable treatment measures to Taiwan banks are included in the Commitments of the Mainland Side on Liberalization of Financial Service Sectors, in Annex IV of the ECFA, Sectors and Liberalization Measures under the Early Harvest for Trade in Services.[145]

1. For Taiwan banks to set up wholly-Taiwan-funded banks or branches (not branches affiliated to a wholly-Taiwan-funded bank) in the Mainland with reference to the FFB Regulation, they shall have representative offices in the Mainland for more than one year before application.
2. For the operating branches of Taiwan banks in the Mainland to apply to conduct RMB business, they shall have been operating in the Mainland for more than two years and be profitable in the preceding year before application.
3. For the operating branches of Taiwan banks in the Mainland to apply to conduct RMB business for Taiwan corporations in the Mainland, they shall fulfil the following conditions: they should have been operating in the Mainland for more than one year and been profitable in the preceding year.
4. The operating branches of Taiwan banks in the Mainland may set up special agencies providing financial services to small businesses, the specific requirements of which shall follow relevant rules in the Mainland.
5. Fast tracks shall be established for Taiwan banks applying to set up branches (not branches affiliated to wholly-Taiwan-funded banks) in central and western, as well as northeastern regions of the Mainland.
6. In conducting profitability assessment on the branches of Taiwan banks in the Mainland, the relevant authorities shall take into account the overall performance of the Taiwan bank under assessment.

At the end of 2010, five Taiwan banks were approved by the CBRC to open branches in the Mainland, including the First Commercial Bank Shanghai Branch, Cathay United Bank Shanghai Branch, The Land Bank Shanghai Branch, Chang Hwa Commercial Bank Kunshan Branch, Taiwan Cooperative Bank Suzhou

Region of the People's Republic of China, April 4, 1990 (entered into force July 1, 1997), art. 109, available at http://www.info.gov.hk/basic_law/fulltext/.

144 Http://tga.mofcom.gov.cn/accessory/201009/1285058725620.pdf.

145 Http://tga.mofcom.gov.cn/accessory/201009/1285058759312.pdf.

Branch.[146] In January, 2011, the CBRC approved Hua Nan Commercial Bank Shenzhen Branch to open business.[147] In February, 2012, the CBRC approved Chinatrust Commercial Bank Shanghai Branch to open business.[148] On June 21, 2012 Mega International Commercial Bank Suzhou Branch opened business.[149] On September 3, 2012 Taiwan E.Sun Bank Dongguan Branch opened business.[150]

V. Concluding Remarks

Foreign-funded banks may enter China's financial market in different forms. They have a firm legal status in the territory of China. Like Chinese-funded banks, they are able to get access to people's courts for protection of their legal rights. They can take the form of a limited liability company recognized by the PRC Corporation Law. They can choose the form of a foreign bank branch, which is under the protection of Chinese law, as well as the protection of their home country law. In practice, the legal status of foreign-funded banks has been reaffirmed and illustrated by many cases dealt with by people's courts of China.

Hong Kong and Macao banks are accorded more favourable legal status in establishing branches and subsidiaries in Mainland China based on the CEPAs than ordinary foreign banks based on the WTO. The banks from Taiwan also get more favourable treatment based on the ECFA. As a matter of fact, before establishment of the ECFA, Taiwan-funded enterprises (including Taiwan-funded banks) in Mainland China had already been accorded some more favourable treatment with respect to the standards of compensation for expropriation.[151]

---

146 Http://www.cbrc.gov.cn/chinese/home/docView/2010121726B6E16787A0D899FFF092DD915C5500.html (published December 17, 2010).

147 CBRC *Yinjianhan* [2011] No. 2, available at http://www.cbrc.gov.cn/govView_3ECF1444E93C43E9864C23BEB7DDCC98.html (published January10, 2011).

148 CBRC *Yinjianfu* [2012] No. 83, available at http://www.cbrc.gov.cn/govView_3E089C46471640FCA1C5CFC0561D1062.html (published February 27, 2012).

149 Http://www.szstx.org/Article/ShowArticle.asp?ArticleID=593 (June 24, 2012).

150 Http://www.esunbank.com.tw/about/614.board (September 3, 2012).

151 Compare Article 5 of Wholly-Foreign-Funded Enterprise Law and Article 24 of the Detailed Rules for Implementation of Law of the Protection of Investment from Taiwan Compatriots.

CHAPTER 4
China's Banking Law Framework: Different Positions of Foreign-Funded Banks and Chinese-Funded Banks

Chapter 3 focused on the market access, forms and legal status of foreign-funded banks in China. This chapter examines the status quo of China's banking law framework, the position of foreign-funded banks and Chinese-funded banks in that framework, and then discusses the problems of the framework.

I. Overview of China's Law Structure

According to the PRC Legislation Law (2000),[1] in China there are seven types of law in the broadest sense, including laws [*falü*], administrative regulations [*xingzheng fagui*], local regulations [*difangxing fagui*], autonomous regulations [*zizhi tiaoli*], separate regulations [*danxing tiaoli*], rules of departments under the State Council [*guowuyuan bumen guizhang*], and rules of local governments [*difang zhengfu guizhang*].[2]

A. Laws

In the strict sense, laws only refer to "laws" enacted by the NPC and its Standing Committee.[3] The NPC enacts and amends basic laws governing criminal offences, civil affairs, State institutions and other basic laws,[4] while the Standing Committee of the NPC enacts and amends laws other than those within the power of the NPC.[5] Because the NPC only holds one national conference each year, which lasts about two weeks, its Standing Committee enacts most laws in practice. The laws enacted

---

1 PRC Legislation Law [*Lifafa*], adopted at the Third Session of the Ninth NPC on March 15, 2000, effective July 1, 2000, *in* Falü Huibian 2000, at 2–23 (People's Publishing House 2001).

2 Id. art.2.

3 Id. art. 7, ¶ 1.

4 PRC Constitution, art. 62 (3), adopted at the Fifth Session of the Fifth NPC on December 4, 1982, effective December 4, 1982, amended in 1988, 1993, 1999, 2004, in Falü Huibian 2004, at 1–34 (People's Publishing House 2005); PRC Legislation Law, art. 7, ¶ 2.

5 PRC Constitution, art. 67 (2); PRC Legislation Law, art. 7, ¶ 3.

by the NPC and its Standing Committee make up the apex of the whole body of China's law.

B. Administrative Regulations

Administrative regulations are formulated by the State Council in accordance with the Constitution and laws enacted by the NPC and its Standing Committee.[6] The main purpose of administrative regulations is to implement the laws and deal with the administrative matters within the powers of the State Council, so they are binding on the whole territory of China. Administrative regulations take the form of "regulations" [*tiaoli*], "provisions" [*guiding*], "measures" [*banfa*], etc.[7] The legal effect of administrative regulations is lower than that of laws.[8]

C. Local Regulations

China's local regions under the State Council include three forms: provinces [*sheng*],[9] autonomous regions [*zizhiqu*],[10] and municipalities directly under the Central Government [*zhixiashi*],[11] all of which have their own local People's Congresses and corresponding Standing Committees. These local People's Congresses and Standing Committees may formulate local regulations, provided such local regulations do not conflict with the Constitution, national laws, or administrative regulations.[12] In contrast to the nationally binding scope of laws and administrative regulations, local regulations are effective only within relevant local areas. Furthermore, the local People's Congresses at the level of larger cities [*jiaoda de shi*][13] may also formulate local regulations, subject to approval by the

---

6 PRC Constitution, art. 89 (1); PRC Legislation Law, art. 56.

7 Regulation on Procedures for Formulating Administrative Regulations [*Xingzheng Fagui Zhiding Chengxu Tiaoli*], promulgated on November 16, 2001, effective January 1, 2002, Decree No. 321 of the State Council, art. 4, GAZETTE OF THE STATE COUNCIL 5–7 (2002, no. 1).

8 PRC Legislation Law, art. 79, ¶ 1.

9 The PRC has 23 provinces. ZHONGHUA RENMIN GONGHEGUO XINGZHENG QŪHUA JIANCE [SHORT MANUAL OF ADMINISTRATIVE DIVISIONS OF THE PRC 2005] 1 (Ministry of Civil Affairs of the PRC (ed.), SinoMaps Press 2005).

10 The PRC has 5 autonomous regions, including Inner Mongolia, Guangxi, Tibet, Ningxia and Xinjiang. SHORT MANUAL OF ADMINISTRATIVE DIVISIONS OF THE PRC 2005, id.

11 The PRC has 4 municipalities directly under the Central Government, including Beijing, Tianjin, Shanghai and Chongqing. SHORT MANUAL OF ADMINISTRATIVE DIVISIONS OF THE PRC 2005, id.

12 PRC Constitution, art. 100; PRC Legislation Law, art.63, ¶ 1.

13 PRC Legislation Law, art. 63, ¶ 4 (providing that larger cities refer to capitals of the provinces and autonomous regions, the cities where special economic zones are located, and other larger cities approved by the State Council). There are 27 capitals of the provinces and autonomous regions (besides Taiwan, HK and Macao), 6 cities where special economic

People's Congresses at the provincial level.[14] The legal effect of local regulations is less than that of administrative regulations.[15]

D. Autonomous Regulations and Separate Regulations

With respect to the political, economic and cultural characteristics of China's nationalities, local People's Congresses in autonomous areas, including autonomous regions and autonomous prefectures [*zizhizhou*][16] or autonomous counties [*zizhixian*],[17] may formulate autonomous regulations and separate regulations.[18] Autonomous regulations and separate regulations must be approved by higher People's Congresses. Autonomous regulations and separate regulations shall apply in the autonomous areas concerned in accordance with laws, administrative regulations and local regulations.[19]

E. Rules of Departments

Article 71 of the Legislation Law states:

> The ministries and commissions of the State Council, the People's Bank of China, the State Audit Administration as well as the other organs endowed with

zones are located (including Shenzhen, Xiamen, Zhuhai, Shantou, Hainan and Kashi), and 18 larger cities approved by the State Council. See ZHONGHUA RENMIN GONGHEGUO LIFAFA SHIYI [EXPLANATIONS OF THE LEGISLATION LAW OF THE PRC] 187 (Zhang Chunsheng (ed.), Law Press China 2000).

14 PRC Legislation Law, art. 63, ¶ 2.

15 Id. art. 79, ¶ 2.

16 The PRC has 30 autonomous prefectures. SHORT MANUAL OF ADMINISTRATIVE DIVISIONS OF THE PRC 2005, supra note 9. It must be noted that the autonomous prefectures are mainly located in the provinces. Among the 5 autonomous regions, only Xinjiang has autonomous prefectures.

17 The PRC has 120 autonomous counties. China's Ethnic Policy and Common Prosperity and Development of All Ethnic Groups, issued by the State Council Information Office of the PRC, September 2009, http://www.gov.cn/zwgk/2009-09/27/content_1427930.htm (September 27, 2009).

18 PRC Constitution, art. 116; PRC Legislation Law, art. 66; Law of the PRC on Regional National Autonomy [*Minzu Quyu Zizhifa*], art. 19, adopted May 31, 1984 at the Second Session of the Sixth NPC, effective from October 1, 1984, amended on February 28, 2001 at the 20th Meeting of the Standing Committee of the Ninth NPC, in LAW OF THE PRC ON REGIONAL NATIONAL AUTONOMY (Chinese Ethnic Publishing House 2001).

19 For further information on autonomous regulations and separate regulations, see ZHONGGUO MINZU QUYU ZIZHI FALÜ FAGUI TONGDIAN [GENERAL COMPILATIONS OF AUTONOMOUS LAWS AND REGULATIONS OF CHINA'S ETHNIC AREAS] (Secretariat of the Standing Committee of the NPC & Legal Department of the State Ethnic Affairs Commission of the PRC (eds), Publishing House of the Central University for Nationalities 2002).

> administrative functions directly under the State Council may, in accordance with laws as well as administrative regulations, decisions and orders of the State Council and within the limits of their power, formulate rules.
>
> Matters governed by rules of departments shall be those for the enforcement of laws or administrative regulations, decisions and orders of the State Council.

The binding scope of rules of departments is similar to that of administrative regulations, i.e. the whole territory of China. Administrative regulations refer only to the regulations issued by the State Council, with titles such as "regulations", "provisions", or "measures".[20] Rules of departments refer only to the rules, often with titles such as "provisions" or "measures",[21] issued by departments or ministries under the State Council. Rules of departments are the general title of the normative documents formulated by the departments under the State Council, within the scope of their power and in accordance with relevant procedures, such as provisions, measures, detailed rules for implementation, rules, etc.[22] The legal effect of administrative regulations is higher than that of rules of departments. This subtle difference between the regulations and rules of departments is often ignored,[23] especially due to the common use of the titles of "provisions" and "measures". Moreover, the relationship between local regulations and rules of departments is more complicated than that between administrative regulations and rules of departments. If there is an inconsistency between local regulations and rules of departments, the State Council shall give its opinion. The legal effect of the opinions of the State Council depends on two conditions. If the State Council considers that local regulations should be applied, the local regulations shall be applied. If the State Council considers that rules of departments should be applied, the case shall be submitted to the Standing Committee of the NPC for a final ruling.[24]

F. Rules of Local Governments

The local governments of the provinces, autonomous regions, municipalities directly under the Central Government and the comparatively larger cities may

---

20 Regulation on Procedures for Formulating Administrative Regulations, supra note 7.

21 Article 6 of the Regulation on Procedures for Formulating Rules [*Guizhang Zhiding Chengxu Tiaoli*], promulgated on November 16, 2001, effective January 1, 2002, Decree No. 322 of the State Council, GAZETTE OF THE STATE COUNCIL 8–10 (2002, no. 1).

22 See Article 2(2) of the Provisions for Putting Regulations and Rules on Record [*Fagui Guizhang Bei'An Guiding*], issued on February 18, 1990, effective February 18, 1990, State Council Decree No. 48, GAZETTE OF THE STATE COUNCIL 86–89 (1990, no. 3).

23 For example, the USTR misused the term "regulations" in one of its reports, i.e., USTR 2003 National Trade Estimate Report on Foreign Trade Barriers, at 64, http://www.ustr.gov/Document_Library/Reports_Publications/2003/2003_NTE_Report/Section_Index.html.

24 PRC Legislation Law, art. 86 (2).

formulate rules of local governments.[25] The effect of rules of departments and the effect of rules of local governments is equal, and if there is a conflict, the State Council shall make a decision on which will prevail.[26] The effect of rules of local governments is lower than that of local regulations.

II. The Vertical Banking Law Framework of China

The above-mentioned types of law in the broad sense are categorized vertically based on their legal effects. However, not all of them are relevant to regulating China's banking. It seems that China's banking law is out of reach of local regulations, autonomous regulations, separate regulations and rules of local governments. Article 8 of the Legislation Law provides that nine matters, one of which is "basic system of finance",[27] are in the exclusive legislative power of the NPC and its Standing Committee. The Legislation Law does not define the "basic system of finance", which opens the door for the State Council to make administrative regulations on non-basic system of finance.[28] As to the powers of the CBRC and the PBC to make banking rules, they are derived from the two banking laws made by the NPC and its Standing Committee.[29] By contrast, there are no laws or administrative regulations authorizing local governments to make local banking regulations or local banking rules. It must be noted that the two early administrative regulations allowing foreign banks to set up foreign-funded banks in the four Special Economic Zones of the time (Shenzhen, Xiamen, Zhuhai and Shantou) and Shanghai, i.e., the Regulation on Administration of Wholly-Foreign-Funded Banks and Sino-Foreign Equity Joint Venture Banks in the Special Economic Zones (1985) and the Regulation on Administration of Wholly-Foreign-Funded Financial Institutions and Sino-Foreign Equity Joint Venture Financial Institutions in Shanghai (1990), were not local regulations or rules promulgated by local governments, but the regulations by the State Council. In June 2009, the Standing Committee of Shanghai Municipal People's Congress passed a local financial regulation, i.e., the Regulation of Shanghai on Promoting the Construction of International Financial Centre [Shanghai Shi Tuijin Guoji Jinrong Zhongxin Jianshe Tiaoli], the first local financial regulation in China. However, the regulation contains few substantive rules.

---

[25] Id. art. 73.

[26] Id. art. 82.

[27] Id. art. 8(8).

[28] Paragraph 1 of Article 89 of the PRC Constitution states that the State Council may formulate administrative regulations, make administrative measures in accordance with the Constitution and laws.

[29] See PBC Law 2003, art. 4(1), GAZETTE OF THE NPC 26–30 (2004, no. 1); Banking Supervision Law 2006 [*Yinhangye Jiandu Guanlifa*], art. 15, adopted at the Sixth Meeting of the Standing Committee of the Tenth NPC on December 27, 2003, effective February 1, 2004, amended at the Twenty-fourth Meeting of the Standing Committee of the Tenth NPC on October 31, 2006, amendment effective as of January 1, 2007.

Local governments are not entitled to set up local banking regulators. The regulatory power to supervise local banks, such as city commercial banks and rural commercial banks, is in the hands of local offices of the CBRC. The CBRC is the leading banking regulator of China's central government.[30] The local offices of the CBRC are under the direct leadership of the CBRC head office located in Beijing.[31] Moreover, local governments cannot interfere in the work of the CBRC and its local offices.[32] Actually, in China, all licences of local commercial banks shall be issued by the CBRC.[33] A local government has no power to approve the establishment of a bank, or issue a banking licence.

As a whole, from the vertical perspective, China's banking law framework is composed of four tiers, i.e. banking laws (in the narrow sense) made by the NPC and its Standing Committee, banking administrative regulations by the State Council, banking rules by the CBRC and the PBC, and other banking normative documents by the CBRC and the PBC.[34] The four-tiered banking law framework is shown in table 4.1.

Table 4.1 China's vertical banking law framework

Tier	Category	Maker
1	Banking Laws	NPC or its Standing Committee
2	Banking Regulations	State Council
3	Banking Rules	CBRC or PBC
4	Other Banking Normative Documents	CBRC or PBC

A. Banking Laws

Nineteen ninety-five is the watershed in PRC's banking law history. There were no banking laws in the narrow sense prior to that year. In that year, the NPC enacted

30 Banking Supervision Law 2006, art. 2.

31 Id. art. 8, ¶ 1.

32 Id. art. 5.

33 Commercial Banking Law 2003, art. 11. Decision on the Amendment of the Law on Commercial Banks, adopted at the Sixth Meeting of the Standing Committee of the Tenth NPC on December 27, 2003, GAZETTE OF THE STATE NPC 32–35 (2004, no. 1).

34 It is noteworthy that occasionally the CBRC and the PBC jointly issue banking rules with some ministries or commissions under the State Council. For example, the PBC, CBRC and China Securities Regulatory Commission [hereinafter the CSRC] jointly issued the Measures for Administration of Pilots of Fund Management Companies Established by Commercial Banks [*Shangye Yinhang Sheli Jijin Guanli Gongsi Shidian Guanli Banfa*] on February 20, 2005, *PBC, CBRC and CSRC Decree* [2005] No. 4, GAZETTE OF THE STATE PBC 3–5 (2005, no. 3).

the Law on the People's Bank of China (PBC Law 1995),[35] and the Standing Committee of the NPC enacted the Law on Commercial Banks (Commercial Banking Law 1995).[36] Therefore, 1995 is called China's Financial Legislation Year.[37] The PBC Law 1995 assigned both banking regulatory powers and monetary policy functions to the central bank, i.e. the PBC.[38] The Commercial Banking Law 1995 applied to both Chinese-funded banks and foreign-funded banks,[39] meaning that China tried to place foreign banking law and domestic banking law under the umbrella of a general commercial banking law. In March 2003, the NPC decided to separate the banking regulatory function from the PBC to a new agency – the CBRC,[40] thus necessitating the amendment of the PBC Law 1995 and the Commercial Banking Law 1995, as well as other relevant banking regulations, rules, etc.[41] On December 27, 2003, the Standing Committee of the NPC passed China's first separate banking supervision law, the Law on Banking Regulation and Supervision (Banking Supervision Law 2003),[42] together with the 2003 amendments to the PBC Law 1995 (PBC Law 2003)[43] and the 2003 amendments to the Commercial Banking Law 1995 (Commercial Banking Law 2003),[44] all of which took effect as of February 1, 2004. Banking Supervision Law 2003 was

---

35 PBC Law 1995 [*Renin Yinhang Fa*], adopted at the Third Session of the Eighth NPC on March 18, 1995, effective on the same day, Falü Huibian 1995, at 142–50 (People's Publishing House 1996).

36 Commercial Banking Law 1995 [*Shangye Yinhangfa*], adopted at the Thirteenth Meeting of the Standing Committee of the Eighth NPC on May 10, 1995, effective July 1, 1995, Falü Huibian 1995, 152–70 (People's Publishing House 1996).

37 Wu Zhipan, *Jinrong Fazhi Shinian* [*Ten Years of the Financial Law*], ZHONGGUO JINRONG [CHINA FINANCE] 11 (2005, no. 13).

38 PBC Law 1995, art. 2, ¶ 2.

39 Commercial Banking Law 1995, art. 88.

40 Decision of the First Session of the Tenth NPC on the Plan of Reforming the State Council Institutions, March 10, 2003, GAZETTE OF THE NPC 190–94 (2003, no. 2).

41 Decision on the Exercise of Regulatory Duty by CBRC in Place of PBC [*Guanyu Zhongguo Yinhangye Jiandu Guanli Weiyuanhui Lüxing Yuan You Zhongguo Renmin Yinhang Luxing de Jiandu Guanli Zhize de Jueding*], adopted at the Second Meeting of the Standing Committee of the Tenth NPC on April 26, 2003, GAZETTE OF THE NPC 326 (2003, no. 3).

42 Banking Supervision Law 2003 [*Yinhangye Jiandu Guanlifa*], adopted at the Sixth Meeting of the Standing Committee of the Tenth NPC on December 27, 2003, effective February 1, 2004, GAZETTE OF THE NPC 4–9 (2004, no. 1); also available in Falü Huibian 2003, at 131–42 (People's Publishing House 2004).

43 Decision on the Amendment of the Law on the PBC, adopted at the Sixth Meeting of the Standing Committee of the Tenth NPC on December 27, 2003, GAZETTE OF THE NPC 23–25 (2004, no. 1). For the whole text of the PBC Law 2003, see GAZETTE OF THE NPC26–30 (2004, no. 1); also available in Falü Huibian 2003, at 150–60 (People's Publishing House 2004).

44 Decision on the Amendment of the Law on Commercial Banks, adopted at the Sixth Meeting of the Standing Committee of the Tenth NPC on December 27, 2003, GAZETTE OF

amended in 2006 (Banking Supervision Law 2006).[45] Additionally, on October 25, 2005, the NPC Standing Committee passed the Law on Judicial Immunity of Compulsory Measures for Assets of Foreign Central Banks. On October 31, 2006, China promulgated the Anti-Money Laundering Law (Anti-Money Laundering Law 2006).[46] The five banking laws are at the highest level in China's banking law framework, shown in table 4.2.

Table 4.2 China's banking laws

Year	Title	Maker	No.
2003	PBC Law	NPC Standing Committee	President Decree No. 12
2003	Commercial Banking Law	NPC Standing Committee	President Decree No. 13
2005	Law on Judicial Immunity of Compulsory Measures for Assets of Foreign Central Banks	NPC Standing Committee	President Decree No. 41
2006	Anti-Money Laundering Law	NPC Standing Committee	President Decree No. 56
2006	Banking Supervision Law	NPC Standing Committee	President Decree No. 58

Note: PBC Law was made by the NPC in 1995, but amended by the NPC Standing Committee in 2003.

B. Banking Administrative Regulations

Next to the five banking laws are banking administrative regulations made by the State Council. Currently there exist at least six banking administrative regulations,

THE NPC 32–35 (2004, no. 1). For the Commercial Banking Law 2003, see GAZETTE OF THE NPC 36–44 (2004, no. 1).

45 Decision on the Amendment of the Banking Supervision Law, adopted at the Twenty-fourth Meeting of the Standing Committee of the Tenth NPC on October 31, 2006, effective as of January 1, 2007 (adding some articles and paragraphs so that the CBRC has more powers to investigate and inspect banking institutions).

46 Anti-Money Laundering Law [*Fan Xiqian Fa*], adopted at the Twenty-fourth Meeting of the Standing Committee of the Tenth NPC on October 31, 2006, effective as of January 1, 2007.

including the Regulation on Administration of Savings,[47] the Measures for Clamping Down Illegal Financial Institutions and Illegal Financial Activities,[48] the Measures for Punishment of Illegal Financial Activities,[49] the Provisions on the True Name System of Personal Deposit Accounts,[50] the Regulation on Dissolution of Financial Institutions,[51] the FFB Regulation 2006.[52] The banking administrative regulations are at the second level of China's banking law framework. Table 4.3 shows China's existing banking regulations.

Table 4.3 China's banking regulations

Year	Title	Maker	No.
1992	Regulation on Administration of Savings	State Council	Decree 107
1998	Measures for Clamping Down Illegal Financial Institutions and Illegal Financial Activities	State Council	Decree 247 (revised in 2011)
1999	Measures for Punishment of Illegal Financial Activities	State Council	Decree 260
2000	Provisions on the True Name System of Personal Deposit Accounts	State Council	Decree 285
2001	Regulation on Dissolution of Financial Institutions	State Council	Decree 324
2006	FFB Regulation 2006	State Council	Decree 478

[47] Regulation on Administration of Savings [*Chuxu Guanli Tiaoli*], State Council Decree No. 107, promulgated on December 11, 1992, effective March 1, 1993, GAZETTE OF THE STATE COUNCIL 1339–44 (1992, no. 31).

[48] The Measures for Clamping Down Illegal Financial Institutions and Illegal Financial Activities [*Feifa Jinrong Jigou he Feifa Jinrong Yewu Huodong Qudi Banfa*], State Council Decree No. 247, promulgated on July 13, 1998, revised on January 8, 2011, GAZETTE OF THE STATE COUNCIL 339–341 (2011, No. 1, Supplement).

[49] Measures for Punishment of Illegal Financial Activities [*Jinrong Weifa Xingwei Chufa Banfa*], State Council Decree No. 260, promulgated on February 22, 1999, effective on the same day, GAZETTE OF THE STATE COUNCIL 244–51 (1999, no. 8).

[50] Provisions on the True Name System of Personal Deposit Accounts [*Geren Cunkuan Zhanghu Shimingzhi Guiding*], State Council Decree No. 285, promulgated on March 20, 2000, effective April 1, 2000, GAZETTE OF THE STATE COUNCIL 10–11 (2000, no. 15).

[51] Regulation on Dissolution of Financial Institutions [*Jinrong Jigou Chexiao Tiaoli*], Decree No. 324 of the State Council, promulgated on November 23, 2001, effective December 15, 2001, GAZETTE OF THE STATE COUNCIL 13–16 (2002, no. 1).

[52] Regulation on Administration of Foreign-Funded Banks [*Waizi Yinhang Guanli Tiaoli*] (FFB Regulation 2006), State Council Decree 478, promulgated on November 11, 2006, effective as of December 11, 2006, GAZETTE OF THE STATE COUNCIL 13–19 (2007, no. 1).

C. Banking Rules

The third level of China's banking law framework refers to relevant banking regulatory rules issued by banking regulatory institutions.

Banking Regulatory Institutions
Because China adopts a sector supervision system, Chinese financial regulatory institutions include the CBRC, the PBC, the China Securities Regulatory Commission (CSRC), and the China Insurance Regulatory Commission (CIRC). The CBRC and the PBC are banking regulatory institutions. In 2004, the CBRC, CSRC and CIRC signed the Memorandum of Understanding on Separation and Cooperation of Financial Supervision among the CBRC, CSRC and CIRC.[53]

Since the establishment of the CBRC in April 2003, most powers or duties to issue "orders and rules relating to financial regulation" have been transferred from the PBC to the CBRC.[54] In addition to the rule-making power, the CBRC is in charge of examing and approving the establishment, change or winding-up of banking institutions, and of their business scope.[55] The CBRC takes off-site surveillance and on-site examination on banks.[56] The CBRC headquarter is in Beijing, including, inter alia, Bank Supervision Department I (supervising large commercial banks, i.e., state-owned commercial banks), Bank Supervision Department II (supervising joint-stock commercial banks, city commercial banks and city cooperatives), Bank Supervision Department III (supervising foreign-funded banks), Bank Supervision Department IV (supervising policy banks). Under the CBRC headquarters, there are 36 agencies in provinces, autonomous regions and some big cities.[57]

However, the PBC, as China's central bank whose main function is to issue and implement monetary policy, to prevent and resolve financial crisis, to maintain financial stability,[58] still preserves some banking regulatory and supervisory functions.[59]

---

[53] Memorandum of Understanding on Separation and Cooperation of Financial Supervision among the CBRC, CSRC and CIRC, available at http://www.cbrc.gov.cn/chinese/home/docView/717.html (published June 28, 2004).

[54] Decision of the Standing Committee of the NPC on the Performance by the CBRC of the Supervisory and Administrative Duties Originally Performed by the PBC, § 1, adopted at the Second Meeting of the Standing Committee of the Tenth NPC on April 26, 2003, GAZETTE OF THE NPC 326 (2003, no. 3); see also Banking Supervision Law 2006, art. 15.

[55] Banking Supervision Law 2006, art. 16.

[56] Banking Supervision Law 2006, arts. 23, 24.

[57] Http://www.cbrc.gov.cn/index.html.

[58] PBC Law 2003, art. 2.

[59] Id. art. 4. The People's Bank of China shall perform the following functions and responsibilities: (1) to issue and carry out the orders and regulations related to its functions and responsibilities; (2) to formulate and implement monetary policies in accordance with law; (3) to issue Renminbi (RMB) and control its circulation; (4) to supervise and

Now the CBRC takes the main responsibility for making China's banking regulatory rules. The Banking Supervision Law 2006 states that, in accordance with the law and the administrative regulations, the banking regulatory institution of the State Council, i.e. the CBRC, shall formulate and issue rules governing the supervision over banking institutions and their operations.[60] This article clearly empowers the CBRC to formulate banking rules.

Forms of Banking Rules

The forms of banking rules include "provisions" [*guiding*], "measures" [*banfa*], "Detailed Rules for Implementation" [*shishi xize*], etc.[61] There is a subtle difference between "provisions" and "measures". Generally speaking, the title of "provisions" is suitable for financial activities in part or in whole. The title of "measures" is suitable for detailed rules on financial activities.[62]

China's Existing Banking Rules

The current banking rules in China are a mixture of rules issued by both the PBC and the CBRC. This situation adds difficulty in finding proper banking regulatory rules, considering the huge amount of rules that had been issued by the PBC before the establishment of the CBRC. The PBC and the CBRC have recognized the problem and since 2003 have begun to sort out the banking rules of the PBC. On December 17, 2004, the PBC and the CBRC jointly issued an announcement declaring the initial result of sorting out one hundred and ten rules originally made by the PBC,[63] among which eleven PBC banking rules remain valid under the common monitoring and enforcement by the PBC and the CBRC,[64] sixty-one PBC

administer the inter-bank lending market and the inter-bank bond market; (5) to exercise control of foreign exchange and supervise and administer the inter-bank foreign exchange market; (6) to supervise and administer the gold market; (7) to hold, administer and manage the state foreign exchange reserve and gold reserve; (8) to manage the State Treasury; (9) to maintain the normal operation of the system for making payments and settling accounts; (10) to guide and make plans for anti-money laundering; (11) to be responsible for statistics, investigation, analysis and forecasting concerning the banking industry; (12) to engage in relevant international banking operations in its capacity as the central bank of the State; and (13) other functions and responsibilities prescribed by the State Council.

60 Banking Supervision Law 2006, art. 15.

61 Interim Rules on the Formulation Procedures of Basic Financial Rules [*Jinrong Yewu Jiben Guizhang Zhiding Chexu Guiding Shixing*], art. 8, issued by the PBC on March 30, 1991, effective July 1, 1991, *Yinfa* [1991] No.166, http://www.law-lib.com/lawhtm/1991/7506.htm.

62 Id.

63 Announcement of the PBC and the CBRC, [2004] No. 20, December 17, 2004, GAZETTE OF THE PBC 3–8 (2004, no. 18–19) [hereinafter the Announcement of the PBC and the CBRC].

64 Id. Section 1, and Annex 1.

banking rules are succeeded by the CBRC,[65] thirty-eight PBC banking rules were repealed from date of the announcement.[66]

In addition to the PBC banking rules jointly enforced by the PBC and the CBRC and those succeeded by the CBRC, the CBRC itself has issued a series of new banking regulatory rules since 2003.[67] On July 3, 2007, the CBRC issued the Announcement on Formulating, Amending, Repealing and not Applying Some Rules and Normative Documents, [68] sorting out a number of banking rules and normative documents. In 2011, the CBRC issued the Announcement on the Result of Sorting Out Banking Rules.[69]

Table 4.4 shows the main body of China's existing banking rules.

Table 4.4 China's banking rules

Year	Title	Maker	No.
1994	Provisions on Administration of Financial Institutions	PBC	Yinfa 198
1996	General Rules for Loans	PBC	Decree No. 2
1997	Measures for Payment and Settlement	PBC	Yinfa 393
1999	Measures for Administration of Bank Card Business	PBC	Yinfa 17
1999	Guidelines for Commercial Banks to Carry out a Unified Credit-Granting System (trial implementation)	PBC	Yinfa 31
2000	Guidelines for Risk Management of Off-Balance Sheet Business of Commercial Banks	PBC	Yinfa 344
2001	Measures of the PBC for Procedure of Administrative Punishment	PBC	Decree 3
2001	Measures of the PBC for Administrative Reconsideration	PBC	Decree 4
2002	Provisions on Administration of Financial Institutions in the Work of Assisting Inquiry, Freezing, Seizing and Transferring	PBC	Yinfa 1
2002	Interim Measures for Information Disclosure of Commercial Banks (not applicable from July 3, 2007)	PBC	Decree 6
2002	Guidelines for Corporate Governance of Joint-Stock Commercial Banks	PBC	Announcement 15
2002	Guidelines for the System of Independent Director and External Supervisor of Joint-Stock Commercial Banks	PBC	Announcement 15

[65] Id. Section 2, and Annex 2.

[66] Id. Section 3, and Annex 3.

[67] See Zhongguo Yinhangye Jianguan Guizhang Huibian 2003–2006 [Compendium of China Banking Rules 2003–2006] (Policy and Law Department of the CBRC (ed.), Law Press China 2006).

[68] *Yinjianfa* [2007] 56.

[69] Announcement on the Result of Sorting Out Banking Rules [*Guanyu Fabu Yinhangye Guizhang Qingli Jieguo de Gonggao*] Yinjianfa [2011] No. 1, http://www.cbrc.gov.cn/chinese/home/docView/201101133B97ACB14F04E4EBFF9A98E2F2E5DB00.html (published January 1, 2011).

Year	Title	Maker	No.
2002	Measures for Administration of Accounting Archives of Banks	PBC	Yinfa 374
2002	Guidelines for Internal Control of Commercial Banks (not applicable from July 3, 2007)	PBC	Announcement 19
2002	Guidelines for Provisioning Loan Loss Reserves	PBC	Yinfa 98
2003	Measures for Administration of Renminbi Bank Settlement Accounts	PBC	Decree 5
2003	Decision on Adjusting Administrative Means and Procedures of Banking Market Access	CBRC	Decree 1
2003	Measures for Administration of Financial Licences (revised in 2007 by CBRC Decree 8 of 2007)	CBRC	Decree 2
2003	Interim Measures for Administration of Service Price of Commercial Banks	CBRC NDRC	Decree 3
2003	Guidelines for Administration of Credit-granting Risks for Group Customers (Revised in 2007, 2010)	CBRC	Decree 5
2003	Measures for Administration of Equity Investment of Overseas Financial Institutions in Chinese-Funded Financial Institutions	CBRC	Decree 6
2004	Measures for Administration of Auto Loans	PBC & CBRC	Degree 2
2004	Measures for Administration of Linked Transactions between Commercial Banks and Insiders, Shareholders	CBRC	Decree 3
2004	Measures for Administration of Foreign Debt of Foreign-Funded Banks in Chinese Territory	NDRC, PBC & CBRC	Decree 9
2004	Interim Measures for Administration of Supervisory Statistics of Commercial Banks	CBRC	Decree 6
2004	Measures of the CBRC for Administrative Punishment (revised in 2007 by Decree 5 of 2007)	CBRC	Decree 7
2004	Measures of the CBRC for Administrative Reconsideration	CBRC	Decree 8
2004	Guidelines for Administration of Market Risk of Commercial Banks	CBRC	Decree 10
2004	Implementation Measures of the PBC for Administrative Licencing	PBC	Decree 3
2004	Provisions for administration of Reserves for Foreign Exchange Deposit of Financial Institutions	PBC	Yinfa 252
2005	Measures for Administration of Pilot of Fund Management Companies Established by Commercial Banks	PBC, CBRC & CSRC	Decree 4
2005	Guidelines for Performance of Duties of Board of Directors of Joint-Stock Commercial Banks (Interim)	CBRC	N/A
2005	Interim Measures for Administration of Credit Assets Securitization Pilots	PBC & CBRC	Announcement 7

continued ...

Table 4.4 concluded

Year	Title	Maker	No.
2005	Interim Measures for Administration of Personal Financial Management Services Provided by Commercial Banks	CBRC	Decree 2
2005	Measures for Supervising Credit Assets Securitization Pilots of Financial Institutions	CBRC	Decree 3
2006	Provisions of the CBRC on Implementation Procedures of Administrative Licencing	CBRC	Decree 1
2006	Measures of the CBRC for Granting Administrative Licences to Chinese-Funded Commercial Banks	CBRC	Decree 2
2006	Measures of the CBRC for Granting Administrative Licences to Foreign-Funded Financial Institutions	CBRC	Decree 4
2006	Administrative Measures Governing E-Banking Business	CBRC	Decree 5
2006	DRI 2006	CBRC	Decree 6
2006	Provisions on Anti-Money Laundering by Financial Institutions	PBC	Decree 1
2006	Measures for Administration of Reporting Large-Value Transactions and Suspicious Transactions of Financial Institutions	PBC	Decree 2
2007	Measures for Administration of Inter-bank Loans	PBC	Decree 3
2007	Guidelines for Internal Control of Commercial Banks	CBRC	Decree 6
2007	Measures for Information Disclosure of Commercial Banks	CBRC	Decree 7
2009	Interim Measures for Administration of Fixed Assets Loans	CBRC	Decree 2
2010	Procedural Rules for Examination on Execution of Law by the PBC	PBC	Decree 1
2010	Interim Measures for Administration of Current Fund Loans	CBRC	Decree 1
2010	Interim Measures for Administration of Personal Loans	CBRC	Decree 2
2011	Measures for Administration of Financial Derivatives Transactions of Banking Financial Institutions	CBRC	Decree 1
2011	Measures for Administration and Supervision of Credit Card Business of Commercial Banks	CBRC	Decree 2
2011	Measures for Administration of Leverage Ratio of Commercial Banks	CBRC	Decree 3
2011	Measures for Administration of Loan Loss Provisions of Commercial Banks	CBRC	Decree 4
2011	Measures for Administration of Sale of Financing Products of Commercial Banks	CBRC	Decree 5
2012	Measures for Administration of Capital of Commercial Banks (interim)	CBRC	Decree 1

Note: compiled by the author.

D. Other Banking Normative Documents

One of China's legal characteristics is the existence of a great number of "other normative documents" [*qita guifanxing wenjian*], such as circulars or notices [*tongzhi*], letters or replies [*han* or *pifu*], announcements [*gonggao*], or other measures [*cuoshi*], issued by ministries, commissions of the State Council or by other institutions endowed with administrative functions directly under the State Council, which should not be ignored as they often revise or supplement higher level administrative regulations and rules. Because the normative documents are not in the scope of the Legislation Law, they do not have a formal status in the Chinese legal system. But they may be invoked in administrative judgements at the discretion of people's courts.[70] In fact, those administrative measures have binding force.[71]

According to Article XXVIII (a) of the GATS, "measure" means any measure by a WTO Member, whether in the form of a law, regulation, rule, procedure, decision, administrative action, or any other form. Any other form is an all-inclusive expression. Furthermore, Part I:2(2) of the China Accession Protocol states:

> China shall apply and administer in a uniform, impartial and reasonable manner all its *laws, regulations and other measures* of the central government as well as *local regulations, rules and other measures* issued or applied at the sub-national level (collectively referred to as "*laws, regulations and other measure*") pertaining to or affecting trade in goods, services, trade-related aspects of intellectual property rights ("TRIPS") or the control of foreign exchange (emphasis added).

The expression in the China Accession Protocol implies that "measure" includes any measure, such as a law, a regulation, a rule, a procedure, a decision, an administrative action, etc., which echoes the definition in the GATS. From the expression in the China Accession Protocol, *laws* and *regulations* are parallel to *other measures*, so *other measures* include any measures "pertaining to or affecting trade in goods, services, TRIPS or the control of foreign exchange", except for laws and regulations.

---

70 Paragraph 2 of Article 62 of the Interpretations of the Supreme People's Court on Relevant Issues of the Administrative Procedural Law of the PRC [*Zuigao Renmin Fayuan guanyu Zhixing Zhonghua Renmin Gongheguo Xingzheng Susongfa Ruogan Wenti de Jieshi*], adopted at the 1088th Meeting of the Adjudication Committee of the Supreme People's Court on November 24, 1999, http://www.court.gov.cn/lawdata/explain/executivecation/200303200097.htm.

71 Hu Jianmiao, Xingzhengfa Xue [Administrative Law] 245–46 (Law Press China 2nd edn, 2003).

During the negotiations relating to China's entry to the WTO, some WTO Members expressed concerns about the lack of transparency regarding the laws, regulations and other measures that applied to matters covered in the WTO Agreement. In particular, some Members noted the difficulty in finding and obtaining copies of regulations and other measures undertaken by various ministries.[72] China promised that none of the information required by the WTO Agreement or the China Accession Protocol to be disclosed would be withheld as confidential information except for very special reasons.[73] China further promised only those laws, regulations and other measures "that are published and readily available to other WTO Members, individuals and enterprises" can be enforced.[74] Therefore, it is China's obligation to publish all normative measures affecting trade in financial services.[75]

In *China-Publications*, China argued as follows:

> China maintains that pursuant to its *Legislation Law*, the hierarchy of Chinese laws and regulations at central government level is composed of three levels: (i) laws enacted by the National People's Congress or its Standing Committee; (ii) administrative regulations enacted by the State Council; (iii) departmental rules enacted by ministries or agencies under the State Council. According to China, the *Several Opinions* does not fit into any of the three categories of laws and regulations within China and as an internal guideline is not applicable in the context of administrative acts.[76]

As to whether "Several Opinions" can be in the scope of Chinese legal system, the panel found as follows:

> With respect to China's argument that the *Several Opinions* does not fall within any of the three categories of laws or regulations within China, we recall that although an understanding of China's administrative law system is useful, what is important for purposes of our analysis is not the nomenclature used by the domestic legal system of the Member, but whether the act falls within the meaning of the term "measure" as it is used in Article 3.3 of the DSU.[77]
>
> Even accepting China's arguments that the *Several Opinions* merely provides internal guidance and is not directly applicable would not be enough to exclude it from review by this Panel. It is already well established that internal government documents that provide administrative guidance to agencies in how they carry

72 Working Party Report, WT/ACC/CHN/49, ¶ 324.

73 Id. ¶ 333.

74 China Accession Protocol, WT/L/432, Part I :2(C).1.

75 Id.

76 WT/DS363R, ¶ 7.182.

77 WT/DS363R, ¶ 7.188.

out their duties can be "measures" within the meaning of Article 3.3 of the DSU. Additionally, accepting that the restrictions described in the *Several Opinions* do not have direct effect, but must be implemented by government agencies promulgating regulations, does not mean that they do not set forth rules or norms that are intended to have general and prospective application.[78]

The panel found that "Several Opinions" sets forth rules or norms intended to have general and prospective application and is a "measure" within the meaning of Article 3.3 of the DSU.[79]

So far, China has enhanced the transparency in banking laws, regulations, rules and other banking normative documents. Table 4.5 is based on my personal knowledge. It must be noted that it is not complete and only indicative.

Table 4.5 China's other banking normative documents

Year	Title	Maker	No.
1993	Relevant Provisions on the enforcement of Regulation on Administration of Savings	PBC	Yinfa 7
1994	Interim Provisions on the Investment to Financial Institutions	PBC	Yinfa 186
1996	Interim Measures for Authorization and Credit-Granting Business of Commercial Banks	PBC	Yinfa 403
2000	Notice on Relevant Issues of Administration of Market Access and Qualification for Senior Management of Joint-Stock Commercial Banks (not applicable from July 3, 2007)	PBC	Yinbanfa 192
2000	Notice on Relevant Issues of Examining Qualification for Shareholders of Joint-Stock Commercial Banks and City Commercial Banks (not applicable by CBRC 2011 Yinjianfa 1)	PBC	Yinbanfa 246
2001	Notice of the PBC on Further Enhancing Administration of Market Access of Foreign Exchange Business of Wholly-State-Owned Commercial Banks	PBC	Yinfa 33
2001	Recommendation Letter for Resolving the Issue of Super-National Treatment of Foreign-Funded Banks	PBC	Yinfa 69
2001	Notice of the PBC on Further Regulating Market Access of Branches and Sub-branches of Joint-Stock Commercial Banks (not applicable by CBRC 2011 Yinjianfa 1)	PBC	Yinfa 173
2001	Guidelines for Principles of Loan Risk Categories	PBC	Yinfa 416
2001	Announcement by the PBC on the Related Issues of Foreign-Funded Financial Institutions' Market Access	PBC	Announcement 1

78 WT/DS363R, ¶ 7.196.

79 WT/DS363R, ¶ 7.198.

Table 4.5 continued

Year	Title	Maker	No.
2002	Unifying the Administrative Policy of Interest Rates of Foreign Currency Deposits and Loans for Chinese-funded and Foreign-Funded Financial Institutions	PBC	Announcement 4
2002	Notice of the PBC on the Business of Letter of Credit and Letter of Guarantee of Commercial Banks	PBC	Yinfa 51
2002	Notice of the PBC on Chinese-Funded Commercial Banks to Purchase Foreign Exchange to Supplement Foreign Exchange Capital	PBC	Yinfa 106
2002	Notice on Relevant Issues of Adjusting the System of Examining and Approving New Branches of Joint-Stock Commercial Banks (not applicable from July 3,2007)	PBC	Yinfa 244
2003	Notice on Relevant Issues of Opening Special RMB Cash Accounts for Settlement and Sale of Exchange by Foreign-Funded Banks	PBC	Yinfa 180
2003	Interim Provisions of Administration of Rural Commercial Banks	CBRC	Yinjianfa 10
2003	Notice on Strengthening Administration of Share Right of City Commercial Banks	CBRC	Yinjianbanfa 105
2003	Notice on Normalizing Chinese Names of Branches and Sub-branches of Foreign Banks in China (repealed on July 3, 2007)	CBRC	Yinjiantong 27
2004	Measures for Administration of Consolidated Regulation of Foreign-Funded Banks (repealed by CBRC 2011 Yinjianfa 1)	CBRC	Yinjianfa 10
2004	Guidelines for Fulfilling Duties in Credit-Granting Business of Commercial Banks	CBRC	Yinjianfa 51
2004	Guidelines for Risk Management of Real Estate Loans of Commercial Banks	CBRC	Yinjianfa 57
2004	Procedures of Off-Site Surveillance on Joint-Stock Commercial Banks (Interim)	CBRC	Yinjianfa 21
2004	Measures for Administration of Issuing Secondary Bonds by Commercial Banks	PBC & CBRC	Announce-ment 4
2004	Notice of the PBC on Adjusting Interest Rates of Deposits and Loans of Financial Institutions	PBC	Yinfa 251
2004	Notice of the PBC on Strengthening Administration of Deposit Reserves	PBC	Yinfa 302
2005	Guidelines for the Work of Banking Associations	CBRC	N/A
2005	Guidelines for Fulfilling Duties in Disposing Non-Performing Financial Assets	CBRC & MOF	Yinjianfa 72
2005	Procedures of the CBRC for Statistics of On-Site Examination (Interim)	CBRC	Yinjianbanfa 79

Year	Title	Maker	No.
2005	Guidelines for Risk Management of Personal Finance Business of Commercial Banks	CBRC	N/A
2005	Guidelines for Supervising Risks of Derivative Business of Foreign-Funded Banks (Interim)	CBRC	Yinjianfbanfa 313
2005	Announcement on the Market Access Procedures for the Custody Business for Share Assets of Insurance Companies by Foreign-Funded Banks in China	CBRC	Yinjianfa 13
2005	Reply of the CBRC General Office on Relevant Issues of Pledge of Commercial Bank Stock Right	CBRC	Yinjianbanfa 60
2005	Opinions on Supervisory Work for Rural Commercial Banks	CBRC	Yinjianfa 28
2005	Guidelines for External Sale Business of Commercial Banks	CBRC	Yinjianfa 20
2005	Guidelines for Corporate Governance of Foreign-Funded Banks with Legal Personality	CBRC	Yinjianfa 21
2005	Notice of the CBRC General Office on Handling Wrongful Activities of Joint-Stock Commercial Banks such as Watered Deposits	CBRC	Yinjianbanfa 320
2006	Guidelines for E-Banking Security Evaluation	CBRC	Yinjianfa 9
2006	Guidelines for Corporate Governance and Relevant Supervision of State-owned Commercial Banks	CBRC	Yinjianfa 22
2006	Guidelines on Fulfilling Duties in Credit-Granting Business for Small Enterprises by Commercial Banks (Interim)	CBRC	Yinjianfa 69
2006	Guidelines for Management of Compliance Risk of Commercial Banks	CBRC	Yinjianfa 76
2006	Guidelines for Financial Innovations of Commercial Banks	CBRC	Yinjianfa 87
2006	Announcement of the CBRC on Related Issues after Promulgation of the Detailed Rules for Implementation of the FFB Regulation	CBRC	Yinjianfa 82
2007	Guidelines for Administration of Operational Risks of Commercial Banks	CBRC	Yinjianfa 42
2007	Guidelines for Credit-Granting Business for Small Enterprises by Banks	CBRC	Yinjianfa 53
2007	Procedures of On-site Examination by the CBRC	CBRC	Yinjianfa 55
2007	Guidelines for Syndicated Loans	CBRC	Yinjianfa 68
2008	Guidelines for Consolidated Supervision of Banks (Interim)	CBRC	Yinjianfa 5
2008	Guidelines for Business Cooperation between Banks and Trust Companies	CBRC	Yinjianfa 83
2008	Guidelines for Administration of Risk of M&A Loans of Commercial Banks	CBRC	Yinjianfa 84

continued ...

Table 4.5 concluded

Year	Title	Maker	No.
2009	Guidelines for Administration of Liquidity Risk of Commercial Banks	CBRC	Yinjianfa 87
2009	Guidelines for Administration of Information Technology Risk of Commercial Banks	CBRC	Yinjianfa 19
2009	Guidelines for the Business of Project Finance	CBRC	Yinjianfa 71
2009	Guidelines for Administration of Reputation Risk of Commercial Banks	CBRC	Yinjianfa 82
2009	Measures for Administration of Investment of Commercial Banks to the Shares of Insurance Companies	CBRC	Yinjianfa 98
2009	Guidelines for Administration of Interest Rate Risk of Banking Accounts in Commercial Banks	CBRC	Yinjianfa 106
2010	Guidelines for Supervision of Sound Salary of Commercial Banks	CBRC	Yinjianfa 14
2010	Guidelines for Administration of State or District Risks of Financial Institutions of Banking	CBRC	Yinjianfa 45
2011	Guidelines for Management of Risks of Off-balance Sheet Business of Commercial Banks	CBRC	Yinjianfa 31
2011	Guidelines for Implementing New Supervision Standards by Chinese Banking	CBRC	Yinjianfa 44
2012	Guidelines for Green Credit	CBRC	Yinjianfa 4

Note: compiled by the author.

III. The Horizontal Banking Law Framework of China

China's vertical banking law framework is different from its horizontal banking law framework. The former refers to the top-down structure, i.e. the four tiers composed of banking laws, banking regulations, banking rules and other banking normative documents. The latter refers to the framework based on the different scope of application of China's banking law. One can find that the vertical banking law framework is generally based on the PRC Legislation Law, that is to say, the vertical banking law framework is a de jure framework. However, the horizontal banking law framework is based on the practice of China's banking law, so it can be regarded as a de facto framework. From the horizontal perspective, China's banking law framework can be described as a tripartite law framework shown in table 4.6, including foreign banking law, domestic banking law, and common banking law.

Table 4.6 China's horizontal banking law framework

Tier	Foreign banking law	Domestic banking law	Common banking law
1	FFB Regulation 2006	Part of Banking Laws	Part of Banking Laws
2	Part of Banking Laws	Domestic banking regulations	Common banking regulations
3	Special Rules for foreign-funded banks	Special rules for Chinese-funded banks	Common banking rules
4	Special normative documents for foreign-funded banks	Special normative documents for Chinese-funded banks	Common banking normative documents

A. Foreign Banking Law

The first part of China's banking law framework includes banking law applicable only to foreign-funded banks. According to the Commercial Banking Law 2003 and the Banking Supervision Law 2006, special foreign banking laws and/or administrative regulations shall prevail over general banking laws.[80] Therefore, with respect to foreign-funded banks, the primary legal sources are not the three general banking laws enacted by the NPC or its Standing Committee, but special foreign banking regulations and rules.[81] So far, the NPC and its Standing Committee have not enacted any special foreign banking "law". Currently, China's foreign banking law in the broad sense includes a special administrative regulation issued by the State Council, several banking rules and other normative documents, especially the FFB Regulation 2006 and the Detailed Rules for Implementation of the Regulation on Administration of Foreign-Funded Banks of 2006 (DRI 2006). Table 4.7 gives an illustrative list of China's existing foreign banking regulations, rules and other normative documents.

[80] Commercial Banking Law 2003, art.92; Banking Supervision Law 2006, art. 51.

[81] In fact, the role of the banking laws (enacted by the NPC and its Standing Committee) in foreign banking supervision is so insignificant that some Chinese banking law scholars ignore the banking laws when introducing China's foreign banking law framework. See, e.g., QIANG LI, JINRONGFA [FINANCIAL LAW] 186 (Law Press China 1997); ZHONGGUO JINRONGFA [CHINESE FINANCIAL LAW] 127–28 (Lu Zefeng et al. (eds), Wuhan Univ. Press 1997).

Table 4.7 China's foreign banking law

Year	Title	Maker	No.
2003	PBC Law 2003 (Part)	NPC	President Decree 12
2003	Commercial Banking Law 2003 (Part)	NPC Standing Committee	President Decree 13
2003	Notice on Relevant Issues of Opening Special RMB Cash Accounts for Settlement and Sale of Exchange by Foreign-Funded Banks	PBC	Yinfa 180
2003	Measures for Administration of Equity Investment of Overseas Financial Institutions in Chinese-Funded Financial Institutions	CBRC	Decree 6
2003	Notice on Normalizing Chinese Names of Branches and Sub-branches of Foreign Banks in China	CBRC	Yinjiantong 27
2004	Measures for Administration of Consolidated Regulation of Foreign-Funded Banks (repealed by CBRC 2011Yinjianfa 1)	CBRC	Yinjianfa 10
2004	Measures for Administration of Foreign Debt of Foreign-Funded Banks in Chinese Territory	NDRC, PBC & CBRC	Decree 9
2005	Announcement on the Market Access Procedures for the Custody Business for Share Assets of Insurance Companies by Foreign-Funded Banks in China	CBRC	Yinjianfa 13
2005	Guidelines for Corporate Governance of Foreign-Funded Banks with Legal Personality	CBRC	Yinjianfa 21
2005	Guidelines for Supervising Risks of Derivative Business of Foreign-Funded Banks (Interim)	CBRC	Yinjianbanfa 313
2006	Banking Supervision Law (Part)	NPC Standing Committee	President Decree 58
2006	FFB Regulation	State Council	Decree 478
2006	Detailed Rules for Implementation of the FFB Regulation	CBRC	Decree 5
2006	Announcement of the CBRC on Related Issues after Promulgation of the Detailed Rules for Implementation of the FFB Regulation	CBRC	Yinjianfa 82
2007	Circular of the CBRC concerning Conduction of the Bank Card Business by Wholly Foreign-Funded Banks and Sino-Foreign Equity Joint Venture Banks	CBRC	Yinjianfa 49
2009	Guiding Opinions on Strengthening Corporate Governance of Banks with Legal Entity Transformed from Foreign Bank Branches	CBRC	Yinjianbanfa 276

Note: compiled by the author.

B. Domestic Banking Law

Before going further, it is necessary to clarify the scope of Chinese-funded banks. In this book, Chinese-funded banks refer to Chinese-funded commercial banks [*zhongzi shangye yinhang*], namely, domestic-funded commercial banks [*neizi shangye yinhang*]. After the PBC stopped doing credit business with enterprises and persons and began to exercise only the function of a central bank in 1983,[82] the system of the big four specialized state banks [*guojia zhuanye yinhang*] was set up,[83] including (1) Industrial and Commercial Bank of China [*Zhongguo Gongshang Yinhang*, ICBC]; (2) Agricultural Bank of China [*Zhongguo Nongye Yinhang*, ABC]; (3) Bank of China [*Zhongguo Yinhang*, BOC]; (4) China Construction Bank [*Zhongguo Jianshe Yinhang*, CCB]. In the 1990s, the big four state specialized banks were transformed into state-owned commercial banks [*guoyou shangye yinhang*],[84] which constitute the main body of Chinese-funded banks. In addition, there are 12 nationwide joint-stock commercial banks [*quanguoxing gufenzhi shangye yinhang*],[85] more than one hundred city commercial banks [*chengshi shangye yinhang*], and some rural commercial banks [*nongcun shangye yinhang*], all of which are Chinese-funded banks.

Generally speaking, rural credit cooperative banks [*nongcun hezuo yinhang*] are not commercial banks. Therefore, in this book, Chinese-funded banks do not include rural credit cooperative banks. However, it must be noted that the definition of Chinese-funded commercial banks in Measures of the CBRC for Granting administrative Licences to Chinese-Funded Commercial Banks is of minor difference. Article 2 of the Meansures provides that Chinese-funded commercial banks in the Measures refer to state-owned commercial banks, joint-

---

[82] The Decision of the State Council on the People's Bank of China to Exercise only the Function of Central Bank [*Guowuyuan Guanyu Zhongguo Renmin Yinhang Zhuanmen Xingshi Zhongyang Yinhang Zhineng de Jueding*], *Guofa* [1983] No. 146, promulgated on September 17, 1983, effective September 17, 1983, GAZETTE OF THE STATE COUNCIL 965–68 (1983, no. 21).

[83] YANG XITIAN ET AL., 6 ZHONGGUO JINRONG TONGSHI: 1949–1996 [GENERAL HISTORY OF CHINA'S FINANCE: 1949–1996] 223–27 (Li Fei et al. (eds), China Financial Publishing House 2002).

[84] Decision of the State Council on Reforming the Financial System [*Guowuyuan Guanyu Jinrong Tizhi Gaige de Jueding*], §3, promulgated on December 25, 1993, effective December 25, 1993, *Guofa* [1993] No. 91, GAZETTE OF THE STATE COUNCIL 1488–96 (1993, no. 31).

[85] The 12 nationwide joint-stock commercial banks include: China CITIC Bank, China Everbright Bank, Huaxia Bank, China Guangfa Bank, China Merchants Bank, Shanghai Pudong Development Bank, Industrial Bank, China Minsheng Banking Corp., Evergrowing Bank, China Zheshang Bank, China Bohai Bank and PingAn Bank.

stock commercial banks, city commercial banks and city credit cooperative limited companies [*chengshi xinyongshe gufen youxian gongsi*], etc.[86]

The second part of China's tripartite banking law framework consists of domestic banking law applicable only to the Chinese-funded banks. For example, in August 1994, the PBC issued the Provisions on Administration of Financial Institutions,[87] applicable only to Chinese-funded banks.[88] This administrative rule was not replaced by the Commercial Banking Law 1995,[89] and is still effective to the extent not inconsistent with the Commercial Banking Law 2003. This rule, which has been succeeded by the CBRC from the PBC,[90] is an important banking regulatory measure for Chinese-funded commercial banks.

Table 4.8 shows the existing banking law applicable only to Chinese-funded banks.

Table 4.8 China's domestic banking law

Year	Title	Maker	No.
1994	Interim Provisions on Investing in Financial Institutions	PBC	Yinfa 186
1994	Provisions on Administration of Financial Institutions	PBC	Yinfa 198
1996	Interim Measures for Administration of Authorization, Credit-Granting of Commercial Banks	PBC	Yinfa 403
1997	Measures for Administration of Offshore Banking Business	PBC	Yinfa 438
1998	Notice on Name Change of City Cooperative Banks	PBC	Yinfa 94
1999	Guidelines for Commercial Banks to Carry out a Unified Credit-Granting System (trial implementation	PBC	Yinfa 31

[86] Measures of the CBRC for Granting administrative Licences to Chinese-Funded Commercial Banks [*Zhongzi Shangye Yinhang Xingzheng Xuke Shixiang Shishi Banfa*], CBRC Decree [2006] No. 2, effective from Februrary 1, 2006, available at http://www.cbrc.gov.cn/upload/zwgk/ml4/1/zhongzishangye.doc.

[87] Provisions on Administration of Financial Institutions [*Jinrong Jigou Guanli Guiding*], PBC *Yinfa* [1994] No. 198, issued on August 9, 1994, effective August 9, 1994.

[88] Id. art 63 (stating that "PBC will formulate rules applicable to foreign-funded financial institutions", implying that this rule is not applicable to foreign banks).

[89] In a PBC's reply to an enquiry, the PBC clearly indicated that non-conflicting regulations and rules with the Commercial Banking Law 1995 shall be enforced. See the Reply to the enquiry of execution of Law on Commercial Banks and the Rules on Administration of Financial Institutions, PBC (Legal Department) No. 26, 1995.

[90] Announcement of the PBC and the CBRC, Annex 2, [2004] No. 20, GAZETTE OF THE PBC 3–8 (2004, no. 18–19).

Year	Title	Maker	No.
2000	Notice on Abolishing Limitations on Working Capital of Foreign Exchange for Branches and Sub-branches of Banks	PBC	Yinfa 9
2000	Notice on Relevant Issues of Administration of Market Access and Qualification for Senior Management of Joint-Stock Commercial Banks (not applicable from July 3, 2007)	PBC	Yinbanfa 192
2000	Notice on Relevant Issues of Examining Qualification for Shareholders of Joint-Stock Commercial Banks and City Commercial Banks (not applicable by CBRC 2011 Yinjianfa 1)	PBC	Yinbanfa 246
2001	Notice of the PBC on Further Enhancing Administration of Market Access of Foreign Exchange Business of Wholly-State-Owned Commercial Banks	PBC	Yinfa 33
2001	Notice of the PBC on Further Regulating Market Access of Branches and Sub-branches of Joint-Stock Commercial Banks (not applicable by CBRC 2011 Yinjianfa 1)	PBC	Yinfa 173
2001	Notice of the PBC and the SAFE on Registration of Usane Letters of Credit of the Chinese-Funded Banks Appointed	PBC	Yinfa 235
2002	Notice of the PBC on Relevant Issues of Administration of Market Access of Chinese-Funded Commercial Banks (not applicable by CBRC 2011 Yinjianfa 1)	PBC	Yinfa 105
2002	Notice of the PBC on Chinese-Funded Commercial Banks to Purchase Foreign Exchange to Supplement Foreign Exchange Capital	PBC	Yinfa 106
2002	Notice on Relevant Issues of Adjusting the System of Examining and Approving New Branches of Joint-Stock Commercial Banks (not applicable from July 3, 2007)	PBC	Yinfa 244
2002	Guidelines for Corporate Governance of Joint-Stock Commercial Banks	PBC	Announcement 15
2002	Guidelines for the System of Independent Director and External Supervisor of Joint-Stock Commercial Banks	PBC	Announcement 15
2002	Measures for Administration of Accounting Archives of Banks	PBC	Yinfa 374
2003	PBC Law 2003 (Part)	NPC	President Decree 12
2003	Commercial Banking Law 2003 (Part)	NPC	President Decree 13
2003	Banking Supervision Law (Part)	NPC	President Decree 11

continued ...

Table 4.8 concluded

Year	Title	Maker	No.
2003	Notice on Strengthening Administration of Share Right of City Commercial Banks	CBRC	Yinjianbanfa 105
2003	Interim Provisions of Administration of Rural Commercial Banks	CBRC	Yinjianfa 10
2004	Risk Assessment System of Joint-Stock Commercial Banks (Interim) (repealed by CBRC 2011 Yinjianfa 1)	CBRC	Yinjianfa 3
2004	Notice of the CBRC on Regulating Annual Report Contents of Joint-Stock Commercial Banks	CBRC	Yinjianfa 8
2004	Notice of the PBC on Relevant Issues Concerning RMB Business Between Mainland Banks and Hong Kong Banks	PBC	Yinfa 36
2004	Procedures of Off-Site Surveillance on Joint-Stock Commercial Banks (Interim)	CBRC	Yinjianfa 21
2005	Notice on Strengthening the Work of Preventing Operational Risk	CBRC	Decree 4
2005	Measures for Administration of Pilot of Fund Management Companies Established by Commercial Banks	PBC, CBRC & CSRC	Decree 4
2005	Guidelines for Performance of Duties of Board of Directors of Joint-Stock Commercial Banks (Interim)	CBRC	Yinjianfa 61
2005	Opinions on Supervisory Work for Rural Commercial Banks	CBRC	Yinjianfa 28
2005	Notice of the CBRC General Office on Handling Wrongful Activities of Joint-Stock Commercial Banks such as Watered Deposits	CBRC	Yinjianbanfa 320
2006	Measures of the CBRC for Granting administrative Licences to Chinese-Funded Commercial Banks	CBRC	Decree 2
2006	Measures of the CBRC for Granting Administrative Licences to Cooperative Financial Institutions (repealed in 2011)	CBRC	Decree 3
2006	Guidelines for Corporate Governance and Relevant Supervision of State-owned Commercial Banks	CBRC	Yinjianfa 22
2006	Decision of the CBRC on Amending the Measures of the CBRC for Granting administrative Licences to Chinese-Funded Commercial Banks	CBRC	Decree 7

Note: compiled by author

It must be noted that the banking law applicable only to Chinese-funded banks can be further divided into several groups, including those applicable only to state-owned commercial banks, those only to joint-stock commercial banks, those only to city commercial banks, those only to rural commercial banks,[91] those to both state-owned commercial banks and joint-stock commercial banks,[92] and those to all Chinese-funded banks.[93] This internal segregation of Chinese-funded banks and domestic banking law is partly demonstrated in table 4.9 and table 4.10.

Table 4.9 China's domestic banking law applicable only to state-owned commercial banks

Year	Title	Maker	No.
2001	Notice of the PBC on Further Enhancing Administration of Market Access of Foreign Exchange Business of Wholly-State-Owned Commercial Banks	PBC	Yinfa 33
2006	Guidelines for Corporate Governance and Relevant Supervision of State-owned Commercial Banks	CBRC	Yinjianfa 22

Table 4.10 China's domestic banking law applicable only to joint-stock commercial banks

Year	Title	Maker	No.
2000	Notice on Relevant Issues of Administration of Market Access and Qualification for Senior Management of Joint-Stock Commercial Banks (not applicable from July 3, 2007)	PBC	Yinbanfa 192

continued ...

91 See, e.g., Interim Provisions of Administration of Rural Commercial Banks [*Nongcun Shangye Yinhang Guanli Zanxing Guiding*], CBRC *Yinjianfa* [2003] No. 10, issued on September 12, 2003, effective September 12, 2003, Gazette of the State Council 29–35 (2004, no. 15).

92 See, e.g., the Notice of the PBC on Relevant Issues of Administration of Market Access of Chinese-Funded Commercial Banks [*Guanyu Zhongzi Shangye Yinhang Shichang Zhunru Guanli Youguan Wenti de Tongzhi*], art. 7, issued by the PBC on April 14, 2002, effective at the same date, PBC *Yinfa* [2002] No. 105, in Gazette of the PBC 11–12 (2002, no. 11) (applying only to "wholly-state-owned commercial banks and joint-stock commercial banks" and not applying to "city commercial banks" and "rural commercial banks").

93 See, e.g., the Notice of the PBC on Chinese-Funded Commercial Banks to Purchase Foreign Exchange to Supplement Foreign Exchange Capital [*Guanyu Zhongzi Shangye Yinhang Gouhui Buchong Waihui Zibenjin de Tongzhi*], issued by the PBC on April 14, 2002, in Gazette of the PBC 13 (2002, no. 11) (applying to all Chinese-funded commercial banks, including wholly-state-owned commercial banks, joint-stock commercial banks, city commercial banks, and rural commercial banks).

Table 4.10 concluded

Year	Title	Maker	No.
2001	Notice of the PBC on Further Regulating Market Access of Branches and Sub-branches of Joint-Stock Commercial Banks (not applicable by CBRC 2011 Yinjianfa 1)	PBC	Yinfa 173
2002	Guidelines for Corporate Governance of Joint-Stock Commercial Banks	PBC	Announcement 15
2002	Guidelines for the System of Independent Director and External Supervisor of Joint-Stock Commercial Banks	PBC	Announcement 15
2002	Notice on Relevant Issues of Adjusting the System of Examining and Approving New Branches of Joint-Stock Commercial Banks (not applicable from July 3, 2007)	PBC	Yinfa 244
2004	Risk Assessment System of Joint-Stock Commercial Banks (Interim) (repealed by CBRC 2011 Yinjianfa 1)	CBRC	Yinjianfa 3
2004	Notice of the CBRC on Regulating Annual Report Contents of Joint-Stock Commercial Banks	CBRC	Yinjianfa 8
2004	Procedures of Off-Site Surveillance on Joint-Stock Commercial Banks (Interim)	CBRC	Yinjianfa 21
2005	Notice of the CBRC General Office on Handling Wrongful Activities of Joint-Stock Commercial Banks such as Watered Deposits	CBRC	Yinjianbanfa 320
2005	Guidelines for Performance of Duties of Board of Directors of Joint-Stock Commercial Banks (Interim)	CBRC	Yinjianfa 61

C. Common Banking Law

The third part of the tripartite banking law framework refers to the overlaps between foreign banking law and domestic banking law, i.e. banking laws, regulations and rules applicable to both Chinese-funded banks and foreign-funded banks.

The third part of the tripartite banking law framework can be called common banking law which is prima facie consistent with national treatment obligations of the GATS/WTO, unless it can be proved that the common banking law is *formally identical treatment* but *modifies the conditions of competition*[94] in favour of Chinese-funded banks.

Based on my research, the following banking laws, regulations, rules and other normative documents listed in Table 4.11 apply to both Chinese-funded and foreign-funded banks.

[94] GATS, art. XVII:3.

Table 4.11 China's common banking law

Year	Title	Maker	No.
1992	Regulation on Administration of Savings (1992)	State Council	Decree 107
1996	Interim Measures for Authorization and Credit-Granting Business of Commercial Banks	PBC	Yinfa 403
1997	Measures for Payment and Settlement	PBC	Yinfa 393
1999	Measure for Punishment of Illegal Financial Activities	State Council	Decree 260
1999	Provisions on the True Name System of Personal Deposit Accounts	State Council	Decree 285
1999	Measures for Administration of Bank Card Business	PBC	Yinfa 17
2000	Guidelines for Risk Management of Off-Balance Sheet Business of Commercial Banks	PBC	Yinfa 344
2001	Regulation on Dissolution of Financial Institutions	State Council	Decree 324
2001	Measures of the PBC for Administrative Punishment	PBC	Decree 3
2001	Measures of the PBC for Administrative Reconsideration	PBC	Decree 4
2002	Measures for Administration of Establishment of Operation Networks in the Same City by Commercial Banks	PBC	Decree 3
2002	Interim Measures for Information Disclosure of Commercial Banks (not applicable from July 3, 2007)	PBC	Decree 6
2002	Unifying the Administrative Policy of Interest Rates of Foreign Currency Deposits and Loans for Chinese-funded and Foreign-Funded Financial Institutions	PBC	Announcement 4
2002	Guidelines for Internal Control of Commercial Banks (not applicable from July 3, 2007)	PBC	Announcement 19
2002	Guidelines for Provisioning Loan Loss Reserves	PBC	Yinfa 98
2003	PBC Law 2003 (Part)	NPC	President Decree 12
2003	Commercial Banking Law 2003 (Part)	NPC	President Decree 13
2003	Measures for Administration of Renminbi Bank Settlement Accounts	PBC	Decree 5
2003	Decision on Adjusting Administrative Means and Procedures of Banking Market Access	CBRC	Decree 1
2003	Measures for Administration of Financial Licences (revised in 2007 by Decree 8 of 2007)	CBRC	Decree 2

continued ...

Table 4.11 continued

Year	Title	Maker	No.
2003	Interim Measures for Administration of Service Price of Commercial Banks	CBRC & NDRC	Decree 3
2003	Guideline for Administration of Credit-Granting Risks for Group Customers (Revised in 2007 by Decree 12 of 2007)	CBRC	Decree 5
2004	Interim Measures for Administration of Derivative Products Business of Financial Institutions (revised in 2007 and 2011)	CBRC	Decree 1
2004	Measures for Administration of Linked Transactions between Commercial Banks and Insiders, Shareholders	CBRC	Decree 3
2004	Interim Measures for Administration of Supervisory Statistics of Commercial Banks	CBRC	Decree 6
2004	Measures of the CBRC for Administrative Punishment (revised in 2007 by Decree 5 of 2007)	CBRC	Decree 7
2004	Measures of the CBRC for Administrative Reconsideration	CBRC	Decree 8
2004	Guidelines for Market Risk of Commercial Banks	CBRC	Decree 10
2004	Implementation Measures of the PBC for Administrative Licencing	PBC	Decree 3
2004	Notice of the PBC on Implementing the System of Different Rates of Deposit Reserves	PBC	Yinfa 60
2004	Notice of the PBC on Administrative Works of Foreign Exchange Settlement and Sold	PBC	Yinfa 62
2004	Notice of the PBC on Increasing the Deposit Reserve Ratio	PBC	Yinfa 73
2004	Notice of the PBC on Adjusting Interest Rates of Deposits and Loans of Financial Institutions	PBC	Yinfa 251
2004	Provisions for administration of Reserves for Foreign Exchange Deposit	PBC	Yinfa 252
2004	Notice of the PBC on Strengthening Deposit Reserve Administration	PBC	Yinfa 302
2004	Guidelines for Fulfilling Duties in Credit-Granting Business of Commercial Banks	CBRC	Yinjianfa 51
2004	Guidelines for Risk Management of Real Estate Loans of Commercial Banks	CBRC	Yinjianfa 57
2004	Measures for Administration of Auto Loans	PBC & CBRC	Announcement 2
2004	Measures for Administration of Issuing Secondary Bonds by Commercial Banks	PBC & CBRC	Announcement 4
2005	Guidelines for External Sale Business of Commercial Banks	CBRC	Yinjianfa 20

Year	Title	Maker	No.
2005	Rules for Examination of Entry of Banking Institutions to the National Inter-Bank Loan Market	PBC	Announcement 3
2005	Interim Measures for Administration of Personal Financial Management Services Provided by Commercial Banks	CBRC	Decree 2
2005	Measures for Supervising Credit Assets Securitization Pilots of Financial Institutions	CBRC	Decree 3
2005	Reply of the CBRC General Office on Relevant Issues of Pledge of Commercial Bank Stock Right	CBRC	Yinjianbanfa 60
2005	Procedures of the CBRC for Statistics of On-Site Examination (Interim)	CBRC	Yinjianbanfa 79
2005	Guidelines for Risk Management of Personal Finance Business of Commercial Banks	CBRC	N/A
2005	Guidelines for Fulfilling Duties in Disposing Non-Performing Financial Assets	CBRC	Yinjianfa 72
2006	Banking Supervision Law (Part)	NPC Standing Committee	President Decree 58
2006	Anti-Money Laundering Law	NPC Standing Committee	President Decree No. 56
2006	Key Indicators for Risk-based Supervision of Commercial Banks (Interim)	CBRC	N/A
2006	Provisions of the CBRC on Implementation Procedures of Administrative Licencing	CBRC	Decree 1
2006	Administrative Measures Governing E-Banking Business	CBRC	Decree 5
2006	Guidelines for E-Banking Security Evaluation	CBRC	Yinjianfa 9
2006	Guidelines for Financial Innovations of Commercial Banks	CBRC	Yinjianfa 87
2006	Provisions on Anti-Money Laundering by Financial Institutions	PBC	Decree 1
2006	Measures for Administration of Reporting Large-Value Transactions and Suspicious Transactions of Financial Institutions	PBC	Decree 2
2007	Guidelines for Administration of Operational Risks of Commercial Banks	CBRC	Yinjianfa 42
2007	Measures for Administration of Inter-bank Loans	PBC	Decree 3
2007	Guidelines for Internal Control of Commercial Banks	CBRC	Decree 6
2007	Measures for Information Disclosure of Commercial Banks	CBRC	Decree 7

continued ...

Table 4.11 continued

Year	Title	Maker	No.
2007	Guidelines for Credit-Granting Business for Small Enterprises by Banks	CBRC	Yinjianfa 53
2007	Procedures of On-site Examination by the CBRC	CBRC	Yinjianfa 55
2007	Guidelines for Syndicated Loans	CBRC	Yinjianfa 68
2008	Guidelines for Consolidated Supervision of Banks (Interim)	CBRC	Yinjianfa 5
2008	Guidelines for Business Cooperation between Banks and Trust Companies	CBRC	Yinjianfa 83
2008	Guidelines for Administration of Risk of M&A Loans of Commercial Banks	CBRC	Yinjianfa 84
2009	Interim Measures for Administration of Fixed Assets Loans	CBRC	Decree 2
2009	Guidelines for Administration of Information Technology Risk of Commercial Banks	CBRC	Yinjianfa 19
2009	Guidelines for the Business of Project Finance	CBRC	Yinjianfa 71
2009	Guidelines for Administration of Reputation Risk of Commercial Banks	CBRC	Yinjianfa 82
2009	Guidelines for Administration of Liqudity Risk of Commercial Banks	CBRC	Yinjianfa 87
2009	Measures for Administration of Investment of Commercial Banks to the Shares of Insurance Companies	CBRC	Yinjianfa 98
2009	Guidelines for Administration of Interest Rate Risk of Banking Accounts in Commercial Banks	CBRC	Yinjianfa 106
2010	Guidelines for Supervision of Sound Salary of Commercial Banks	CBRC	Yinjianfa 14
2010	Guidelines for Administration of State or District Risks of Financial Institutions of Banking	CBRC	Yinjianfa 45
2010	Interim Measures for Administration of Current Fund Loans	CBRC	Decree 1
2010	Interim Measures for Administration of Personal Loans	CBRC	Decree 2
2011	Measures for Administration of Financial Derivatives Transactions of Banking Financial Institutions	CBRC	Decree 1
2011	Measures for Administration and Supervision of Credit Card Business of Commercial Banks	CBRC	Decree 2
2011	Measures for Administration of Leverage Ratio of Commercial Banks	CBRC	Decree 3
2011	Measures for Administration of Loan Loss Provisions of Commercial Banks	CBRC	Decree 4

Year	Title	Maker	No.
2011	Measures for Administration of Sale of Financing Products of Commercial Banks	CBRC	Decree 5
2011	Guidelines for Management of Risks of Off-balance Sheet Business of Commercial Banks	CBRC	Yinjianfa 31
2012	Measures for Administration of Capital of Commercial Banks (interim)	CBRC	Decree 1
2012	Guidelines for Green Credit	CBRC	Yinjianfa 4

Note: compiled by the author.

IV. Shortcomings of China's Banking Law Framework

China's banking law framework has been gradually set up since 1979, when the PRC started to allow foreign banks into the Chinese market. China's major banking legislative activities which started in 1995 and developed in 2003 have not changed the four-tiered and tripartite banking law framework. However, because of China's entry to the WTO, China's banking law framework is exposed to close scrutiny of the WTO obligations, especially GATS/WTO national treatment obligations. The following shortcomings are only some problems of China's banking law framework, which concern mainly the national treatment issue.

A. Susceptibility to Violation of GATS/WTO National Treatment Obligations

As Norton pointed out, "differing regulatory treatment can create competitive advantages and disadvantages among differently regulated banking institutions".[95] China's tripartite banking law framework with semi-segregated regulatory treatment tends to be unsuitable for creating an equal competition environment for foreign-funded and Chinese-funded banks. It is difficult for such a law framework to stand up to the test of national treatment obligations of the WTO.

Moreover, Chinese-funded banks are not fully regulated by a uniform domestic banking law system. In fact, the tripartite law framework contains many fragmented sub-frameworks, which also impair the equality of competition among Chinese-funded banks. Indeed, the national treatment issue in the field of banking services becomes complicated due to the fact that sometimes different treatment is given to different Chinese-funded banks. Because there is not a uniform treatment for Chinese-funded banks, a special treatment for foreign-funded banks lacks a definite counterpart for Chinese-funded banks. In other words, there are too many domestic counterparts. One method of treatment for foreign banking may be compared with several for domestic banking, which increases the possibilities of inconsistency with GATS/WTO national treatment obligations. For example,

[95] Joseph Jude Norton, *Capital Adequacy Standards: A Legitimate Regulatory Concern for Prudential Supervision of Banking Activities*? 49 Ohio St. L.J. 1299, 1355 (1989).

even if the treatment of foreign-funded banks is the same as the treatment of the state-owned commercial banks, it is still possible to be in violation of GATS/WTO national treatment if China grants more favourable treatment to the joint-stock commercial banks.

Furthermore, there is not a clear standard to determine whether a banking rule should be made only for Chinese-funded banks, or only for foreign-funded banks, or for all kinds of commercial banks. Even for a common banking rule, it is still possible that the rule is not completely "common" because some common banking rules apply *mutatis mutandis* to foreign-funded banks, and there is not a clear standard to determine whether a common banking rule should apply directly or *mutatis mutandis* to foreign-funded banks. Under the current tripartite banking law framework, China's banking regulators have broad discretion to adopt separate banking rules or common banking rules, which increases the potentialities of inconsistency with GATS/WTO national treatment obligations.

As a matter of fact, the China Service Schedule under the WTO itself has determined that a uniform banking law is preferred, with the exception of the specific commitments in the market access column and national treatment column, as well as the exception of the subsectors that China does not want to be inscribed into the Service Schedule.

It must be noted that, although a separate foreign banking law is susceptible to violating GATS/WTO national treatment obligations, such a separate foreign banking law itself is not sufficient to constitute a violation of national treatment obligations. In *China – Electronic Payment Services*, Document No. 49 was the Circular of the CBRC concerning Conduction of the Bank Card Business by Wholly Foreign-Funded Banks and Sino-Foreign Equity Joint Venture Banks, a typical foreign banking rule. The United States argued that Document No. 49 required that a wholly foreign-funded bank or a Sino-foreign equity joint venture bank that planned to issue bank cards should comply with the bank card business and technical standards formulated by the PBC, and this requirement to follow uniform business specifications and technical standards established a mandate that CUP be used to process all RMB bank card transactions.[96] The panel found that the special foreign banking rule "on its own" did not constitute a discriminatory treaetment to foreign-funded banks.[97]

B. Difficulty in Application

The confusions created by the four-tiered and tripartite law framework deeply affect the application of Chinese banking law. For bankers, especially foreign bankers who are not familiar with China's complex law framework, it is difficult to find a complete banking law list relating to foreign banking regulation. Even for Chinese bankers or Chinese banking law experts, it is usually a laborious job

96 *China – Electronic Payment Services*, WT/D413/R, ¶ 7.442.

97 *China – Electronic Payment Services*, WT/D413/R, ¶ 7.445.

to tell whether a banking rule is applicable only to Chinese-funded banks, or to foreign-funded banks, or to both. In fact, there is not an official banking law list to exhibit which law is applicable only to foreign-funded banks, which law is applicable only to Chinese-funded banks, or which law is applicable to both of them. It is hard to say that this is a transparency issue because now almost each banking law of the PRC is transparent and available to the public in many ways, including, inter alia, official journals and gazettes, such as the Gazette of the CBRC and the Gazette of the PBC. The issue is, in essence, a system shortcoming. There is neither a uniform mode to show clearly the application scope of banking regulations and rules, nor a presumption of general application.

The Commercial Banking Law 2003 and the Banking Supervision Law 2006 use a proviso clause, i.e., a *mutatis mutandis* mode, to apply to foreign-funded banks,[98] but the proviso clause which gives priority to foreign banking law brings about another question: how can one make certain whether there is a special rule for foreign-funded banks with respect to a banking activity? In other words, a *mutatis mutandis* approach itself cannot resolve the issue of scope of application. To make things more complex is the fact that many banking rules do not use the *mutatis mutandis* mode, but use uncertain ways to identify their scope of application. Some banking rules and normative documents apply to both Chinese-funded banks and foreign-funded banks by adding a clear definition article in the rules,[99] while some banking rules and normative documents do not have such a clear definition article, which makes it difficult to determine their application scope. For instance, it is hard to say whether the Guidelines for Banks to Develop Loan Business to Small Enterprises apply to foreign-funded banks.[100] Article 2 of the Guidelines only provides that banks in the Guidelines include policy banks, commercial banks

[98] See Commercial Banking Law 2003, art. 92; Banking Supervision Law 2006, art. 51.

[99] See, e.g., Guidelines for External Sale Business of Commercial Banks [*Shangye Yinhang Waibu Yingxiao Yewu Zhidao Yijian*], ¶ 2, issued by the CBRC on April 25, 2005, effective at the same date, CBRC *Yinjianfa* [2005] No. 20, GAZETTE OF THE CBRC 5–7 (2005, no. 4) (defining "commercial banks" as state-owned commercial banks, joint-stock commercial banks, city commercial banks, wholly-foreign-funded banks, Sino-foreign equity joint venture banks and foreign bank branches); see also Interim Measures for Information Disclosure of Commercial Banks [*Shangye Yinhang Xinxi Pilu Zanxing Banfa*], art. 2, issued on May 15, 2002, effective May 15, 2002, not applicable from July 3, 2007, *PBC Decree* [2002] No.6, art. 2, GAZETTE OF THE STATE COUNCIL 26–28 (2003, no. 6) (defining "commercial banks" as Chinese-funded commercial banks and foreign-funded commercial banks); Interim Measures for Administration of On-line Bank Business [*WangShang Yinhang Yewu Guanli Zanxing Banfa*], art. 2, PBC Decree [2001] No. 6, issued on June 29, 2001, effective June 29, 2001, GAZETTE OF THE STATE COUNCIL 45–47 (2002, no. 11).

[100] Guidelines for Banks to Develop Loan Business to Small Enterprises [*Yinhang Kaizhan Xiaoqiye Daikuan Yewu Zhidao Yijian*], issued by the CBRC on July 25, 2005, GAZETTE OF THE CBRC 2–5 (2005, no. 7), replaced by Guidelines on Credit-Granting Business for Small Enterprises by Banks, CBRC, Yinjianfa 53, 2007.

and rural cooperative banks.[101] However, according to the CBRC Notice on the Guidelines for Banks to Develop Loan Business to Small Enterprises,[102] foreign-funded banks are not included as the addressees of the Guidelines.[103] It may imply that "commercial banks" in the Guidelines exclude foreign-funded banks.

C. Legal Levels in Disorder

The normal legal levels of Chinese banking laws, regulations and rules are inconsistent with the current banking law framework. The Legislation Law provides that the effect of laws is higher than that of administrative regulations, local regulations and rules,[104] and administrative regulations should not conflict with laws.[105] As a consequence, under the regular order, the legal effect of the Commercial Banking Law 2003 should be higher than all banking regulations and banking rules. According to China's Legislation Law, the level of "laws" enacted by the NPC and its Standing Committee should be the core of the financial law system.[106] However, this is not the case for China's foreign banking law.

Under the current banking law framework, the legal effect of the FFB Regulation 2006 formulated by the State Council is higher than that of the Commercial Banking Law 2003 enacted by the Standing Committee of the NPC. The primary banking law with respect to foreign-funded banks in China is not the superior law, i.e., Commercial Banking Law 2003, but the subordinate regulation, i.e., FFB Regulation 2006. The disorder originates from the delegated legislation by the Commercial Banking Law itself.[107] From Article 92 of the Commercial Banking Law 2003, one cannot find the scope of the delegated legislation to the State Council. There is not any limitation on the delegated legislation right of State Council to make foreign banking regulations. Moreover, there is no expiry date for the delegated legislation; that is to say, the delegated legislation is short of a sunset law or a sunset provision.

---

[101] Id. art. 2, ¶ 3.

[102] CBRC Notice on the Guidelines for Banks to Develop Loan Business to Small Enterprises [CBRC Guanyu Yinfa *Yinhang Kaizhan Xiaoqiye Daikuan Yewu Zhidao Yijian de Tongzhi*], July 25, 2005, GAZETTE OF THE CBRC 2 (2005, no. 7).

[103] Id (addressing to only "policy banks, state-owned commercial banks, joint-stock commercial banks, city commercial banks, rural commercial banks and rural cooperative banks and city credit cooperatives).

[104] PRC Legislation Law, art. 79, ¶ 1.

[105] State Council Notice on Implementation of the PRC Legislation Law [*Guowuyuan Gongyu Guanche Shishi Zhonghua Renmin Gongheguo Lifafa de Tongzhi*], June 8, 2000, *Guofa* [2000] No. 11, Section 2, http://www.chinaiprlaw.com/flfg/flfg58.htm.

[106] PRC Legislation Law, art. 8(8).

[107] Commercial Banking Law 2003, art. 92; See also Commercial Banking Law 1995, art. 88.

This disorder erodes the authority and supremacy of the Commercial Banking Law 2003 and disrupts China's vertical banking framework. On the one hand, the Commercial Banking Law 2003 allows inferior regulations to prevail over superior laws, and makes the Commercial Banking Law 2003 a mere shell for regulating foreign-funded banks. With respect to foreign banking regulation, the Commercial Banking Law 2003 performs no function in practice. It is outshone, if not replaced, by the FFB Regulation 2006 and the DRI 2006. On the other hand, the Commercial Banking Law 2003 is also outweighed by the FFB Regulation 2006 and the DRI 2006. The FFB Regulation 2006 with seventy-three articles and the DRI 2006 with one hundred and thirty-four articles far outnumber the Commercial Banking Law 2003, which has only ninety-five articles.

Furthermore, the disorder may lead to internal conflicts among banking laws, regulations and rules, which may increase the risk of inconsistency with GATS/WTO national treatment obligations. For example, in the Measures for Punishment of Illegal Financial Activities (1999),[108] and the Regulation on Dissolution of Financial Institutions (2000),[109] both of which are effective, the PBC is still the sole banking regulator. This is one of the main problems of China's banking regulations issued by the State Council. Indeed, it is generally recognized that internal conflicts are present in many banking laws, regulations and rules of China.[110]

The CBRC has realized the disorder problem among Chinese banking law. In 2011, the CBRC issued the Announcement on the Result of Sorting Out Banking Rules.[111] The purpose of the sorting-out work was to harmonize the internal disorder and external disorder among Chinese banking law (mainly banking rules and other normative documents).[112] However, the effect of such work is limited due to the fact that the CBRC has no power to harmonize the banking laws enacted by the Standing Committee of the NPC or the banking regulations issued by the State Council.

---

108 Measures for Punishment of Illegal Financial Activities, State Council Decree No. 260.

109 Regulation on Dissolution of Financial Institutions, Decree No. 324 of the State Council.

110 Huang Yi, *Wei Shangye Yinhang Gaige he Fazhan Tigong Genghao de Falü Baozhang: Jinian Shangye Yinhangfa Banbu Shizhounian* [Providing Better Legal Protection for the Reform and Development of Commercial Banks: Commemorating the Tenth Anniversary of the Commercial Banking Law], ZHONGGUO JINRONG [CHINA FINANCE] 22 (2005, no. 13).

111 Announcement on the Result of Sorting Out Banking Rules [*Guanyu Fabu Yinhangye Guizhang Qingli Jieguo de Gonggao*] Yinjianfa [2011] No. 1, http://www.shui5.cn/article/41/47646.html (published January 5, 2011).

112 CBRC Replies to Reporters on the Result of Sorting Out Banking Rules, http://www.cbrc.gov.cn/chinese/home/docView/201101133B97ACB14F04E4EBFF9A98E2F2E5DB00.html (published January 1, 2011).

D. Lack of Stability

China's banking law framework is unstable. There is not a foreign banking law enacted by the NPC or its Standing Committee in the current banking law framework. China's foreign banking law system is mainly composed of the FFB Regulation 2006 and a great deal of foreign banking rules and normative documents, with the Commercial Banking Law 2003 only as a supplement. From the history of China's banking legislation, China's banking regulations and rules are very changeable. For instance, the PBC issued the Detailed Rules for Implementation of the Regulation on Administration of Foreign-Funded Financial Institutions in 1996 (DRI 1996),[113] but six years later, it was replaced by the Detailed Rules for Implementation of the Regulation on Administration of Foreign-Funded Financial Institutions (DRI 2002).[114] Only after two years was the DRI 2002 replaced by the Detailed Rules for Implementation of the Regulation on Administration of Foreign-Funded Financial Institutions (DRI 2004).[115] Then two years later, the DRI 2004 was replaced by the Detailed Rules for Implementation of the Regulation on Administration of Foreign-Funded Banks of 2006 (DRI 2006).[116] Moreover, in 2002, the PBC issued the Notice on Relevant Issue of Market Access of Foreign-Funded Bank after Promulgation of the DRI 2002.[117] Only after one year was the rule superseded by other banking rules.[118] The speed of the change of foreign

---

113 DRI 1996, PBC *Yinfa* [1996] No. 153, April 30, 1996, effective on the same day, http://www.people.com.cn/zixun/flfgk/item/dwjjf/falv/3/3-1-21.html.

114 DRI 2002, issued by China's former banking regulator, the PBC, on January 29, 2002, effective February 1, 2002, void on September 1, 2004, PBC Decree [2002] No. 1, Gazette of the State Council 37–45 (2002, no. 35).

115 DRI 2004, issued by the CBRC on July 26, 2004, effective September 1, 2004, void on December 11, 2006, CBRC Decree [2004] No. 4, in Gazette of the CBRC 1–20 (bound vol. 7–12, 2004, no. 7).

116 DRI 2006, issued by the CBRC on Novemeber 24, 2006, effective as of December 11, 2006, CBRC Decree [2006] No. 6, http://www.cbrc.gov.cn/chinese/home/jsp/docView.jsp?docID=2878 (Nov. 28, 2006).

117 Notice of the PBC on Relevant Issue of Market Access of Foreign-Funded Bank after Promulgation of the DRI 2002 [*Zhongguo Renmin Yinhang Guanyu Zhonghua Renmin Gongheguo Waizi Jinrong Jigou Guanli Tiaoli Shishi Xize Banbu hou Waizi Jinrong Jigou Shichang Zhunru Youguan Wenti de Tongzhi*], PBC *Yinfa* [2002] No. 22, January 29, 2002, http://www.fdi.org.cn/ltlaw/lawinfodisp.jsp?appId=1&language=gb&id=ABC00000000000003526.

118 Decision on Adjusting Administrative Means and Procedures of Banking Market Access [*Guanyu Tiaozheng Yinhang Shichang Zhunru Guanli Fangshi he Chengxu de Jueding*], CBRC Decree [2003] No. 1, issued on May 29, 2003, effective July 1, 2003, http://www.cbrc.gov.cn/mod_cn00/jsp/cn004002.jsp?infoID=277&type=1; Measures for Administration of Financial Licences [*Jinrong Xuekezheng Guanli Banfa*], CBRC Decree [2003] No.2, issued on May 31, 2003, effective July 1, 2003, http://www.cbrc.gov.cn/mod_cn00/jsp/cn004002.jsp?infoID=279&type=1.

banking rules often gives people the impression that China's banking law issued in the morning may be changed in the evening [*zhaoling xigai*].[119] The changeability of the banking rules makes China's banking law framework unstable, vertically and horizontally. The changeability of China's banking rules also increases the risk that it will be inconsistent with national treatment obligations.

V. Concluding Remarks

From the point of view of GATS/WTO national treatment, the main issue of China's banking law is not a simple issue that one or two articles in an individual banking law are inconsistent with national treatment obligations, but a system issue that the contemporary banking law framework is incongruous with the GATS/WTO national treatment as a whole. In the vertical banking law framework, the level of foreign banking law is lower than that of domestic banking law. The power of making foreign banking law is mainly in the hands of the administrative agency, i.e. the State Council, and the CBRC under the State Council. The three general banking laws enacted by the Congress, i.e. the NPC and its Standing Committee, are applicable to foreign-funded banks only in name, not in reality. Foreign-funded banks in China are regulated mainly by the FFB Regulation 2006 which is lower than the three general banking laws, and the DRI 2006 which is lower that the FFB Regulation 2006. Such discriminatory treatment in the framework for foreign-funded banks results in the lower status, less stability and less authority of foreign banking law.

In addition, looking at China's banking law framework from the horizontal perspective, one can find a framework in confusion. There is not a guideline or a legislative philosophy concerning the application of banking law. Sometimes it is difficult to identify precisely the scope of application of a banking regulation or a banking rule, let alone to predict its impact. In China, few people are able to demarcate clearly the boundary line between foreign banking law and domestic banking law. It is not fair to blame Chinese banking law experts. The confusing banking law framework itself is to blame. Indeed, China's banking law framework consists of a jumbled mishmash of laws, regulations, rules and other normative documents which are hard, if not impossible, to categorize. The tables in this chapter, which show vertically and horizontally China's banking laws, regulations,

[119] In Wu Zhipan's view, China's current banking law system is transitional. WU ZHIPAN, JINRONG QUANQIUHUA YU ZHONGGUO JINRONGFA [FINANCIAL GLOBALIZATION AND CHINESE BANKING LAW] 207 (Guangzhou Publishing House 2000); see also ZHONGHUA RENMIN GONGHEGUO YINHANGYE JIANDU GUANLIFA JIANGZUO [LECTURES ON THE BANKING SUPERVISION LAW OF THE PRC] 107 (Huang Yi (ed.), Zhongguo fazhi chubanshe 2004) (stating that there are many banking normative documents which only "treat the head when the head aches, treat the foot when the foot hurts" [*toutong yitou, jiaotong yijiao*]).

rules and other normative documents, are based on my research and study. They are neither exhaustive nor authoritative, but illustrative and indicative.

China's existing banking law framework can be further split up into several sub-frameworks based on the ownerships of banks, including law for state-owned banks, law for joint-stock banks, law for city commercial banks and law for rural commercial banks. The treatment for banks with different categories is often different, which further raises the possibilities of inequality between Chinese-funded banks and foreign-funded banks or, in other words, increases the risk of inconsistency with GATS/WTO national treatment obligations.

CHAPTER 5
More Favourable Treatment of Foreign-Funded Banks

While chapter 4 discusses the different positions of foreign-funded banks and Chinese-funded banks in China's existing banking law framework, i.e. the differences in form, this chapter focuses on one side of the different treatment between foreign-funded banks and Chinese-funded banks, i.e., more favourable treatment of foreign-funded banks, which are scattered throughout the four-tiered and tripartite banking law framework. The other side of the different treatment, i.e., less favourable treatment of foreign-funded banks is discussed in chapter 6.

In comparison with treatment of Chinese-funded banks, treatment of foreign-funded banks in China can be divided into three categories, i.e., identical treatment, more favourable treatment, and less favourable treatment. More favourable treatment and less favourable treatment are different treatment. On the one hand, identical treatment does not mean national treatment. According to GATS Article XVII:2, formally identical treatment may lead to discrimination against foreign-funded banks. On the other hand, different treatment does not necessarily mean the violation of national treatment obligations. Based on GATS Article XVII:2, formally different treatment may lead to national treatment. However, national treatment normally takes the form of identical treatment, while different treatment usually, albeit unnecessarily, indicates inconsistency with national treatment. Based on this assumption, I think that an emphasis must be placed on different treatment of foreign-funded banks in order to examine whether contemporary treatment of foreign-funded bank in China is consistent with national treatment. Thus the two types of different treatment – more favourable treatment and less favourable treatment – are the centre of chapter 5 and chapter 6.

I. More Favourable Treatment of Foreign-Funded Enterprises

The birth of more favourable treatment of foreign-funded enterprises is closely related to China's "reform and open" policy adopted at the end of the 1970s. The PRC promulgated the Sino-Foreign Equity Joint Venture Law in 1979,[1] the Wholly-

[1] PRC Sino-Foreign Equity Joint Venture Law, adopted at the Second Session of the Fifth NPC on July 1, 1979, effective July 1, 1979, Falü Huibian 1979–1984, at 168–71 (People's Publishing House 1985); Amended in 1990 and 2001, Falü Huibian 2001, at 58–62 (People's Publishing House 2002).

Foreign-Funded Enterprise Law in 1986,[2] and the Sino-Foreign Contractual Joint Venture Law in 1988.[3] In order to promote and encourage foreign investment in China, the three laws provide that foreign-funded enterprises enjoy more favourable treatment, such as a reduction of or exemption from taxes.[4] Because the more favourable treatment enjoyed by foreign-funded enterprises exceeds the treatment of Chinese-funded enterprises, it is called super-national treatment [*chao guomin daiyu*] by Chinese scholars.[5]

A. Income Tax Rates

The primary more favourable treatment enjoyed by foreign-funded banks in China is the preferential income tax rates. According to the Interim Regulation of Enterprise Income Tax,[6] Chinese-funded enterprises, including, inter alia, Chinese-funded banks, should pay income tax at the rate of 33 per cent.[7] In contrast, generally speaking, according to the Income Tax Law of Foreign-Funded Enterprises and Foreign Enterprises,[8] and the Detailed Rules for Implementation of the Income Tax Law of Foreign-Funded Enterprises and Foreign Enterprises,[9]

---

2 PRC Wholly-Foreign-Funded Enterprise Law [*Waizi Qiyefa*], adopted at the Fourth Session of the Sixth NPC on April 12, 1986, effective April 12, 1986, Falü Huibian 1986, at 63–66 (People's Publishing House 1987); Amended in 2000, Falü Huibian 2000, at 206–09 (People's Publishing House 2001).

3 PRC Sino-Foreign Contractual Joint Venture Law [*Zhongwai Hezuo Jingying Qiyefa*], adopted at the First Session of the Seventh NPC on April 13, 1988, effective April 13, 1988, Falü Huibian 1988 (People's Publishing House 1989); Amended in 2000, Falü Huibian 2000, at 198–203.

4 PRC Sino-Foreign Equity Joint Venture Law, supra note 1, art. 8; PRC Wholly-Foreign-Funded Enterprise Law, supra note 2, art. 17; PRC Sino-Foreign Contractual Joint Venture Law, supra note 3, art. 20.

5 Wang Fuquan, *Waishang Touzi Qiye yu Guomin Daiyu* [Foreign-Funded Enterprises and National Treatment], Yatai Jingji [Asian Economy] 59, 60–61 (1994, no. 4); Shan Wenhua, *Shichang Jingji yu Waishang Touzi Qiye de Guomin Daiyu Yanjiu* [Study on Market Economy and National Treatment of Foreign-Funded Enterprises] Zhongguo Faxue [Chinese Legal Science] 23, 25 (1994, no. 5).

6 Interim Regulation of Enterprise Income Tax [*Zhonghua Renmin Gongheguo Qiye Suodeshui Zanxing Tiaoli*], State Council Decree [1993] No. 137, issued on December 13, 1993, effective January 1, 1994, Gazette of the State Council 1393–96 (1993, no. 29).

7 Id. arts. 3, 18.

8 Income Tax Law of Foreign-Funded Enterprises and Foreign Enterprises [*Zhonghua Renmin Gongheguo Waishang Touzi Qiye he Waiguo Qiye Suodeshui Fa*], adopted at the Fourth Session of the Seventh NPC, President Decree No. 45, promulgated on April 9, 1991, effective July 1, 1991, Gazette of the State Council 533–37 (1991, no. 14).

9 Detailed Rules for Implementation of the Income Tax Law of Foreign-Funded Enterprises and Foreign Enterprises [*Zhonghua Renmin Gongheguo Waishang Touzi Qiye*

foreign-funded banks paid income tax at the rate of 15 per cent,[10] no matter whether they were established in the Special Economic Zones[11] or other regions in China.[12] From 1997 to 2007 the treatment of income tax of foreign-funded banks was divided into two rates. For the foreign currency business of foreign-funded banks, the income tax rate was still 15 per cent. For the local currency (RMB) business of foreign-funded banks, the income tax rate was the same as for Chinese-funded banks, i.e., 33 per cent.[13]

In March 2007, in order to equalize income tax rates of Chinese-funded enterprises and foreign-funded enterprises, the NPC promulgated the Enterprise Income Tax Law of the People's Republic of China (Enterprise Income Tax Law 2007),[14] combining two different income tax rates into one, i.e., 25 per cent.[15] According to Article 57 of the Enterprise Income Tax Law 2007, the enterprises which had been established before March 2007 could continue to enjoy the preferential income tax rates granted by relevant laws and regulations at that time till December 2012. That is to say, the income tax law provided a five year transitional period for those enterprises. From January 2013, both Chinese-funded enterprises and foreign-funded enterprises should pay income tax at that same rate (25 per cent),[16] unless otherwise provided by laws or treaties. The Income Tax Law of Foreign-Funded Enterprises and Foreign Enterprises of 1991 (for foreign-funded enterprises) and the Interim Regulation of Income Tax of Enterprises of 1993 (for Chinese-funded enterprises) were invalid in January 2008.[17]

---

he Waiguo Qiye Suodeshui Fa Shishi Xize], State Council Decree No. 85, promulgated on June 30, 1991, effective July 1, 1991, GAZETTE OF THE STATE COUNCIL 885–906 (1991, no. 25).

10 Income Tax Law of Foreign-Funded Enterprises and Foreign Enterprises, supra note 8, art. 7; Detailed Rules for Implementation of the Income Tax Law of Foreign-Funded Enterprises and Foreign Enterprises, id. art. 73(3).

11 There are six Special Economic Zones in China which enjoy special economic policy, including Shenzhen, Xiamen, Zhuhai, Shantou, Hainan and Kashi.

12 Notice on the Application of Income Tax Preference for Foreign-Funded Financial Institutions Established Outside the Special Economic Zones [*Guojia Shuiwu Zongju Guanyu Shezai Jingji Tequ Zhiwai Diqu de Waizi Jinrong Jigou Shiyong Suodeshui Youhui Wenti de Tongzhi*], issued by the State Administration of Taxation, April 3, 1995, *Guoshuihanfa* [1995] No. 138, http://www.gddoftec.gov.cn/wjmzc/Detail.asp?ID=949.

13 Notice on Relevant Tax Issues of RMB Business of Foreign-Funded Financial Institutions, issued by the Ministry of Finance, the State Administration of Taxation, the PBC [*Caizhengbu, Guojia Shuiwu Zongju, Zhongguo Renmin Yinhang Guanyu Waizi Jinrong Jigou Jingying Renminbi Yewu Shuishou Wenti de Tongzhi*], *Caishui* [1997] No. 52, ¶2, effective January 1, 1997, http://www.chinatax.gov.cn/view.jsp?code=200309241007458537.

14 Enterprise Income Tax Law 2007 [*Zhonghua Renmin Gongheguo Qiyue Suodeshui Fa*], adopted at the Fifth Session of the Tenth NPC on March 16, 2007, effective on January 1, 2008, President Decree No. 63, GAZETTE OF THE NPC 319–324 (2007, no. 3).

15 Enterprise Income Tax Law 2007, id. art. 4.

16 Enterprise Income Tax Law 2007, id. art. 57.

17 Enterprise Income Tax Law 2007, id. art. 60.

B. Income Tax Exemption and Reduction

The second more favourable treatment was related to foreign currency business. In addition to preferential income tax rate, foreign-funded banks also enjoyed "one-year exemption, two-year reduction" treatment, which means that, from the year of obtaining profits, foreign-funded banks would pay zero income tax in the first year, and would pay half income tax in the second year and the third year.[18] It must be noted that foreign-funded banks could not enjoy the "one-year exemption, two-year reduction" treatment for their RMB business.[19] The income tax exemption and reduction have been progressively repealed since the enforcement of the Enterprise Income Tax Law 2007.[20]

II. Trend of Repealing More Favourable Treatment of Foreign-Funded Banks

In November 2006, China revised its foreign banking regulation and detailed rules, which resulted in not only repealing non-prudential limitations on market access of foreign-funded banks, but also abolishing more favourable treatment of foreign-funded banks.

A. Lending Ratio Ceiling

According to Article 39 (4) of the Commercial Banking Law 2003, the ratio of the outstanding of loans granted to a single borrower to the balance of the capital of a Chinese domestic commercial bank may not exceed 10 per cent. But for a foreign-funded bank, the ratio was raised to 25 per cent by the FFFI Regulation 2001,[21] meaning that a foreign-funded bank could lend more to a single borrower under the same circumstances. However, the more favourable treatment of foreign-funded banks has been deleted by the FFB Regulation 2006, which means that the lending ratio ceiling for foreign-funded banks is also 10 per cent. On November 24, 2006, the CBRC issued an announcement to allow a one year grace period for a foreign bank branch to be incorporated into a wholly-foreign-funded commercial bank in China to meet the 10 per cent lending ratio ceiling.[22]

---

18 Detailed Rules for Implementing the Income Tax Law of Foreign-funded Enterprises and Foreign Enterprises, supra note 9, art. 75 (5).

19 Notice on Relevant Tax Issues of RMB Business of Foreign-Funded Financial Institutions, supra note 13, ¶ 2.

20 Enterprise Income Tax Law 2007, art. 57.

21 FFFI Regulation 2001, art. 26.

22 Announcement of the CBRC on Relevant Issues after Promulgation of the DRI 2006 [*Zhongguo Yinhangye Jiandu Guanli Weiyuanhui guanyu Zhonghua Renmin Gongheguo Waizi Yinhang Guanli Tiaoli Shishi Xize gongbuhou youguan wenti de gonggao*], CBRC

B. Legal Liability

Prior to December 2006, to some extent, the legal liability of foreign-funded banks was less than that of Chinese-funded banks. In the first place, those who established banks without the approval of the banking regulator would be prosecuted if committing a crime.[23] There was no difference at this point. But if the misconduct was not serious enough to constitute a crime, there would be a big difference. For foreign-funded banks, the unlawful income would be confiscated and a fine of one to five times unlawful income should be imposed. If there was no unlawful income or the unlawful income was less than RMB 100,000, a fine in the amount of RMB 100,000 to RMB 500,000 should be imposed.[24]

For Chinese-funded banks, the unlawful income would be confiscated, and a fine from one to five times unlawful income would be imposed for unlawful income higher than RMB 500,000. A fine to the amount of RMB 500,000 to RMB 2,000,000 would be imposed for the case of no unlawful income or the unlawful income lower than RMB 500,000.[25] Compared with the legal liability under the same condition, Chinese-funded banks had been exposed to a heavier fine, than foreign-funded banks had been.

The liability for failure to submit financial reports and relevant documents was also different. The fine on foreign-funded banks was not as heavy as that on Chinese-funded banks. For foreign-funded banks, the fine was from RMB 10,000 to RMB 100,000.[26] For Chinese-funded banks, from RMB 100,000 to RMB 300,000.[27]

However, since December 2006, according to the FFB Regulation 2006, foreign-funded banks have been exposed to a fine as heavy as that of Chinese-funded banks.[28] The revisions repealing more favourable treatment of foreign-funded banks reflect a trend that the Chinese government has begun to equalize competition conditions based on an understanding that national treatment implies identical treatment.

C. A Problematic Policy Recommendation from the PBC

In 2001, the PBC, i.e., the Chinese central bank, and the sole banking regulator in China at the time, issued a recommendation letter to the National Development

Yinjianfa [2006] No. 82, promulgated on November 24, 2006, para. 5, available at http://www.cbrc.gov.cn/chinese/home/jsp/docView.jsp?docID=2879.

23 FFFI Regulation 2001, art. 42; Commercial Banking Law 2003, art. 81.

24 FFFI Regulation 2001, art. 42.

25 Commercial Banking Law 2003, art. 83.

26 Id. art. 47.

27 Commercial Banking Law 2003, art. 80.

28 See FFB Regulation 2006, chapter 6.

and Plan Commission (NDPC),[29] the Ministry of Finance, the MOFTEC, the Legislative Affairs Office of the State Council, appealing for the elimination of more favourable treatment granted to foreign-funded banks.[30] The core of the letter was to eliminate the more favourable tax treatment enjoyed by foreign-funded banks and to establish a uniform tax regime for Chinese-funded banks and foreign-funded banks. It is understandable that the PBC aimed to equalize competitive conditions between Chinese-funded banks and foreign-funded banks with a uniform tax treatment, and the recommendation for a uniform tax treatment was not a wrong proposal per se, at least from the perspective of Chinese-funded banks.[31] The PBC's recommendation was also consistent with the trend of China's general tax reform, i.e., gradually unifying tax systems for different types of enterprise.[32] In fact, the NPC has unified the income tax rates by enacting the Enterprise Income Tax Law 2007. However, the PBC failed to justify its recommendation.

The PBC's rationale as indicated in the recommendation letter was China's WTO accession commitments. In fact, China did not make a WTO commitment to increase foreign-funded banks' tax rates or, in other words, to equalize tax treatment between Chinese-funded banks and foreign-funded banks. All Chinese WTO banking commitments were for the purpose of reducing limitations on foreign-funded banks, rather than increasing the limitations. Moreover, the WTO itself does not require or encourage its Members to eliminate more favourable treatment of foreign service suppliers. Although the more favourable treatment of foreign-funded banks may constitute reverse discrimination on Chinese-funded banks, such reverse discrimination has nothing to do with the WTO. China has begun to

---

[29] The NDPC [*Guojia Fazhan Jihua Weiyuanhui*] became the NDRC [National Development and Reform Commission, *Guojia Fazhan Gaige Weiyuanhui*] in 2003. See Decision of the First Session of the Tenth NPC on the Plan of Reforming the State Council Institutions, March 10, 2003, Gazette of the NPC 190–94 (2003, no. 2).

[30] Recommendation Letter of the People's Bank of China on Resolving the Preferential Treatment Issue Concerning Foreign-Funded Banks, March 12, 2001, PBC *Letter* [2001] No. 69.

[31] For example, some Chinese-funded banks launched an appeal for a uniform tax treatment in September 2005, http://finance.people.com.cn/GB/1040/3671623.html.

[32] Decision of the State Council on Reforming the Financial System, promulgated on December 25, 1993, effective December 25, 1993, *Guofa* [1993] No. 91, Gazette of the State Council 1488–96 (1993, no. 31); also available in 1 Shisida yilai Zhongyao Wenxian Xuanbian [Selections of Important Documents since the Fourteenth Conference] 593, 600 (Document Study Office of the Central Committee of the CCP (ed.), People's Publishing House 1996); see also Decision of the Central Committee of the CCP on Relevant Issues of the Socialist Market Economy [*Zhonggong Zhongyang guanyu Wanshan Shehui Zhuyi Shichang Jingji Tizhi Ruogan Wenti de Jueding*], adopted at the Third Plenum of the Sixteenth Central Committee of the CCP on October 14, 2003, ¶ 20, in 1 Shiliuda yilai Zhongyao Wenxian Xuanbian [Selections of Important Documents Since the Sixteenth Conference] 464, 472–73 (Document Study Office of the Central Committee of the CCP (ed.), Central Document Press 2005).

eliminate the reverse discrimination, such as imposing the same income tax rate (25 per cent) for both Chinese-funded enterprises and foreign-funded enterprises. This increase does not result from China's WTO obligations or commitments, but from China's sovereignty.[33] The WTO concern is whether China increases the income tax rate for foreign-funded banks without limit. The problem with the PBC's recommendation is not the recommendation itself, but its legal basis.

In my opinion, the legal basis for equalizing income tax rates of foreign-funded banks and Chinese-funded banks is neither China's WTO commitments, nor WTO national treatment obligations, but China's sovereignty, or more precisely, China's banking regulatory power. WTO national treatment obligations do not require absolute and formal equality between foreign-funded enterprises and Chinese-funded enterprises. WTO national treatment obligations neither require China to provide more favourable treatment to foreign-funded banks, nor demand China to repeal more favourable treatment.

It must be pointed out that misunderstanding the legal basis of equalizing the income tax rate of foreign enterprises with that of domestic enterprises is not only the problem of the PBC, but also that of the CBRC and the State Council. For example, the CBRC considered resolving the issue of more favourable treatment enjoyed by foreign-funded banks based on the same reason.[34] Former PRC Premier Zhu Rongji confused WTO national treatment with identical treatment and took the view that more favourable treatment was inconsistent with national treatment.[35]

III. Concluding Remarks

More favourable treatment of foreign-funded banks still exists in the current legal system of China. However, there is a trend to repeal the more favourable treatment so as to create equally competitive conditions for all kinds of enterprises. This trend is not inconsistent with WTO national treatment obligations. WTO national

---

33 For the relationship between sovereignty and the WTO, see John H. Jackson, *Sovereignty, the WTO, and Changing Fundamentals of International Law*, translated by Zhao Longyue, Zuo Haicong and Sheng Jianming, Social Sciences Academic Press (China), 2009.

34 Huang Yi, *Wei Shangye Yinhang Gaige he Fazhan Tigong Genghao de Falü Baozhang: Jinian Shangye Yinhangfa Banbu Shizhounian* [Providing Better Legal Protection for the Reform and Development of Commercial Banks: Commemorating the Tenth Anniversary of the Commercial Banking Law], ZHONGGUO JINRONG [CHINA FINANCE] 22 (2005, no. 13), at 24.

35 Zhu Rongji, *Shiying Xinqingkuang Xinrenwu, Nuli ba Liyong Waizi Gongzuo Tigao dao Xinshuiping* [Adapting to the New Situations and New Tasks, Striving to Improve the Work of Foreign Fund Use to a New Level], Speech at the National Working Conference on Foreign Fund, July 4, 2001, in 2 Shiwuda yilai Zhongyao Wenjian Xuanbian [Selections of Important Documents since the Fifteenth Conference] 1932, 1942 (Document Study Office of the Central Committee of the CCP (ed.), People's Publishing House 2003).

treatment obligations aim to prevent less favourable treatment of foreigners, rather than more favourable treatment.

More favourable treatment is not a reincarnation of the prerogative treatment enjoyed by foreigners (including foreign banks) in the late Qing Dynasty and the early ROC period discussed in chapter 1. More favourable treatment is granted by China of her own accord, while the prerogative treatment was given under the force of arms.

CHAPTER 6
Less Favourable Treatment of Foreign-Funded Banks

Less favourable treatment is the counterpart to preferential treatment. Chinese scholars usually call less favourable treatment sub-national treatment [*ci guomin daiyu* or *di guomin daiyu*].[1] Less favourable treatment refers to treatment accorded to foreigners and foreign enterprises less favourable than that accorded to Chinese and Chinese domestic enterprises. According to Article XVII of the GATS and the Annex on Financial Services, less favourable treatment of foreign-funded banks is incompatible, at least prima facie, with WTO national treatment obligations unless it is prudential. Less favourable treatment and more favourable treatment, as two types of different treatment, coexist in China's banking law framework. Chapter 5 analyses more favourable treatment accorded to foreign-funded banks while this chapter discusses less favourable treatment of foreign-funded banks in China.

I. Less Favourable Treatment of Foreign-Funded Banks

A. Limitations on Banking Investors

Under China's current banking law framework, for the establishment of wholly-foreign-funded banks or Sino-foreign equity joint venture banks, foreign investors must be financial institutions,[2] and the sole shareholder or majority shareholder of such a foreign-funded bank must be a commercial bank.[3] Furthermore, the

---

[1] For the early use of the term sub-national treatment, see Yu Meizhen, *Lun Woguo Liyong Waizi zhong Shishi Guomin Daiyu de Ruogan Wenti* [Relevant Issues of Implementing National Treatment When Using Foreign Investment in China], JOURNAL OF SOUTH CHINA NORMAL UNIVERSITY (Social Science Edition) 10 (1997, no. 1); Li Jianmei, *Yinjin Waizi yu Guomin Daiyu* [Introduction of Foreign Investment and National Treatment], YUNNAN FINANCE AND TRADE COLLEGE JOURNAL 29, 30 (1997, no. 6).

[2] FFB Regulation 2006, arts 10, 11; see also the Measures of the CBRC for Granting Administrative Licences to Foreign-Funded Financial Institutions [*Zhongguo Yinhangye Jiandu Guanli Weiyuanhui Waizi Jinrong Jigou Xingzheng Xuke Shixiang Shishi Banfa*], art. 8(1), issued on January 12, 2006, effective from February 1, 2006, CBRC Decree [2006] No. 4, in COMPENDIUM OF CHINA BANKING RULES 309–50.

[3] FFB Regulation 2006, arts. 10, 11; see also the Measures of the CBRC for Granting Administrative Licences to Foreign-Funded Financial Institutions, id. art. 8(2).

sole foreign shareholder or majority shareholder should have established a representative office in China and its total assets shall not be less than USD 10 billion.[4]

However, Chinese banking investors are not limited to Chinese banks or other financial institutions. Chinese industrial enterprises can also be banking investors.[5] In comparison with conditions on investment made by Chinese banking investors, China imposes stricter limitations on foreign banking investors. The scope of foreign banking investors is narrower than that of Chinese banking investors. It is unnecessary for the biggest Chinese shareholder of a Chinese bank or an equity joint venture bank to be a commercial bank. The different treatment, or the stricter requirement for the qualification of foreign banking investors, seems to be inconsistent with national treatment obligations of the GATS.

Nevertheless, the inconsistency may be offset to some extent by China's specific WTO commitments in banking services. In the China Schedule, there are two special sentences. One is "foreign financial institutions who meet the following condition are permitted to establish a subsidiary of a foreign bank …".[6] The other is "foreign financial institutions who meet the following condition are permitted to establish a Chinese-foreign joint bank …".[7] It is clear that China used the term "foreign financial institutions" rather than "foreigners or foreign institutions" when China made the banking specific commitments on market access. Thus, China may argue that China only allows "foreign financial institutions" to make investment in Sino-foreign equity joint venture banks and wholly-foreign-funded banks, and this argument seems reasonable. But "foreign financial institutions" are not equivalent to foreign commercial banks. Indeed, the concept of "foreign financial institutions" is broader than the term of foreign commercial banks. "Foreign financial institutions" refer to financial institutions that have registered and established outside the territory of China, approved or recognized by the financial

---

4 FFB Regulation 2006, arts 10, 11.

5 Interim Provisions on Investing in Financial Institutions [*Guanyu xiang Jinrong Jigou Touzi Rugu de Zanxing Guiding*], PBC *Yinfa* [1994] No. 186, http://finance.sina.com.cn/roll/20040310/1454664849.shtml. The Interim Rules shall be implemented, interpreted, or revised by the CBRC, see Announcement of the PBC and the CBRC [2004] No. 20, December 17, 2004, Gazette of the PBC 3–8 (2004, nos 18–19), Annex 2; see also the Measures of the CBRC for Granting Administrative Licences to Chinese-Funded Commercial Banks [*Zhongguo Yinhangye Jiandu Guanli Weiyuanhui Zhongzi Shangye Yinhang Xingzheng Xuke Shixiang Shishi Banfa*], issued on January 12, 2006, effective as of February 1, 2006, CBRC Decree [2006] No. 2, in Compendium of China Banking Rules 229–60, art. 8 (providing that promoters of Chinese-funded joint-stock commercial banks can be inland financial institutions, overseas financial institutions, inland non-financial institutions and other promoters approved by the CBRC).

6 The China Schedule, WT/ACC/CHN/49/Add.2, 7B.

7 Id.

regulators of the home countries or home regions,[8] including financial holding companies, commercial banks, securities firms, insurance companies, funds, all of which have been registered and established in foreign countries, and other foreign financial institutions recognized by the CBRC.[9] The requirement in the FFB Regulation 2006 of being a commercial bank to be the biggest shareholder or the sole shareholder of an equity joint venture bank or a wholly-foreign-funded bank is stricter than the condition of being a "foreign financial institution" in China's WTO Schedule. The State Council has not provided the background, purpose or intention of this requirement.

Although China has loosened the limitations on foreign banking investors,[10] allowing overseas financial institutions, including "international financial institutions" and "foreign financial institutions" to make equity investment in Chinese-funded financial institutions,[11] China has not changed the strict limitations on foreign banking investors when they invest to establish equity joint venture banks or wholly-foreign-funded banks in China.

Furthermore, foreign-funded enterprises, including, inter alia, Sino-foreign equity joint venture banks or wholly-foreign-funded banks, which register in China as Chinese legal persons, and do not belong to "foreign financial institutions", are forbidden to invest in Chinese-funded financial institutions.[12] But Chinese-funded commercial banks, except the four state-owned commercial banks, are allowed to invest in Chinese-funded financial institutions.[13] Chinese-funded enterprises are also permitted to make investment in Chinese-funded financial institutions.[14] This different treatment between Chinese-funded banks and foreign-funded banks investing in Chinese-funded financial institutions may be in violation of national treatment obligations of the GATS/WTO, unless China proves that it is prudential.

---

8 FFB Regulation 2006, art. 3, ¶ 1.

9 Measures for Administration of Equity Investment in Chinese-Funded Financial Institutions by Overseas Financial Institutions [*Jingwai Jinrong Jigou Touzi Rugu Zhongzi Jinrong Jigou Guanli Banfa*], issued by the CBRC on December 5, 2003, effective December 31, 2003, CBRC *Decree* [2003] No. 6, GAZETTE OF THE STATE COUNCIL 27–29 (2004, no. 15), art. 2, ¶ 2.

10 Id. art. 2, ¶ 1.

11 Foreign financial institutions refer to financial holding companies, commercial banks, securities companies, insurance companies, funds, and other foreign financial institutions registered in foreign countries and approved to invest in Chinese-funded financial institutions by the CBRC; Chinese-funded financial institutions refer to Chinese-funded commercial banks, city credit cooperatives, rural credit cooperatives, trust and investment companies, enterprise group finance companies, finance leasing companies, or other Chinese-funded financial institutions which have been approved and established in China. See id. art. 2, ¶¶ 2, 3.

12 Interim Provisions on Investing in Financial Institutions [*Guanyu Xiang Jinrong Jigou Touzi Rugu de Zanxing Guiding*], PBC *Yinfa* [1994] No. 186, art. 12, http://www.hecom.gov.cn/wtofadian/wen/fagui/d1bf/d13p/d13p116.htm.

13 Id. art. 5.

14 Id. art. 11.

Wang Zhaoxing, then assistant to the CBRC Chairman, stated in a press conference held by the State Council on November 16, 2006, that the reason for the different treatment is based on the fact that commercial banks were financial enterprises with high risks and should have shareholders with high qualification.[15]

B. Special RMB Capital Adequacy Ratio

The Commercial Banking Law 2003 and the FFB Regulation 2006 stipulate that the capital adequacy ratio of foreign-funded banks shall not be less than 8 per cent.[16] Before 2013, the Measures for Administration of Capital Adequacy Ratio of Commercial Banks,[17] which contained an 8 per cent capital adequacy ratio requirement,[18] applied to Chinese-funded banks, wholly-foreign-funded banks and Sino-foreign equity joint venture banks.[19] On the surface, it seems that the 8 per cent capital adequacy ratio is equally applicable to Chinese-funded banks and foreign-funded banks in China.

In addition to the general 8 per cent capital adequacy ratio requirement for foreign-funded banks, there is a special 8 per cent RMB capital adequacy ratio requirement for foreign-funded banks. Article 45 of the FFB Regulation 2006 states as follows:

> For a foreign bank branch, the ratio of the share of RMB assets in the total amount of its working capital- plus reserves to the share of RMB assets in its risk assets shall not be less than 8 per cent.
> The banking regulatory institution of the State Council may increase the above ratio for those foreign bank branches with higher risks and weaker risk management ability.

The special 8 per cent ratio for RMB assets, in fact, adds a new capital requirement for foreign bank branches. As a result, foreign bank branches cannot make up the inadequacy of RMB assets through provision of additional foreign currency assets. More importantly, there is no counterpart requirement for Chinese bank branches to keep a separate 8 per cent ratio for foreign currency assets, implying that Chinese-funded banks may offset the inadequacy of foreign

---

15 Wang Zhaoxing, Press Conference on the FFB Regulation 2006, November 16, 2006, http://zhuanti.cbrc.gov.cn/subject/subject/duiwai/main.do?newsclass=8a8183d60f529195010f5648c28b0009&levelnum=2.

16 Commercial Banking Law 2003, art. 39(1); FFB Regulation 2006, art. 40.

17 Measures for Administration of Capital Adequacy Ratio of Commercial Banks, CBRC Decree [2004] No. 2, issued on February 23, 2004, effective from March 1, 2004, amended on July 3, 2007, repealed on January 1, 2013 by Measures for Administration of Capital of Commercial Banks (Interim).

18 Id. art. 7.

19 Id. art. 2.

currency assets by increasing their RMB assets. Is the measure prudential and compatible with paragraph 2 of the Annex on financial services? At least in the view of Chinese delegation to the WTO, such special requirement for RMB assets is to reduce the risks for RMB assets of foreign-funded financial institutions.[20]

C. Limitations on Foreign Exchange Working Capital

It is unnecessary for a Chinese-funded bank to allocate a minimum amount of foreign exchange working capital to its branches to engage in foreign exchange business.[21] Article 37(5) of Measures of the CBRC for Granting Administrative Licences to Chinese-Funded Commercial Banks (CBRC 2006 Decree no. 2) only provides that a state-owned commercial bank or a joint-stock commercial bank must allocate its branch working capital no less than RMB 100 million or other convertible currencies with equal value.

It seems that a wholly-foreign-funded bank or a Sino-foreign equity joint venture bank has the same treatment as to working capital for its branch.[22] However, if a foreign bank wants to set up a branch in China, it should allocate both RMB working capital and foreign exchange working capital to its Chinese branch, and the minimum working capital requirements are higher. If a foreign bank branch wants to engage in all foreign exchange business and all RMB business in China, the working capital of the foreign bank branch shall not be less than RMB 300 million or other convertible currencies with equal value, among which RMB working capital shall not be less than 100 million.[23] As a result, a foreign bank branch has to bear the burden of not only the high working capital requirements, but also double working capital requirements, i.e., RMB working capital requirement and foreign exchange working capital requirement. The burden is obviously heavier than that of a Chinese-funded bank branch.

---

[20] GUOWUYUAN FAZHI BANGONGSHI CAIZHENG JINRONG FAZHISI [FINANCIAL LAW DEPARTMENT OF THE LEGISLATIVE AFFAIRS OFFICE OF THE STATE COUNCIL], ZHONGHUA RENMIN GONGHEGUO WAIZI JINRONG JIGOU GUANLI TIAOLI WENDA [QUESTIONS & ANSWERS OF THE REGULATION ON ADMINISTRATION OF FOREIGN-FUNDED FINANCIAL INSTITUTIONS OF THE PRC] 52 (CITIC Publishing House 2002).

[21] Notice on Abolishing Limitations on Working Capital of Foreign Exchange for Branches and Sub-branches of Banks [*Quxiao Yinhang Fenzhi Jigou Waihui Yingyun Zijin Xianzhi de Tongzhi*], issued by the PBC on January 4, 2000, PBC *Yinfa* [2000] No. 9, http://www.szjr.net/szjr/control/ProcessServlet?eventId=239&article_id=113, not applicable from July 3, 2007.

[22] FFB Regulation 2006, art. 8(2).

[23] DRI 2006, art. 50.

D. Information Disclosure Requirement

In general, commercial banks in China, including Chinese-funded commercial banks, wholly-foreign-funded banks, Sino-foreign equity joint venture banks and foreign bank branches, are obliged to disclose information according to the Interim Measures for Information Disclosure of Commercial Banks issued by the PBC in 2002[24] and the Measures for Information Disclosure of Commercial Banks issued by the CBRC in 2007.[25] According to an exception clause in the banking rules, commercial banks whose total assets are lower than RMB 1 billion or whose deposit balance is lower than RMB 500 million are exempt from information disclosure.[26] It seems that the exception clause is equally applicable to Chinese-funded and foreign-funded banks.[27] However, in practice, it is impossible for foreign-funded banks in China to take advantage of the exception clause owing to the fact that foreign-funded banks in China are usually large banks. This fact is caused by China's market access limitations on foreign banking services in the GATS/WTO. For example, a foreign financial institution is permitted to establish a subsidiary or a Sino-foreign equity joint venture bank in China only if its total assets are more than USD 10 billion.[28] Furthermore, article 8(1) of the FFB Regulation 2006 provides that the minimum registered capital of a wholly-foreign-funded bank or a Sino-foreign equity joint venture bank is RMB 1 billion. Thus the total assets of a wholly-foreign-funded bank or a Sino-foreign equity joint venture bank are definitely higher than RMB 1 billion so that a foreign-funded bank is not qualified to be exempt from information disclosure, while it is possible for small and medium Chinese-funded banks to be exempt from information disclosure. Thus, the exception clause may constitute a *formally identical treatment* resulting

---

24 Interim Measures for Information Disclosure of Commercial Banks [*Shangye Yinhang Xinxi Pilu Zanxing Banfa*], art. 2, issued on May 15, 2002, effective May 15, 2002, PBC Decree [2002] No. 6, GAZETTE OF THE STATE COUNCIL 26–28 (2003, no. 6). From the end of 2004, the PBC rule was exercised by the CBRC, Announcement of the PBC and the CBRC, Annex 2 [2004] No. 20, December 17, 2004. From July 2007, the PBC rule was not applicable.

25 Measures for Information Disclosure of Commercial Banks, CBRC Decree [2007] No. 7, http://www.cbrc.gov.cn/chinese/files/2007/200707253587F2C2CEDEF631FFA512 30C0343C00.doc.

26 Interim Measures for Information Disclosure of Commercial Banks, art. 29, PBC Decree [2002] No.6; Measures for Information Disclosure of Commercial Banks, art. 30, CBRC Decree [2007] No. 7.

27 Measures for Information Disclosure of Commercial Banks, art. 2, CBRC Decree [2007] No. 7.

28 The China Schedule, WT/ACC/CHN/49/Add.2, 7B, Column of Limitations on Market Access (3).

in less favourable treatment to foreign-funded banks, i.e., de facto discrimination against foreign-funded banks.[29]

E. Examination Period for Establishment Application

The examination periods for the application for establishment of Chinese-funded banks and foreign-funded banks are different. On the one hand, upon receipt of application documents for establishment of a foreign-funded bank, the CBRC shall make decision, within six months, on whether to accept or reject the application.[30] On the other hand, for the application for establishment of a Chinese-funded bank, the CBRC shall make such a decision within a shorter period of time, i.e. four months.[31] The longer examination period may be justified by China for the complicated and difficult process of investigating and examining the application information provided by foreign investors.

F. Limitation on the Amount of an Individual Time Deposit

According to Paragraph 2 of Article 31 of the FFB Regulation 2006, a foreign bank branch in China may take in a time deposit from an individual in the territory of China of no less than RMB 1 million per transaction. In contrast, there is not a similar limitation on a Chinese domestic bank branch for the same business. In light of the CBRC's interpretation, such a limitation on the amount of a time deposit is prudential because it aims to protect the interests of the Chinese depositors, or, in other words, such a limitation is not a less favourable treatment, but a more favourable treatment to foreign banks.[32] Such an interpretation lacks sufficient legal foundation.

II. Less Favourable Treatment of Foreign-Funded Banks Before 2007

China revised its foreign-funded banking regulation and rules at the end of 2006. Some articles according less favourable treatment of foreign-funded banks in the FFFI Regulation 2001 and DRI 2004 were deleted.

---

29 GATS, art. XVII:2.

30 FFB Regulation 2006, art. 15; see also the Measures of the CBRC for Granting Administrative Licences to Foreign-Funded Financial Institutions, supra note 2, art. 11, ¶ 3.

31 Measures of the CBRC for Granting Administrative Licences to Chinese-Funded Commercial Banks, CBRC Decree [2006] No. 2, art. 15, revised on December 28, 2006.

32 Wang Zhaoxing, Press Conference on the FFB Regulation 2006, November 16, 2006, http://zhuanti.cbrc.gov.cn/subject/subject/duiwai/main.do?newsclass=8a8183d60f529195010f5648c28b0009&levelnum=2.

A. Minimum Business Operation Period and Profitability Requirements

According to the DRI 2004, two of the conditions for wholly-foreign-funded banks and Sino-foreign equity joint venture banks to set up branches in China were more than three years' business operations in China and being profitable for two consecutive financial years.[33] However, one could not find similar conditions for Chinese-funded banks to set up branches. Furthermore, the two conditions also deviated from China's GATS/WTO commitments. In accordance with the China Schedule, "Qualifications for foreign financial institutions to engage in *local currency business* are as follows: three years' business operations in China and being profitable for two consecutive years prior to the application, otherwise, none".[34] Evidently, the three years' business operation requirement and being profitable for two consecutive years should be conditions for foreign-funded banks to do *local currency business* in China, not qualifications for foreign banks to set up branches in China. The DRI 2004 kept the two conditions, but changed their places of application, which is like, as a Chinese saying goes, putting Zhang's hat on Li's head [*Zhangguan Lidai*]. This limitation in the DRI 2004 is replaced by Article 13 of DRI 2006 stating: "To set up a branch, a wholly-foreign-funded bank or a Sino-foreign equity joint venture bank shall meet the prudential conditions formulated by the CBRC." Although the DRI 2006 does not clearly declare the deletion of the limitation in the DRI 2004, its disappearance from the DRI 2006 itself shows the limitation has been relinquished.

B. Limitation on Accumulated Working Capital for Branches

Before the end of 2006, in addition to the minimum business operation period and profitability requirements, for establishing a branch in China a wholly-foreign-funded bank or an equity joint venture bank shall inject no less than RMB 100 million as working capital [*yingyun zijin*] for the new branch, but accumulated working capital of the bank for setting up branches should not exceed 60 per cent of its registered capital [*zhuce ziben*].[35] As for Chinese-funded banks to establish branches in China, the accumulated working capital allocated to all branches should not exceed 60 per cent of the total amount of capital [*zibenjin zong'e*] of

---

[33] DRI 2004, art. 17(1); Measures of the CBRC for Implementing Administrative Licensing Matters of Foreign-Funded Financial Institutions [*Zhongguo Yinhangye Jiandu Guanli Weiyuanhui Waizi Jinrong Jigou Xingzheng Xuke Shixiang Shishi Banfa*], arts 38 (1) (2), issued on January 12, 2006, effective from February 1, 2006, CBRC Decree [2006] No. 4, http://www.cbrc.gov.cn/mod_cn00/jsp/cn004002.jsp?infoID=2234&type=1.

[34] The China Schedule, WT/ACC/CHN/49/Add.2, 7B, Column of Limitations on Market Access (3).

[35] DRI 2004, art. 17(3); Measures of the CBRC for Implementing Administrative Licensing Matters of Foreign-Funded Financial Institutions, CBRC Decree [2006] No. 4, art. 38 (4).

the bank.[36] Although the ratio was the same, the denominators were different. The former's denominator was *registered capital*, while the latter's denominator was *total amount of capital*.

The *total amount of capital* consisted of core capital and supplementary capital.[37] Core capital comprised paid-up capital or common stocks, reserves, capital surplus, retained earnings and minority interests.[38] Supplementary capital was composed of revaluation reserves, general loan-loss reserves, preference shares, convertible bonds and long-term subordinated debt.[39] According to the Commercial Banking Law 2003, the *registered capital* of a commercial bank was equal to *paid-up capital*,[40] which was part of the core capital in the *total amount of capital*. In other words, *registered capital* was only one of the components of the *total amount of capital*. Thus, the amount of registered capital was lower than the total amount of capital. As a consequence, under the same conditions, 60 per cent of registered capital was below 60 per cent of the total amount of capital, which would mean that the working capital allocated by a foreign-funded bank to set up branches would be less than the working capital allocated by a Chinese-funded bank to set up branches. It also meant that, in like circumstances, Chinese-funded banks were able to establish more branches than foreign-funded banks. Undoubtedly, this would modify the conditions of competition in favour of Chinese-funded banks, which was likely to be inconsistent with national treatment obligations under Article XVII of the GATS.

This limitation in the DRI 2004 was not adopted by the DRI 2006.

C. Foreign Exchange Deposit Limitation

Article 30 of the FFFI Regulation 2001 provided: "Foreign currency deposits taken within the territory of China by any foreign-funded financial institution shall not exceed 70 per cent of its total foreign exchange assets in China." The purpose of this limitation was to encourage foreign-funded banks to use foreign exchange

---

36 Commercial Banking Law 2003, art. 19, ¶ 2; see also the Interim Provisions of Administration of Rural Commercial Banks [*Nongcun Shangye Yinhang Guanli Zanxing Guiding*], art. 13, CBRC *Yinjianfa* [2003] No. 10, issued on September 12, 2003, effective September 12, 2003, Gazette of the State Council 29–35 (2004, no. 15) (providing that the accumulated working capital allocated to all branches of a rural commercial bank shall not exceed 60 per cent of the total amount of capital of the rural commercial bank).

37 Measures for Administration of Capital Adequacy Ratio of Commercial Banks, CBRC Decree [2004] No. 2, art. 12, ¶ 1.

38 Id. art. 12, ¶ 2.

39 Id. art. 12, ¶ 3.

40 For the definitions of paid-up capital and other definitions of components of capital, see id. Annex 1, "Capital Definitions".

funds from overseas so as to facilitate China's domestic economic development.[41] But this foreign exchange deposit limitation on foreign-funded banks was not listed as a limitation measure for market access or national treatment in the China Schedule. In contrast, there was no foreign exchange deposit limitation on Chinese-funded banks. Theoretically, Chinese-funded banks could take as many foreign exchange deposits as possible. Therefore, the 70 per cent ceiling ratio for foreign-funded banks[42] was inconsistent with GATS/WTO market access and national treatment obligations, unless Chinese authorities were able to prove that the ceiling ratio is a prudential regulatory measure. The less favourable treatment of foreign-funded banks in the FFFI Regulation 2001 does not exist in the FFB 2006, which means that the limitation has been deleted from Chinese banking law.

III. Less Favourable Treatment and China's WTO Practice in Banking Services

A. Transitional Reviews of the WTO

In order to monitor China's compliance with WTO obligations, the WTO designed the Transitional Review Mechanism (TRM) for China.[43] The TRM was unique. Nothing similar could be found in any other WTO agreements or in WTO history.[44] With this mechanism, the General Council and the subsidiary bodies of the WTO reviewed the implementation by China of the WTO agreements and the provisions of the China Accession Protocol.[45] The review took place after Chinese accession to the WTO in each year for eight years. A final review was made in year 10 (2011).

---

41 Questions & Answers of the Regulation on Administration of Foreign-Funded Financial Institutions of the PRC 55 (CITIC Publishing House 2002).

42 It must be noted that the foreign exchange deposit ratio of foreign banks was 40 per cent in the FFFI Regulation 1994, stricter than the current 70 per cent limitation. See the FFFI Regulation 1994, art. 30.

43 Id. Part I:18.

44 See a Chinese representative's speech in the meeting of Committee on Trade in Financial Services of the WTO on 22 July 2002, S/FIN/M/36, ¶ 56 (September 26, 2002).

45 There are in total sixteen WTO subsidiary bodies to be involved in TRM, including: Council for Trade in Goods, Council for Trade-Related Aspects of Intellectual Property Rights, Council for Trade in Services, Committee on Balance-of-Payments Restrictions, Committee on Market Access (covering also ITA), Committee on Agriculture, Committee on Sanitary and Phytosanitary Measures, Committee on Technical Barriers to Trade, Committee on Subsidies and Countervailing Measures, Committee on Anti-Dumping Measures, Committee on Customs Valuation, Committee on Rules of Origin, Committee on Import Licensing, Committee on Trade-Related Investment Measures, Committee on Safeguards, Committee on Trade in Financial Services.

Compared with the Trade Policy Review Mechanism (TPRM)[46] applicable to other WTO Members, the TRM was relatively strict.[47] Through the TRM, other WTO Members could monitor and urge China to make its laws, regulations, rules and relevant measures consistent with the WTO agreements. For China, the TRM was both a burden and an opportunity. In each year's review process, China had to face challenges from other WTO Members, answer various difficult questions on its domestic laws, regulations, rules, or policies, and defend itself with every possible reason. In view of the importance of the TRM, the General Office of the State Council of the PRC [*Zhonghua Renmin Gongheguo Guowuyuan Bangongting*][48] issued to local governments at provincial level, departments and commissions of the central government a special circular on how to deal with this matter.[49] In this circular, the General Office pointed out the main reason for the significance of the TRM affairs; that is, the TRM, as well as notification and enquiry matter, had a direct impact on China's reputation in the WTO.[50]

From 2002 to 2011, the WTO made nine rounds of transitional reviews relating to China. With respect to China's financial services, some WTO members showed an interest in China's treatment of foreign-funded banks, including the United

---

[46] TPRM, in THE LEGAL TEXTS: THE RESULTS OF THE URUGUAY ROUND OF MULTILATERAL TRADE NEGOTIATIONS 380–82 (Cambridge Univ. Press 1999).

[47] Under the TPRM, the ordinary frequency of reviews is once every two years, four years, mostly six years, or even longer for least-developed-country Members, based on the impact of individual Members on the functioning of the multilateral trading system. See TPRM, id. § C(ii).

[48] The State Council [*Guowuyuan*] is China's highest administrative agency and responsible for the National People's Congress and its Standing Committee. See Articles 85 and 92 of the PRC Constitution [*Xianfa*], adopted at the Fifth Session of the Fifth NPC on December 4, 1982, effective December 4, 1982, amended in 1988, 1993, 1999, 2004, in Falü Huibian 2004, at 1–83 (People's Publishing House 2005). The General Office of the State Council is the internal organ led by the secretary-general of the State Council, dealing with routine business of the State Council. See Article 7 of the Organic Law of the State Council [*Guowuyuan Zuzhi Fa*], adopted at the Fifth Session of the Fifth NPC on December 10, 1982, effective December 10, 1982, Zhonghua Renmin Gongheguo Guowuyuan Gongbao [Gazette of the State Council of the PRC, hereinafter GAZETTE OF THE STATE COUNCIL] 948–49 (1982, no. 20).

[49] Circular of the General Office of the State Council on Accomplishing the Work of Notification, Enquiry and Review of Trade Policies after China's Accession to the WTO [*Guowuyuan Bangongting Guanyu Zuohao Woguo Jiaru Shijie Maoyi Zuzhi Youguan Maoyi Zhengce Tongbao Zixun he Shenyi Gongzuo de Tongzhi*], *Guobanfa* [2002] No. 50, September 29, 2002, GAZETTE OF THE STATE COUNCIL 16 (2002, no. 31).

[50] Id. § 1.

States, European Communities,[51] Canada, Australia, Japan and Chinese Taipei.[52] Table 6.1 shows the concerns that were expressed in the nine-round TRM meetings relating to national treatment and China's banking law. The table is compiled on relevant TRM meeting reports and communications from those WTO members.[53]

Table 6.1 Less favourable treatment issues relating to foreign banks in the WTO TRM meetings, 2002–2011

Year	Questions	China's replies
2002	1. EC's Questions: (1) Are the high minimum capital requirements for foreign bank branches consistent with national treatment? (2) 7% business tax on the gross margin foreign banks earn when they use capital to fund loans to customers, but only 7% of the net margin when the beneficiary of the loan is a Chinese bank.	1. To EC's questions: (1) National treatment was observed for the minimum capital requirement for both foreign and domestic banks; (2) No such a regulation or measure applied differently between domestic and foreign banks.
	2. Canada's Questions: Is the drafted 40% limit on inter-bank borrowing in RMB consistent with national treatment?	2. To Canada's Question: 40% limit on inter-bank borrowing in RMB in the drafted rules is in conformity with WTO national treatment.

51 In the WTO, the European Union (EU) was known known officially as the European Communities (EC) for legal reasons until November 30, 2009. Its 27 member States are also WTO members in their own rights. See the European Communities and the WTO. See the European Union and the WTO, http://www.wto.org/english/thewto_e/countries_e/european_communities_e.htm (last visited September 20, 2012).

52 The official name of Chinese Taipei in the WTO is the Separate Customs Territory of Taiwan, Penghu, Kinmen and Matsu, and it became a WTO Member on January 1, 2002. See Protocol of Accession of the Separate Customs Territory of Taiwan, Penghu, Kinmen and Matsu, WT/L/433 (Nov. 23, 2001).

53 These TRM reports and communications include: (1) S/FIN/M/37, S/FIN/W/18, S/FIN/W/19, S/FIN/W/20, S/FIN/W/21, S/FIN/W/21/Add.1 (for 2002 review); (2) S/FIN/M/43, S/FIN/W/30, S/FIN/W/32, S/FIN/W/33, S/FIN/W/34, S/FIN/W/35 (for 2003 review); (3) S/FIN/M/47, S/FIN/W/36, S/FIN/W/37, S/FIN/W/39, S/FIN/W/40, S/FIN/W/41, S/FIN/W/42 (for 2004 review); (4) S/FIN/M/50, S/FIN/W/44, S/FIN/W/45, S/FIN/W/46, S/FIN/W/48, S/FIN/W/49, S/FIN/W/50 (for 2005 review); (5) S/FIN/M/53, S/FIN/W/51, S/FIN/W/52, S/FIN/W/53, S/FIN/W/54, S/FIN/W/55, S/FIN/W/56 (for 2006 review); (6) S/FIN/M/55, S/FIN/M/58, S/FIN/W/59, S/FIN/W61 (for 2007 review); (7) S/FIN/M/57, S/FIN/W/66 (for 2008 review); (8) S/FIN/M/61, S/FIN/W/70, S/FIN/W/71, S/FIN/W/72 (for 2009 review); (9) S/FIN/W/79, S/FIN/W/81, S/FIN/W/83, S/FIN/M/71 (for 2011 review).

Year	Questions	China's replies
2003	1. EC's Questions: (1) Why should 30% of the working capital of foreign bank branches be deposited at a Chinese local bank rather than a foreign bank? (2) Foreign banks are limited to opening only one new branch per year. Are Chinese banks also bound by such a limit?	1. To EC's Questions: (1) 30% working capital deposit at a local bank is based on prudential regulation and to keep away financial risks. (2) No Reply to the one new branch per year limit.
	2. Canada's Questions: (1) Are Chinese banks also bound by the limit to open only one new branch per year? (2) Although the drafted 40% limit on inter-bank borrowing in RMB also applies to Chinese banks, it may still be inconsistent with WTO national treatment if it changes equal competitive opportunities.	2. To Canada's Questions: (1) No Reply to the one new branch per year limit. (2) The 40% limit on inter-bank borrowing does not exist because it is still in the drafting stage. Therefore, it should not be discussed in the context of the TRM.
2004	1. EC's Question: Why should 30% of the working capital of foreign bank branches be deposited at a Chinese local bank rather than a foreign bank?	1. To EC's Question: Due to the frequent capital inflows and outflows in foreign bank branches in China, the authorities could not ensure effective supervision of those funds if they were deposited in foreign bank branches.
	2. Canada's Question: (1) New limitations on the amount of foreign exchange funding foreign banks may acquire from abroad through the imposition of a quota system. Can China explain how the measure respects GATS national treatment? (2) According to Article 30 of the FFFI Regulation 2001, a foreign bank can only fund up to 70% of its foreign currency loans with funds deposited in China, and at least 30% of its loan funding must be from abroad, which limits the ability of foreign banks to lend foreign currency without bringing in foreign currency from abroad. Can China indicate how it satisfies China's GATS national treatment commitments?	2. To Canada's Question: (1) No reply to the long-term borrowing quota question. (2) 70% limit on foreign bank holding of foreign currency deposits is needed for prudential considerations.
	3. Australia's Questions: Same as Canada's questions.	3. To Australia's Questions: Same as reply as to Canada's questions.

continued ...

Table 6.1 continued

Year	Questions	China's replies
2004	4. Japan's Question: Will China introduce flexibility in applying a long-term borrowing quota to foreign banks in light of equal competitive opportunities (as defined in GATS Article XVII:3)?	4. To Japan's Question: No reply to the long-term borrowing quota question.
	5. Chinese Taipei's Question: Does a minimum of RMB 100 million of working capital for each branch of a foreign-funded bank also apply to Chinese banks?	5. To Chinese Taipei's Question: Minimum capital requirements applied to domestic banks as well.
2005	1. EC's Questions: (1) Why should 30% of the working capital of foreign bank branches be deposited at a Chinese local bank rather than a foreign bank? (2) China's regulatory regime in subsector (k) "provision and transfer of financial information, and financial data processing and related software by suppliers of other financial services" is applied only to foreign suppliers.	1. To EC's Questions: (1) Due to the frequent capital inflow and outflow from foreign bank branches in China, Chinese authorities could not ensure effective supervision of the funds if they were placed with the foreign banks established in China. (2) No reply to the subsector (k) question.
	2. Australia's Question: Limitations on the amount of foreign exchange funding foreign banks may acquire from abroad through the imposition of a quota system. Is the quota system consistent with GATS national treatment obligations?	2. To Australia's Question: No reply.
2006	1. US's and Japan's Question: China currently maintains a policy limiting the equity share of a single foreign investor in a Chinese-foreign joint venture bank to 20 per cent, with the proviso that the equity share of the total foreign investment be lower than 25 per cent.	1. To US's and Japan's question: The issue of foreign equity participation in China's domestic banks was an issue of cross-border merger and acquisitions (M&A), which was beyond the scope of China's WTO accession commitments, and therefore irrelevant for the TRM.

Year	Questions	China's replies
2006	2. EC's and US's Question: China has made full national treatment commitments in banking sub-sector (k) *Provision and transfer of financial information, and financial data processing and related software by suppliers of other financial services*. China's regulatory regime in this subsector is, however, applied only to foreign suppliers. Would China consider alternative supervisory approaches covering both domestic and foreign suppliers? On September 10, 2006, Xinhua issued the *Administrative Measures on News and Information Release by Foreign News Agencies within China*, by which Xinhua now precludes foreign providers of financial information services from contracting directly with or providing financial information services directly to domestic Chinese clients. Instead, foreign financial information service providers must now operate through a Xinhua-designated agent. These new restrictions do not apply to domestic financial information service providers. Please explain how China justifies the 2006 measure's imposition of restrictions on the market access of foreign but not domestic financial information service providers in light of China's commitment to remove national treatment limitations.	2. To EC's and US's question: The purpose of the Measures was to administer the release of news and information by foreign news agencies. They were not especially aimed at regulating foreign financial information providers. It was not intended to impose any restriction on the access of financial information provided by foreign news agencies to China's market.

continued ...

Table 6.1 continued

Year	Questions	China's replies
2007	1. Japan's question: whether or not China plans to introduce flexibility in applying long-term borrowing quotas to foreign invested banks;	2. To Japan's question: the possibility of giving more flexibility on long-term borrowing quotas to foreign invested banks was irrelevant to China's commitments.
	2. EC's questions: (1) whether China permits foreign-funded banks to use the same structure of "second-tier" branches and sub-branches that is used by state-owned commercial banks; (2) whether China will permit foreign-funded banks to take the 30% capital deposits from other banks on an equal basis with local banks; (3) whether China intends to further reduce minimum capital requirements for branches; (4) why China has introduced a one-branch cap and when it intends to lift it.	2. To EC's questions: (1) There was no difference in the approval requirements for establishing sub-branches in the same city for both Chinese and foreign banks; (2) 30 percent of the operating capital of a foreign bank's branch must be held at no more than three Chinese commercial banks within the territory of China; (3) The current requirement was reasonable and in line with the principle of prudential regulation; China did not intend to further reduce the minimum capital requirements for branches; (4) One-branch cap was in line with the principle of prudential supervision and regulation.
2008	1. EC's questions: (1) Does China intend to permit foreign-funded banks to fulfil the requirement to deposit 30% of their capital in foreign banks incorporated in China, on an equal basis with local banks? (2) Why China has introduced a one-branch cap, given that its schedule does not contain a quantitive restriction on branch licences.	1. To EC's questions: (1) For prudential purposes, China had adopted more stringent requirements for the branches of foreign banks. However, China offered equal treatment to locally incorporated subsidiaries of foreign banks and to domestic banks. (2) no answer;
	2. US's question: Are the criteria for calculating branch capital requirements the same for domestic and foreign-affiliated institutions?	2. To US's question: The new regulation met the diversified needs of foreign banks while maintaining prudential supervision and regulation.

Year	Questions	China's replies
2009	EC's questions: (1) Why branch applications are only allowed one at a time, given that its schedule does not appear to contain a quantitative restriction on branch licences; (2) When will China treat branches of foreign banks in China as part of a consolidated network, and not as separate legal entities as regards calculation of prudential ratios?	To EC's questions: (1) Foreign banks were allowed to submit applications for establishing sub-branches simultaneously in several cities; (2) As the branches of various foreign banks were in different development conditions and their head offices gave different authorizations to the branches, most of these branches were relatively independent in carrying out business. In order to increase the branches' capacity of risk prevention as much as possible, China implemented stricter prudential requirements for these branches, including separate assessment of branches of foreign banks.
2011	1. US' Questions: China does not publish "internal guidance"; China sometimes does not seek comments before enacting; China sometimes does not provide English translations of measures; 2. Japan's Questions: How can 20% restriction of foreign equity participation in a Chinese-funded financial institution be justified while China's schedule does not stipulate such a limitation? 3. EU's Questions: (1) How can China streamline the regulatory oversight of the banking sector and ensure coordination and consistency among the different actors? (2) How can China ensure that regulation in the financial services sector is transparent and takes account of the views of the industry? (3) Can China explain the 20% cap on equity investment by a single overseas financial institution in a Chinese-funded financial institution? (4) Why are branch applications only allowed one at a time?	Replies to EU's and Japan's Questions: (1) There is a multi-tiered regulation and coordination system to facilitate the regulatory cooperation in the financial industry. A regulation and coordination system had been established at the level of the State Council, and the financial regulators at various levels had signed memoranda of understanding on regulation cooperation. (2) All regulatory rules and standards shall be made public in the official journal and website of the CBRC. Public opinions are to be solicited for all laws and regulations before their official promulgation. (3) China does not make commitments on the acquisition of domestic banks by foreign financial institutions, but allows foreign investors to acquire equities of domestic banks up to a certain level. The restrictions on foreign financial institutions meet the requirements of prudent banking regulation, aiming to protect the interests of depositors and safeguard financial stability. (4) Foreign banks wishing to establish branches must comply with laws and regulations as well as prudent conditions.

From table 6.1, three characteristics can be drawn. Firstly, WTO members have attached great importance on the less favourable treatment of foreign banks. Those problems have been continuously raised since the first TRM.

Secondly, China often avoids answering some of the questions. Even if China replies to the questions, China's replies are not always persuasive. For example, China answered that national treatment was observed for the minimum capital requirements because they applied to both foreign and domestic banks.[54] This answer was immediately queried by the representative of the EC who wanted to know to what extent the minimum capital requirements were in conformity with national treatment.[55] The Chinese representative did not give any further explanation. In fact, before the end of 2006, in comparison with the minimum capital requirements for a foreign bank branch from RMB 100 million to 400 million,[56] the minimum capital requirement for a domestic bank branch was only RMB 100 million.[57]

Thirdly, the last resort taken by China against other WTO Members' complaints about China's less favourable treatment of foreign-funded banks is always the simple and omnipotent "principle of prudential regulation".

It must be noted that not all less favourable treatment measures discussed in this chapter have been questioned during the nine-round TRMs. This may be partly due to WTO members' comprehension of China's banking law. In my view, on the surface less favourable treatment is inconsistent with WTO national treatment obligations. Less favourable treatment is a piece of prima facie evidence that it is inconsistent with WTO national treatment obligations unless it constitutes an exception to the WTO obligations, such as prudential carve-out.

B. China – Electronic Payment Services

On September 15, 2010 the United States requested consultations with China, under the WTO dispute settlement mechanism, with respect to "certain restrictions and requirements maintained by China pertaining to electronic payment services for payment card transactions and the suppliers of those services". The United States alleged that China permits only "China UnionPay" to supply electronic payment services for payment card transactions denominated and paid in renminbi in China. The United States alleged that China acted inconsistently with its

---

[54] WTO Committee on Trade in Financial Services, Report of the Meeting Held on October 21, 2002, S/FIN/M/37, ¶ 21:2(a), at 4.

[55] Id. ¶ 22.

[56] DRI 2004, arts. 31–36, revised by the Announcement of the CBRC on Further Opening Banking, [*Guanyu Jinyibu Kaifang Yinhangye Xiangguan Shixiang de Gonggao*], issued by the CBRC on December 3, 2005, effective December 5, 2005, http://www.cbrc.gov.cn/mod_cn00/jsp/cn004002.jsp?infoID=1765&type=1.

[57] Measures of the CBRC for Granting Administrative Licences to Chinese-Funded Commercial Banks, CBRC Decree [2006] No. 2, art. 37(5).

obligations under Articles XVI (market access) and XVII (national treatment) of the GATS. The United States claimed that China's requirements treated foreign suppliers of electronic payment services (EPS) less favourably than China UnionPay (CUP), by providing formally different treatment between CUP and like EPS suppliers of other Members, and that the different treatment modified the conditions of competition to the detriment of the latter.[58] A number of states as third parties were highly concerned with the case, including Australia, Ecuador, European Union, Guatemala, Japan, Korea, Republic of India. [59]

China defended as follows:

> China UnionPay had not monopolized the e-payment transactions market, but it had been the only service provider of e-payment inter-bank clearing of bank cards. China had not made any WTO commitment on the payment clearing services provided by non-financial institutions such as Visa. The payment clearing services of bank cards belonged to the clearing services of monetary assets as well as the "settlement and clearing services for financial assets, including securities, derivative products, and other negotiable instruments" in the classification of financial services. China had not made any commitment on payment clearing services of bank cards in its Schedule of Specific Commitments in services ... China would gradually open up payment clearing services of bank cards according to the development of bank cards in China, but would not provide any specific timetable.[60]

In this case, China required that RMB bank cards and dual currency bank cards, that are issued in China by commercial banks and usable in domestic inter-bank RMB transactions, must bear the *Yin Lian*/UnionPay logo on the front of the cards. The panel found that those requirements (called *issuer requirements*) modified the conditions of competition in favour of CUP, which resulted in like EPS suppliers of other WTO Members being treated less favourably than CUP.[61] Furthermore, the panel found that China's *terminal equipment requirements* modified the conditions of competition in favour of CUP, and accorded to like EPS suppliers of other WTO Members less favourable treatment than that to CUP.[62] Thirdly, China's *acquirer requirements* were also found to result in different and less favourable treatment of like EPS and EPS suppliers of other WTO Members. [63] It is interesting to note that the US raised a special request that the above different kinds of requirement should be considered not only individually, but also jointly. In the view of the US, "the requirements at issue are not just WTO-inconsistent

58 WT/DS/AB/R, ¶ 7.294.

59 Http://www.wto.org/english/tratop_e/dispu_e/cases_e/ds413_e.htm.

60 S/FIN/M/71, ¶ 30.

61 Panel Report, *China – Electronic Payment Services*, WT/DS413/R, ¶ 7.318.

62 Panel Report, *China – Electronic Payment Services*, WT/DS413/R, ¶ 7.331.

63 Panel Report, *China – Electronic Payment Services*, WT/DS413/R, ¶¶ 7.339, 7.346.

when analysed individually, but operate together in a manner that is also WTO-inconsistent".[64] The panel declined to make a separate conclusion on whether those requirements, when considered jointly, were also inconsistent with GATS national treatment obligations.[65]

IV. Less Favourable Treatment and Prudential Carve-out

Undoubtedly, GATS Article XVII applies to financial service sector and sub-sectors inscribed in a WTO Member's service schedule, which means that less favourable treatment of foreign-funded banks may be inconsistent with the WTO national treatment obligations. However, less favourable treatment may be acceptable if it is prudential. That is the so-called prudential carve-out.

A. Negotiating History of Prudential Carve-out under the WTO

During the Uruguay Round negotiations, the chairman of the working group on financial services introduced a number of important elements that banking and financial services could cover, including the prudential carve-out.[66] Many developing countries emphasized the need for a prudential safeguard.[67] Korea, Switzerland, the United States, and the EC also paid close attention to this concept.[68]

The negotiators presented five prudential carve-out options.[69] The first option was a prudential carve-out only for national treatment provision. The second option was a broader one that included all *reasonable* prudential and fiduciary measures. The third option listed examples of prudential measures based on the second option. The fourth option was an unqualified prudential carve-out. The fifth option "aimed at defining as precisely as possible the prudential actions that would be permitted, so as to reduce legal uncertainties".[70] Among the five options, the fourth option was an unlimited prudential carve-out that seemed impossible to be adopted.[71]

The representatives of Canada and Japan were of the view that "a prudential carve-out should not be limited to national treatment but also apply to other articles

---

64 Panel Report, *China – Electronic Payment Services*, WT/DS413/R, ¶ 7.353.

65 Panel Report, *China – Electronic Payment Services*, WT/DS413/R, ¶ 7.354.

66 Working Group on Financial Services Including Insurance, Note on the Meeting of June 11–13, 1990, MTN.GNS/FIN/1, ¶ 2 (July 5, 1990).

67 Id. ¶ 77.

68 Id. ¶¶ 32, 34, 39.

69 Id. ¶ 2.

70 Id. ¶ 78.

71 Id. ¶¶ 85, 87, 88.

of the framework".[72] Therefore, they supported the second option, and so did the representative of the United States.[73] Sweden preferred the combination of the second option and the third option. Because Sweden recognized the difficulties of having criteria based on a reasonableness test,[74] it preferred to add an illustrative list of legitimate objectives for prudential regulations. South Africa supported the second option with a precise definition of the reasonableness test.[75] In the end, the prudential carve-out was written in the Annex on Financial Services under the WTO, which seems to be the combination of the second option and the third option.

B. Paragraph 2(a) of the Annex on Financial Services

The Annex on Financial Services, as treaty text itself,[76] is one of the eight Annexes to the main text of the GATS and an integral part of the GATS.[77] Both the GATS and the Annex on Financial Services apply to WTO Members.[78] The Annex on Financial Services contains five paragraphs. Paragraph 1 is "Scope and Definition", further interpreting GATS Article I in the context of financial services. Paragraph 2 is "Domestic Regulation", and its counterpart in the GATS is GATS Article VI. Paragraph 3 is "Recognition", which is the application of GATS Article VII in financial services. Paragraph 4 is "Dispute Settlement", providing that panels for disputes on prudential issues and other financial matters shall have the necessary expertise relevant to the specific financial service under dispute. Paragraph 5, "Definitions" includes three definitions: financial service, financial service supplier, and public entity.

Paragraph 2(a) of the Annex on Financial Services reads as follows:

> Notwithstanding any other provisions of the Agreement, a Member shall not be prevented from taking measures for prudential reasons, including for the protection of investors, depositors, policy holders or persons to whom a fiduciary duty is owed by a financial service supplier, or to ensure the integrity and stability of the financial system. Where such measures do not conform with

---

72 Id. ¶¶ 79, 80; see also Working Group on Financial Services Including Insurance: Note on the Meeting of July 12–13, 1990, MNT.GNS/FIN/2, ¶ 55 (August 10, 1990).

73 The United States submitted to the working group an informal paper entitled Provisions Regarding Financial Services, in which the United States suggested that all of the provisions in the future agreement be subject to prudential consideration. See MNT.GNS/FIN/2, id, ¶ 46.

74 Singapore also claimed that the "reasonableness" standard was very subjective. See MTN.GNS/FIN/1, ¶ 91.

75 See MNT.GNS/FIN/2, ¶ 88.

76 Panel Report, China-Electronic Payment Services, WT/DS/413R, adopted August 31, 2012, ¶ 7.139.

77 GATS, art. XXIX.

78 Panel Report, *Mexico – Telecoms*, WT/DS/204/R, adopted June 1, 2004, ¶ 7.4.

the provisions of the Agreement, they shall not be used as a means of avoiding the Member's commitments or obligations under the Agreement.

The first sentence of paragraph 2(a) is the so-called prudential carve-out which empowers a Member to take prudential regulatory measures on financial service trade.[79] The second sentence is a trade-off of the first sentence, providing that such measures allowed by the first sentence shall not be used as a means of avoiding the Member's commitments or obligations under the GATS. From the text of paragraph 2(a) of the Annex on Financial Services, the final version of prudential carve-out adopted by the WTO seems to be the combination of the second option and the third option proposed during the Uruguay Round negotiations, but the second sentence of paragraph 2(a) contains the extent of the first sentence and makes the scope of prudential carve-out elusive. In GATS Article XIV (General Exceptions), there is a necessity test, which means that a Member must prove that it is "necessary" to take an exceptional measure.[80] But the necessity test is not included in the final text of the prudential carve-out, which may imply that it is unnecessary for a Member to prove that a prudential measure is necessary. Compared with general exceptions of the GATS, which have an objective necessity standard,[81] prudential carve-out is flexible and, to some extent, subjective. In other words, prudential carve-out lacks detailed standards and limitations.

C. Relationship between Prudential Carve-out and National Treatment

The starting point to analyse prudential carve-out is to identify its relationship with other GATS/WTO obligations. Obviously, the bigger the scope of prudential carve-out, the narrower the scope of national treatment obligations in financial service trade, and vice versa. In fact, the core of the issue is the relationship between the first sentence and the second sentence of paragraph 2(a) of the Annex on Financial Services, i.e. how much could the second sentence narrow down the scope of the first sentence? Or, to put it another way, could a prudential measure be discriminatory? Should a prudential measure be non-discriminatory? For example, in a Member's Schedule of Specific Commitments on Services, if there is a "None" entry (full commitment) in both the market access column and the national treatment column, can the Member take a limitation measure on market access or national treatment in the name of prudential carve-out?

The GATS text and other provisions of the Annex on Financial Services fail to resolve the issue, and it is still highly debated among WTO Members. For instance, during the WTO meetings, Colombia took the view that paragraph 2 of

79 WTO Secretariat, Guide to the Uruguay Round Agreements 176 (Kluwer Law International 1999).

80 For the legal standard of "necessity" in Article XIV of the GATS, see Appellate Body Report, *U.S. – Gambling*, WT/DS285/AB/R, adopted April 20, 2005, ¶¶ 304–27.

81 Id. ¶ 304.

the Annex on Financial Services and Article VI of the GATS (domestic regulation) should allow Members to take both prudential and non-prudential measures to ensure the stability and integrity of the financial system.[82] Malaysia insisted that there be "no flexibility to introduce any changes to the so-called prudential carve-out".[83] Japan, as a typical developed country, also claimed that Members should be cautious when discussing limitations respecting the right to take prudential measures.[84] However, the EC and its Member States emphasized that prudential measures should not be used "as a means of avoiding GATS market access and national treatment commitments".[85]

The centre of the second sentence of paragraph 2 (a) of the Annex on Financial Services is that prudential measures shall not be used as means of avoiding the Member's commitments or obligations under the GATS. This sentence implies that prudential measures should not aim intentionally to avoid a Member's commitments and obligations, one of which is national treatment under GATS Article XVII. Logically, it denotes that prudential carve-out should not be used to derogate from national treatment obligations. This conclusion, however, seems to be in contradiction to the first sentence which describes the scope of prudential carve-out with the wording "[n]otwithstanding any other provisions of the Agreement". In a word, the scope of prudential carve-out is unclear.[86]

Theoretically, there are four modes of prudential carve-out with different scope. According to the degree of domestic regulation power, against the degree of financial trade liberalization, they are full prudential carve-out, partly overlapping prudential carve-out, non-discriminatory prudential carve-out and wholly overlapping prudential carve-out.

Full Prudential Carve-out

The first mode is full prudential carve-out. In the view of the WTO Secretariat, prudential carve-out is a further exception to the GATS rules, "similar to the general exceptions in both the GATS and the GATT".[87] It is obvious that the WTO Secretariat's view is that prudential carve-out is an exception to any of the obligations in the GATS. However, the WTO Secretariat is not an official authority

---

[82] Communication from Colombia, S/CSS/W/96 (July 9, 2001).

[83] Report of the Meeting Held on December 3–6, 2001, S/CSS/M/13, at 60 (February 26, 2002).

[84] Id. at 57.

[85] Communication from the EC and their Member States, *GATS 2000: Financial Services*, S/CSS/W/39, ¶ 21 (November 22, 2000).

[86] Kalypso Nicolaidis and Joel P. Trachtman, *From Policed Regulation to Managed Recognition in GATS*, in GATS 2000, NEW DIRECTIONS IN SERVICE TRADE LIBERALIZATION 241, 255 (Pierre Sauve and Robert M. Stern (eds), Brookings Institution Press 2000).

[87] WTO Secretariat, GUIDE TO THE URUGUAY ROUND AGREEMENTS 176 (Kluwer Law International 1999).

to interpret the WTO agreements.[88] In the 2001 Scheduling Guidelines, a prudential measure is deemed to be an exception to the GATS and should not be scheduled.[89] Therefore, according to the WTO official understanding (not interpretation), the measures listed in a Member's service schedule as limitations on market access and national treatment should not be prudential measures. In other words, even if there are some limitation measures listed in a Member's service schedule, the Member still has a right to take more stringent measures based on prudential carve-out. From this guidance, it could be inferred that the WTO Secretariat and the Council for Trade in Services take the view that prudential carve-out is an exception to all GATS obligations, inter alia, national treatment. Accordingly, a Member which utilizes prudential carve-out can take discriminatory measures against foreign financial services and service suppliers. This view is a broad understanding of prudential carve-out, which necessarily limits the effects of financial trade liberalization. In the process of striking a balance between trade liberalization and policy flexibility, such a view could be deemed conservative, tending to give maximum power to WTO Members to protect domestic financial services and service suppliers.

Partly Overlapped Prudential Carve-out

The second mode is partly overlapped prudential carve-out. Under this mode, some prudential measures are subject to GATS obligations, while others are not. This possibility comes from the second sentence of Paragraph 2(a) of the Annex on Financial Services, stating "[where] such measures do not conform to the provisions of the Agreement ...". It may imply that some other prudential measures may conform to the provisions of the GATS, which may constitute the overlap between GATS obligations and prudential carve-out.

Non-discriminatory Prudential Carve-out

The third mode is non-discriminatory prudential carve-out, which subjects prudential carve-out to GATS national treatment obligations. It means that prudential measures can derogate from most GATS obligations, except national treatment. All prudential measures must be applicable to domestic and foreign services and service suppliers without discrimination. As a result, prudential carve-out could not be the means to protect domestic services and service suppliers. This mode is adopted by the OECD Code of Liberalisation of Current Invisible

[88] It should be noted that the WTO Secretariat specifically indicated that its understanding in this guide must not be taken to constitute legal interpretation of the agreement. See id., *Foreword.*

[89] 2001 Scheduling Guidelines, S/L/92, ¶ 20.

Operations,[90] and some free trade agreements (FTAs), such as the EFTA-Mexico FTA,[91] the CARICOM-Dominica FTA,[92] and the EC-Mexico FTA.[93]

Wholly Overlapped Prudential Carve-out

The fourth mode is wholly overlapped prudential carve-out. Under such a mode, all prudential measures must be subject to GATS obligations, which results in maximum liberalization of financial service trade and minimum national policy flexibility. Actually, such prudential measures are not called "carve-out" or "exceptions" since they are not beyond the scope of GATS obligations. It is almost impossible for WTO Members to adopt this mode.

From the above analysis, the scope of prudential carve-out depends on the distance between prudential measures and GATS obligations. The greater the distance is, the broader the scope of prudential carve-out is, and vice versa. To identify the scope of prudential carve-out is, in essence, to identify the distance between GATS obligations and prudential measures, or to strike a balance between the two. Paragraph 2(a) of the Annex on Financial Services does not define the concept of prudential carve-out, or clearly identify the distance between the carve-out and GATS obligations, so there is much room for WTO Members to manoeuvre.

D. Standards of Prudential Carve-out

The Annex on Financial Services fails to set standards for determining whether a measure taken by a WTO Member is prudential or non-prudential. Moreover, it does not mention any of the so-called international standards or the role of international organizations. Unlike GATS Article VII, the Annex on Financial Services is silent on the point of international standards.

GATS Article VII:5 states as follows:

> Wherever appropriate, recognition should be based on multilaterally agreed criteria. In appropriate cases, Members shall work in cooperation with

---

[90] See OECD Code of Liberalization of Current Invisible Operations, September 2004, Annex II to Annex A: Conditions for the Establishment and Operation of Branches, Agencies, etc. of Non-Resident Investors in the Banking and Financial Services Sector, ¶8(f), http://www.oecd.org/dataoecd/41/21/2030182.pdf.

[91] See EFTA-Mexico FTA, signed on November 27, 2000, entered into force on July 1, 2001, WT/REG126/1 (August 24, 2001), WT/REG126/3 (March 11, 2003), Section III (Financial Services), art. 36.

[92] See Article VIII (General Exceptions) of Annex II of the Agreement Establishing the Free Trade Area between the Caribbean Community and the Dominican Republic, signed in August 1998, http://www.caricom.org/archives/history.htm.

[93] See Decision No 2/2001 of the EU-Mexico Joint Council of February 27, 2001 to Implement Articles 6, 9, 12(2)(b) and 50 of the Economic Partnership, Political Coordination and Cooperation Agreement, art. 19, WT/REG109/4 (March 31, 2003).

> relevant intergovernmental and non-governmental organizations towards the establishment and adoption of common international standards and criteria for recognition and common international standards for the practice of relevant services trades and professions.

It must be noted that the role of international standards in GATS Article VII should not be exaggerated to be international standards directly applicable to the service trade. GATS Article VII:5 only provides that Members shall make efforts "towards the establishment and adoption of common international standards and criteria". Therefore, international standards, if any, cannot be directly applied to trade in services under the legal framework of the GATS. There must be a process of "establishment and adoption", which denotes the need to have multilateral negotiations on the application of international standards in the GATS. Even if GATS Article VII:5 generally applies to the Annex on Financial Services, there is no legal position to use international standards in determining whether a measure is prudential or not.

Some may invoke GATS Article VI:5(b) to support the legal status of international standards in service trade. GATS Article VI:5(b) reads: "In determining whether a Member is in conformity with the obligation under paragraph 5(a), account shall be taken of international standards of relevant international organizations applied by that Member."[94] This paragraph indeed emphasizes the role of international standards in domestic regulation relating to service trade and it seems also to be a general obligation because it is in Part II of the GATS (General Obligations and Disciplines). However, in my opinion, GATS Article VI:5(b) has little influence on prudential measures.

Prudential carve-out provision is in the paragraph of Domestic Regulation (paragraph 2) of the Annex on Financial Services, which may suggest it relate to GATS Article VI, also entitled Domestic Regulation. What is the relationship between GATS Article VI and paragraph 2 of the Annex on Financial Services? Is paragraph 2 of the Annex on Financial Services an extension of or supplement to GATS Article VI? Or is it also an exception to GATS Article VI as well as to other GATS articles? There is no clear answer from the GATS text. Paragraph 2(a) uses the wording "notwithstanding any *other* provisions of the Agreement" (emphasis added), therefore it seems to suggest that paragraph 2(a) is not an exception to GATS Article VI. If this logic is right, then the limitations on domestic regulation also apply to prudential carve-out. In my view, for the following reasons, the limitations on domestic regulations do not necessarily apply to prudential measures.

94 The footnote of GATS Article VI:5(b) further states that relevant international organizations refer to international bodies whose membership is open to the relevant bodies of at least all Members of the WTO.

Firstly, it is generally acknowledged that the core obligation of the GATS is national treatment,[95] so the real meaning of prudential carve-out focuses on the carve-out of national treatment obligations. Secondly, GATS Article XVII, as well as Article XVI, is placed in Part III of the GATS, not Part II of the GATS, suggesting that national treatment obligations are not in the scope of GATS Article VI:5(b). The Working Party on Professional Services (WPPS), while drafting accountancy disciplines, came to the conclusion that "there should not be any overlap between [GATS] Article XVI and XVII on the one hand and Article VI on the other hand".[96] Most WTO Members believe that GATS Article VI only deals with non-discriminatory restrictive measures.[97] Moreover, in discussing GATS Article VI, several Members specifically stated that "the development of rules on domestic regulation should not in any way affect the financial services prudential carve-out".[98]

Furthermore, international standards to be taken into account in GATS Article VI are closely related to the necessity test. The necessity test is one of the requirements provided by GATS Article VI:4(b) and covered by Article VI:5(a). The necessity test in Article VI applies only to non-discriminatory trade restrictive measures.[99] Since the necessity test is not a stated requirement for prudential measures, it seems to be premature to adopt international standards in determining whether a prudential measure is necessary or not.

From the practice of the WTO agreements, the role of international standards is based on a bottom-up approach, not a top-down approach. For example, there is no general obligation to apply international standards in the GATT 1994. As to GATS, no general obligation apply international standards exists. GATS Article VI:5 merely uses the wording "account shall be taken of", which is a typical non-obligatory expression. International standards appear sporadically, not generally, in agreements on trade in services. For example, the Annex on Telecommunications includes a special paragraph on international standards and international organizations,[100] while the Annex on Financial Services does not include such a provision. This bottom-up approach strongly suggests that prudential carve-out

---

95 Mitsuo Matsushita, Thomas J. Schoenbaum and Petros C. Mavroidis, The World Trade Organization, Law, Practice, and Policy 230 (Oxford Univ. Press 2003).

96 *Article VI:4 of the GATS: Disciplines on Domestic Regulation Applicable to All Services*, Note by the Secretariat, S/C/W/96, ¶ 14 (March 1, 1999).

97 Working Party on Domestic Regulation, Report on the Meeting Held on July 3, 2001, Note by the Secretariat, S/WPDR/M/12, ¶¶ 26, 33, 34, 37 (August 16, 2001); see also Communication from the European Communities and Their Member States, *Domestic Regulation: Necessity and Transparency*, S/WPDR/W/14, ¶¶ 7, 8 (May 1, 2001).

98 Working Party on Domestic Regulation, Report on the Meeting Held on July 3, 2001, Note by the Secretariat, S/WPDR/M/12, Annex, *Informal Summary of Discussions on the Checklist of Issues for WPDR*, at 16 (August 16, 2001).

99 S/C/W/96, ¶ 22.

100 GATS, Annex on Telecommunication, ¶ 7.

in financial services is not subject to international standards at the current stage, which gives WTO Members broad right to adopt prudential regulations to meet national policy objectives.

So far, many WTO Members have taken the view that there is no need to define prudential carve-out contained in the Annex on Financial Services.[101] For instance, the representative of the Philippines said that the language in paragraph 2(a) of the Annex on Financial Services was "quite clear", and the wide discretion granted to Members was "intentional".[102] Thailand also expressed that there was no problem with the definition of prudential measures contained in the Annex on Financial Services.[103] Malaysia was of the view that prudential carve-out is a "fine balance reached in the Uruguay Round",[104] and even objected to the initiative raised by Japan to gather information on prudential regulation from international financial organizations because "the exercise would impinge on the right of national governments to take prudential measures independently, as provided for in the Financial Services Annex".[105] Mexico supported Malaysia's view.[106]

On the other hand, Australia suggested developing a definition of prudential regulation or a common understanding of that term.[107] The Japanese representative said that there was ambiguity as to the definition of prudential regulation, so the representative suggested collecting information on prudential regulation from the international financial organizations. However, he admitted that it was difficult and unrealistic to achieve a definition of prudential regulation.[108] The EC also felt it difficult or not realistic to define what prudential regulation was under prudential carve-out, but it supported Japan's proposal to collect information from international financial organizations.[109] Canada supported Japan's proposal provided that such exercise did not touch on prudential carve-out in any way.[110]

The third view, expressed by both the United States and India is whether there is a need to define prudential carve-out. According to this cautious view, there is no compelling evidence that prudential carve-out has been abused, or used as

---

[101] See S/FIN/W/16, ¶ 4 (November 3, 2000).

[102] Report of the Meeting Held on July 13, 2000, Note by the Secretariat, ¶ 32, S/FIN/M/27 (August 23, 2000).

[103] Id. ¶ 35.

[104] Report of the Meeting Held on May 25, 2000, Note by the Secretariat, ¶ 25, S/FIN/M/26 (June 29, 2000); see also Report of the Meeting Held on April 13, 2000, Note by the Secretariat, ¶ 22, S/FIN/M/25 (May 8, 2000).

[105] Report of the Meeting Held on November 29, 2000, Note by the Secretariat, ¶ 22, S/FIN/M/29 (March 14, 2001).

[106] Id. ¶ 23.

[107] S/FIN/M/26, ¶ 21.

[108] Id. ¶ 22.

[109] S/FIN/M/27, ¶ 27.

[110] Report of the Meeting Held on April 2, 2001, Note by the Secretariat, S/FIN/M/30, ¶ 22 (May 8, 2001).

disguised protection, so it is premature to consider the definition of prudential carve-out.[111]

E. Changes in Prudential Carve-out in China

China's power to resort to the prudential carve-out may be cut down by its WTO commitments because prudential carve-out in China's WTO financial commitments seems subtly different from that in the GATS/WTO. Generally speaking, as analysed above, from the language of the text in the Annex on Financial Services, prudential carve-out is not restrained by the necessity test, which leaves the door open for a WTO Member to regulate banking services based on prudential reasons. However, it seems that this advantage or loophole cannot be freely used by China's banking regulatory authorities due to China's special WTO commitments. Paragraph 308 of the Working Party Report states: "[U]pon accession [to the WTO] China would ensure that China's licensing procedures and conditions would not act as barriers to market access and would not be more trade restrictive than necessary." The difference between paragraph 308 of the Working Party Report and GATS Article VI:4 is that the former is related to market access (so as to connect with national treatment through GATS Article XX:2), but the latter is separated from market access and national treatment. Therefore, China's special commitment in paragraph 308 should not be seen as a repeat of GATS Article VI:4, but a commitment beyond GATS Article VI:4. According to the commitment, "China's licensing procedures and conditions" should not be "more trade restrictive than necessary", so China's licensing procedures and conditions on banking services are subject to the necessity test. Since China made this commitment as one of the terms to get access to the WTO, its legal force, as *lex specialis*, should go beyond the articles in the GATS or its annexes. In other words, China has undertaken more restrictive obligations through its WTO access commitments than the general WTO obligations in the GATS. Although China did not indicate that it was intended to change the rule of prudential carve-out, China's special commitment in paragraph 308 of the Working Party Report, as a binding paragraph annexed to the China Accession Protocol,[112] may limit China's manoeuvrability in taking advantage of the prudential carve-out in regulating foreign financial institutions.

On September 9, 2012 China and Canada concluded the Agreement for the Promotion and Reciprocal Protection of Investment (Sino-Canadian BIT).[113] Article 33(3) of the Sino-Canadian BIT states as follows:

---

[111] S/FIN/M/26, ¶¶ 29, 30.

[112] See Working Party Report, WT/ACC/CHN/49, ¶ 342 (October 1, 2001).

[113] Http://www.international.gc.ca/trade-agreements-accords-commerciaux/agr-acc/fipa-apie/china-text-chine.aspx?lang=eng&view=d.

> Nothing in this Agreement shall be construed to prevent a Contracting Party from adopting or maintaining reasonable measures for prudential reasons, such as:
>
> (a) the protection of depositors, financial market participants and investors, policy-holders, policy-claimants, or persons to whom a fiduciary duty is owed by a financial institution;
> (b) the maintenance of the safety, soundness, integrity or financial responsibility of financial institutions; and
> (c) ensuring the integrity and stability of a Contracting Party's financial system.

Article 20(2) of the Sino-Canadian BIT gives the right to determine whether the measures are prudential to the joint decision of Sino-Canadian financial services authorities. If Sino-Canadian financial services authorities cannot reach a joint decision on the issue, the issue shall be referred by China or Canada to a State-State arbitral tribunal (rather than the Investor-State arbitral tribunal). The decision of the State-State arbitral tribunal shall be transmitted to the Investor-State arbitral tribunal, and shall be binding on the Investor-State arbitral tribunal.

V. Concluding Remarks

Less favourable treatment is prima facie incompatible with GATS/WTO national treatment obligations. It is China's GATS/WTO duty to remove less favourable treatment of foreign-funded banks unless it is prudential. China has repealed some banking rules according less favourable treatment to foreign-funded banks since China entered the WTO. However, there are still some provisions less favourable to foreign-funded banks in China's banking law framework. Whether China can justify them depends on the definition of prudential carve-out. The core of the prudential carve-out issue is the relationship between the first sentence and the second sentence of paragraph 2(a) of the Annex on Financial Services. The GATS text and other provisions of the Annex on Financial Services fail to resolve the issue. The scope of prudential carve-out depends on the distance between prudential measures and GATS obligations. The longer the distance is, the broader the scope of prudential carve-out is, and vice versa. To identify the scope of prudential carve-out is, in essence, to identify the distance between GATS obligations and prudential measures, or to strike a balance between them. Paragraph 2(a) of the Annex on Financial Services does not define the concept of prudential carve-out, or clearly identify the distance between the carve-out and GATS obligations, so there is much room for WTO Members to manoeuvre. Prudential carve-out may open the door for China's banking law to keep some flexibility when meeting the GATS/WTO national treatment obligations. However, the flexibility is limited by China's WTO-plus national treatment commitments. This limitation has weakened the willingness of the Chinese government to use the special shield against the complaints of other WTO members. For example, in *China – Electronic Payment Services*, China did not cite the prudential carve-out clause as a reason to justify China's financial measures providing foreign services and service suppliers less favourable treatment. In the end, China lost the case. No one could predict whether China would win if citing the prudential carve-out. However, if China had raised the prudential carve-out, that case would become the first case to test the practical effect of the prudential carve-out in the history of the WTO. It is a pity, if not a mistake, for China not to use the prudential carve-out in the WTO dispute settlement. In my view, China is too prudential to use prudential carve-out.

CHAPTER 7

Identical Treatment between Foreign-Funded Banks and Chinese-Funded Banks

Chapter 5 and Chapter 6 analysed different treatment (more favourable treatment and less favourable treatment) of foreign-funded banks. In China, the treatment of foreign-funded banks is a mixture of more favourable treatment, less favourable treatment, and identical treatment. Chapter 7 focuses on identical treatment, or the same treatment, between foreign-funded banks and Chinese-funded banks.

I. Identical Treatment in the Common Banking Law

A. Banking Laws

Generally speaking, China's three banking laws (Commercial Banking Law 2003, PBC Law 2003, and Banking Supervision Law 2006) apply to both Chinese-funded and foreign-funded banks. Firstly, the definition of commercial banks in Commercial Banking Law 2003 is broad enough to include Chinese-funded and foreign-funded banks in the territory of China. Commercial banks refer to enterprises with legal personality that are established in conformity with China's Commercial Banking Law and the Corporation Law, and that take in deposits from the general public, provide loans, handle settlement, etc.[1] Furthermore, Article 92 of the Commercial Banking Law 2003 states: "Wholly-foreign-funded commercial banks, Sino-foreign equity joint venture commercial banks and branches of foreign commercial banks shall be governed by the provisions of this Law; if other laws and administrative regulations provide otherwise, the provisions of those laws and regulations shall prevail."

Secondly, the PBC Law 2003 also covers Chinese-funded and foreign-funded banks. Article 52 of the PBC Law 2003 is a definition clause for the term of *banking institutions*. According to the article, *banking institutions* under the PBC Law 2003 are financial institutions established in China that take deposits from the general public, including, commercial banks, urban credit cooperatives and rural credit cooperatives, and policy banks. This definition of banking institutions is the same as that in the Banking Supervision Law 2006. Foreign-funded banks are included in the PBC Law 2003 due to the fact that they belong to commercial banks. However, it must be noted that not all articles of the three banking laws are

---

1 Commercial Banking Law 2003, art. 2.

applicable to foreign-funded banks. As mentioned above, special foreign banking laws and administrative regulations, if any, shall prevail over the three general banking laws.

Thirdly, both Chinese-funded banks and foreign-funded banks are within the scope of the Banking Supervision Law 2006. China's banking regulatory authority is responsible for the supervision of *banking institutions* in China.[2] As part of commercial banks, foreign-funded banks belong to banking institutions under the Banking Supervision Law 2006. Article 51 of the Banking Supervision Law 2006 is similar to Article 92 of the Commercial Banking Law 2003, which reads: "Where the laws and administrative regulations provide otherwise for the regulation and supervision of the wholly-foreign-funded banking institutions, Sino-foreign equity joint venture banking institutions and branches of foreign banking institutions that are established in the PRC, those provisions shall prevail."

In addition, the Anti-Money Laundering Law 2006 applies to all kinds of financial institutions in China, including policy banks, commercial banks, credit cooperatives, postal savings institutions, trust investment corporations, securities companies, future brokerage companies, insurance companies, and other institutions engaging in financial business.[3] There is not a special article in the Anti-Money Laundering Law 2006 to exclude foreign-funded banks, which means that foreign-funded banks are equally covered as part of commercial banks in China.

B. Application of Common Banking Law: *mutatis mutandis*

China's common banking law is listed in table 4.11 (in Chapter 4). However, it must be noted that some of the common banking laws, regulations, rules in table 4.11 apply *mutatis mutandis* [*canzhao shiyong*] to foreign-funded banks,[4] and some directly and completely apply to foreign-funded banks.[5] Therefore, table 4.11 only provides an outline for the application scope of the common banking law. To

---

[2] Banking Supervision Law 2006, art. 2, ¶ 1.

[3] Anti-Money Laundering Law 2006, art. 34.

[4] See, e.g., Guidelines for Fulfilling Duties in Credit-Granting Business of Commercial Banks [*Shangye Yinhang Shouxin Gongzuo Jinzhi Zhiyin*], art. 53, CBRC *Yinjianfa* [2004] No. 51, issued on July 16, 2004, effective at the same date, in GAZETTE OF THE CBRC 30–35 (bound vols 7–12, 2004, no. 7) (applying directly to Chinese-funded commercial banks and *mutatis mutandis* to other banking institutions).

[5] See, e.g., Interim Measures for Review of Internal Control of Commercial Banks [*Shangye Yinhang Neibu Kongzhi Pingjia Shixing Banfa*], art. 69, CBRC Decree [2004] No. 9, issued on December 25, 2004, effective from February 1, 2005, in GAZETTE OF THE CBRC 196–208 (bound volume 2004, no. 12) (stating that the banking rule applies to state-owned commercial banks, joint-stock commercial banks, foreign-funded commercial banks, city commercial banks, rural commercial banks, etc.); see also Measures for Administration of Capital Adequacy Ratio of Commercial Banks [*Shangye Yinhang Ziben Chongzulü Guanli Banfa*], art. 2, CBRC Decree [2004] No. 2, issued on February 23, 2004, effective from March 1, 2004, in GAZETTE OF THE CBRC 44–47 (bound vols. 1–6, 2004, no. 2) (providing

find the exact application scope of an individual banking law in table 4.11, it is necessary to look at the specific application article in the banking law. If there is a *mutatis mutandis* article in the common banking law, the application effect on foreign-funded banks is uncertain unless one can find whether there is a special foreign banking law with necessary changes on the common banking law.

II. Overlaps between Foreign Banking Law and Domestic Banking Law

Under the Chinese tripartite banking law framework, the whole body of China's banking law is artificially divided into three parts and more sub-parts based on the categories of commercial banks. However, it does not mean that the foreign banking law and domestic banking law are totally different. In fact, there are many overlaps between the foreign banking law and domestic banking law, which can be demonstrated in table 7.1.

Although the overlaps, as identical treatment, tend to be consistent with national treatment obligations, the extensive overlaps and repetitions, on the one hand, undermine the basis of China's banking law framework, on the other hand, raise the cost of banking law-making, and the cost of banking law-observing.[6] GATS/WTO national treatment obligations do not mean duplicate legislation or repeated law-making at all costs.

The CBRC has realized that banking rules should not repeat existing banking laws, regulations and other banking rules. According to Article 45 (5) of the Provisions of the CBRC on Legal Works,[7] the legal department of the CBRC shall return the drafted banking rules which simply repeat existing laws, regulations and rules to the drafting department. However, the overlaps and repeats are doomed under the existing four-tiered and tripartite banking law framework. Article 45 (5) of the Provisions of the CBRC on Legal Works cannot resolve the systemic weakness.

---

that the banking rule applies to Chinese-funded banks, wholly-foreign-funded banks and Sino-foreign equity joint venture banks).

[6] See LECTURES ON THE BANKING SUPERVISION LAW OF THE PRC (Huang Yi (ed.), Zhongguo fazhi chubanshe 2004).

[7] Provisions of the CBRC on Legal Works [*Zhongguo Yinhangye Jiandu Guanli Weiyuanhui Falü Gongzuo Guiding*], issued on November 26, 2005, effective from February 1, 2006, CBRC Decree [2005] No. 4, in GAZETTE OF THE CBRC 13–25 (2005, no. 11).

Table 7.1 Overlaps between Commercial Banking Law 2003 and FFB Regulation 2006

Overlap	Commercial Banking Law 2003	FFB Regulation 2006
Business Scope	Art. 3: Commercial banks may engage in some or all of the following business activities: (1) Taking in public deposits; (2) Offering short-term, medium-term and long-term loans; (3) Handling domestic and foreign settlements; (4) Handling acceptance and discount of negotiable instruments; (5) Issuing financial bonds; (6) Acting as an agent for issuing, honouring and underwriting government bonds; (7) Buying and selling government bonds or financial bonds; (8) Undertaking inter-bank loans; (9) Buying and selling foreign exchange by itself or as an agent; (10) Engaging in bank card business; (11) Providing letter of credit services and guaranty services; (12) Acting as an agent for receipt and payment and acting as an insurance agent; (13) Providing safe box services; (14) Other businesses approved by the banking regulatory institution of the State Council.	Art. 29: Wholly-foreign-funded and Sino-foreign equity joint-venture banks may engage in some or all of the following foreign currency business or RMB business: (1) Taking in public deposits; (2) Offering short-term, medium-term and long-term loans; (3) Handling acceptance and discount of negotiable instruments; (4) Buying and selling government bonds or financial bonds, and foreign currency securities except stocks; (5) Providing letter of credit services and guaranty services; (6) Handling domestic and foreign settlements; (7) Buying and selling foreign exchange by itself or as an agent; (8) Insurance agency; (9) Undertaking inter-bank loans; (10) Engaging in bank card business; (11) Providing safe box services; (12) Credit investigation and consulting services; (13) Other businesses approved by the banking regulatory institution of the State Council.
Law-abidance Requirement	Art. 8: Commercial banks shall abide by laws and administrative regulations, and may not harm the interests of the State or of the public.	Art. 4: Foreign-funded banks shall abide by laws and administrative regulations of the PRC, and may not harm the interests of the state or of the public.

Overlap	Commercial Banking Law 2003	FFB Regulation 2006
Registered Capital	Art. 13: The minimum amount of registered capital required for establishing a national commercial bank shall be RMB 1 billion … . Registered capital shall be paid-up capital. The banking regulatory institute of the State Council may adjust the minimum amount of registered capital in light of prudential regulation; however, the adjusted amount may not be lower than the amount specified in the preceding paragraph.	Art. 8: The minimum amount of registered capital required for establishing a wholly-foreign-funded bank or a Sino-foreign equity joint venture bank shall be RMB 1 billion or foreign currency with equivalent value. Registered capital shall be paid-up capital. … The banking regulatory institute of the State Council may increase the minimum amount of registered capital in light of business scope of the foreign-funded bank and prudential regulation, and require the portion of RMB currency in the capital.
Registration Procedure	Art. 16: Upon approval, the commercial bank shall be issued a licence, and then it shall register at the state administration for industry and commerce by the licence, and get a business licence.	Art. 19: Upon approval, the foreign-funded bank shall register with the state administration for industry and commerce and get a business licence.
Limitation on Working Capital of Branches	Art. 19 (2): The total amount of working capital allocated to all branches and sub-branches by a bank shall be not higher than 60 per cent of the total capital of the bank.	Art. 8(2): The total amount of working capital allocated to all branches and sub-branches by a wholly-foreign-funded bank or a Sino-foreign equity joint venture bank shall be not higher than 60 per cent of the total capital of the bank.
Civil Liability of Branches and Sub-branches	Art. 22: Branches and sub-branches of commercial banks shall not have the status of a legal person and shall lawfully conduct their business operations within the scope authorized by their head offices, and their civil liability shall be borne by their head offices.	Art. 32: Civil liability of branches or sub-branches of foreign-funded banks shall be borne by their head offices.

continued ...

Table 7.1 continued

Overlap	**Commercial Banking Law 2003**	**FFB Regulation 2006**
Bank Changes	Art. 24: A commercial bank shall obtain the approval of the banking regulatory institution of the State Council for making any of the following changes: 1. change of name; 2. change in the registered capital; 3. change of location of the head office or a branch; 4. adjustment of the scope of business; 5. change of shareholders that hold 5 per cent or more of the total capital or total amount of shares; 6. revision of the articles of association; or 7. changes in other matters provided by the banking regulatory institution of the State Council. If a director or a senior manager is to be replaced, the qualifications of the substitute for the position shall be submitted to the banking regulatory institute of the State Council for examination.	Art. 27: A foreign-funded bank shall obtain the approval of the banking regulatory institution of the State Council for making any of the following changes: 1. change in the registered capital or working capital; 2. change of name, location; 3. adjustment of the scope of business; 4. change of shareholders or adjustment of proportion of shares held by shareholders. 5. revision of the articles of association; or 6. changes in other matters provided by the banking regulatory institution of the State Council. If a director, a senior manager, or a chief representative of a foreign-funded bank is to be replaced, the qualifications of the substitute for the position shall be submitted to the banking regulatory institute of the State Council for examination.
Deposit Interest Rate	Art. 31: Commercial banks shall determine their deposit interest rates in accordance with the upper and lower limits for deposit interest rates set by the PBC.	Art. 38: Foreign-funded banks shall determine their deposit interest rates and service fees in accordance with relevant provisions.
Deposit Reserve Fund	Art. 32: Commercial banks should provide a certain amount of deposit reserve funds to the PBC and keep adequate payment funds in accordance with PBC rules.	Art. 41: To conduct deposit-taking business, foreign-funded banks should provide deposit reserve funds in accordance with PBC rules.
Capital Adequacy Ratio	Art. 39 Commercial banks shall abide by the provisions on the ratios of assets to debts: The capital adequacy ratio of a commercial bank shall not be less than 8 per cent.	Art. 40: Wholly-foreign-funded banks and Sino-foreign equity joint-venture banks shall abide by the provisions on the ratios of assets to debts in accordance with the Commerical Banking Law.
Ratio of Liability	Art. 39 (3): The proportion of the balance of current assets and the balance of current liabilities shall not be lower than 25 per cent.	Art. 40: The Same.
Bad Debt Reserves	Art. 57: Commercial banks shall draw reserves against bad debts to offset bad debts in accordance with relevant rules.	Art. 41: Foreign-funded banks shall draw reserves against bad debts in accordance with relevant rules.

Overlap	Commercial Banking Law 2003	FFB Regulation 2006
Report of Financial Statements	Art. 61: Commercial banks shall report balance sheets, statements of profits and other financial statements and statistical reports and documents to the banking regulatory institution of the State Council and the PBC.	Art. 52: Foreign-funded banks shall report financial statements and other relevant documents to the banking regulatory institution.
Examination	Art. 62: The banking regulatory institution of the State Council shall have the right to examine and supervise the deposits, loans, settlement, bad debts, and other conditions of commercial banks at any time … . The PBC has the right to examine and supervise commercial banks in accordance with the PBC Law.	Art. 53: Foreign-funded banks shall accept the supervision and investigation of the banking regulatory institution.
Legal Liability	Arts. 74, 81, 83: Those who establish a bank, a branch, or engage in banking business without approval of the banking regulatory institution shall be prosecuted if committing a crime. Such illegal banks shall be closed by the banking regulatory institution of the State Council. If the activity is not serious enough to constitute a crime, its unlawful income would be confiscated and a fine of one to five times unlawful income should be imposed. If there is no unlawful income or the unlawful income is less than RMB 500,000, a fine in the amount of RMB 500,000 to RMB 2,000,000 should be imposed. Art. 80: If a commercial bank does not provide relevant documents and materials, the banking regulatory institution of the State Council will order it to make a correction; otherwise a fine in the amount of RMB 100,000 to 300,000 should be imposed.	Arts. 63, 64: Those who establish a foreign-funded bank, a branch, or engage in banking business without approval of the banking regulatory institution shall be prosecuted if committing a crime. Such illegal banks shall be closed by the banking regulatory institution of the State Council. If the activity is not serious enough to constitute a crime, its unlawful income would be confiscated and a fine of one to five times unlawful income should be imposed. If there is no unlawful income or the unlawful income is less than RMB 500,000, a fine in the amount of RMB 500,000 to RMB 2,000,000 should be imposed. Art. 66: If a foreign-funded bank does not provide relevant documents and materials, the banking regulatory institution of the State Council will order it to make a correction; otherwise a fine in the amount of RMB 100,000 to 300,000 should be imposed.

Note: Compiled by the author.

One typical example is the parallel formulation of rules for granting administrative licences to Chinese-funded banks and foreign-funded banks. On January 12, 2006, only about one month after issuing the Provisions of the CBRC on

Legal Works, the CBRC issued four decrees concerning banking licencing matters. The first decree is the Provisions of the CBRC on Implementation Procedures of Administrative Licencing, applicable to all kinds of commercial banks.[8] The second decree is the Measures of the CBRC for Granting Administrative Licences to Chinese-Funded Commercial Banks, applicable only to state-owned commercial banks, joint-stock commercial banks, city commercial banks and city cooperatives.[9] The third decree is the Measures of the CBRC for Granting Administrative Licences of Cooperative Financial Institutions,[10] applicable only to rural commercial banks and several kinds of rural cooperatives.[11] The fourth decree is the Measures of the CBRC for Granting Administrative Licences to Foreign-Funded Financial Institutions,[12] applicable only to wholly-foreign-funded commercial banks, Sino-foreign equity joint venture commercial banks, foreign bank branches, foreign bank representative offices, and foreign-funded finance companies.[13] There are many overlaps among the four decrees, especially between the second decree (for Chinese-funded banks) and the fourth decree (for foreign-funded banks).

III. Identical Treatment and WTO De Facto Discrimination

The common banking law and the overlaps between the foreign banking law and domestic banking law do not guarantee that China's banking law is consistent with WTO national treatment obligations. The WTO itself does not adopt the concept of *the same treatment* or *identical treatment* for both national treatment obligations and MFN treatment obligations. GATT Articles I, III, GATS Articles II, XVII, TRIPS Article III, and TRIMs Article II use the wording *no less favourable treatment*. Identical treatment is only the same treatment in form, that is, the formally identical treatment.

---

8 Provisions of the CBRC on Implementation Procedures of Administrative Licencing [*Zhongguo Yinhangye Jiandu Guanli Weiyuanhui Xingzheng Xuke Shishi Chengxu Guiding*], issued on January 12, 2006, effective from February 1, 2006, CBRC Decree [2006] No. 1, in COMPENDIUM OF CHINA BANKING RULES [ZHONGGUO YINHANGYE JIANGUAN GUIZHANG HUIBIAN] (2003–2006) 224–28 (Law Press China 2006) (hereinafter COMPENDIUM OF CHINA BANKING RULES).

9 Measures of the CBRC for Granting Administrative Licences to Chinese-Funded Commercial Banks, art. 2, issued on January 12, 2006, effective as of February 1, 2006, CBRC Decree [2006] No. 2, in COMPENDIUM OF CHINA BANKING RULES 229–60.

10 Measures of the CBRC for Granting Administrative Licences to Cooperative Financial Institutions [*Zhongguo Yinhangye Jiandu Guanli Weiyuanhui Hezuo Jinrong Jigou Xingzheng Xuke Shixiang Shishi Banfa*], issued on January 12, 2006, effective from February 1, 2006, CBRC Decree [2006] No. 3, in COMPENDIUM OF CHINA BANKING RULES 261–308.

11 Id. art. 2.

12 Measures of the CBRC for Granting Administrative Licences to Foreign-Funded Financial Institutions, issued on January 12, 2006, effective from February 1, 2006, CBRC Decree [2006] No. 4, in COMPENDIUM OF CHINA BANKING RULES 309–50.

13 Id. art. 2.

A. GATS Article XVII:2

GATS Article XVII:2 reads:

> A Member may meet the requirement of paragraph 1 by according to services and service suppliers of any other Member, either formally identical treatment or formally different treatment to that it accords to its own like services and service suppliers.

The text of GATS Article XVII:2 is modelled on a GATT Panel Report concerning Article III of the GATT 1947.[14] In *US – Section 337 of the Tariff Act of 1930*,[15] the Panel used the wording *formally identical*.[16] It is generally recognized that GATT Article III:4 covers both de jure and de facto inconsistency.[17] This is also the case for GATS Article XVII. GATS Article XVII:2, in fact, has incorporated both de jure and de facto discrimination. The notion of *treatment no less favourable* is interpreted by paragraphs 2 of GATS Article XVII to include both *formally identical treatment* and *formally different treatment*.[18]

In the beginning of the Uruguay Round negotiations, there were three options for national treatment. The first option was a traditional definition of national treatment which tended to be de jure, supported by Japan and Korea.[19] The second option was the equality of competitive opportunities, supported by the EC, Switzerland, Canada and the United States.[20] The third option was the equivalent treatment.[21] In the end, the second option was accepted; that is, national treatment should go beyond de jure and guarantee equality of competitive opportunities.

---

[14] Z. Werner Zdouc, *WTO Dispute Settlement Practice Relating to the GATS*, 2(2) J. INT'L ECON. L. 295, 335 (1999); see also Aaditya Mattoo, *National Treatment in the GATS, Corner-stone or Pandora's Box*? 31 J. WORLD TRADE 107, 123 (1997).

[15] Panel Report, *US – Section 337 of the Tariff Act of 1930*, adopted November 7, 1986, BISD 36S/345, L/6439.

[16] Id. ¶ 5.11 (The panel further stated that the wording "treatment no less favourable" in paragraph 4 of GATT Article III called for "effective equality of opportunities for imported products", and that application of formally identical legal provisions would in practice accord less favourable treatment to imported products, or application of different legal treatment to imported products may in fact be no less favourable).

[17] Id.

[18] In the view of the Panel of *EC – Banana III*, paragraphs 2 and 3 of GATS Article XVII do not impose new obligations on WTO Members additional to those contained in paragraph 1. See Panel Report, *EC – Banana III*, ¶ 7.301.

[19] Working Group on Financial Services Including Insurance, Note on the Meeting of June 11–13, 1990, MTN.GNS/FIN/1, ¶¶ 44, 46, 49 (July 5, 1990).

[20] Id. ¶¶ 44, 45, 57, 59; see also Working Group on Financial Services Including Insurance: Note on the Meeting of July 12–13, 1990, MNT.GNS/FIN/2, ¶¶ 18, 33, 58 (August 10, 1990).

[21] MTN.GNS/FIN/1, ¶ 44.

De jure discrimination is easily identified through comparison of treatment between domestic and foreign services or service suppliers. However, it is difficult to determine de facto discrimination. According to GATS Article XVII:2, formally identical treatment might result in less favourable treatment, i.e. de facto discrimination, whereas formally different treatment can result in no less favourable treatment. Therefore, there are four possible permutations, as follows:

a. Formally identical treatment results in no less favourable treatment;
b. Formally identical treatment results in less favourable treatment;
c. Formally different treatment results in no less favourable treatment;
d. Formally different treatment results in less favourable treatment.

In the four permutations, (a) and (c) are compatible with GATS national treatment obligations, while (b) and (d) run counter to GATS national treatment obligations. With respect to (b), it seems that a complaining party, usually a foreign country which claims that its services or services suppliers are discriminated against by a host country, should bear the burden of proof to show that "formally identical treatment results in less favourable treatment". On the other hand, with respect to (d), formally different treatment itself constitutes prima facie evidence that the disputed measure may be inconsistent with national treatment obligations. It is the turn of the defendant party to take the burden to prove that "formally different treatment results in no less favourable treatment", which is also the view of the GATT Panel in *U. – Section 337 of the Tariff Act of 1930*.[22]

B. GATS Article XVII:3: Modifying the Conditions of Competition

GATS Article XVII:3 reads:

> Formally identical or formally different treatment shall be considered to be less favourable if it modifies the conditions of competition in favour of services or service suppliers of the Member compared to like services or service suppliers of any other Member.

GATS Article XVII:3 goes further to try to provide a criterion to determine what measures will accord less favourable treatment to foreign services or service suppliers. The criterion is whether the formally identical or formally different treatment modifies the conditions of competition.[23] The wording of GATS Article

[22] Panel Report, *US – Section 337 of the Tariff Act of 1930*, ¶ 5.11, BISD 36S/345, L/6439.

[23] It is worth noting that the NAFTA also uses a similar standard, i.e., "equal competitive opportunities" standard, to determine whether the treatment is less favourable in financial services. NAFTA Article 1405(5) reads: "A Party's treatment of financial institutions and cross-border financial service providers of another Party, whether different or identical to

XVII:3 also originated from GATT cases. Some scholars even consider that GATS Article XVII:3 "is inspired by the GATT case law".[24] In the case of *Italian Discrimination against Imported Agricultural Machinery*,[25] the Panel for the first time used the wording "modify the conditions of competition".[26] However, the notion of modification of the conditions of competition is as vague as the notion of like services and service suppliers,[27] all of which may be the focus of disputes in cases relating to the GATS under the WTO dispute settlement mechanism. Actually, the new concept of modification of conditions of competition or its predecessor *equality of competitive opportunities* was intentionally left for the dispute settlement mechanism to interpret.[28]

C. The Same Treatment in China's Working Party Report

Paragraph 18 of the Working Party Report states:

> The representative of China further confirmed that China would provide *the same treatment* to Chinese enterprises, including foreign-funded enterprises, and foreign enterprises and individuals in China .... (emphasis added)

Paragraph 53 of the Working Party Report states:

---

that accorded to its own institutions or providers in like circumstances, is consistent with paragraphs 1 through 3 if the treatment affords *equal competitive opportunities*." (emphasis added). For the text of the NAFTA, see http://www.nafta-sec-alena.org/DefaultSite/index_e.aspx?DetailID=78 (Modified July 9, 2003).

24 Mitsuo Matsushita, Thomas J. Schoenbaum and Petros C. Mavroidis, The World Trade Organization, Law, Practice, and Policy 248 (Oxford Univ. Press 2003).

25 Panel Report, *Italian Discrimination against Imported Agricultural Machinery*, adopted October 23, 1958, BISD 7S/60.

26 Id. at 64, ¶ 12 (stating that the drafters of GATT Article III "intended to cover in paragraph 4 not only the laws and regulations which directly governed the conditions of sale or purchase but also any laws or regulations which might adversely *modify the conditions of competition* between the domestic and imported products.") (emphasis added).

27 In Hudec's view, the text of GATS Article XVII:3 seems to introduce an economic analysis of the competitive impact of the regulation in question. Robert E. Hudec, *GATT/WTO Constraints on National Regulation: Requiem for an "Aim and Effects" Test*, 32 Int'l Law 619, 639 (Fall 1998).

28 Working Group on Financial Services Including Insurance, Note on the Meeting of June 11–13, 1990, MTN.GNS/FIN/1, ¶ 59 (July 5, 1990). For the discussions of modification of the conditions of competition, see China-Electronic Payment Services, Panel Report, WT/DS413/R (July 16, 2012), ¶ ¶ 7.687–7.688, 7.700, 7.712–7.39.

> … All the enterprises and individuals enjoyed *the same treatment* in terms of participating in the process of setting government prices and government guidance prices. (emphasis added)

Paragraph 222 of the Working Party Report is as follows:

> Members of the Working Party expressed concern that imported products introduced from these special economic areas into other parts of China's customs territory should be subject to *the same treatment* in the application of all taxes, import restrictions and customs duties and other charges as that normally applied to imports into the other parts of China's customs territory …. (emphasis added)

Different from the concept used in the China Accession Protocol and in GATS Article XVII, i.e. *no less favourable treatment*, Paragraphs 18, 53 and 222 of the Working Party Report, all of which have legally binding force,[29] adopt the concept of *the same treatment. The same treatment* is not equal to *no less favourable treatment* because the latter provides an opportunity for foreign individuals and enterprises and foreign-funded enterprises to enjoy more favourable treatment than that accorded to domestic individuals and enterprises. From the above three paragraphs, it seems that China downgrades WTO national treatment (no less favourable treatment) to *the same treatment*. However, under most circumstances, the concept of *no less favourable treatment*, rather than the concept of *the same treatment*, is used by China in the context of non-discrimination, especially in the leading WTO accession document, i.e., the China Accession Protocol. In contrast, there is no wording using *the same treatment* in the China Accession Protocol. On the contrary, the wording *no less favourable treatment* is frequently used in the China Accession Protocol.[30] In the Working Party Report, the wording *no less favourable treatment* is also used in two paragraphs, i.e. paragraphs 81 and 215.[31]

---

[29] Id.

[30] See China Accession Protocol, Part I:3, Part I:5(2), Part I:8(2) and Part I:11(4), WT/L/432 (November 23, 2001)

[31] Paragraph 81 of the Working Party Report reads: "Some members of the Working Party also noted China's commitment to accord foreign enterprises and individuals, including those not invested or registered as enterprises in China, *no less favourable treatment* than that accorded enterprises in China with respect to the right to trade except as otherwise provided for in the Draft Protocol. Members of the Working Party requested that China provide detailed information regarding the process for such enterprises and individuals to obtain the right to import and export goods."

Paragraph 215 of the Working Party Report reads: "The representative of China further confirmed that access to supplies of raw materials in the textiles sector would remain at conditions *no less favourable* than for domestic users, and gave his assurance that access to supplies of raw materials as enjoyed under existing arrangements would not be adversely affected following China's accession …."

Moreover, the WTO itself does not adopt the concept of *the same treatment* or *identical treatment* for both national treatment obligations and MFN treatment obligations. GATT Articles I, III, GATS Articles II, XVII, TRIPS Article III, and TRIMs Article II use the wording *no less favourable treatment*. In accordance with Article XVI:5 of the WTO Agreement, "[r]eservations in respect of any of the provisions of the Multilateral Trade Agreements may only be made to the extent provided for in those Agreements". When China entered the WTO, China did not make any statement of reservation on any provision of the Multilateral Trade Agreements, therefore, *no less favourable treatment* should be observed by China. Strictly speaking, *no less favourable treatment* includes two possibilities. One is *the same treatment* or identical treatment. Another is *more favourable treatment*. Identical treatment for foreign products and foreign services and service suppliers is the bottom line of WTO *no less favourable treatment*. The WTO does not encourage a Member to grant more favourable treatment to foreign products or foreign services or service suppliers, nor prevent a Member from adopting more favoured treatment to them as well. If China had tried to reduce the two possibilities to one, which would be equivalent to reducing China's obligations under the WTO, other WTO Members would have objected during China's accession negotiations. Under the current WTO framework, it is possible for a Member to undertake WTO-plus obligations through negotiations with other WTO Members or based on a Member's free will, but it is impossible for a Member to undertake WTO-minus obligations without obtaining consensus from other WTO Members.

IV. Concluding Remarks

Comparing the FFFI Regulation 2001 and the FFB Regulation 2006, one can find that the latter has more articles overlapping the Commercial Banking Law 2003. Moreover, from the perspective of quantity, the number of common banking laws is more than that of either foreign banking law or domestic banking law. More and more identical treatment between foreign-funded banks and Chinese-funded banks reflects a trend that the legal status and treatment of foreign-funded banks will be at an equal level (though not absolutely identical) with that of Chinese-funded banks. It is interesting to note that the more overlaps there are between foreign banking law and Chinese banking law, the less reasons there are to keep parallel legal frameworks. Substantive equality between foreign-funded banks and Chinese-funded banks cannot justify the necessity of a formally independent and separate foreign banking law system.

CHAPTER 8
Integrating China's Banking Law Framework

Chapter 5, Chapter 6 and Chapter 7 examined the treatment of foreign-funded banks under China's existing banking law framework. This chapter discusses how to restructure China's banking law framework so as to be consistent with GATS/WTO national treatment obligations. This chapter puts forward three options to restructure China's existing banking law framework, including a single banking law framework, a dual banking law framework, and an integrated banking law framework.

I. Three Options for Restructuring China's Banking Law Framework

A. A Single Banking Law Framework

To redress the problems created by the existing banking law framework, there are three options. The first option is to unify domestic banking law and foreign banking law so that all commercial banks in China are regulated by a single banking law framework. To achieve this purpose, it is necessary to repeal the FFB Regulation 2006, the DRI 2006, and other special banking rules and measures solely for foreign-funded banks. It is also necessary to repeal special banking regulations, rules and measures merely for Chinese-funded banks. With this option, the tripartite banking law framework will become a single banking law framework in the end, under which all banking laws, regulations and rules are equally applied to foreign-funded banks and Chinese-funded banks.

The advantages of this option are efficiency and equality, while the disadvantages of the option are inflexibility, and lack of speciality and particularity. This option is supported by some Chinese scholars.[1] Argentina and Korea may be regarded as

[1] Lu Jiongxing, *Lun Wanshan Waishang Touzi Falü Zhidu* [Improving the Legal System of Foreign Merchant Investment], ZHONGGUO FAXUE [CHINESE LEGAL SCIENCE] 69, 71 (1996, no. 3); Ding Wei, "*Chao Guomin Daiyu Heli Hefa Lun*" *Pingxi*: *Waishang Touzi Lingyu guomin Daiyu Zhidu de Lixing Sibian* [An Argumentation against the Validity and Reasonableness of Super-National Treatment and the Rational Consideration for National Treatment in the Fields of Foreign Direct Investment], 22 TRIBUNE OF POLITICAL SCIENCE AND LAW [JOURNAL OF CHINA UNIV. OF POLITICAL SCIENCE AND LAW] 164, 169 (2004, no. 2) (regarding a completely uniform law framework as the final result); Wang Li, *Shijie Maoyi Zuzhi Falü Kuangjia xia Zhongguo Jinrong Shichang de Kaifang* [Opening Chinese

examples of the single banking law framework, in which, with minor exceptions, there is no distinction between the treatment of domestic and foreign banks.[2] A single banking law framework is formally consistent with the national treatment obligations. However, it must be noted that a single banking law framework does not guarantee conformity with the national treatment obligations.

B. A Dual Banking Law Framework

The second option is a dual banking law framework. The supporters of this option take the view that the division of foreign banking law and domestic banking law is consistent with the special characteristics of foreign-funded banks and China's legislative history.[3] Under the dual banking law framework, the Commercial Banking Law 2003 will become a purely domestic Commercial Banking Law, while the FFB Regulation 2006 will become a purely foreign banking law, i.e., Foreign-Funded Banking Law, both of which will be formulated by the NPC or its Standing Committee. Therefore, they have equal status. Below the two parallel laws are domestic banking regulations, rules, and foreign banking regulations, rules respectively. The two parallel law systems are separated from each other and each functions in its own way.

The advantage of the dual banking law framework is that it can satisfy to the fullest extent the requirements of the special characteristics of foreign-funded banks and Chinese-funded banks. However, the main disadvantage of the second option is that the dual banking law framework is susceptible to the national treatment issue of the GATS/WTO. In a dual banking law framework,

---

Financial Market under the WTO Legal Framework], ZHONG DE FAXUE LUNTAN [Jahrbuch des Deutsch-Chinesischen Instituts für Rechtswissenschaft der Universitaten Gottingen and Nanjing], Vol. 2, 2003, at 259, 275 (Nanjing Univ. Press 2004); Chen Yongmei, *Waishang Laihua Touzi Daiyu de falü Wenti Yanjiu* [On the Legal Issues of Foreign Investment Treatment in China], in 2 JINGJIFA LUNTAN [A Symposium on Economic Law] 441, 458, 461 (Qunzhong Press 2004).

2 See Guillermo Cabanellas, *Banking Regulation in Argentina and the Treatment of Foreign Banks*, in 2 REGULATION OF FOREIGN BANKS, UNITED STATES AND INTERNATIONAL, ch. 1, at 27–28 (Michael Gruson and Ralph Reisner (eds), 3rd edn, Lexis Publishing 2000); Kye Sung Chung and Chun Pyo Jhong, Banking Regulation in Korea, in 3 REGULATION OF FOREIGN BANKS: BANKING LAWS OF MAJOR COUNTRIES AND THE EUROPEAN UNION 577–628 (Michael Gruson and Ralph Reisner (eds), 4th edn, LexisNexis, 2005).

3 Li Yan, *Zhongguo Jiaru WTO yu Waizi Yinhang de Falü Guizhi* [China's Entering WTO and the Supervision of Foreign Banks] JOURNAL OF SHANGHAI UNIV. OF FINANCE & ECONOMICS 45,49 (2000, no. 4); Zhang Jianwei and Li Yan, *Zhongguo Jiaru WTO yu Waizi Yinhang de Falü Guizhi* [Regulation on the Foreign Banks after China entered WTO], FINANCIAL LAW FORUM 41, 43–44 (2001, no. 12); see also ZHONGFEI ZHOU, CHINESE BANKING LAW AND FOREIGN FINANCIAL INSTITUTIONS 199–200 (Kluwer Law International 2001) (arguing that China should adopt an all-inclusive foreign banking law in order to overcome the existing confusion in application and conflicts).

there are three kinds of banking measures in two related but separate banking rules: overlap (the same treatment), preferences (more favourable treatment), and discriminations (less favaourable treatment). For overlap part, it is necessary to coexist in two separate rules. For preference part, it is objected by domestic banks as adverse discrimination. For discrimination part, it is inconsistent with national treatment obligations unless it is within the scope of the reservations. Therefore, a dual banking law framework is in a dilemma: if it is intended to give preferences to foreign banks, it will be objected to by domestic banks; if it is intended to give favours to domestic banks, it will be complained about by foreign banks; if it is intended to make a copy of another banking rule, domestic or international, it will be criticized by both domestic banks and foreign banks as futile repeat. As a whole, such a dilemma can be described as a no-win situation.

Besides, the cost of making a dual banking law framework is as high as the cost of making a tripartite banking law framework. No matter how many differences there are between foreign-funded banks and Chinese-funded banks, there will be considerable overlaps between the two groups. A dual law framework can easily result in the waste of legislation resources, and the increase of the regulatory cost of the banking regulators. Legislation cost was not considered by the drafters of China's Legislation Law 2000. However, the Enforcement Outline for Overall Promotion of Administration by Law states that the governmental legislation shall consider legislation process cost, enforcement cost and social cost.[4] A dual banking law framework is not a copying machine of legislation. In China, a foreign banking law and a domestic banking law, even if they are totally the same, must pass two separate legislation proceedings, which are usually time-consuming and resource-consuming.

The Chinese legislators realized the problems of dual or tripartite law framework decades ago. Before 1999, there were three kinds of contract laws in China, including Economic Contract Law, Foreign-Related Economic Contract Law and Technology Contract Law, applicable to different kinds of contracts, i.e., domestic contracts, foreign-related contracts and technology contracts. In 1999, China passed a uniform Contract Law after integrating the three kinds of special contract laws. According to Gu Ang'ran, who was in charge of the work of drafting the Contract Law, the integrated Contract Law was a reflection of social and economic changes and the deepening of the "reform and open" policy in China, and for a demand of developing a socialist market economy.[5]

---

[4] The Enforcement Outline for Overall Promotion of Administration by Law [*Quanmian Tuijin Yifa Xingzheng Shishi Gangyao*], para.17, Guofa [2004] No. 10, http://www.gov.cn/ztzl/yfxz/content_374160.htm.

[5] Gu Ang'ran, An Introduction to the Draft of Contract Law of the PRC, Second Session of Ninth NPC, March 9, 1999, http://www.npc.gov.cn/wxzl/gongbao/2000-12/06/content_5007082.htm

Some people may use the US federal foreign banking law framework, including the International Banking Act of 1978 (IBA)[6] and the Foreign Bank Supervision Enhancement Act of 1991 (FBSEA),[7] as an example to support the dual banking law framework.[8] But after looking at the two acts, one can find that the two special foreign banking laws cannot be used as evidence to support the argument that the United States has a dual banking law framework. On the contrary, the IBA and the FBSEA are examples showing that the United States has a uniform banking law framework which provides equal treatment between domestic banks and foreign banks. In fact, the IBA is the codification of national treatment.[9] The FBSEA also accords national treatment to foreign banks. For example, the FBSEA sets out that foreign banks must meet the same standards as US domestic banks when acquiring bank or nonbank subsidiaries in the United States.[10] Indeed, one purpose of the FBSEA is to ensure that foreign banks in the United States are regulated and supervised within the same broad framework as US domestic banks.[11] As Alan Greenspan stated: "It has been the policy of the United States at least since the adoption of the International Banking Act of 1978 to apply the principle of national treatment to the regulation of foreign banks in the United States."[12]

The IBA and FBSEA do not constitute an independent and exclusive foreign banking law framework in the United States. They, especially the IBA, lay the foundation of national treatment in the banking area of the United States at the federal level.[13] The two Acts can never be regarded as the whole set of rules regulating foreign banks in the United States, nor the majority of such rules.

---

6 Pub. L. No. 95–369, 92 Stat. 607 (1978).

7 Pub. L. No. 102–242, 105 Stat. 2236 (1991).

8 For example, Zhou Zhongfei is of the view that the US has a separate and parallel foreign banking law framework. JINRONG JIANGUANXUE YUANLI [PRINCIPLES OF FINANCIAL REGULATION] ch. 9, at 222 (Ding Bangkai and Zhou Zhongfei (eds), Peking Univ. Press 2004).

9 Daniel B. Gail, Joseph J. Norton and Michael K. O'Neal, *The Foreign Bank Supervision Act of 1991: Expanding the Umbrella of "Supervisory Reregulation"*, 26 INT'L LAW. 993, 995 (1992); see also Joseph J. Norton and Christopher D. Olive, *A By-Product of the Globalization Process: The Rise of Cross-Border Bank mergers and Acquisitions: The US Regulatory Framework*, 56 BUS. LAW. 591, 597 (2001) (stating that the IBA in reality "imposed" national treatment to foreign banks); John C. Dugan, Peter L. Flanagan and E. Jason Albert, *FDIC Insurance and Regulation of US Branches of Foreign Bank*, in 1 REGULATION OF FOREIGN BANKS: UNITED STATES AND INTERNATIONAL 331, 333 n. 7 (Michael Gruson and Ralph Reisner (eds), LexisNexis 4th edn, 2003).

10 US Department of the Treasury, *National Treatment Study Report 1998*, at 31, http://www.treas.gov/offices/international-affairs/nts/.

11 Id. at 30.

12 Statement of Board Chairman Alan Greenspan before the House Committee on Banking, Finance and Urban Affairs, June 11, 1991.

13 See K.N. SCHEFER, INTERNATIONAL TRADE IN FINANCIAL SERVICES: THE NAFTA PROVISIONS 79 (Kluwer Law International 1999) (stating that the US banking regulations benefit foreign banks as much as they do domestic banks).

According to a review made by the GAO, foreign bank branches and agencies in the United States are subject to substantially the same laws and regulations as US domestic banks,[14] notwithstanding some adaptations.[15] For instance, the Riegle-Neal Interstate Banking and Branching Efficiency Act of 1994 (Riegle-Neal Act)[16] applies to both US and foreign banks, [17] and foreign banks enjoy the benefits of the Riegle-Neal Act "to much the same extent as domestic banks".[18] The Gramm-Leach-Bliley Act of 1999 (GLBA)[19] also generally applies to both US and foreign banking organizations.[20] Furthermore, foreign branches and agencies in the United States are subject to the same consumer protection law as US banks.[21]

The Office of the Comptroller of the Currency (OCC), as the regulator of US national banks and the federal branches and agencies of foreign banks, issued a manual including a sentence on national treatment policy of the OCC that reads as:

> Except as otherwise provided by the International Banking Act of 1978 (IBA), other federal laws or regulations, or OCC policy, a federal branch or agency [of foreign banks] generally is authorized to operate under the same rights and privileges and subject to the same duties, restrictions, penalties, liabilities, conditions and limitations that apply to a national bank in the same location.[22]

Although there is a dual banking system in the United States, it refers to the division between the federal banking system and the state banking system, not domestic banking system and foreign banking system.[23] A dual banking law system

[14] Report to the Banking Minority Member, Committee on Banking, Housing and Urban Affairs, US Senate, February, 1996, Foreign Banks: Assessing Their Role in the US Banking System, GAO/GGD-96–26, "Executive Summary", at 4, http://www.gao.gov/archive/1996/gg96026.pdf.

[15] Id. ch. One: Introduction, at 17–18.

[16] Pub. L. No. 103–328, 108 Stat. 2338 (1994).

[17] John C. Dugan and James A. McLaughlin, *Forms of Entry, Operation, Expansion, and Supervision of Foreign Banks in the United States*, in 1 Regulation of Foreign Banks: United States and International 14 (Michael Gruson and Ralph Reisner (eds), LexisNexis 4th edn, 2003); see also National Treatment Study Report 1998, supra note 10, at 37 (stating that the Riegle-Neal Act affords foreign banks national treatment with respect to interstate banking and branching).

[18] Dugan and McLaughlin, id. at 34.

[19] Pub. L. No. 106–102, 113 Stat. 1338 (1999).

[20] See Dugan and McLaughlin, supra note 17, at 18; see also Norton and Olive, supra note 9, at 627–28.

[21] GAO/GGD-96–26, supra note 14, at 44.

[22] *Federal Branches and Agencies: Entry/Expansionary Activities/Other Changes and Activities*, Comptroller's Corporate Manual, at 2–3, Washington, D.C., December 1999, http://www.occ.treas.gov/corpbook/group4/public/pdf/fba.pdf.

[23] Alfred M. Pollard et al., Banking Law in the United States 44–45 (Butterworth Legal Publishers 1988); see also Norton and Olive, supra note 9, at 597 (stating that the

for domestic banks and foreign banks does not exist in the United States. Therefore, the US foreign banking law framework cannot be used as an example to support the segregation of the domestic banking law framework and the foreign banking law framework. This conclusion does not necessarily mean that China should have a banking law framework similar to that of the United States. Fundamentally, the mode of China's banking law framework should be based on the whole picture of China's law framework in the context of China's legal history, economic situation, political situation, not on a mode adopted by some other countries with different situations and backgrounds. The US mode, as well as other countries' modes, can only provide references, not standards.

C. An Integrated Banking Law Framework

Based on the above analysis of the single banking law framework and the dual banking law framework, I propose the third option, i.e., an integrated banking law framework. The core of the banking law framework is to make an integrated banking law framework based on vertical integration and horizontal integration, which is generally applicable to both Chinese-funded banks and foreign-funded banks, without ignoring special considerations for foreign-funded banks.

Vertical Integration

First of all, I suggest adding a special chapter relating to foreign-funded banks in the Commercial Banking Law 2003, incorporating mainly the prudential measures in the FFB Regulation 2006 and the DRI 2006, which will upgrade the measures to the level of "law" enacted by the NPC or its Standing Committee. I call this process the vertical integration. The special foreign banking law chapter in the Commercial Banking Law 2003 may contain minimum registered capital requirements for foreign bank subsidiaries and equity joint venture banks, minimum working capital requirements for foreign bank branches in China, and other prudential considerations for foreign-funded banks, which are deemed to be necessarily different from those for Chinese-funded banks. Through vertical integration, China's banking law framework will be more stable than the current banking law framework because the basic rules for foreign-funded banks are upgraded to the "law" level by being incorporated in the Commercial Banking Law under the integrated banking law framework. Certainly, laws enacted by the NPC and its Standing Committee are more stable than regulations and rules. Meanwhile, the vertical integration does not mean that all foreign banking supervisory measures must be upgraded to the "law" level as part of the Commercial Banking Law. Only fundamental measures, such as capital requirements, can be incorporated into the "law" level. Other less fundamental and less significant measures concerning

IBA national treatment attempted to adapt the dual banking system, i.e., state and federal systems, to foreign bank operations in the United States).

foreign-funded banks can be horizontally integrated into corresponding common banking regulations and rules.

As to the more favourable treatment measures to foreign-funded banks, Chinese authorities may decide on their own whether to maintain or to repeal them. If it is necessary to maintain those more favourable treatment measures in order to attract foreign investment to China's banking market, those measures may also be integrated into the special foreign banking chapter(s).[24] As a result, the special foreign banking chapters in general banking laws, regulations and rules may include both less favourable treatment which can be justified by prudential carve-out and more favourable treatment.

The vertical integration has a historical basis in China's banking legislation. As introduced in Chapter 1, there is a special chapter on foreign banks in the Banking Law 1947 promulgated by the ROC government.[25] The special foreign banking law chapter remains in Taiwan's existing Banking Law 2005.[26] However, a vertically integrated foreign banking law chapter in China's Commercial Banking Law should be different from the foreign banking law chapter in Taiwan's Banking Law. In fact, China's foreign banking law chapter should be a foreign-funded banking law chapter applicable to Sino-foreign equity joint venture banks, wholly-foreign-funded banks, and foreign bank branches; while Taiwan's foreign banking law chapter is a foreign banking law chapter applicable only to foreign bank branches.[27]

Another aspect of the vertical integration is to repeal the fourth level of China's vertical banking law framework, i.e., "other banking normative documents". Strictly speaking, there is no legal position of "other banking normative documents" in China's de jure legal framework. "Other banking normative documents" do not constitute part of formal legal sources of China. In practice, "other banking normative documents" in forms of "notice", "letter", or "reply" take effect and legally bind upon relevant commercial banks. Sometimes, some of the normative documents, like notices and letters, are deemed to be confidential information

---

[24] It is noteworthy that some preferential treatment measures related to foreign-funded banks are not solely covered by the banking law framework, but concurrently or predominantly covered by tax law framework, such as the preferential tax rates.

[25] The Banking Law 1947, promulgated on September 1, 1947, effective at the same day, in 3 ZHONGHUA MINGUO LIUFA LIYOU PANJIE HUIBIAN [A COMPILATION OF THE SIX CODES OF THE REPUBLIC OF CHINA] 541–59 (Wu Jingxiong (ed.), Guo Wei revised, Huiwentang Xinji Shujü 1947).

[26] Banking Law [*Yinhangfa*], amended in 2005, ch. 7 (Foreign Banks), in JIN TONGLIN, YINHANGFA [BANKING LAW] 506–31 (5th edn, Sanmin shujü 2005), also available at http://web.ntit.edu.tw/~beatrice/f-law1.pdf.

[27] Id. art. 116 (defining foreign banks in the Banking Law as foreign bank branches in Taiwan). For Taiwan's banking law, see generally, YANG CHENGHOU, YINHANGFA SHIYI [INTERPRETING THE BANKING LAW] (Sanmin shujü 1993); JIN TONGLIN, supra note 26; XIAO CHANGRUI, YINHANG FALING SHIWU [Practice of Banking Laws and Regulations] (Huatai wenhua shiye gongsi 4th edn, 2000).

available only to insiders, which will inevitably annoy outsiders, especially some foreigners. For example, a notice is often issued to particular parties, not to the public, but the legal effect of the notice is not always precisely predictable, especially for potentially affected parties, like foreign-funded banks. Furthermore, there is not a clear, reasonable, substantive distinction between "banking rules" and "other banking normative documents". Banking rules of the CBRC are defined as normative documents formulated by the CBRC, signed by the Chairman of the CBRC in the form of "decree" [*ling*], [28] while other banking normative documents are formulated and issued by the CBRC or its local branches.[29] Because the fourth tier of China's banking law framework is not covered by the Legislation Law, "other banking normative documents" lack a set of legal proceedings to make, revise, monitor, and repeal. Thus, "other banking normative documents" are unstable, interim, arbitrary, opaque, sometimes allusive, or even partly dependent on the preference or taste of leaders of regulators. The application of other banking normative documents by Chinese courts is also unstable. In 2004, the Supreme People's Court issued the Minutes of Meetings on the Application of Law in Administrative Cases.[30] According to the internal document made by the Supreme People's Court, if a court finds "other normative documents" lawful, effective, reasonable and proper, it should confirm their binding force. The courts have broad discretion to determine the validity of "other normative documents".

To make a stable banking law framework, I suggest removing the fourth tier of China's banking framework as a whole and, if necessary, upgrading some of them to the third level, i.e., the level of banking rules. Accordingly, China's four-tiered banking law framework will become a three-tiered banking law framework, including, from top to bottom, banking laws, banking regulations, and banking rules.

Horizontal Integration

The horizontal integration includes two aspects, i.e., the internal integration and the external integration. The internal integration takes place between different banking regulations and rules for different Chinese-funded commercial banks, especially between the state-owned commercial banks and the joint-stock commercial banks.

---

28 Measures of the CBRC for Administrative Reconsideration [*CBRC Xingzheng Fuyi Banfa*], art. 6, para. 2, CBRC Decree [2004] No. 8, issued by the CBRC on December 28, 2004, effective February 1, 2005, in GAZETTE OF THE CBRC 190–95 (bound vols. 7–12, 2004, no. 12); see also Provisions of the CBRC on Legal Works [*Falü Gongzuo Guiding*], art. 51, issued on November 26, 2005, effective from February 1, 2006, CBRC Decree [2005] No. 4, in GAZETTE OF THE CBRC 13–25 (2005, no. 11), also available at http://www.cbrc.gov.cn/govView_704BD678A4A24FB1B7DDDB82D5EFE534.html.

29 Measures of the CBRC for Administrative Reconsideration, art. 6, para. 2, id; see also Provisions of the CBRC on Legal Works, id. arts. 57, 58, 114.

30 Minutes of Meetings on the Application of Law in Administrative Cases [*Guanyu Shenli Xingzheng Anjian Shiyong Falv Guifan Wenti de Zuotanhui Jiyao*], Supreme People's Court, May 18, 2004, [2004] No. 96.

The aim of the internal integration is to create *tertium comparationis* for the normal operation of GATS/WTO national treatment by way of unifying treatment of Chinese-funded commercial banks. The internal integration is a prerequisite for the external integration. As Wang Yi pointed out, in order to give national treatment to foreign-funded enterprises, it is necessary to give "national treatment" to all kinds of national enterprises.[31] However, it must be noted, the internal integration should have flexibility to give special treatment to rural commercial banks and city commercial banks, such as lower registered capital requirements.

The external integration is to integrate China's foreign banking law and domestic banking law into common, general banking law. During this process, China should examine and review its current less favourable treatment measures to foreign-funded banks and determine whether they are necessary and prudential. If some measures are not consistent with GATS/WTO national treatment obligations, they should be repealed. The external integration will put foreign-funded banks and Chinese-funded banks on the same footing to the utmost extent. Meanwhile, as discussed in Chapter 7, there are many overlaps between domestic banking law and foreign banking law under the existing banking law framework. Through the external integration, the overlaps between existing foreign banking law and domestic banking law will be wiped out by being integrated into one, while the special considerations for foreign-funded banks will be put into a special chapter of the Commercial Banking Law 2003, or special chapters of general banking regulations and rules.

Moreover, by way of horizontal integration, China's banking legislation cost and banking regulatory cost can be largely reduced by the integrated banking law framework which equally applies to Chinese-funded and foreign-funded banks.

Table 8.1 The integrated banking law framework

Tier	Integrated banking law framework
1	Banking Laws (including special chapters on foreign-funded banks)
2	Banking Regulations (including special chapters or special articles on foreign-funded banks)
3	Banking Rules (including special chapters or special articles on foreign-funded banks)

[31] Wang Yi, WTO Guomin Daiyu de Falü Jiqi zai Zhongguo de Shiyong [WTO National Treatment Rules and Their Application in China] 180 (Chinese Social Science Press and the People's Court Press 2005); see also Han Caizhen, Waishang Touzi Zhengce Yu FAlü Huanjing [Policy and Law Environment of Foreign Investment] 210 (Zhongguo qinggongye chubanshe 2000).

Table 8.1 is the proposed integrated banking law framework. Compared with table 4.1 (China's vertical banking law framework) and table 4.6 (China's horizontal banking law framework), one can find the differences between China's four-tiered and tripartite banking law framework and the proposed integrated banking law framework.

Characteristics

The integrated banking law framework is different from the dual banking law framework. Under the integrated banking law framework, it is unnecessary for the NPC or its Standing Committee to make an all-inclusive special foreign banking law, or for the State Council to make an all-inclusive special foreign banking regulation (like the FFB Regulation 2006), or for the CBRC to make an all-inclusive special foreign banking rule (like the DRI 2006). The general banking laws, especially the Commercial Banking Law 2003, shall equally cover all commercial banks. On the one hand, no banking regulations can conflict with superior banking laws and no banking rules can conflict with superior banking regulations. On the other hand, banking regulations shall not repeat other banking regulations, or overlap with banking laws, and banking rules shall not repeat other banking rules, or overlap with banking regulations.

The integrated banking law framework is also different from the single banking law framework. The single banking law framework lacks flexibility for foreign-funded banks and Chinese-funded banks. The single banking law framework means identical treatment between foreign-funded banks and Chinese-funded banks, regardless of the special nature of foreign-funded banks, especially foreign bank branches. Such kind of identical treatment has been gradually replaced by the concept of *equivalent treatment* to take into account situations where identical treatment cannot be accorded because of the special nature of the beneficiaries of national treatment.[32] The GATS/WTO also allows Members to provide different treatment to foreign-funded banks according to prudential carve-out discussed in Chapter 6. The integrated banking law framework does not exclude special and different measures for foreign-funded banks, which makes it different from the rigid single banking law framework. The integrated banking law framework may incorporate the advantages of the single banking law framework and the dual banking law framework, and avoid the disadvantages of the two. Theoretically, the integrated banking law framework can combine the universality and particularity of foreign-funded banks and Chinese-funded banks.

---

[32] For example, in 1991, the OECD recognized that differences in treatment in favour of domestic entities may be justified under particular situations to be equivalent to national treatment. See OECD, NATIONAL TREATMENT FOR FOREIGN-CONTROLLED ENTERPRISES 14, 22 (Paris 1993).

Compatibility with GATS/WTO National Treatment

The integrated banking law framework may largely reduce the possibilities of potential conflicts between Chinese banking law and the GATS/WTO national treatment obligations, because Chinese banking law will apply generally and equally to both Chinese-funded banks and foreign-funded banks. The issue of WTO national treatment consistency will focus merely on the special chapter in the Commercial Banking Law or the special chapters or articles in other banking regulations or rules.

It must be kept in mind that the integrated banking law framework itself does not guarantee full consistency with GATS/WTO national treatment obligations. It depends on the detailed contents of the special chapters or articles on foreign-funded banks. Although the integrated banking law framework can reduce to the largest extent the possibilities of violating GATS/WTO national treatment obligations, it cannot eradicate the possibility of inconsistency between them. Even though the integrated banking law framework can fundamentally give foreign-funded banks *formally identical treatment*, it does not mean that it can definitely give foreign-funded banks de facto national treatment.

In form, the integrated banking law framework can largely reduce the overlaps between the existing foreign banking law and domestic banking law, and the difficulties and uncertainties in application. More significantly, it can lower the risk of inconsistency with national treatment obligations as much as possible without weakening prudential regulation of foreign-funded banks. The integrated banking law framework is a balance between national treatment obligations and national banking regulation. The basic idea is that the general application of banking law is a general rule, while special consideration for foreign-funded banks or Chinese-funded banks is an exception. In this regard, China may establish a presumption of general application in its banking laws, regulations and rules; that is, China's banking laws, regulations and rules are presumed to apply generally to both Chinese-funded banks and foreign-funded banks, unless there are special provisions. Such a presumption of general application may be incorporated as an article in the first chapter (General Provisions [*Zongze*]) of the Commercial Banking Law 2003, or in the first chapter of the Banking Supervision Law 2006. For example, Article 4 of the Banking Supervision Law 2006 provides four principles for banking supervision, i.e., law-abidance [*yifa*], openness [*gongkai*], fairness [*gongzheng*], and efficiency [*xiaolü*]. It is unclear whether fairness means national treatment, or includes, inter alia, national treatment. From the practice of BITs, especially China's BITs, "fair and equitable treatment" and "national treatment" usually stand side by side, which implies that they are two different kinds of treatment.[33] It is strongly recommended that a national treatment article be included in the Commercial Banking Law 2003, or the Banking Supervision Law 2006, or both, so as to establish a presumption of general application of banking law.

---

[33] For the discussion of the relationship between "fair and equitable treatment" and national treatment in BITs, see Wenhua Shan, The Legal Framework of EU-China Investment Relations: A Critical Appraisal 148–56 (Hart Publishing 2005).

II. Economic Basis of an Integrated Banking Law Framework

Banking reform connects with economic and political reforms, and so does banking law reform.[34] China's economic and political reforms provide bases for integrating China's banking law framework. Meanwhile, integrating the Chinese banking law framework is a reflection and inherent requirement of China's economic and political reforms.

A. Traditional Ownership Structure of the PRC

Historically, the segregation or semi-segregation of banking law is closely related to China's distinction and segregation between different ownerships. According to the traditional socialist concept, public ownership was the basis of the socialist economy system,[35] while individual economy [*geti jingji*] was only a supplement.[36] With the development of the economic reform, the PRC government began to recognize the status of private economy [*siying jingji*] as a supplement to the public ownership economy.[37] Finally, China's basic economic system has been changed into the coexistence of multiple ownerships with the public ownership as its main body.[38] Under the multiple ownerships, different economic subjects are usually conferred different rights and imposed different obligations, covered by different laws, regulations and rules.[39] By the standard of ownerships, enterprises

---

34 LIU GUANGDI, ZHONGGUO DE YINHANG [CHINA'S BANKS] 174, 176 (Beijing Publishing House 1984); see also Zhang Qinglin and Peng Zhongbo, *Lun Woguo Waizi Falü Tixi de Chonggou Moshi* [Reconstruction Pattern of Foreign Investment Law System in China], 24 FAXUE PINGLUN [Wuhan Univ. Law Review] 121, 124 (2006, no. 1) (stating that economic development and economic system determine to a large extent law-making pattern).

35 PRC Constitution 1982, art. 6, adopted at the Fifth Session of the Fifth NPC on December 4, 1982, effective December 4, 1982; see also PRC Constitution 1975, art. 5, adopted at the First Session of the Fourth NPC, January 13, 1975, in THE CONSTITUTION OF THE PEOPLE'S REPUBLIC OF CHINA (Commercial Press 1975); PRC Constitution 1978, art. 5, adopted at the First Session of the Fifth National People's Congress, March 5, 1978, in THE CONSTITUTION OF THE PEOPLE'S REPUBLIC OF CHINA (People's Publishing House 1978) (providing that there were mainly two kinds of ownership in the PRC: socialist ownership by the whole people and socialist collective ownership by working people).

36 PRC Constitution 1982, art. 11.

37 PRC Constitution (amendment 1988), art. 11 (permitting the existence and development of private economy).

38 PRC Constitution (amendment 1999), art. 6.

39 Li Shishi, *Bilateral Investment Promotion and Protection Agreements: Practice of the People's Republic of China*, in INTERNATIONAL LAW AND DEVELOPMENT 163, 167 (Paul De Waart, Paul Peters and Erik Denters (eds), Martinus Nijhoff Publishers 1988); see also Li Shishi, *On Bilateral Investment Protection Treaties Entered by China with Other Countries*, supra note 215 of Chapter 1, at 115–16.

are divided into three categories and several sub-categories which can be shown in the following table:

Table 8.2 Enterprise categories and sub-categories in China

Categories of enterprises	Sub-categories of enterprises
Chinese-funded enterprises	(1) State-owned enterprises; (2) Collective enterprises; (3) Joint-stock cooperative enterprises; (4) Joint operation enterprises; (5) Limited liability companies; (6) Joint-stock companies; (7) Private enterprises; (8) Other enterprises.
Enterprises funded by Hong Kong, Macao or Taiwan merchants	(1) Equity joint ventures (funded by HK, Macao or Taiwan); (2) Contractual joint ventures (funded by HK, Macao or Taiwan); (3) Enterprises wholly-funded by HK, Macao or Taiwan merchants; (4) Joint-stock companies funded by HK, Macao or Taiwan merchants
Foreign-funded Enterprises	(1) Sino-foreign equity joint ventures; (2) Sino-foreign contractual joint ventures; (3) Wholly-foreign-funded enterprises; (4) Foreign-funded joint-stock companies.

Source: Compiled based on the Provisions on Dividing Enterprises Categories for Registration. [*Guanyu Huafen Qiye Dengji Zhuce Leixing de Guiding*], jointly issued by the National Bureau of Statistics of China and the State Administration of Industry and Commerce on August 28, 1998, http://www.stats.gov.cn/tjbz/jjcfhf/t20021125_46792.htm.

From the above table, one can find that fund sources and ownerships, especially the latter, are the main standards of categorizing enterprises in China.[40] As a consequence, commercial banks in China are divided into several categories based on different forms of ownerships and different geographical positions, including wholly-state-owned commercial banks, joint-stock commercial banks, city commercial banks, rural commercial banks and foreign-funded commercial banks. Correspondingly, China's banking law is also divided into several categories.

[40] CAO LI, HUNHE SUOYOUZHI YANJIU [A STUDY OF THE MIXED OWNERSHIP] 73 (Guangdong People's Publishing House 2004).

Some banking regulations and rules apply only to wholly-state-owned commercial banks, some to joint-stock commercial banks, some to city commercial banks, some to rural commercial banks, some to foreign-funded commercial banks and some to all kinds of banks. This is the economic origin of the tripartite banking law framework, a semi-segregated framework.

Obviously, the standard for dividing banks is not a single standard, but a mixed standard, including simultaneously the ownership standard and geographic standard. As to geographic standard, it is also not a clear-cut standard, such as domestic banks versus foreign banks, but a mixed standard to include simultaneously domestic rural banks, domestic city banks, and foreign-funded banks, etc., which are paralleled. In a word, the current standard of dividing commercial banks in China is illogical and confusing. Under such a banking structure and banking law structure, it is difficult, if not impossible, to find domestic *tertium comparationis* with which foreign-funded banks can compare their treatment. If foreign-funded banks receive treatment as favourable as the worst-treated Chinese-funded banks (e.g., joint-stock commercial banks) but less favourable than the best-treated Chinese-funded banks (e.g., the big four state-owned commercial banks), is China in violation of GATS/WTO national treatment obligations? There is not a clear answer to this question.[41]

B. Economic System Changes

Nowadays, the traditional ownership structure is undergoing great changes and the difficult question arising from it will gradually disappear from view by a process of integration. On the whole, the PRC's economic system has experienced three stages, i.e., the planned economy (1949–1983),[42] the commodity economy with plans (1984–1991),[43] and finally the socialist market economy (1992–present).[44]

---

41 According to the OECD's Committee on International Investment and Multinational Enterprises (CIME), such kind of cases should be examined pragmatically. See OECD, NATIONAL TREATMENT FOR FOREIGN-CONTROLLED ENTERPRISES 17 (OECD 1985).

42 See, e.g., PRC Constitution 1982, art. 15 (providing that China adopted planned economy based on the socialist public ownership).

43 Decision of the Central Committee of the CCP on Economic System Reform [*Zhonggong Zhongyang guanyu Jingji Tizhi Gaige de Jueding*], adopted at the Third Plenum of the Twelfth Central Committee of the CCP on October 20, 1984, in 2 Shiyijie Sanzhong Quanhui yilai Zhongyao Wenxian Xuandu [Selections of Important Documents after the Third Plenum of the Eleventh Central Committee of the CCP] 766, 777 (Document Study Office of the Central Committee of the CCP (ed.), People's Publishing House 1987).

44 Jiang Zemin's Report to the Fourteenth National Conference of the CCP, October 12, 1992, in 1 Shisida yilai Zhongyao Wenxian Xuanbian [Selections of Important Documents since the Fourteenth Conference] 1, 18–19 (Document Study Office of the Central Committee of the CCP (ed.), People's Publishing House 1996) (stating that the aim of the economic system reform is to establish the socialist market economy); see also PRC Constitution (amendment 1993), art. 15; Working Party Report, WT/ACC/CHN/49,

Under the planned economy, which was generally recognized to be unsuitable for national treatment,[45] and incompatible with the WTO,[46] Chinese banks became a tool of the state to realize its social, political and economic goals. The planned economy was unsuitable for the operations of foreign-funded banks, which was the main reason for different treatment of Chinese-funded banks and foreign-funded banks.[47] Thus, fair play had to yield to unfair plan. However, from the second stage, China started to understand the significance of equal competition, and began to treat all types of enterprises equally without discrimination. At the current socialist market economy stage, in spite of the continuing existence of multiple ownerships, most traditional enterprises in China are under the restructuring process by way of corporationization [*gongsihua*] based on a uniform Corporation Law in order to establish a modern enterprise system. PRC Corporation Law applies to all kinds of enterprises which adopt the form of a limited liability company or the form of a joint-stock company, or the form of a wholly-state-owned company in the territory of the PRC.[48] China's state-owned enterprises basically operate in accordance with rules of the market economy.[49] The Chinese Government promised that it would no longer directly administer the human, finance and material resources and operational activities of state-owned enterprises.[50] This change of economic system has a strong impact on China's attitude to equal competition, national treatment and China's legal framework.

¶¶ 4, 6, 24, 41, 43, 221, and 263 (October 1, 2001). For the definition of the socialist market economy, see the Decision of the Central Committee of the CCP on Relevant Issues of the Socialist Market Economy, adopted at the Third Plenum of the Fourteenth Central Committee, November 14, 1993, in 1 Shisida yilai Zhongyao Wenxian Xuanbian [Selections of Important Documents Since the Fourteenth Conference] 519–48 (Document Study Office of the Central Committee of the CCP (ed.), People's Publishing House 1996).

45 Shan Wenhua, *Waizi Guomin Daiyu Jiben Lilun Wenti Yanjiu* [Studies on Basic Theoretical Issues of National Treatment on Foreign Investment], 1 GUOJI JINGJIFA LUNCONG [CHINESE J. INT'L. ECON. L.] 240, 262 (Chen An (ed.), Law Press China 1998); see also Li Hui, *Shuangbian Cujin he Baohui Touzi Tiaoyue Bijiao Yanjiu* [Comparative Study on Bilateral Treaties of Investment Promotion and Protection] 1995 CHINESE Y.B. INT'L. L. 159,166; GUOJI TOUZI FA [INTERNATIONAL INVESTMENT LAW] 291 (Yu Jinsong and Zhou Chengxin (eds), Law Press China 1997) (arguing that granting national treatment is dependent on two factors, i.e. economic system and economic development level).

46 The three Bretton Woods institutions (the IMF, the World Bank and the GATT) came from the idea of free market economy. See ANTONIO CASSESE, INTERNATIONAL LAW IN A DIVIDED WORLD § 201, at 343 (Clarendon Press 1986).

47 WU ZHIPAN, SHANGYE YINHANGFA LUN [ON COMMERCIAL BANKING LAW] 67 (Zhongguo renshi chubanshe 1993).

48 See PRC Corporation Law 2005, arts. 218.

49 Working Party Report, WT/ACC/CHN/49, ¶ 43.

50 Id.

C. Mixed Ownership and Joint-Stock System

The traditional segregation of different ownerships has been broken by the introduction of a mixed ownership [*hunhe suoyouzhi*] with the joint-stock system [*gufenzhi*] as an interface. In 1992, China promulgated the Pilot Measures for Joint-Stock Enterprises[51] to encourage joint-stock enterprises in China. In 1999, the concept of the mixed ownership appeared in an authoritative document of the CCP.[52] The joint-stock system is no longer regarded as a form of private ownership, but a form of capital organization which can be used by both socialism and capitalism, or public ownership or private ownership.[53] In 2002, the mixed ownership and joint-stock system was reaffirmed in China.[54]

The trend of developing the mixed ownership and joint-stock system is also reflected in China's banking industry. Currently, there is a tendency for integrating China's complex banking ownerships into one form, that is, the form of an integrated banking ownership by the joint-stock system.[55] Firstly, the PRC government has transformed its big four state-owned commercial banks to become joint-stock banks. The speed of the reform is very fast. In the beginning, two banks, the Bank of China and the China Construction Bank, were chosen as pilots of the joint-stock

---

[51] Pilot Measures for Joint-Stock Enterprises [*Gufenzhi Qiye Shidian Banfa*], issued by the State Commission for Structural Reforms [*Guojia Tigaiwei*], the State Plan Commission [*Guojia Jiwei*], the Ministry of Finance, the PBC, the Office of Production of the State Council [*Guowuyuan Shengchanban*], *Tigaisheng* [1992] No. 30, GAZETTE OF THE STATE COUNCIL 549–53 (1992, no. 16).

[52] Jiang Zemin, Holding the Flag of the Deng Xiaoping Theory, Promoting the Socialist Project with Chinese Characteristics to the 21st Century [*Gaoju Deng Xiaoping Lilun Weida Qizhi, ba Jianse you Zhongguo Tese Shehui Zhuyi Shiye Quanmian Tuixiang 21 Shiji*], Report to the Fifteenth National Conference of the CCP, September 12, 1997, in 1 Shiwuda yilai Zhongyao Wenjian Xuanbian [Selections of Important Documents since the Fifteenth Conference] 1, 21 (Document Study Office of the Central Committee of the CCP (ed.), People's Publishing House 2000).

[53] Id. at. 22.

[54] Jiang Zemin, Establishing a Comfortable Society, Opening up a New Prospect for the Socialist Cause with Chinese Characteristics [*Quanmian Jianshe Xiaokang Shehui, Kaichuang Zhongguo Tese Shehui Zhuyi Shiye Xin Jümian*], Report to the Sixteenth National Conference of the CCP, November 8, 2002, in 1 Shiliuda yilai Zhongyao Wenxian Xuanbian [Selections of Important Documents Since the Sixteenth Conference] 1, 20 (Document Study Office of the Central Committee of the CCP (ed.), Central Document Press 2005).

[55] See Chi Fulin, Zhu Huayou and Xia Xunge, *Jiakuai yi Shichanghua wei Mubiao de Zhongguo Shangye Yinhang Tizhi Gaige* [Accelerating the System Reform of China's Commercial Banks with the Target of Marketization], in ZHONGGUO SHANGYE YINHANG TIZHI GAIGE [SYSTEM REFORM OF CHINA'S COMMERCIAL BANKS] 62, 73 (China Hainan Reform and Development Institute (ed.), Minzhu yu Jianshe Publishing House 1995) (arguing that joint-stock system is an ideal mode for commercial banks, and modern commercial banks should be categorized by property formation forms and legal liabilities, rather than by ownerships).

system reform.[56] The CBRC issued guidelines for the joint-stock system reform of the two pilot banks.[57]

On September 17, 2004, the China Construction Bank Corporation (CCB) was set up, succeeding to all assets and liabilities of the former China Construction Bank.[58] On October 27, 2005, CCB was officially listed on the Hong Kong Exchanges and Clearing Limited (HKEx) and CCB became the first Chinese state-owned commercial bank launching the IPO after the State Council decided to make shareholding reform in its wholly-state-owned commercial banks.[59] On September 25, 2007, CCB was listed in the Shanghai Stock Exchange (SSE).[60]

On August 26, 2004, the Bank of China (BOC) Limited was established, which fully succeeded to all assets, liabilities and business of the former Bank of China.[61]

---

56 Tang Shuanning, Several Questions on the Reform of the State-Owned Commercial Banks [*Guanyu Shangye Yinhang Gaige de Jige Wenti*], Address at the Annual Conference of China Finance Academy (March 25, 2005), http://www.cbrc.gov.cn/chinese/con_main/main1.jsp#.

57 Guidelines for Corporate Governance Reform and Supervision of the Bank of China and the China Construction Bank [*Zhongguo Yinhang, Zhongguo Jianshe Yinhang Gongsi Zhili Gaige yu Jianguan Zhiyin*], effective March 11, 2004, in Gazette of the CBRC 99–100 (bound vols. 1–6, 2004, no. 3), replaced by the Guidelines for Corporate Governance and Relevant Supervision of State-owned Commercial Banks [*Guoyou Shangye Yinhang Gongsi Zhili ji Xiangguan Jianguan Zhiyin*], issued by the CBRC on April 18, 2006, effective as of April 24, 2006, CBRC *Yinjianfa* [2006] No. 22, http://www.cbrc.gov.cn/mod_cn00/jsp/cn004002.jsp?infoID=2504&type=1; see also Guidelines of the CBRC General Office for the Work of Reorganization, Reform and Market Access of the Bank of China and the China Construction Bank [*Guanyu Zhongguo Yinhang, Zhongguo Jianshe Yinhang Chongzu Gaizhi Shichang Zhunru Gongzuo Zhidao Yijian*], issued on August 31, 2004, in Gazette of the CBRC 75–79 (bound vols. 1–12, 2004, no. 8) (applying *mutatis mutandis* to other state-owned commercial banks).

58 Notice on the Incorporation of China Construction Bank Corporation, September 17, 2004, http://www.ccb.cn/portal/cn/home/moreinfo.jsp; see also the Reply of the CBRC on the Reorganization, Reform of the China Construction Bank and Establishment of China Construction Bank Corporation [*Guanyu Zhongguo Jianshe Yinhang Chongzu Gaizhi Sheli Zhongguo Jianshe Yinhang Gufen Youxian Gongsi de Pifu*], in Gazette of the CBRC 106–107 (bound vols. 7–12, 2004, no. 9).

59 CCB Gets Listed in Hong Kong Investors Show Strong Interest, http://www.ccb.com/en/newccbtoday/whatsnew/1133749853100.html (published November 3, 2005).

60 CCB Successfully Listed in the A-Share Market, http://www.ccb.com/en/newccbtoday/whatsnew/1193626974100.html (published September 25, 2007).

61 Reply of the CBRC on Relevant Issues of Transforming the Bank of China into A Joint-stock Company [*Guanyu Zhongguo Yinhang Gaizhi wei Gufen Youxian Gongsi Youguan Wenti de Pifu*], issued by the CBRC on August 22, 2004, in Gazette of the CBRC 67 (bound vols. 7–12, 2004, no. 8).

In June and July 2006, BOC was listed on HKEx and SSE respectively, becoming the first Chinese commercial bank listed in both the mainland and Hong Kong.[62]

In 2005, the Industrial and Commercial Banking of China became the Industrial and Commercial Bank of China Limited (ICBC), a joint-stock commercial bank.[63] On October 27, 2006, ICBC was listed on the SSE and the HKEx simultaneously.[64]

On January 15, 2009, the Agriculture Bank of China (ABC) was transformed into a joint stock company, i.e., the Agriculture Bank of China Ltd., and on July 15 and 16, 2010, ABC was listed on the SSE and HKEx respectively.[65] Since the joint-stock reform, the sole ownership structure of the big four state-owned commercial banks has become a mixed ownership structure by introducing multiple and strategic investors.[66]

Secondly, the city commercial banks are, by their very nature, also joint-stock banks.[67] In 1995, the State Council issued the Notice of the State Council on Organizing City Cooperative Banks,[68] defining city cooperative banks as joint-stock commercial banks invested by city enterprises, city residents and local finance.[69] Because the owners of city commercial banks include both public shareholders and private shareholders, city commercial banks take the form of mixed ownership. In 1998, the name of "city cooperative bank" was changed to "joint-stock company of city commercial bank",[70] "city commercial bank" for

---

[62] Bank of China Overview, http://www.boc.cn/en/aboutboc/ab1/200809/t20080901_1601737.html (last visited Sept. 18, 2012).

[63] Reply of the CBRC on Transforming the Industrial and Commercial Banking of China into A Joint-Stock Corporation [*Guanyu Zhongguo Gongshang Yinhang Gaizhi wei Gufen Youxian Gongsi de Pifu*], issued by the CBRC on October 26, 2005, in GAZETTE OF THE CBRC 18–19 (2005, no. 10).

[64] Http://www.icbc-ltd.com/icbcltd/ (published October 30, 2006).

[65] About ABC, Company Overview, http://www.abchina.com/en/about-us/about-abc/Overview/ (last visited September 18, 2012).

[66] For example, the promoters of the China Construction Bank Corporation include five shareholders, i.e., the Central Huijin Investment Company Ltd, China Jianyin Investment Company Ltd, State Grid Corporation of China, Shanghai Baosteel Group Corporation, China Yangtze Power Co., Ltd, in GAZETTE OF THE CBRC 107 (bound vols. 7–12, 2004, no. 9).

[67] Tang Shuangning, *It Takes Ten Years to Grow Trees, But a Hundred to Rear People*, Address at the Working Conference of City Commercial Banks and the Sixth Conference of the Development Forum of City Commercial Banks (June 22, 2005), http://www.cbrc.gov.cn/chinese/con_main/main1.jsp#.

[68] Notice of the State Council on Organizing City Cooperative Banks [*Guowuyuan Guanyu Zujian Chengshi Hezuo Yinhang de Tongzhi*], issued by the State Council on September 7, 1995, effective September 7, 1995, *Guofa* [1995] No. 25, http://202.202.96.84/WTO/1/fagui/d1bf/d12p/d12p271.htm.

[69] Id.

[70] Notice on Name Change of City Cooperative Banks [*Guanyu Chengshi Hezuo Yinhang Biangeng Mingcheng Youguan Wenti de Tongzhi*], jointly issued by the PBC and

short, given the fact that city cooperative banks were, by their very nature, not "cooperative banks", but joint-stock commercial banks.[71]

Thirdly, rural commercial banks are also joint-stock banks by their nature. Rural commercial banks originated from rural cooperative banks. Rural cooperative banks are joint-stock commercial banks.[72] According to the definition in the Interim Provisions of Administration of Rural Commercial Banks,[73] rural commercial banks are local joint-stock financial institutions established jointly by peasants, rural industrialists and businessmen, enterprises with legal personality and other economic organizations, with the purpose of providing financial services to local peasants, agriculture and rural economic development.[74] For example, on October 18, 2005, the CBRC approved the setting up of the Beijing Rural Commercial Bank Joint-Stock Corporation.[75] In 2009, 43 rural commercial banks opened business.[76] From the perspective of the multiple owners, rural commercial banks also take the form of mixed ownership by way of the joint-stock system.

Fourthly, China's traditional joint-stock commercial banks (not including the big four banks) have developed smoothly. In 1986, the first joint-stock commercial bank, i.e., the Bank of Communications [*Jiaotong Yinhang*] was set up.[77] In 1996, China Minsheng Banking Corp. Ltd (CMBC) became the first joint-stock

---

the State Administration for Industry and Commerce on March 12, 1998, PBC *Yinfa* [1998] No. 94, http://www.pbc.gov.cn/detail_frame.asp?col=340&id=166&keyword=&isFromDetail=1. This rule issued by the PBC has been succeeded by the CBRC. See Announcement of the PBC and the CBRC, [2004] No. 20, Annex 2, December 17, 2004, GAZETTE OF THE PBC 3–8 (2004, no. 18–19).

71 Id. § 1.

72 Decision of the State Council on the Reform of the Rural Financial System [*Guowuyuan Guanyu Nongcun Jinrong Gaige de Jueding*], August 22, 1996, in 3 Shisida yilai Zhongyao Wenxian Xuanbian [Selections of Important Documents since the Fourteenth Conference], at 1996, 2001 (Document Study Office of the Central Committee of the CCP (ed.), People's Publishing House 1999).

73 Interim Provisions of Administration of Rural Commercial Banks [*Nongcun Shangye Yinhang Guanli Zanxing Guiding*], CBRC *Yinjianfa* [2003] No. 10, issued on September 12, 2003, effective September 12, 2003, GAZETTE OF THE STATE COUNCIL 29–35 (2004, no. 15).

74 Id. art. 2.

75 Reply of the CBRC to the Opening of the Beijing Rural Commercial Bank Joint-Stock Corporation [*Guanyu Beijing Nongcun Shangye Yinhang Gufen Youxian Gongsi Kaiye de Pifu*], CBRC, October 18, 2005, GAZETTE OF THE CBRC 14 (2005, no. 10) (stating that the bank's nature is a joint-stock commercial bank).

76 The CBRC Annual Report 2009, at 35.

77 See Notice of the State Council on Setting Up the Bank of Communications [*Guowuyuan Guanyu Zujian Jiaotong Yinhang de Tongzhi*], July 24, 1986, in ZHONGHUA RENMIN GONGHEGUO JINRONG FAGUI HUIBIAN [COMPILATION OF FINANCIAL REGULATIONS OF THE PRC] 202 (Regulation Compilation Office of the Legal Affairs Bureau of the State Council ed., Law Press China 1992).

commercial bank whose main investors are non-state-owned enterprises. On December 19, 2000, A-shares of CMBC were listed on the SSE, and on November 26, 2009, CMBC was listed on Hong Kong Exchanges.[78]

To sum up, China's domestic banking reform can be deemed as a joint-stock reform with the aim of establishing joint-stock commercial banks.[79] In essence, joint-stock commercial banks are commercial banks with mixed ownership. For example, in the China Zheshang Bank, private shares amount to 85.71 per cent of the total shares.[80] Moreover, Sino-foreign equity joint venture banks can also be regarded as banks with mixed ownership.[81] Under the mixed ownership, the segregation of different ownerships becomes meaningless; therefore, the different rights and obligations for different subjects of different ownerships become groundless. Thus, uniform *tertium comparationis* can be provided as the basis of comparing treatment of Chinese-funded banks and foreign-funded banks. In a word, the economic system and ownership changes lay the economic foundation for integrating China's banking law framework. Meanwhile, an integrated banking law framework will promote China's banking reform, i.e., the joint-stock reform.

III. Political Basis of an Integrated Banking Law Framework

As analysed in Chapter 1, historically, the political reason is the main reason for the lack of national treatment in PRC's commercial treaties and laws from 1949 to 1978, during which China's political environment was unsuitable for national treatment. After the CCP[82] adopted the "reform and open" policy in the late 1970s,[83] China's political environment also changed.

---

78 About CMBC, http://www.cmbc.com.cn/en/about/jianjie.shtml (last visited September 18, 2012).

79 See Tang Shuangning, Several Questions on the Reform of the State-Owned Commercial Banks [*Guanyu Shangye Yinhang Gaige de Jige Wenti*], Address at the Annual Conference of China Finance Academy (Mar. 25, 2005), http://www.cbrc.gov.cn/chinese/con_main/main1.jsp#.

80 Wei Rongzhi, *The 12th Joint-Stock Commercial Bank, 85.71 per cent Private Capital*, Guoji Jinrong Bao [International Finance News] (in Chinese), August 17, 2004, at 1.

81 See CAO LI, supra note 40, at 96 (stating that both Sino-foreign equity joint ventures and Sino-foreign contractual joint ventures are enterprises with mixed ownership).

82 According to the PRC Constitution, the CCP is the permanent leading party of the PRC. See PRC Constitution, preamble.

83 Communiqué of the Third Plenum of the Eleventh Central Committee of the CCP, December 22, 1978, 1 Selections of Important Documents since the Third Plenum of the Eleventh Central Committee of the CCP 1–14 (Document Study Office of the Central Committee of the CCP (ed.), People's Publishing House, 1987).

In 1993, the Central Committee of the CCP pointed out the necessity to grant national treatment to foreign-funded enterprises by creating conditions.[84] The CCP also recognized the different treatment between Chinese-funded enterprises and believed that one of the conditions for granting national treatment to foreign-funded enterprises was to treat all kinds of enterprises equally without discrimination.[85] As a result of the policy making, China began to gradually eliminate the different rights and obligations of different enterprises with different ownerships.[86]

In 1995, the CCP reaffirmed to treat all kinds of enterprises without discrimination so as to create an equally competitive environment,[87] and promised to gradually grant national treatment to foreign-funded enterprises.[88] This policy of the CCP was reiterated in a national economic conference of the Central Committee of the CCP and the State Council,[89] and was finally adopted by the NPC in 1996.[90]

In 1997, equal competition and equal status of all kinds of enterprises and the implementation of national treatment were viewed by the CCP as economic reform strategies.[91] In 2003, the CCP further announced that non-state-owned enterprises,

---

84 Decision of the Central Committee of the CCP on Relevant Issues of the Socialist Market Economy, supra note 44, at 541.

85 Id.

86 E.g., on January 1, 1994, China unified the income tax rate for all kinds of domestic enterprises, including state-owned enterprises, collective-owned enterprises, joint-stock enterprises, private-owned enterprises. See Article 1 and Article 2 of the Interim Regulation for Enterprise Income Tax [*Qiye Suodeshui Fa Zanxing Tiaoli*], the State Council Decree No.137, promulgated by the State Council on December 13, 1993, effective January 1, 1994, http://www.chinatax.gov.cn/jibenfa/jibenfa0201.htm.

87 Proposal of the Central Committee of the CCP on Formulating the Ninth Five-Year Plan of National Economy and Social Development and Prospective Objectives to 2010, adopted at the Fifth Plenum of the Fourteenth Central Committee of the CCP, September 28, 1995, in 2 Selections of Important Documents Since the Fourteenth Conference 1477, 1497 (Document Study Office of the Central Committee of the CCP (ed.), People's Publishing House 1997).

88 Id. at 1501.

89 *Report on the 1995 Economic Conference Held in Beijing*, RENMIN RIBAO [PEOPLE'S DAILY], Dec. 8, 1995.

90 Report on the Ninth Five-Year Plan of National Economy and Social Development and Prospective Objectives to 2010, adopted at the Fourth Session of the Eighth NPC on March 17, 1996, ¶ 4(5), in 2 Selections of Important Documents Since the Fourteenth Conference, at 1821, 1882 (People's Publishing House 1997) (requiring gradual implementation of national treatment to foreign enterprises and gradual unification of policies for Chinese-funded and foreign-funded enterprises).

91 Jiang Zemin, Holding the Flag of the Deng Xiaoping Theory, Promoting the Socialist Project with Chinese Characteristics to the 21st Century, supra note 52, at 22, 29.

including, inter alia, foreign-funded enterprises, should enjoy the same treatment concerning finance, tax, land use rights and foreign trade as other enterprises.[92]

In 2005, the State Council issued Relevant Opinions on Encouraging, Supporting and Guiding Personal, Private and other Non-Public Ownership Economies.[93] One of the purposes of the policy is to "remove systemic barriers influencing development of non-public economies, establish the equal status of market subjects, and realise fair competition."[94] An eye-catching feature of the policy is that market access limitations on non-public economies have been relaxed by introducing a principle of equal access and equal treatment,[95] including the following provisions.

1. Non-public economies are allowed to enter industries and areas which are not prohibited by laws and regulations. The industries and areas open to foreign capital are also open to non-public economies.[96]
2. Non-public economies and other enterprises with different ownerships shall be put on an equal footing with respect to investment examinations, financing services, financial policies, land use policies, foreign trade policies, etc.[97]
3. Regulations, rules and policies restraining the market access of non-public economies shall be sorted out and revised.[98]
4. Non-public economies are allowed to enter financial service areas, including regional joint-stock banks. They can also participate in reorganization and restructuring of banks.[99]

In order to implement the policy and create a level playing field, the State Council, in another policy document, required relevant ministries and departments, certainly including the CBRC and the PBC, to sort out and revise rules and other normative documents limiting non-public economies.[100]

---

92 Decision of the Central Committee of the CCP on Relevant Issues of the Socialist Market Economy, supra note 44, at 466, 474.

93 Relevant Opinions on Encouraging, Supporting and Guiding Personal, Private and other Non-Public Ownership Economies [*Guowuyuan Guanyu Guli Zhichi he Yindao Geti Siying deng Feigongyouzhi Jingji Fazhan de Ruogan Yijian*], February 19, 2005, *Guofa* [2005] No. 3, Renmin Ribao [People's Daily], Feb. 25, 2005.

94 Id. preamble.

95 Id. § 1(1).

96 Id.

97 Id.

98 Id.

99 Id. § 1(5).

100 Opinions of the State Council on Deepening the Economic System Reform in 2005 [*Guowuyuan Guanyu 2005 Nian Shenhua Jingji Tizhi Gaige de Yijian*], issued on April 4, 2005, People's Daily, Apr. 18, 2005.

Before the NPC passed the Enterprise Income Tax Law 2007, the Minister of Finance of China at that time, Jin Renqing, explained:

> Nowadays, Chinese economic and social conditions have made great changes, and the socialist market economy has been fundamentally established. Since China entered the WTO, Chinese domestic market has been further open to foreign investment, and Chinese-funded enterprises have gradually integrated into the world economy system, facing more and more competitive pressure. If China continued its different tax policies for domestic-funded and foreign-funded enterprises, China would put domestic-funded enterprises in an unfair playing field so as to negatively influence the establishment of a uniform, orderly, and fairly competitive market environment.[101]

In 2012, the CCP reiterated the relationship between state-owned economy and non-state-owned economy:

> We should thus steadily enhance the vitality of the state-owned sector of the economy and its capacity to leverage and influence the economy. At the same time, we must unswervingly encourage, support and guide the development of the non-public sector, and ensure that economic entities under all forms of ownership have equal access to factors of production in accordance with the law, compete on a level playing field and are protected by the law as equals.[102]

From the above policy evolution, one can find that there is a trend in China's political environment to treat different ownerships of domestic enterprises, foreign and domestic enterprises, equally without discrimination. Undoubtedly, this trend guided and supported by the CCP will have a great impact on China's law framework, including, inter alia, China's banking law framework, because China's legislation must insist on the principle of the leadership of the CCP,[103] which means that the CCP's policies will be finally embodied in China's laws, regulations and rules.[104] According to Provisions of the CBRC on Legal Works, banking rule-

---

[101] Jin Renqing, Explanation on the Draft Enterprise Income Tax Law, March 18, 2007, at the Fifth Session of the Tenth NPC, GAZETTE OF THE NPC 324, 325 (2007, no. 3).

[102] Hu Jintao, Firmly March on the Path of Socialism with Chinese Characteristics and Strive to Complete the Building of A Moderately Prosperous Society in All Respects [*Jianding Buyi Yanzhe Zhongguo Tese Shehui Zhuyi Daolu Qianjin, wei Quanmian Jiancheng Xiaokang Shehui er Fendou*], Report to the Eighteenth National Conference of the CCP, November 8, 2012, http://news.xinhuanet.com/english/special/18cpcnc/2012-11/17/c_131981259_5.htm (November 17, 2012).

[103] PRC Legislation Law, art. 3.

[104] For the leading role played by the CCP in China's legislation process, see Several Opinions on Further Strengthening Legislation Work of the State Council [*Guanyu Jinyibu Jiaqiang Guowuyuan Lifa Gongzuo de Jidian Yijian*], State Council *Guobanfa* [1999] No. 9,

making should be based on laws and administrative regulations, and directed by national economic and financial policy.[105] Under the positive political environment in favour of equal treatment, it is time to restructure China's four-tiered and tripartite banking law framework into an integrated banking law framework so as to provide equal treatment to Chinese-funded enterprises and foreign-funded enterprises, which is consistent with GATS/WTO national treatment obligations.

IV. Concluding Remarks

In order to create a level playing field and minimize the different treatment (in form and in substance) between foreign-funded banks and Chinese-funded banks, I suggest integrating China's four-tiered and tripartite banking law framework, vertically and horizontally, internally and externally. The integrated banking law framework is more likely to conform to GATS/WTO national treatment obligations and has strong economic and political bases in China. It must be noted, however, that the integrated banking law framework is an imperfect framework, which itself does not guarantee all of China's banking laws, regulations, rules under the framework are consistent with GATS/WTO national treatment obligations. Moreover, under the integrated banking law framework, special and prudential measures for foreign-funded banks are incorporated into a single chapter or into a few special articles in some common banking laws, regulations, rules, which may bring about another problem: If there is a new issue concerning foreign-funded banks which needs to be resolved immediately but there is not a legal base from the "existing" foreign banking law chapters or articles, this will result in a legislation vacuum and delay the effective banking regulation on foreign-funded banks. Although this defect may be remedied through legislative interpretation or amendment, the process of interpretation and amendment in China is too slow to be relied upon. China's legislation interpretation or amendment, to some extent, takes much more time than legislation itself. Thus, it seems to be necessary to design some "pocket articles" [*koudai tiaokuan*] to give some discretion to the banking regulators. However, these "pocket articles" may be abused as an excuse to discriminate against foreign-funded banks. Such a dilemma cannot be resolved by the integrated banking law framework, but by improving the whole level of Chinese legal system, especially enhancing the interpretation rights and procedures of the NPC Standing Committee, the State Council, the CBRC, the PBC and the people's courts for banking laws, regulations, and rules respectively.

---

issued on January 29, 1999, effective January 29, 1999, GAZETTE OF THE STATE COUNCIL 137–39 (1999, no. 5) (providing that the legislation work of the State Council must be "voluntarily" subject to the overall situations of the CCP and the State, consistent with the work plans of the CCP, adaptable to new decisions and policies of the CCP).

[105] Provisions of the CBRC on Legal Works, art. 6, para. 2, CBRC Decree [2005] No. 4.

It seems that China's banking regulators have realized the significance of national treatment in China's banking law framework. Tang Shuangning, former vice-Chairman of the CBRC, once pointed out that, in the context of the WTO, foreign-funded banks should get national treatment, and should be subject to a uniform regulation with Chinese-funded banks.[106] On November 26, 2005, the CBRC issued Provisions of the CBRC on Legal Works.[107] According to Article 39 of the Provisions of the CBRC on Legal Works, when reviewing and examining a banking rule draft, the legal department of the CBRC should take into account whether the banking rule draft treats financial institutions, other units and individuals equally. This implies that the CBRC has paid attention to the internal equality between domestic banks, and external equality between domestic banks and foreign banks. Although Article 39 of Provisions of the CBRC on Legal Works applies to only CBRC's banking rules, not to PBC's banking rules, or the State Council's banking regulations, or the NPC and its Standing Committee's banking laws, it may be a sign that China's future banking law will equally apply to all kinds of commercial banks.

---

[106] Tang Shuangning, *Jiaqiang Jinrong Jianguan, Yingjie Rushi Tiaozhan* [Strengthening Financial Regulation, Preparing for the Challenge of the Entry to the WTO], in A TREATISE TO COMMEMORATE THE FIFTH ANNIVERSARY OF THE PBC LAW 63, 65 (Treaty and Law Department of the PBC (ed.), China Finance Publishing House 2000).

[107] Provisions of the CBRC on Legal Works, CBRC Decree [2005] No. 4.

Conclusion

Banking is one of the service sectors that China promised to open to the WTO. Except for the banking reservations made by China and listed in the China Schedule under the GATS, national treatment under the GATS/WTO has relative generality. China's banking law, therefore, is restrained by GATS/WTO national treatment obligations and China's specific banking commitments under the WTO, that is to say, the GATS/WTO-plus obligations.

In comparison with the treatment of Chinese-funded banks, the treatment of foreign-funded banks in China can be divided into three categories: identical treatment, more favourable treatment, and less favourable treatment. According to the GATS/WTO law, different treatment is not tantamount to violation of GATS/WTO national treatment obligations. On the one hand, more favourable treatment itself, i.e., preferential treatment of foreign-funded banks, does not run counter to GATS/WTO national treatment obligations. On the other hand, less favourable treatment of foreign-funded banks is only prima facie evidence that the treatment could be inconsistent with GATS/WTO national treatment obligations. If less favourable treatment is due to prudential consideration, it may constitute a prudential carve-out under the GATS/WTO. Generally speaking, identical treatment and more favourable treatment are consistent with GATS/WTO national treatment obligations, while less favourable treatment is inconsistent with the obligations unless it constitutes an exception to the obligations.

Vertically, China's banking law framework includes four tiers, i.e., banking laws, banking regulations, banking rules, and other banking normative documents. Horizontally, China's banking law framework includes three types of banking law, i.e., foreign banking law applicable only to foreign-funded banks, domestic banking law applicable to Chinese-funded banks, and common banking law for both. Accordingly, China's existing banking law framework can be described as a four-tiered and tripartite banking law framework. On the whole, identical treatment takes the form of common banking law, while more favourable treatment and less favourable treatment take the form of special banking law. Such a four-tiered and tripartite banking law framework has resulted in many problems.

In my view, under the impact of the GATS/WTO national treatment obligations and with the development of China's economic and political reform, the four-tiered and tripartite banking law framework should be gradually integrated into a three-tiered framework under which Chinese-funded banks and foreign-funded banks are treated equally. However, it must be noted that GATS/WTO national treatment obligations themselves neither mandate an integrated banking law framework, nor compel China to abolish its existing banking law framework. It is within China's sovereignty to determine its law framework as long as that framework is sustainable under the test of the WTO rules. By promoting equality of treatment between Chinese-funded banks and foreign-funded banks in China, and by thus eliminating to the maximum extent discriminatory measures against foreign-funded banks, especially those imposed through parallel but separate banking regulations and rules, the integrated banking law framework serves to enhance consistency with the GATS/WTO national treatment obligations. Meanwhile, China's far-reaching economic reform and political development smooth the way for integrating China's existing banking law framework.

For this purpose, on the one hand, the current banking regulations, rules and other normative documents which apply only to foreign-funded banks or Chinese-funded banks respectively could be integrated into banking regulations, rules commonly applicable to all kinds of banks, no matter whether they are Chinese-funded, or foreign-funded, publicly-owned, privately-owned, or jointly-owned. As a result, different kinds of banks in the territory of China will be equally treated under the integrated banking law framework unless specifically provided otherwise. This is the process of horizontal integration, which aims to achieve horizontal equality.

On the other hand, in selected circumstances, it may be necessary to restrain foreign-funded banks, or, in other words, to protect Chinese-funded banks. For this purpose, China may put together the prudential measures in the existing banking laws, regulations, rules and other normative documents by adding a special foreign banking chapter or directly adding several foreign banking articles. In other words, some special and prudential provisions and articles for foreign-funded banks in the existing foreign banking regulations and rules could be preserved by being upgraded to and enshrined in a special chapter on foreign-funded banks in China's Commercial Banking Law. Current foreign banking regulations and rules, especially the FFB Regulation 2006 and the DRI 2006, which are lower than banking laws enacted by the NPC and its Standing Committee, should be upgraded to the level of laws. This is the process of vertical integration, which aims to achieve vertical equality. The mode of adding a special chapter or special articles on foreign-funded banks to a general banking law can also be extended to banking regulations and banking rules.

An integrated banking law framework itself will not necessarily influence the safety and stability of China's banking system, because China can make use of GATS exception clauses, especially the effective tool specifically provided for financial services, i.e. prudential carve-out. The proposed special chapter on foreign-funded banks in China's Commercial Banking Law is and should be based on the prudential carve-out under the GATS/WTO, despite the fact that the prudential carve-out rules have not been well developed.

In selected circumstances, it may be necessary to offer foreign-funded banks benefits which Chinese-funded banks do not enjoy in order to attract foreign investment in China's banking market. In this connection, it should be understood that the more favourable treatment of foreign-funded banks is neither required by GATS/WTO national treatment obligations, nor prohibited by them. Whether to accord more favourable treatment, such as preferential tax treatment, to foreign-funded banks is at the Chinese government's discretion.

It is time to think or rethink the real meaning of national treatment under the GATS and, from this perspective, to review laws, regulations, and administrative rules concerning trade in banking services, promulgated or amended by China before and after its accession to the WTO. Meanwhile, research on WTO national treatment may not only disclose its impact on China's banking law system, but also provide some reasonable and legal grounds to protect China's financial stability and security. The restructuring of China's banking law framework under the background of the WTO is not negative, but positive and interactive.

A positive way means China's banking law framework is not an invariable system. China's banking law should change on its own initiative based on WTO national treatment requirements. An interactive way means the restructuring of China's banking law system should not simply and entirely depend on the existing WTO national treatment rules. On the one hand, China should conform to WTO national treatment obligations. On the other hand, China may also take advantage of the WTO rules. China is entitled to keep prudential regulation of foreign-funded banks even if sometimes, on the surface, such regulation may place foreign-funded banks in less favoured conditions. The 2004 amendment to China's Foreign Trade Law of 1994 reflects that the view has been accepted by China's legislature. According to the amended Foreign Trade Law, China may limit or prohibit relevant international services trade for reasons of national security, public interest or public morality.[1] The amended Foreign Trade Law even gives the green light to limiting foreign banking services in China for the purpose of establishing or quickly establishing China's domestic banking industry.[2]

The integrated banking law framework is not a new bottle with old wine, or a new label for the same medicine [*huantang bu huanyao*]. It is neither the process of combining two into one, nor the process of simply moving the FFB Regulation 2006 and the DRI 2006 to the Commercial Banking Law. In fact, the integration process must be to integrate China's banking law, not only in form, but also in

---

1 PRC Foreign Trade Law (amended 2004), art. 26 (1), adopted at the Eighth Meeting of the Standing Committee of the Tenth NPC, April 6, 2004, effective July 1, 2004, GAZETTE OF THE NPC 247–53 (2004, no. 4).

2 Id. art. 26 (3) (providing that China, if necessary for establishing or quickly establishing a special domestic service industry, may limit international service trade). It must be noted that there was a dissenting opinion on this paragraph during the review of the draft of the amendment to the Foreign Trade Law; that is, one could not find a legal base from the existing WTO rules for this protective paragraph. See Li Chong'An, *Quanguo Renda Falü Weiyuanhui guanyu Zhonghua Renmin Gongheguo Duiwai Maoyifa (Xiuding Cao'an) Shenyi Jieguo de Baogao* [Report of the Law Commission of the Standing Committee of the NPC on the Result of the Review on the Draft Amendment to the Foreign Trade Law of the PRC], Eighth Meeting of the Standing Committee of the Tenth NPC, April 2, 2004, GAZETTE OF THE NPC 263, 264 (2004, no. 4).

substance, during which China should examine especially the different treatment to foreign-funded banks, i.e., more favourable treatment and less favourable treatment discussed in Chapter 5 and Chapter 6, and decide which different treatment should be maintained and upgraded to a foreign banking chapter in the Commercial Banking Law. Meanwhile, the overlaps between the foreign banking law and domestic banking law should not exist in the special foreign banking chapter, but exist as general provisions in the Commercial Banking Law, or in other banking regulations or rules.

The final purpose of fulfilling WTO national treatment obligations in the banking sector is to establish a level playing field for Chinese-funded banks and foreign-funded banks in the territory of China, which is also the touchstone of success or failure of China's banking law framework against the background of China's accession to the WTO, and China's banking services accession to the global financial market. An integrated banking law framework is helpful in creating such a level playing field in China. However, it must be noted that the integrated banking law framework itself cannot guarantee consistency with GATS/WTO national treatment obligations. Due to the double requirements of de facto and de jure non-discrimination, China must pay attention not only to equality in form, but also to equality in substance, that is, equal opportunities for competition, a complex issue which has never been thoroughly explored in the area of trade in services.

Moreover, the ambiguous concept of prudential carve-out in financial services trade makes the relationship between GATS/WTO national treatment and China's banking law more complex. Without a clear-cut standard of prudential measures, it is difficult to make a final conclusion whether China's banking law is consistent with GATS/WTO obligations or not. From this perspective, the nature of GATS/WTO national treatment is beyond the traditional nature of national treatment, i.e. relative treatment concerning only a domestic standard. Due to the issue of prudential carve-out, GATS/WTO national treatment is also related to absolute treatment. In other words, GATS/WTO national treatment when applied to financial services demands an international standard of prudential measures. In this regard, this book merely delves into the relationship between prudential carve-out and GATS/WTO national treatment; that is, whether prudential carve-out may constitute an exception to GATS/WTO national treatment obligations. How to establish a generally-accepted standard of prudential measures, which can be a topic for another book, is not covered by this book. Therefore, this book centres on China's banking law framework, i.e. formal equality, although it also gives consideration to substantive equality. It is expected that the formal equality embodied in the integrated banking law framework may facilitate substantive equality in the end.

This book neither touches upon all sides of China's banking law, nor draws the whole picture of GATS/WTO obligations. It only takes one part from each, that is, China's banking law framework on the one hand, GATS/WTO national treatment on the other hand, and put them together to probe into their relationship, especially the impact of GATS/WTO national treatment on China's banking law framework.

To integrate China's banking law framework is a very important step to meet the demands of GATS/WTO national treatment obligations. But it is only the first step, not the final step. In this regard, this book should be deemed as the beginning of a research, not the ending, i.e., a brick thrown by me to attract jade from others [*pao zhuan yin yu*].

Bibliography

English Books

Andersons, Kym, and Bernard Hoekman (eds) *The Global Trading System*. 3 vols. New York: I.B. Tauris Publishers, 2002.
Arrowsmith, Sue. *Government Procurement in the WTO*. London: Kluwer Law International, 2003.
Arup, Christopher. *The New World Trade Organization Agreements: Globalizing Law through Services and Intellectual Property*. Cambridge: Cambridge University Press, 2000.
Aust, Anthony. *Modern Treaty Law and Practice*. Cambridge: Cambridge University Press, 2000.
Barfield, Claude E. *Free Trade, Sovereignty, Democracy: The Future of the World Trade Organization*. Washington, D.C.: AEI Press, 2001.
Beane, Donald G. *The United States and GATT, A Relational Study*. Amsterdam: Pergamon, 2000.
Beveridge, Fiona. *The Treatment and Taxation of Foreign Investment under International Law: Towards International Disciplines*. Manchester: Manchester University Press, 2000.
Bhagwati, Jagdish. *Free Trade Today*. Princeton, NJ: Princeton University Press, 2002.
———, and Robert E. Hudec (eds). *Fair Trade and Harmonization: Prerequisites for Free Trade*? Vol 2, *Legal Analysis*. Cambridge, MA: The MIT Press, 1996.
Brinton, Jasper Yeates. *The Mixed Courts of Egypt*. New Haven and London: Yale University Press, 1968.
Brownlie, Ian. *Principles of Public International Law*. 6th edn. Oxford: Oxford University Press, 2003.
Buckley, Ross P. *The WTO and the Doha Round: The Changing Face of World Trade*. The Hague: Kluwer Law International, 2003.
Cass, Deborah Z., Brett G. Williams, and George Barker (eds). *China and the World Trading System: Entering the New Millennium*. Cambridge: Cambridge University Press, 2003.
Cassese, Antonio, *International Law in a Divided World*, Oxford, Clarendon Press, 1986.
———. *International Law*. Oxford: Oxford University Press, 2001.
Chan, Ming K., and David J. Clark (eds). *The Hong Kong Basic Law: Blueprint for "Stability and Prosperity" under Chinese Sovereignty*? Hong Kong: Hong Kong University Press, 1991.

Chen, Yin Ching (ed.). *Treaties and Agreements between the Republic of China and Other Powers, 1929–1954*. Washington, D.C.: Sino-American Publishing Service, 1957.
Cheng, Linsun. *Banking in Modern China: Entrepreneurs, Professional Managers, and the Development of Chinese Banks, 1897–1937*. Cambridge: Cambridge University Press, 2003.
Choi, Won-Mog. *"Like Products" in International Trade Law: Towards a Consistent GATT/WTO Jurisprudence*. Oxford: Oxford University Press, 2003.
Claessens, Stijn, and Marion Janson (eds). *The Internationalization of Financial Services, Issues and Lessons for Developing Countries*. The Hague: Kluwer Law International, 2000.
Cohen, Jerome Alan (ed.). *China's Practice of International Law: Some Case Studies*. Cambridge, MA: Harvard University Press, 1972.
Collis, Maurice. *Wayfoong, the HongKong and Shanghai Banking Corporation*. Hong Kong: Faber and Faber, 1965.
Cottier, Thomas, and Petros C. Mavroidis (eds). *Regulatory Barriers and the Principle of Non-Discrimination in World Trade Law*. Michigan: University of Michigan Press, 2002.
Croome, John. *Reshaping the World Trading System, A History of the Uruguay Round*. 2nd and revised edn. The Hague: Kluwer Law International, 1999.
Curzon, George N. *Problems of the Far East*. Westminster: Archibald Constable and Co., 1896.
Cruzon, Gerard. *Multilateral Commercial Diplomacy: The General Agreement on Tariffs and Trade and Its Impact on National Commercial Policies and Techniques*. London: Michael Joseph, 1965.
Dam, Kenneth W. *The GATT Law and International Economic Organization*. Chicago: The University of Chicago Press, 1970.
Das, Dilip K. *Global Trading System at the Crossroads*. London: Routledge, 2001.
Dobson, Wendy, and Pierre Jacquet. *Financial Services Liberalization in the WTO*. Washington, D.C.: Institute for International Economics, 1998.
Findlay, Christopher, and Tony Warren (eds). *Impediments to Trade in Services*. London: Routledge, 2001.
Fishel, Wesley R. *The End of Extraterritoriality in China*. New York: Octagon Books, 1974.
Friedmann, Wolfgang. *The Changing Structure of International Law*. London: Stevens & Sons, 1964.
Gallagher, Peter. *Guide to the WTO and Developing Countries*. The Hague: Kluwer Law International, 2000.
Garten, Helen A. *US Financial Regulation and the Level Playing Field*. New York: Palgrave, 2001.
Green, N.A. Maryan. *International Law*. 3rd edn. London: Pitman Publishing, 1987.

Gruson, Michael, and Ralph Reisner (eds). *Regulation of Foreign Banks: United States and International*. 4th edn. Newark, NJ: LexisNexis Metthew Bender, 2003.

Hafner, Gerhard et al. (eds). *Liber Amicorum: Professor Ignaz Seidl-Hohenveldern, in honour of his 80th birthday*. The Hague: Kluwer Law International, 1998.

Hahn, Robert W. *Reviewing Regulatory Reform: A Global Perspective*. Washington, D.C.: Brookings Institution Press, 2001.

Hildreth, Richard. *The History of Banks*. London: Routledge/Thoemmes Press, 1996.

Hoekman, Bernard M., and Michel M. Kostecki. *The Political Economy of the World Trading System: The WTO and Beyond*. 2nd edn. Oxford: Oxford University Press, 2001.

———, Aaditya Mattoo, and Philip English (eds). *Development, Trade, and the WTO, A Handbook*. Washington, D.C.: the World Bank, 2002.

Hsü, Immanuel C.Y. *The Rise of Modern China*. 6th edn. New York: Oxford University Press, 2000.

Hudec, Robert E. *Essays on the Nature of International Trade Law*. London: Cameron May, 1999.

———. *The GATT Legal System and World Trade Diplomacy*. 2nd edn. Salem, N.H.: Butterworth Legal Publishers, 1990.

Jackson, John H. *The Jurisprudence of GATT and the WTO, Insights on Treaty Law and Economic Relations*. Beijing: China Higher Education Press, 2002 (Originally Published by Cambridge University Press in 2000).

———. *Restructuring the GATT System*. London: The Royal Institute of International Affairs, 1990.

———. *World Trade and the Law of GATT*, Indianapolis, Indiana: The Bobbs-Merrill Company, 1969.

———. *The World Trade Organization: Constitution and Jurisprudence*. London: The Royal Institute of International Affairs, 1998.

———. *The World Trading System: Law and Policy of International Economic Relations*. 2nd edn. Cambridge, MA: The MIT Press, 1997.

———, and Alan Sykes (eds). *Implementing the Uruguay Round*. Oxford: Clarendon Press, 1997.

———, William J. Davey, and Alan O. Sykes Jr. *Legal Problems of International Economic Relations, Case, Materials and Text on the National and International Regulation of Transnational Economic Relations*. 4th edn. St Paul, Minn.: West Group, 2002.

———, William J. Davey, and Alan O. Sykes Jr. *2002 Documents Supplement to Legal Problems of International Economic Relations*. 4th edn. St Paul, Minn.: West Group, 2002.

Jennings, Robert, and Arthur Watts (eds). *Oppenheim's International Law*. 9th edn. 2 vols. Harlow, Essex: Longman, 1992.

Ji, Zhaojin. *A History of Modern Shanghai Banking: The Rise and Decline of China's Finance Capitalism*. Armonk, New York/London, England: M.E. Sharpe, 2003.

Johnson, Jon R. *International Trade Law*. Concord, Ont.: Irwin Law, 1998.

Keeton, G.W. *The Development of Extraterritoriality in China*. London: Longmans, Green and Co., 1928.

Kenen, Peter B. *The International Financial Architecture: What's New, What's Missing?* Washington, D.C.: Institute for International Economics, 2001.

Kennedy, Daniel M., and James D. Southwich (eds). *The Political Economy of International Trade Law: Essays in Honor of Robert E. Hudec*. Cambridge: Cambridge University Press, 2001.

Kennedy, Kevin. *Competition Law and the World Trade Organization: The Limits of Multilateralism*. London: Sweet & Maxwell, 2001.

Key, Sydney J. *Financial Services in the Uruguay Round and the WTO*. Washington, D.C.: Occasional Paper 54, Group of Thirty, 1997.

Klabbers, Jan. *The Concept of Treaty in International Law*. The Hague: Kluwer Law International, 1996.

Koo, Wellington. *The Status of Aliens in China*. New York: Columbia University Press, 1912.

Lee, Barn Elmer. *Modern Banking Reforms in China* (1941) (PhD dissertation, Columbia University). Ann Arbor, Michigan: UMI, printed in 2002.

Litan, Robert E., Paul Masson, and Michael Pomerleano (eds). *Open Doors, Foreign Participation in Financial Systems in Developing Countries*. Washington, D.C.: Brookings Institution Press, 2001.

Liu, Shiu Shun. *Extraterritoriality: Its Rise and Its Decline*. New York: Columbia University, 1925.

Long, Olivier. *Law and Its Limitations in the GATT Multilateral Trade System*. Dordrecht: Graham & Trotman/Martinus Nijhoff, 1987.

Lovett, William A., Alfred E. Eckes, Jr, and Richard L. Brinkman. *US Trade Policy, History, Theory, and the WTO*. Armonk, N.Y.: M.E. Sharpe, 1999.

Lowenfeld, Andreas F. *International Economic Law*. Oxford: Oxford University Press, 2002.

Mathis, James H. *Regional Trade Agreements in the GATT/WTO: Article XXIV and the International Trade Requirement*. The Hague: T.M.C. Asser Press, 2002.

Matsushita, Mitsuo, Thomas J. Schoenbaum, and Petros Mavroidis. *The World Trade Organization: Law, Practice, and Policy*. Oxford: Oxford University Press, 2003.

McNair, Lord. *The Law of Treaties*. Oxford: Oxford University Press, 1961.

Menon, P.K. *The law of Treaties between States and International Organizations*. Lewiston: The Edwin Mellen Press, 1992.

Millard, Thomas F. *The End of Exterritoriality in China*. Shanghai: The ABC Press, 1931.

Neufeld, H. *The International Protection of Private Creditors from the Treaties of Westphalia to the Congress of Vienna (1648–1815)*. Leiden: A.W. Sijthoff, 1971.

Norton, Joseph J. *Devising International Bank Supervisory Standards*. London/Dordrecht/Boston: Graham & Trotman/Martinus Nijhoff, 1995.

———. *Financial Sector Law Reform in Emerging Economies*. London: BIICL, 2000.

———, and C.J. Li et al. (eds). *Financial Regulation in the Greater China Area: Mainland China, Taiwan and Hong Kong SAR*. The Hague: Kluwer Law International, 2000.

Nussbaum, Arthur. *A Concise History of the Law of Nations*. Revised edn. New York: The Macmillan Company, 1958.

Palmeter, David, and Petros C. Mavroidis. *Dispute Settlement in the World Trade Organization, Practice and Procedure*. The Hague: Kluwer Law International, 1999.

Panitchpakdi, Supachai, and Mark Clifford. *China and the WTO: How China's Entry is Going to Affect You and the Future of World Trade Organization*. New York: John Wiley & Sons Inc., 2001.

Petersmann, Ernst-Ulrich. *The GATT/WTO Dispute Settlement System, International Law, International Organizations and Dispute Settlement*. The Hague: Kluwer Law International, 1996.

———, and Meinhard Hilf (eds). *The New GATT Round of Multilateral Trade Negotiations, Legal and Economic Problems, Studies in Transnational Economic Law*. The Hague: Kluwer Law International, 1991.

Pollard, Alfred M., Joseph G. Passaic, Jr, Keith H. Ellis, and Joseph P. Daly. *Banking Law in the United States*. Butterworth Legal Publishers, 1988.

Reuter, Paul. *Introduction to the Law of Treaties*. Translated by Jose Mico and Peter Haggenmache. London: Printer Publishers, 1989.

Reynolds, Paul D. *China's International Banking and Financial System*. New York: Praeger, 1982.

Rhode, Grant F., and Reid E. Whitlock (eds). *Treaties of the People's Republic of China, 1949–1978: An Annotated Compilation*. Boulder, Colorado: Westview Press, 1980.

Ruttley, Philip, Iain MacVay, and Ahmad Masa'deh (eds). *Liberalisation and Protectionism in the World Trading System*. London: Cameron May, 1999.

Sauve, Pierre. *Trade Rules behind Borders: Essays on Services, Investment and the New Trade Agenda*. London: Cameron May, 2003.

———, and Robert M. Stern (eds). *GATS 2000 New Direction in Services Trade Liberalization*. Washington D.C.: Brookings Institution Press, 2000.

Schefer, K.N. *International Trade in Financial Services: The NAFTA Provisions*. The Hague/London/Boston: Kluwer Law International, 1999.

Schwarzenberger, Georg. *International Law and Order*. London: Stevens & Sons, 1971.

Shan, Wenhua. *The Legal Framework of EU-China Investment Relations: A Critical Appraisal*. Oxford and Portland, Oregon: Hart Publishing, 2005.
Shearer, I.A. *Starke's International Law*. 11th edn. London: Butterworths, 1994.
Shihata, Ibrahim F.I. *Legal Treatment of Foreign Investment: The World Bank Guidelines*. Dordrecht/Boston/London: Martinus Nijhoff Publishers, 1993.
Starr, Peter. *Citibank: A Century of Asia*. Singapore: Editions Didier Millet, 2002.
Stewart, Terence P. *After Doha, the Changing Attitude & Ideas of the New WTO Round*. Ardsley, N.Y.: Transnational Publishers, 2002.
——— (ed.). *The GATT Uruguay Round: A Negotiating History (1986–1992)*. Vol. 2. The Hague: Kluwer Law and Taxation Publishers, 1993.
——— (ed.). *The GATT Uruguay Round: A Negotiating History (1986–1992)*. Vol. 3. TheHague: Kluwer Law and Taxation Publishers, 1993.
——— (ed.). *The GATT Uruguay Round: A Negotiating History (1986–1994)*. Vol. 4. The Hague: Kluwer Law International, 1999.
Teichova, Alice, Ginette Kurgan-van Hentenryk, and Dieter Ziegler (eds). *Banking, Trade and Industry*. Cambridge: Cambridge University Press, 1997.
Tung, L. *China and Some Phases of International Law*. Oxford: Oxford University Press, 1940.
Tyau, Min-chien Tiz. *The Legal Obligations Arising Out of Treaty Relations between China and Other States*. Taibei: Ch'eng-wen Publishing Company, 1966.
Vincent, John Carter. *The Extraterritorial System in China: Final Phase*. Cambridge, MA.: East Asian Research Center, Harvard University, 1970.
Waart, Paul De, Paul Peters, and Erik Denters (eds). *International Law and Development*. Martinus Nijhoff Publishers, 1988.
Walker, George Alexander. *International Banking Regulation: Law, Policy and Practice*. The Hague: Kluwer Law International, 2001.
Wesley-Smith, Peter, and Albert H Y. Chen (eds). *The Basic Law and Hong Kong's Future*. Hong Kong: Butterworths, 1988.
Wilkinson, Rorden. *Multilateralism and the World Trade Organization*. New York: Routledge, 2000.
World Trade Organization. *The Legal Texts: The Results of the Uruguay Round of Multilateral Trade Negotiations*. Cambridge: Cambridge University Press, 1999.
WTO Secretariat. *Guide to the Uruguay Round Agreements*. The Hague: Kluwer Law International, 1999.
Zhou, Zhongfei. *Chinese Banking Law and Foreign Financial Institutions*. The Hague/London/Boston: Kluwer Law International, 2001.

Chinese Books

Bai Guimei et al. (eds). *Guojifa* [International Law]. Beijing: Peking University Press, 1988.

Cao Jianming, and He Xiaoyong. *Shijie maoyi zuzhi* [The World Trade Organization]. Beijing: Law Press China, 1999.

Cao Li. *Hunhe suoyouzhi yanjiu* [A study of the mixed ownership]. Guangzhou: Guangdong renmin chubanshe, 2004.

Central Archives of China (ed.). *Zhonggong zhongyang wenxian xuanji 1921–1925* [Selected documents of the Central Committee of the Chinese Communist Party 1921–1925]. Vol. 1. Beijing: Zhonggong zhongyang dangxiao chubanshe, 1982.

——— (ed.). *Zhonggong zhongyang wenjian xuanji* [Selected documents of the Central Committee of the Chinese Communist Party 1928]. Vol. 4. Beijing: Zhonggong zhongyang dangxiao chubanshe, 1983.

———, China Second Historical Archives of China, and Jilin Province Social Academy, (eds). *Wangwei zhengquan* [Wang puppet regime]. Beijing: Zhonghua shujü, 2004.

Chao Zhongchen. *Mingdai haijin yu haiwai maoyi* [Ban on maritime trade and overseas trade during the Ming Dynasty]. Beijing: Renmin chubanshe, 2005.

Chen An (ed.). *Guoji jingjifa zonglun* [General review of international economic law]. Beijing: Law Press China, 1991.

Chen Weili, and Chen Jian et al. (eds). *WTO Jinrong fuwu xieyi: guifan yu chengnuo* [Financial services agreements: rules and commitments]. Hefei: Huangshan chubanshe, 2000.

Chen Xulu, Gu Tinglong, and Wang Xi (eds). *Sheng xuanhuai dang'an*. Vol. 5, *zhongguo tongshang yinhang* [Sheng xuanhuai's archives, vol. 5, *The Imperial Bank of China*]. Shanghai: Shanghai renmin chubanshe, 2000.

Chen Yixin. *WTO yu zhongguo jinrong kaifang* [WTO and the openness of China's finance]. Shanghai: Xuelin chubanshe, 2001.

Cheng Lin. *Zhongguo jindai yinhang zhidu jianshe sixiang yanjiu: 1859–1949* [Studies on thoughts of building the banking system in Modern China: 1859–1949]. Shanghai: Shanghai Finance and Economics University Press, 1999.

Chen Zhiqi. *Zhongguo jindai waijiaoshi* [Foreign relations history of Modern China]. Taibei: Nantian Book Press, 1993.

Cheng Daode (ed.). *Jindai zhongguo waijiao yu guojifa* [Diplomacy in Modern China and international law]. Beijing: Xiandai chubanshe, 1993.

CBRC (ed.), Compendium of China Banking Regulations and Supervisory Rules. 3 vols, Beijing: Law Press China, 2011.

China Hainan Reform and Development Institute (ed.), *Zhongguo shangye yinhang tizhi Gaige* [System reform of China's commercial banks]. Beijing: Minzhu yu jianshe chubanshe, 1995.

China Second History Archive Office [Zhongguo di'er lishi dang'an guan] (ed.). *Zhonghua minguoshi dang'an ziliao huibian* [Compilation of archives of the Republic of China]. Vol. 3 (1) (2), *Finance*. Nanjing: Jiangsu guji chubanshe, 1991. 中国第二历史档案馆编，中华民国史档案资料汇编，第三辑，金融（一）（二），南京，江苏古籍出版社

——— (ed.). *Zhonghua minguoshi dang'an ziliao huibian.* Vol. 3, *Diplomacy*, Nanjing: Jiangsu guji chubanshe, 1991. 中华民国史档案资料汇编，第三辑，外交

——— (ed.). *Zhonghua minguoshi dang'an ziliao huibian.* Vol. 5(1), *Diplomacy, Parts I and II,*. Nanjing: Jiangsu guji chubanshe, 1994. 中华民国史档案资料汇编，第五辑第一编，外交 （一） （二）

——— (ed.). *Zhonghua minguoshi dang'an ziliao huibian.* Vol. 5(2), *Diplomacy*. Nanjing: Jiangsu guji chubanshe, 1997. 中华民国史档案资料汇编，第五辑第二编，外交

Chinese National Library [*Zhongguo guojia tushuguan*] (ed.). *Waijiao wendu* [Foreign diplomatic documents]. Vol. 3. Beijing: Chinese National Library Documentary Microfilm Reproduction Center, 2004.

Cui Shuqin. *Guojifa* [International law]. 2 vols. 3rd edn. Shanghai: The Commercial Press, 1948.

Deng Zhenglai (ed.). *Wang Tieya Wenxuan* [Selected papers of Wang Tieya]. Beijing: China University of Political Science and Law Press, 2003.

Department of Treaty and Law of the Ministry of Foreign Affairs of the PRC (ed.). *Zhonghua renmin gongheguo duobian tiaoyue ji* [Collection of the multilateral treaties of the People's Republic of China]. Vols 1–4. Beijing: Law Press China, 1987.

———, *Zhonghua Renmin Gongheguo Duobian Tiaoyue Ji.* Vol.7. Beijing: Law Press China, 2002.

Dewatripont, Mathias, and Jean Tirole. *The Prudential Regulation of Banks*. Translated by Shi Lei, and Wang Yongqin. Shanghai: Fudan University Press, 2002.

Ding Bangkai, and Zhou Zhongfei (eds). *Jinrong jianguanxue yuanli* [Principles of financial regulation]. Beijing: Peking University Press, 2004.

Ding Richu (ed.). *Shanghai jindai jingjishi* [Modern economic history of Shanghai]. Vol. 2 (1895–1927). Shanghai: Shangahi renmin chubanshe, 1997.

Ding Wei, and Chen Zhidong (eds). *Chongtufa lun* [Study on law of conflict]. Beijing: Law Press China, 1996.

Document Study Office of the Central Committee of the Chinese Communist Party [*Zhonggong zhongyang wenxian yanjiushi*] (ed.). *Shiyijie sanzhong quanhui yilai zhongyao wenxian xuandu* [Selections of important documents since the third plenum of the eleventh Central Committee of the Chinese Communist Party]. 2 vols. Beijing: Renmin chubanshe, 1987.

——— (ed.). *Shisida yilai zhongyao wenxian xuanbian* [Selections of important documents since the fourteenth conference]. 3 vols. Beijing: Renmin chubanshe, 1996.

——— (ed.). *Shiwuda yilai zhongyao wenjian xuanbian* [Selections of important documents since the fifteenth conference]. 2 vols. Beijing: Renmin chubanshe, 2000, 2003.

——— (ed.). *Shiliuda yilai zhongyao wenxian xuanbian* [Selections of important documents since the sixteenth conference]. Vol. 1. Beijing: *Zhongyang wenxian chubanshe*, 2005.

Dong Shizhong and Li Renzhen. *Zhongguo jinrongfa* [Chinese financial law]. Hong Kong: Joint Publishing (HK) Co., Ltd., 1998.

Duan Muzheng, Shi Daxin, and Chen Zhizhong (eds). *Guojifa* [International law]. Beijing: Peking University Press, 1989.

Economic Research Division of the Central Bank (eds). *Jinrong fagui huibian* [A compilation of financial laws and regulations]. Shanghai: Commercial Press, 1937.

Fairbank, John King. *The United States and China*, 4th edn. Translated by Zhang Lijing. Beijing: World Affairs Press, 2003.

Fei Chengkang. *Zhongguo zujieshi* [The History of concession in China]. Shanghai: Shanghai Academy of Social Sciences Press, 1991.

Feng Yushu. *Guoji maoyi tizhi xia de guanmao zongxieding yu zhongguo* [GATT and China]. Beijing: Zhongguo duiwai jingji maoyi chubanshe, 1992.

Financial Institute of the People's Bank of China (ed.). *Meiguo huaqi yinhang zai hua shiliao* [Historical materials of the American Citybank in China]. Beijing: China Finance Publishing House, 1990.

Fu Bingchang and Zhou Dingyu (eds). *Zhonghua minguo liufa huibian* [A compilation of the Six Codes of the Republic of China]. Vol. 4. Xinlu Book Company, Taibei, 1964.

Fu Wenling (ed.). *Riben hengbin zhengjin yinhang zai hua huodong shiliao* [Historical materials of activities of the Japanese Yokohama Specie Bank in China]. Beijing: China Finance Publishing House, 1992.

Guo Tingyi [Kuo Ting-yee]. *Jindai zhongguo shigang* [A short history of Modern China]. 3rd edn. 2 vols. Hong Kong: Chinese University Press, 1986.

Guo Weidong. *Zhuanzhe: yi zhaoqi zhangying guanxi he Nanjing tiaoyue wei kaocha zhongxin* [A turning point: focusing on the early Sino-British relations and the Treaty of Nanjing]. Shijiazhuang: Hebei renmin chubanshe, 2003.

Han Caizhen. *Waishang touzi zhengce yu falü huanjing* [Policy and law environment of foreign investment]. Beijing: Zhongguo qinggongye chubanshe, 2000.

Han Depei (ed.). *Guoji sifa xinlun* [New study on private international law]. Wuhan: Wuhan University Press, 1997.

———, Ren Jisheng, and Liu Ding (eds). *Guoji sifa* [Private international law]. revised edn. Wuhan: Wuhan University Press, 1989.

Han Long. *Shijie maoyi zuzhi yu jinrong fuwu maoyi* [WTO and financial service trade]. Beijing: People Court Press, 2003.

He Qinhua, and Li Xiuqing (eds). *Minguo faxue lunwen jingcui: guoji falü pian* [The cream of legal papers of the Republican period: international law]. Beijing: Law Press China, 2004.

He Xiaoyong. *Jinrong quanqiuhua qushi xia jinrong jianguan de falü wenti* [Legal aspects on financial supervision under financial globalization]. Beijing: Law Press China, 2002.

Hevia, James L. *Cherishing Men from Afar*. Durham, NC: Duke University Press, 1995. Translated by Deng Changchun as *Huairou Yuanren: Ma Ge Er Ni Shihua de Zhongying Liyi Congtu* (Beijing: Shehui kexue wenxian chubanshe, 2002)

Hong Jiaguan. *Zhongguo jinrongshi* [History of China's finance]. 2nd edn. Chengdu: Southwestern University of Finance and Economics Press, 2001.

Hu Jianmiao. *Xingzheng faxue* [Administrative law]. 2nd edn. Beijing: Law Press China, 2003.

Hu Kangsheng, and Wang Shengming (eds). *Zhonghua renmin gongheguo yinhangye jiandu guanlifa shiyi* [Explanation of the Law of the People's Republic of China on Banking Regulation and Supervision]. Beijing: Law Press China, 2004.

Huang Jiansen, and Huang Quanxing. *Yinhangfa* [Banking law]. Taibei: Huatai wenhua shiye gongsi, 2003.

Huang Jin, and Liu Weixiang (eds). *Han Depei wenxuan* [Selected works of Han Depei]. Wuhan: Wuhan University Press, 1996.

Huang Yi (ed.). *Zhonghua Renmin Gongheguo yinhangye jiandu guanlifa jiangzuo* [Lectures on the Banking Supervision Law of the PRC]. Beijing: Zhongguo fazhi chubanshe, 2004.

Jackson, John H., Sovereignty, the WTO, and Changing Fundamentals of International Law, Zhao Longyue, Zuo Haicong and Sheng Jianming (trans), Beijing: Social Sciences Academic Press (China), 2009.

Japanese History Group of the Department of History of Fudan University (ed. & trans). *Riben diguo zhuyi duiwai qinlue shiliao xuanbian 1931–1945* [Compilation of the historical materials on Japanese imperialist aggression 1931–1945]. Shanghai: Shanghai renmin chubanshe, 1975.

Japanese Society of International Law (ed.), *Guojifa Cidian* [International law dictionary], Translated by the International Law Unit of China Foreign Affairs University [*Waijiao Xueyuan*]. Beijing: Shijie zhishi chubanshe [World Affairs Press], 1985.

Jiang Tingfu. *Zhongguo jindaishi* [Modern history of China]. Shanghai: Shanghai guji chubanshe, 1999.

Jin Guangyao (ed.). *Wellington Koo and Chinese Diplomacy*. Shanghai: Shanghai guji chubanshe, 2001.

Jin Tonglin. *Yinhangfa* [Banking law]. 5th edn. Taibei: Sanmin shujü, 2005.

Kong Xiangjun. *WTO falü de guonei shiyong* [The implementation of WTO law in China]. Beijing: The People's Court Press, 2002.

Legal History Unit of the Law Faculty of Renmin University (ed.). *Zhongguo Jindai Fazhishi Ziliao Xuanbian* [Selections of materials of China's modern legal history]. Beijing: Legal History Unit of the Law Faculty of Renmin University, 1980.

Legislative Affairs Office of the State Council. *Zhonghua renmin gongheguo waizi jinrong jigou guanli tiaoli wenda* [Questions and answers on the Regulation of Administration of Foreign-Funded Financial Institutions]. Beijing: CITIC Publishing House, 2002.

Li Changchuan. *Zhongguo zhimin shi* [China's history of colony]. Shanghai: Commercial Press, 1937.

Li Chong. *Guojia jinrong fengxian lun* [On the national financial risks]. Beijing: Commercial Press, 2000.

Li Dianjun, Huang Minhong, Yang Wenkai, Wu Zhipan, Li Zhanchen, and Tian Jianhua (eds). *Zhonghua Renmin Gongheguo shangye yinhangfa jiaocheng* [Textbook of the PRC Commercial Banking Law]. Beijing: Zhongguo jinrong chubanshe, 1995.

Li Enhan. *Jindai zhongguo waijiao shishi xinyan* [New study of the diplomacy history of Modern China]. Taibei: Taiwan Commercial Press, 2004.

Li Guo'an. *Guoji huobi jinrong faxue* [International monetary and financial law]. Beijing: Peking University Press, 1999.

Li Fei, Zhao Haikuan, Xu Shuxin, and Hong Jiaguan (eds). *Zhongguo jinrongshi* [General history of China's finance]. Vol. 2. Beijing: China Financial Publishing House, 2003.

Li Ping (ed.). *Yinhangfa xinshi yu lijie* [New interpretation and cases of banking law]. Beijing: Tongxin Press, 2001.

Li Shuangyuan, Jin Pengnian, Zhang Mao and Li Zhiyong (eds). *Zhongguo guoji sifa tonglun* [General study on Chinese private international law]. Beijing: Law Press China, 1996.

Liang Shuying, and Ling Yan (eds). *Guojifa* [International law]. Beijing: China University of Political Science and Law Press, 1993.

Liang Xi, and Wang Xianshu (eds). *Guojifa* [International law]. Wuhan: Wuhan University Press, 1993.

Liang Weiji, and Zheng Zemin (eds). *Zhongguo jindai bupingdeng tiaoyue xuebian yu jieshao* [Compilation and introduction of the unequal treaties in Modern China]. Beijing: Zhongguo guangbo dianshi chubanshe, 1993.

Lin Zengping. *Zhongguo jindaishi* [The history of Modern China]. 2 vols. Changsha: Hunan renmin chubanshe, 1979.

Liu Guanying. *Xiandai yinhang zhidu* [Modern banking system]. Shanghai: Commercial Press, 1936.

Liu Guangdi. *Zhongguo de yinhang* [China's banks]. Beijing: Beijing Publishing House, 1984.

Liu Yan. *Bei qinhai zhi zhongguo* [China under infringement]. Taibei: Wenhai Press, 1987.

Lu Zefeng, Lu Guorong, Zhang Guanghong, Jiang Naihua, and Peng Weidong (eds). *Zhongguo jinrongfa* [Chinese financial law]. Wuhan: Wuhan University Press, 1997.

Ma Weihua (ed.). *Zhonghua renmin gongheguo shangye yinhangfa shijie* [Explanation of the Law of the People's Republic of China on Commercial Banks]. Beijing: Zhongguo minzhu yu fazhi chubanshe, 2004.

Mao Zedong. *Mao Zedong xuanji* [Selected works of Mao Zedong], 4 vols. 2nd edn. Beijing: People's Publishing House, 1991.

Min-Ch'ien T.Z. Tyau. *Zhongguo guoji tiaoyue yiwu lun* [The legal obligations arising out of treaty relations between China and other states]. 4th edn. Shanghai: The Commercial Press, 1927.

Ministry of Civil Affairs of the PRC (ed.). *Zhonghua renmin gongheguo xingzheng quhua jiance 2005* [Short manual of administrative divisions of the PRC 2005]. Beijing: SinoMaps Press, 2005.

Ministry of Foreign Affairs of the PRC (ed.). *Zhonghua renmin gongheguo youhao tiaoyue huibian* [Collection of friendship treaties of the People's Republic of China]. Beijing: World Affairs Press, 1965.

——— (ed.). *Zhonghua renmin gongheguo tiaoyue ji* [Collection of the treaties of the People's Republic of China]. Vol. 7. Beijing: Law Press China, 1959.

———(ed.). *Zhonghua renmin gongheguo tiaoyue ji*. Vol. 9. Beijing: Law Press China, 1961.

——— (ed.). *Zhonghua renmin gongheguo tiaoyue ji*. Vol. 11. Beijing: Law Press China, 1963.

——— (ed.). *Zhonghua renmin gongheguo tiaoyue ji*. Vol. 26. Beijing: World Affairs Press, 1983.

Ministry of Foreign Affairs of the ROC (ed.). *Treaties between the Republic of China and Foreign States, 1927–1957*. Taipei: Taipei Commercial Press, 1958.

Modern History Unit of the History Department of Fudan University (ed.). *Florilegium of Chinese Modern Foreign Relation History: 1840–1949*. Shanghai: Shanghai renmin chubanshe, 1977.

Morse, Hosea Ballou. *Zhonghua diguo duiwai guanxishi* [The international relations of the Chinese empire]. 3 vols. Translated by Zhang Huiwen, Yao Zengyi, Yang Zhixin, Ma Bohuang, and Wu Dange. Shanghai: Shanghai shudian, 2000.

Mu Yaping. *Guoji touzi de falü zhidu* [Legal system of international investment]. Guangzhou: Guangdong renmin chubanshe, 1999.

People's Bank of China (General Office, and Treaty and Law Department) (ed.). *Jinrong falü fagui duben* [Textbook of financial laws and regulations]. Beijing: Zhongguo jinrong chubanshe, 1996.

Policy and Law Department of the CBRC (ed.). *Zhongguo yinhangye jianguan guizhang huibian 2003–2006* [Compendium of China Banking Rules 2003–2006]. Beijing: Law Press China, 2006.

Political Department of the Supreme People's Court (ed.). *Rushi yu renmin fayuan* [Accession to the World Trade Organization and the People's courts]. Beijing: The People's Court Press, 2002.

Politics and Economics Department of Beijing Normal University (ed.). *Zhongguo jindai jingjishi* [Economic history of Modern China]. 2 vols. Beijing: Renmin chubanshe, 1976, 1978.
Qiang Li. *Jinrongfa* [Financial law]. Beijing: Law Press China, 1997.
Qin Xiaoyi (ed.). *Zhonghua minguo zhongyao shiliao chubian: duiri kangzhan shiqi* [Initial compilations of important history materials of the Republic of China: period of the War of Resistance against Japan]. Vol. 3, *Diplomacy in Wartime*. Taibei: Zhongguo Guomindang Zhongyang Weiyuanhui Dangshi Weiyuanhui, 1981.
Qian Hua (ed.). *Guoji sifa* [Private international law]. Beijing: China University of Political Science and Law Press, 1988.
Qian Yishi. *Zhongguo waijiao shi* [Chinese diplomatic history]. Shanghai: Shenghuo shudian, 1947.
Research Department of the Bank of China (ed.). *China Banks Yearbook.* [in Chinese] 2 vols. Shanghai: Research Department of the Bank of China, 1937.
Research Office of the Customs General Administration of the PRC (ed.). *Xinchou heyue yihou de shangyue tanpan* [Commercial treaty negotiations post the Boxer Protocol]. Beijing: Zhonghua shujü, 1994.
Secretariat of the Standing Committee of the NPC, and Legal Department of the State Ethnic Affairs Commission of the PRC (eds). *Zhongguo minzu quyu zizhi falü fagui tongdian* [General compilations of autonomous laws and regulations of China's ethnic areas]. Beijing: Publishing House of the Central University for Nationalities, 2002.
Shai, Aron. *The Fate of British and French Firms in China (1949–1954): Imperialism Imprisoned.* Translated by Zhang Pin et al. Beijing: Zhongguo shehui kexue chubanshe, 2004.
Shang Mingxuan. *Sun Zhongshan Biography*. 2nd edn. Beijing: Beijing chubanshe, 1981.
Shao Jin (ed.). *Guojifa* [International law]. Beijing: Peking University Press and Higher Education Press, 2000.
Shi Jingxia. *WTO fuwu maoyifa zhuanlun* [WTO Law on Trade in Services], Beijing: Law Press China, 2006.
Song Chun (ed.). *Zhongguo guomindang dangshi* [Chinese Nationalist Party history]. Changchun, Jilin wenshi chubanshe, 1990.
Sun Bang (ed.). *"Jiu Yiba" shibian ziliao huibian* [A collection of documents on the "September 18 Incident"], Changchun, Jinlin wenshi chubanshe, 1991.
Sun Yuqin. *Zhongguo duiwai maoyishi* [China's foreign trade history]. Vol. 2. Beijing: University of International Business and Economics Press, 2004.
Song Enfan, and Li Jiasong (eds). Diplomatic Chronicles of the People's Republic of China. Vol. 1, October 1949–December 1956. Beijing: World Affairs Press, 1997.
Tao Wenzhao. *Zhongmei guanxishi* [History of the Sino–US relations] (1911–1949). Shanghai: Shanghai renmin chubanshe, 2004.

Teaching and Research Section of the CCP History of the China Communist Party School (ed.). *Zhonggong dangshi ziliao* [Reference materials of the history of the Chinese Communist Party]. 8 vols. Beijing: Renmin chubanshe, 1979–1980.

Teaching and Research Group on China's Contemporary History of the Department of History of Beijing Normal University (ed.). *Zhongguo xiandaishi* [China's contemporary history]. 2 vols. Beijing: Beijing Normal University Press, 1983.

Teaching and Research Group on China's Modern History of the Department of History of Fudan University (ed.). *Zhongguo jindai duiwai guanxi shi ziliao xuanbian 1840–1949* [Selected materials of China's modern foreign relation history 1840–1949]. Vol. 2. Shanghai: Shanghai renmin chubanshe, 1977.

Wan E'Xiang (ed.). *Zhongguo shewai shangshi haishi shenpan zhidao yu yanjiu* [Guide and study on China's foreign-related commercial and maritime trials]. Vol. 3. Beijing: People Court Press, 2002.

Wang Chaoying, Meng Xiangang, and Zhang Yaomin (eds). *Duiwai maoyifa shiyong wenda* [Practical questions and answers of the Foreign Trade Law]. Bejing: Zhongguo Shangye chubanshe, 1994.

Wang Er'Min. *Wanqing shangyue waijiao* [Commercial treaty diplomacy in the late Qing Dynasty]. Hong Kong: Hong Kong Chinese University Press, 1998.

Wang Jingyu. *Waiguo ziben zai jindai zhongguo de jinrong huodong* [Financial activities of foreign capital in Modern China]. Beijing: Renmin chubanshe, 1999.

Wang Lei (ed.). *Guanmao zongxieding yu zhongguo diyueguo diwei* [GATT basic principles and China]. Beijing: China Economic Publishing House, 1995.

Wang Limin. *Shanghai fazhishi* [Shanghai's Legal History]. Shanghai: Shanghai renmin chubanshe, 1998.

Wang Shengming (ed.). *Zhonghua renmin gongheguo zhongguo renmin yinhangfa shiyi* [Explanation of the Law of the People's Republic of China on the People's Bank of China]. Beijing: Law Press China, 2004.

Wang Tieya (ed.). *Guojifa* [International law]. Beijing: Law Press China, 1995.

——— (ed.). *Zhongwai jiuyuezhang huibian* [Compilation of old Sino-foreign treaties and agreements]. 3 vols. Beijing: Joint Publishing House, 1957, 1959, 1962, reprinted in 1982.

———, and Wei Min (eds). *Guojifa* [International law]. Beijing: Law Press China, 1981.

Wang Wenyu. *Xin jinrongfa* [New Financial Law]. Taibei: Yuanzhao chuban youxian gongsi, 2003.

Wang Xianshu, and Liu Haishan (eds). *Guojifa* [International law]. Beijing: China University of Political Science and Law Press, 1994.

Wang Yi. *WTO guomin daiyu de falü guize jiqi zai Zhongguo de shiyong* [WTO National Treatment Rules and Their Application in China]. Beijing: Zhongguo shehui kexue chubanshe, and Renmin fayuan chubanshe, 2005.

Willoughby, Westel W. *Foreign Right and Interests in China*. Translated by Wang Shaofang. Bejing: Joint Publishing House, 1957.

Wu Dongzhi (ed.). *A Diplomatic History of China: The Period of the Republic of China 1911–1949*. Zhengzhou: Henan renmin chubanshe, 1990.

Wu Jingxiong (ed.), and Guo Wei revised. *Zhonghua Minguo liufa liyou panjie huibian* [A Compilation of the Six Codes of the Republic of China]. Vol. 3. Shanghai: Huiwentang xinji shujü, 1947.

Wu Xiangguang (ed.). *Zhongguo shewai jingji maoyifa* [China foreign-related economic and trade law]. Ji'nan: Ji'nan University Press, 1993.

Wu Zhipan. *Jinrong quanqiuhua yu zhongguo jinrongfa* [Financial globalization and Chinese banking law]. Guangzhou: Guangzhou chubanshe, 2000.

———. *Shangye yinhangfa lun* [On Commercial Banking Law]. Beijing: Zhongguo renshi chubanshe 1993.

Xiang Liling. *Zhongmei guanxishi quanbian* [Complete compilation of Sino-US relations history]. Shanghai: East China Normal University Press, 2002.

Xiao Changrui. *Yinhang faling shiwu* [Practice of Banking Laws and Regulations]. 4th edn. Taibei: Huatai wenhua shiye gongsi, 2000.

Xie Haiping. *Tangdai liuhua waiguoren shenghuo kaoshu* [Study on the Life of Foreigners in China during the Tang Dynasty]. Taibei: Taiwan Commercial Press, 1978.

Yan Huiqing. *Yan Huiqing zizhuan: yiwei minguo yuanlao de lishi jiyi* [East-west kaleidoscope 1877–1944: an autobiography by W.W. Yen]. Beijing: Commercial Press, 2003.

Yang Chenghou. *Yinhangfa shiyi* [Interpreting the banking law]. Taibei: Sanmin shujü, 1993.

Yang Guohua. *Zhongguo jiaru WTO falü wenti zhuanlun* [Legal problems on China's accession to the WTO]. Beijing: Law Press China, 2002.

Yang Shong. *Guojifa yu guoji huobi xinzhixu yanjiu* [Study of international Law and the new international monetary order]. Beijing: Peking University Press, 2002.

Yang Yinpu, *Shanghai Jinrong Zuzhi Gaiyao* [Outlines of Financial Institutions in Shanghai]. Shanghai: Commercial Press, 1930.

Yang Zewei. *Hongguan guojifa shi* [Macroscopic history of international law]. Wuhan: Wuhan University Press, 2001.

Yao Meizhen. *Guoji touzifa* [International investment law]. 2nd edn. Wuhan: Wuhan University Press, 1989.

Ye Shichang, and Pan Liangui. *Zhongguo gujindai jinrongshi* [The ancient and modern history of Chinese finance]. Shanghai: Fudan University Press, 2001.

Ye Zuhao. *Feichu bupingdeng tiaoyue* [Abolishing the unequal treaties]. Taibei: Zhengzhong Press, 1967.

Yi Xianshi, and Zhang Deliang et al. *"Jiu Yiba" shibian shi* [The "September 18 Incident" history]. Shenyang: Liaoning renmin chubanshe, 1981.

Yu Jianlin, Li Ying, and Cao Tong (eds). *Chongfan GATT: guanmao zongxieding yu zhongguo jingji* [Return to the GATT: the GATT and China's economy]. Shanghai: Shanghai renmin chubanshe, 1994.

Yu Jinsong. *Guoji touzifa* [International investment law]. Beijing: Law Press China, 1997.
———, and Wu Zhipan (eds). *Guoji jingji faxue* [International economic law]. Beijing: Peking University Press/Higher Education Press, 2000.
Zeng Huaqun, Lin Zhong, and Xu Chongli. *Guoji touzi faxue* [International investment law]. Beijing: Peking University Press, 1999.
Zeng Lingliang. *Shijie maoyi zuzhi fa* [The WTO law]. Wuhan: Wuhan University Press, 1996.
———, Rao Geping, and Yang Zewei (eds). *Guojifa* [International law]. Beijing: Law Press China, 2005.
Zeng Xianyi, and Li Yuhui (eds). *Guoji jingji maoyi falü da cidian* [Dictionary of International Economy, Trade, and Law]. Beijing: Huaxia chubanshe, 1993.
Zhang Chunsheng (ed.). *Zhonghua renmin gongheguo lifafa shiyi* [Explanation of the Legislation Law of the People's Republic of China]. Beijing: Law Press China, 2000.
———, and Li Fei (eds). *Zhonghua renmin gongheguo xingzheng xukefa shiyi* [Explanation of the Law of the People's Republic of China on Administrative Licensing]. Beijing: Law Press China, 2003.
Zhang Jinfan (ed.). *Zhongguo fazhishi gangyao* [Outline of Chinese legal history]. Beijing: China University of Political Science and Law Press, 1986.
———, Qiao Wei, and You Shaoyi (eds). *Zhongguo fazhishi* [Chinese legal history]. Beijing: Qunzhong Press, 1982.
Zhang Kaiyuan, and Lin Zengping (eds). *Xinhai geming shi* [The Xinhai revolution history]. 3 vols. Beijing: Renmin chubanshe, 1980–1981.
Zhang Naigen. *Xinbian guoji jingjifa daolun* [New edition of introduction to international economic law]. Shanghai: Fudan University Press, 2001.
———. *Guojifa yuanli* [International law principles]. Beijing: China University of Political Science and Law Press, 2002.
Zhang Shicheng (ed.). *Zhonghua renmin gongheguo yinhangye jiandu guanlifa shiyi* [Explanation of the Law of the People's Republic of China on Banking Regulation and Supervision]. Beijing: Intellectual Property Press China, 2004.
Zhang Xiaojian. *Guoji sifa xue* [Private international law]. Beijing: Peking University Press, 2000.
Zhang Yuan (ed.). *Zhonghua renmin gongheguo yinhangye jiandu guanlifa shiyi* [Explanation of the Law of the People's Republic of China on Banking Regulation and Supervision]. Beijing: Zhongguo minzhu yu fazhi chubanshe, 2004.
Zhang Zhengxiong. *Duiwai maoyi jichu zhishi* [Basic knowledge of foreign trade]. Beijing: Foreign Trade Education Press, 1988.
Zhao Jianwen (ed.). *Guojifa* [International law]. Zhengzhou: Zhengzhou University Press, 2004.
Zhao Qihong. *Shangye yinhang fengxian guanli* [Risk management of commercial banks]. Beijing: Economic Management Press, 2001.

Zheng Bin. *Zhongguo guoji shangyue lun* [A Treatise on Commercial Treaty Relations between China and other States]. Shanghai: The Commercial Press, 1925.
Zhou Gengsheng. *Geming de waijiao* [Revolutionary diplomacy]. 3rd edn. Shanghai: Shanghai Pacific Bookshop, 1929.
———. *Guojifa* [International law]. 2 vols. Beijing: Commercial Press, 1976.
Zhou Gucheng. *Zhongguo tongshi* [General history of China]. Shanghai: Shanghai renmin chubanshe, 1957.
Zhou Huibin. *WTO yu woguo yinhang jianguan fazhi wanshan yanjiu* [The study of the WTO and the perfection of China's banking regulation]. Beijing: China fangzheng chubanshe, 2003.
Zhou Ligang, and Zhang Guihong. *Dui waizi jigou de falü jianguan* [Legal supervision on foreign-funded financial institutions]. Beijing: Law Press China, 2001.
Zhou Zhonghai, Ma Chengyuan, and Li Juqian (eds). *Guojifa* [International law]. Beijing: China University of Political Science and Law Press, 2004.
Zhu Zhenhua. *Zhongguo jinrong jiushi* [China's financial matters of the past]. Beijing: China guangbo dianshi chubanshe, 1991.
Zhu Huan, and Wang Hengwei (eds). *Zhongguo Duiwai Tiaoyue Cidian* [Dictionary of China's foreign trade]. Changchun: Jinlin jiaoyu chubanshe, 1994.
Zong Chengkang (ed.). *Bainian zhongguo duiwai guanxi: 1840–1940* [China's foreign relations of the one hundred years: 1840–1949]. Nanjing: Nanjing University Press, 1993.

English Articles

Abu-Akeel, Aly K. "The MFN as it Applies to Service Trade: New Problems for an Old Concept." *Journal of World Trade* 33 (1999): 103–29.
Adolf, Huala. "Financial Services Agreement of the GATS: The Developing Countries' Perspective." *International Trade Law and Regulation* 6 (2000): 207–12.
Aghatise, Esohe. "Services and the Development Process: Legal Aspects of Changing Economic Determinants." *Journal of World Trade* 24 (1990): 103–13.
Ahnlid, Anders. "Comparing GATT and GATS: Regime Creation under and after Hegemony." *Review of International Political Economy* 3 (1996): 65–94.
Alford, Duncan E. "Core Principles for Effective Banking Supervision: an Enforceable International Financial Standard?" *Boston College International and Comparative Law Review* 28 (Spring 2005): 237–96.
Arkell, Julian. "The General Agreement on Trade in Services: A Review of its Textual Clarity and Consistency." *The Geneva Papers on Risk and Insurance* 27 (2002): 337–48.
Atik, Jeffery. "National Treatment in the NAFTA Trucking Case." *South Texas Law Review* 42 (2001): 1249–258.

Bagheri, Mahmood, and Chizu Nakajima. "Optimal Level of Financial Regulation under the GATS: a Regulatory Competition and Cooperation Framework for Capital Adequacy and Disclosure of Information." *Journal of International Economic Law* 5 (2002): 507–30.

Bartels, Lorand. "The WTO Enabling Clause and Positive Conditionality in the European Community's GSP Program." *Journal of International Economic Law* 6, no. 2 (2003): 507–32.

Bhala, Raj. "Enter the Dragon: an Essay on China's WTO Accession Saga." *American University International Law Review* 15 (2000): 1469–533.

Bhuryan, Sharif. "Mandatory and Discretionary Legislation: the Continued Relevance of the Distinction under the WTO." *Journal of International Economic Law* 5 (2002): 571–604.

Biship, Crawford M. "American Extraterritorial Jurisdiction in China." *American Journal of International Law* 20, no. 2 (1926): 281–99.

Bown, Chad P. "Why are Safeguards under the WTO so Unpopular?" *World Trade Review* 1 (2002): 47–62.

Cabanellas, Guillermo. "Banking Regulation in Argentina and the Treatment of Foreign Banks." in *Regulation of Foreign Banks, United States and International*, Michael Gruson, and Ralph Reisner (eds). 3rd edn. Vol. 2. Lexis Publishing, 2000.

Caldwell, Robert, and Carmen Kan. "Foreign Banks in China – towards a Level Playing Field: Administrative Regulations of the PRC on Foreign-funded Financial Institutions." *Journal of International Banking Law* 17, no. 6 (2002): 181–88.

Cao, Jianming. "WTO and the Rule of Law in China." *Temple International and Comparative Law Journal* 16 (2002): 379–90.

Chen, Gretchen Harders. "China MFN: A Reaffirmation of Tradition or Regulatory Reform?" *Minnesota Journal of Global Trade* 5 (1996): 381–413.

Chung, Kye Sung, and Chun Pyo Jhong. "Banking Regulation in Korea", In *Regulations of Foreign Banks: Banking Laws of Major Countries and the European Union*, Michael Gruson, and Ralph Reisner (eds). 4th edn. Vol. 3. LexisNexis, 2005.

Clarke, Donald C. "China's Legal System and the WTO: Prospects for Compliance." *Washington University Global Studies Law Review* 2 (2003): 97–118.

Cohen, Jerome Alan, and Stuart J. Valentine. "Foreign Direct Investment in the People's Republic of China: Progress, Problems and Proposals." *Journal of Chinese Law* 1 (1987): 161–215.

Cooke, John. "Insurance in the WTO Services Negotiations: Proposal for a Model Schedule of GATS Commitments." *International Trade Law and Regulation* 8 (2002): 68–74.

———. "The Emergence of Domestic Regulation as a Focal Issue in the GATS 2000 Services Negotiations." *International Trade Law and Regulation* 6 (2000): 141–45.

D'Amato, Anthony, and Kirsten Engel. "State Responsibility for the Exportation of Nuclear Power Technology." *Virgina Law Review* 74 (1988): 1011–66.

Das, Dilip K. "Trade in Financial Services and the Role of the GATS: Against the Backdrop of the Asian Financial Crises." *Journal of World Trade* 32 (1998): 79–114.

Dugan, John C., and James A. McLaughlin. "Forms of Entry, Operation, Expansion, and Supervision of Foreign Banks in the United States." In *Regulation of Foreign Banks: United States and International*, Michael Gruson, and Ralph Reisner (eds). 4th edn. Vol. 1. LexisNexis, 2003.

———, Peter L. Flanagan, and E. Jason Albert. "FDIC Insurance and Regulation of US Branches of Foreign Bank." In *Regulation of Foreign Banks: United States and International*, Michael Gruson, and Ralph Reisner (eds). 4th edn. Vol. 1. LexisNexis, 2003.

Ehlermann, Claus-Dieter. "Reflections on the Appellate Body of the WTO." *Journal of International Economic Law* 6, no. 3 (2003): 695–708.

Ehring, Lothar. "De Facto Discrimination in World Trade Law: National and Most-Favoured-Nation Treatment – or Equal Treatment?" *Journal of World Trade* 36, no. 5 (2002): 921–77.

Esty, Daniel C. "The World Trade Organization's Legitimacy Crisis." *World Trade Review* 1 (2002): 7–22.

Fitzmaurice, Malgosia "The Identification and Character of Treaties and Treaty Obligations between States in International Law." *The British Yearbook of International Law* 73 (2002): 141–85.

Flader, Jack W., Jr. "A Call for a General Agreement on Trade in Services." *Transnational Lawyer* 3 (1990): 661–95.

Footer, Mary E. "The International Regulation of Trade in Services Following Completion of the Uruguay Round." *The International Lawyer* 29 (1995): 453–75.

———. "The General Agreement on Trade in Services: Taking Stock and Moving Forward." *Legal Issues of Economic Integration* 29 (2002): 7–25.

Gail, Daniel B., Joseph J. Norton, and Michael K. O'Neal. "The Foreign Bank Supervision Act of 1991: Expanding the Umbrella of 'Supervisory Reregulation.'" *The International Lawyer* 26 (1992): 993–1006.

Gerhart, Peter M., and Michael S. Baron. "Understanding National Treatment: The Participatory Vision of the WTO." *Indiana International and Comparative Law Review* 14 (2004): 505–52.

Gudgeon, K. Scott. "United States Bilateral Investment Treaties: Comments on Their Origin, Purposes, and General Treatment Standards." *International Tax and Business Lawyer* 4 (1986): 105–35.

Ho, Daniel E. "Compliance and International Soft Law: Why do Countries Implement BASEL Accord?" *Journal of International Economic Law* 5 (2002): 647–88.

Hoekman, Bernard. "Market Access Through Multilateral Agreement: From Goods to Services." *The World Economy* 15 (1992).

———, Carlos A. Primo Braga. "Trade in Services, the GATS and Asia." *Asia-Pacific Economic Review* 2 (1996): 5–20.

Hudec, Robert E. "Free Trade, Sovereignty, Democracy: the Future of the World Trade Organization." *World Trade Review* 1 (2002): 211–22.

———. "GATT/WTO Constraints on National Regulation: Requiem for an "Aim and Effect: Test." *The International Lawyer* 32 (1998): 619–48.

Jackson, John H. "Constructing a Constitution for Trade in Services." *The World Economy* 11 (1988): 187–202.

———. "Dispute Settlement and the WTO: Emerging Problems." *Journal of International Economic Law* 1 (1998): 329–51.

———. "Global Economics and International Economic Law", *Journal of International Economic Law*, vol.1 (1998) 1–23.

———. "International Economic Law in Times that are Interesting." *Journal of International Economic Law* 3 (2000): 3–14.

———. "National Treatment Obligations and Non-Tariff Barriers." *Michigan Journal of International Law* 10 (1989): 207–24.

———. "Perceptions about the WTO Trade Institutions." *World Trade Review* 1 (2002): 101–14.

———. "The WTO 'Constitution' and Proposed Reforms: Seven 'Mantras' Revisited." *Journal of International Economic Law* 4 (2001): 67–78.

Jarreau, J. Steven. "Interpreting The General Agreement on Trade in Services and the WTO Instruments Relevant to the International Trade of Financial Services: The Lawyer's Perspective." *North Carolina Journal of International Law and Commercial Regulation* 25 (Fall 1999): 1–74.

Kampf, Roger. "Financial Services in the WTO: Third Time Lucky." *International Trade Law and Regulation* 4 (1998): 111–23.

———. "Liberalisation of Financial Services in the GATS and Domestic Regulation." *International Trade Law and Regulation* 3 (1997): 155–66.

Kearns, Jason E., and Steve Charnovitz. "Adjudicating Compliance in the WTO: A Review of DSU Article 21.5." *Journal of International Economic Law* 5 (2002): 331–52.

Kenney, Kevin C. "A WTO Agreement on Investment: A Solution in Search of a Problem?" *University of Pennsylvania Journal of International Economic Law* (spring 2003): 77–188.

Kennedy, Matthew. "Services Join GATT: An Analysis of the General Agreement on Trade in Services." *International Trade Law and Regulation* 1 (1995) 11–20.

Key, Sydney J. "Is National Treatment Still Viable? US Policy in Theory and Practice." *Journal of International Banking Law* 5, no. 9 (1990): 365–81.

———. "Trade Liberalization and Prudential Regulation: The International Framework for Financial Services." *International Affairs* 75 (1999): 61–75.

Lake, Charles D. "Comments Regarding the General Agreement on Trade in Services." *Law and Policy in International Business* 31 (2000): 811–13.

Lazar, Fred. "*Services and the GATT: US Motives and a Blueprint for Negotiations.*" *Journal of World Trade* 24 (1990): 135–45.

Lee, Lawrence L.C. "The Basle Accords as Soft Law: Strengthening International Banking Supervision." *Virginia Journal of International Law* 39 (Fall 1998): 1–40.

Lee, Wei J. "China and the WTO: Moving toward Liberalization in China's Banking Sector." *DePaul Business and Commercial Law Journal* 1 (Spring 2003): 481–507.

Lee, Yong-Shik. "Emergency Safeguard Measures under Article X in GATS: Applicability of the Concepts in the WTO Agreement on Safeguards." *Journal of World Trade* 33 (1999): 47–59.

Lennard, Michael. "Navigating by the Stars: Interpreting the WTO Agreements." *Journal of International Economic Law* 5, no. 1 (2002): 17–89.

Leroux, Eric H. "Trade in Financial Services under the World Trade Organization." *Journal of World Trade* 36 (2002): 413–42.

Malloy, Michael P. "International Financial Services: an Agenda for the Twenty-first Century." *Transnational Lawyer* 15 (2002): 55–61.

Mashayekhi, Mina, and Gibbs, Murray. "Lessons from the Uruguay Round Negotiations on Investment." *Journal of World Trade* 33, no. 6 (1999): 1–26.

Mastel, Greg. "China and the World Trade Organization: Moving Forward without Sliding Backward." *Law and Policy of International Business* 31 (2000): 981–97.

Mattoo, Aaditya. "National Treatment in the GATS: Corner-stone or Pandora Box?" *Journal of World Trade* 31 (1997): 107–35.

———. "China's Accession to the WTO: the Services Dimension." *Journal of International Economic Law* 6, no. 2 (2003): 299–339.

Morrison, Peter. "WTO Financial Services Agreement: A Basis for Further Liberalisation in 2000." *International Trade Law and Regulation* 4 (1998): 188–91.

Mukherjee, Neela. "GATS and the Millennium Round of Multilateral Negotiations, Selected Issues from the perspective of the Developing Countries." *Journal of World Trade* 33, no. 4 (1999): 87–102.

Murinde, Victor. "General Agreement on Trade in Services: Financial Services Issues." *International Banking and Financial Law* 14, no. 3 (1995): 28–30.

Murphy, Sean D. "Contemporary Practice of the United States Relating to International Law, International Economic Law: US Enacts Law on Normalizing Trade Relations with China." *American Journal of International Law* 95 (2001): 145–47.

Norton, Joseph Jude. "Capital Adequacy Standards: A Legitimate Regulatory Concern for Prudential Supervision of Banking Activities?" *Ohio State Law Journal* 49 (1989): 1299–363.

———, and Christopher D. Olive. "A By-Product of the Globalization Process: The Rise of Cross-Border Bank Mergers and Acquisitions – The US Regulatory Framework." *Business Lawyer* 56 (2001): 591–633.

Nottage, Hunter. "Trade and Competition in the WTO: Pondering the Applicability of Special and Differential Treatment." *Journal of International Economic Law* 6 (2003): 23–47.

Palumbo, Homan. "Analysis of the Sino-British Joint Declaration and the Basic Law of Hong Kong: What do They Guarantee the People of Hong Kong after 1997?" *Connecticut Journal of International Law* 6 (1991): 667–713.

Pauwelyn, Joost. "Cross-agreement Complaints before the Appellate Body: A Case Study of the EC-Asbestos Dispute." *World Trade Review* 1 (2002): 63–87.

Qian, Andrew Xuefeng. "Transforming China's Traditional Banking Systems under the New National Banking Laws." *Georgia Journal of International and Comparative Law* 25 (1996): 479–95.

Qin, Julia Ya. "'WTO-Plus' Obligations and Their Implications for the WTO Legal System – An Appraisal of the China Accession Protocol." *Journal of World Trade* 37, no. 3 (2003): 483–522.

Quigley, Harold Scott. "Extraterritoriality in China." *American Journal of International Law* 20, no. 1 (1926): 46–68.

Rajan, Ramkishen S., and Rahul, Sen. "Liberalisation of International Trade in Financial Services in Southeast Asia: Indonesia, Malaysia, Philippines and Thailand." *Journal of International Financial Markets* 4 (2002): 170–80.

Reading, Michael R. "The Bilateral Investment Treaty in ASEAN: A Comparative Analysis." *Duke Law Journal* 42 (1992): 679–705.

Regan, Donald H. "Regulatory Purpose and 'Like Products' in Article III:4 of the GATT." *Journal of World Trade* 36 (2002): 443–78.

Rhodes, Sylvia A., and John H. Jackson. "United States Law and China's WTO Accession Process." *Journal of International Economic Law* 2 (1999): 497–510.

Ruttley, Philip. "The WTO Financial Services Agreement." *Journal of International Financial Markets* 1, no. 3 (1999): 109–27.

Sampson, Gary P., and Richard H. Snape. "Identifying the Issues in Trade in Services." *The World Economy* 8 (1985): 171–82.

Sapir, André. "The General Agreement on Trade in Services: From 1994 to the Year 2000." *Journal of World Trade* 33 (1999): 51–66.

Sauve, Pierre. "Assessing the General Agreement on Trade in Services: Half-Full or Half-Empty?" *Journal of World Trade* 29 (1995): 125–45.

Shan, Wenhua. "National Treatment and the Transformation of FDI Laws and Policies in China." *International Trade Law and Regulation* 6 (2000): 21–27.

Shenkin, Todd S. "Trade-Related Investment Measures in Bilateral Investment Treaties and the GATT: Moving Toward a Multilateral Investment Treaty." *University of Pittsburgh Law Review* 55 (1994): 541–97.

Stahl, Tycho H.E. "Liberalizing International Trade in Services: The Case for Sidestepping the GATT." *Yale Journal of International Law* 19 (1994): 405–53.

Stephenson, Sherry M. "Regional versus Multilateral Liberalization of Services." *World Trade Review* 1 (2002): 187–209.

Simser, Jeffrey. "GATS and Financial Services: Redefining Borders." *Business Journal of International Law* 3 (1996): 33–65.

Spadi, Fabio "Discriminatory Safeguards in the Light of the Admission of the People's Republic of China to the World Trade Organization." *Journal of International Economic Law* 5, no. 2 (2002): 421–43.

Sutherland, Peter D. "Concluding the Uruguay Round-Creating the New Architecture of Trade for the Global Economy." *Fordham International Law Journal* 24 (2000): 15–29.
Tarullo, Daniel K. "Rules, Discretion, and Authority in International Financial Reform." *Journal of International Economic Law* 4 (2001): 613–82.
Vandevelde, Kenneth J. "US Bilateral Investment Treaties: The Second Wave." *Michigan Journal of International Law* 14 (1993): 621–704.
Wagner, Constance Z. "The New WTO Agreement on Financial Services and Chapter 14 of NAFTA: Has Free Trade in Banking Finally Arrived?" *NAFTA: Law and Business Review of Americas* 5 (1999): 5–90.
Walker, Herman, Jr. "Provisions on Companies in United States Commercial Treaties." *American Journal of International Law* 50 (1956): 373–93.
Wallace, Don, Jr, and David B. Bailey. "The Inevitability of National Treatment of Foreign Direct Investment with Increasingly Few and Narrow Exceptions." *Cornell International Law Journal* 31 (1998): 615–30.
Wang, Yi. "Most-Favoured-Nation Treatment under the General Agreement on Trade in Services – and Its Application in Financial Services." *Journal of World Trade* 30 (1996): 91–124.
Wilson, Robert R. "Editorial Comment: A Decade of New Commercial Treaties." *American Journal of International Law* 50 (1956): 927–33.
———. "Postwar Commercial Treaties of the United States." *American Journal of International Law* 43 (1949): 262–87.
Woolfson, Philip. "The WTO Financial Services Agreement and its Impact on Insurers – A European Perspective." *International Trade Law and Regulation* 6 (1998): 189–93.
Wu, Edieth Y. "China Today: Why Its Accession to the World Trade Organization is Relevant and Good for the International Community." *Journal of International Economic Law* 5 (2002): 689–718.
Yang, Guohua, and Cheng Jin. "The Process of China's Accession to the WTO." *Journal of International Economic Law* 4 (2001): 297–328.
Zhang, Xin. "Domestic Effect of the WTO Agreement in China: Trend and Implications." *Journal of World Investment* 3 (2002): 913–34.

Chinese Articles

Bian Yaowu. "Zhongguo caishui jinrong lifa huigu yu qianzhan." [Review and prospective of Chinese legislation of finance and tax] *Journal of Central University of Finance and Economics* (2003, no. 2): 1–2.
Cao Jianming. "WTO yu zhongguo fazhi jianshe." [WTO and the establishment of China's rule of law] *Bijiaofa yanjiu* [Comparative Law Studies] (2002, no. 2): 1–20.
Chen Xianmin. "Jiedu fuwu maoyi zhongxieding de jiben yuanze." [Understanding the basic principles of GATS] *Faxue* [Law Science] (2003, no. 7): 98–104.

Chen Xiaoyun. "Zongjie lifa jingyan, jiaqiang jinrong lifa: jinian zhongguo renmin yinhangfa banbu shishi wu zhounian." [Summing up legislation experience, strengthening financial legislation: commemorating the fifth anniversary of the PBC Law]. In *Zhonghua Renmin Gongheguo Zhongguo Renmin Yinhangfa banbu wu zhounian jinian wenji* [A Treatise to Commemorate the Fifth Anniversary of the PBC Law], the Treaty and Law Department of the PBC (ed.). Beijing: Zhongguo jinrong chubanshe [China Finance Publishing House], 2000: 49–56.

Chen Yongmei. "Waishang Laihua Touzi Daiyu de falü Wenti Yanjiu." [On legal issues of foreign investment treatment in China]. In *Jingjifa Luntan* [A Symposium on Economic Law], Li Changqi (ed.). Vol. 2. Qunzhong chubanshe, 2004: 441–62.

Ding Wei. "'Chao guomin daiyu heli hefa lun' pingxi: waishang touzi lingyu guomin daiyu zhidu de lixing sibian." [An Argument against the validity and reasonableness of more favourable treatment and the rational consideration for national treatment in the fields of foreign direct investment] *Zhengfa luntan* [Tribune of Political Science and Law/Journal of China University of Political Science and Law] 22, no. 2 (2004): 164–70.

Fu Taosheng. "Guanyu jianli zhongguo cunkuan baoxian zhidu de gouxiang." [On the conception of setting up the deposit insurance institution in China] *Journal of Central University of Finance and Economics* (2002, no. 5): 6–11.

Guo Daohui. "Shichang jingji yu faxue lilun, fazhi guannian de biange." [The market economy and the revolution of law theory, legal idea] *Faxue* [Law Science] (1994, no. 2): 2–6.

Han Wanghong, "Xiugai shangye yinhangfa tantao." [Discussing the revision of China's commercial banking law] *Journal of Zhongnan University of Economics and Law* (2002, no. 1): 116–22.

Han Liyu. "WTO guize de shiyong yu zhongguo guonei lifa" [The implementation of WTO rules and China's domestic legislations] *Guoji jingjifa luncong* [Chinese Journal of International Economic Law] 4 (2001): 218–35.

Hu Jian. "Jiaru WTO dui waiguo yinhangye de yingxiang yu woguo yinhang tixi goujian zhong de hexin wenti." [The implications of entry to the WTO on China's banking business and the core issues in the construction of China's banking system] *Jinrong fayuan* [Financial Law Forum] (2000, no. 4): 6–21.

Huang Ke'an, and Zhang Jia'en. "Dui waishang zhijie touzi shixing chao guomin daiyu de yuanyin yu tiaozheng qushi sikao." [Deploring causes of more favourable treatment of foreign direct investment and adjustment trend] Journal of Fuzhou University (Social Science Edition) 14, no. 2 (2000) 21–24, 115.

Huang Yi. "Wei shangye yinhang gaige he fazhan tigong genghao de falü baozhang: jinian shangye yinhangfa banbu shizhounian." [Providing better legal protection for the reform and development of commercial banks: commemorating the tenth anniversary of the Commercial Banking Law] *Zhongguo jinrong* [China Finance] (2005, no.13): 22–24.

Jiang Xinmiao, "Guomin Daiyu Yuanze zai Guoji Banquan Baohu zhong de Shiyong yu Liwai." [Application of and exemption from the national treatment principle in the international copyright protection]. In *2000 Chinese Yearbook of Private International Law and Comparative Law*, Han Depei, Yu Xianyu, and Huang Jin (eds). Vol. 3. Beijing: Law Press China 2000: 164–83.

Li Hui. "Shuangbian cujin he baohui touzi tiaoyue bijiao yanjiu." [Comparative study on bilateral treaties of investment promotion and protection]. In *1995 Chinese Yearbook of International Law*, Wang Tieya (ed.). Beijing: Zhongguo duiwai fanyi chuban gongsi, 1996: 159–76.

Li Jinnan. "Jinrong shichang caifang beijing xia waizi yinhang jianguan zhidu de wanshan." [Perfection of the supervision mechanism over foreign-invested banks in the context of opening financial market] *Journal of Central University of Finance and Economics* (2002, no.7): 20–23.

Li Jinze. "Woguo waizi yinhang shichang zhunru zhidu de juxianxing jiqi kefu." [On the weaknesses and overcoming of China's foreign-funded banking market access] *Falü kexu* [The Science of Law] (2003, no.1): 108–18.

Li Lian. "Woguo waizi guomin daiyu ruogan falü wenti tanTao." [Discussing relevant legal issues relating to national treatment for foreign investment in China] *Guoji jingjifa luncong* [Chinese Journal of International Economic Law] 4 (2001): 422–47.

Li Shishi. "Lun zhongguo dijie de shuangbian touzi baohu xieding." [On bilateral investment protection treaties entered by China with other countries]. *1990 Chinese Yearbook of International Law*, Wang Tieya, and Li Haopei (eds). Beijing: Law Press China, 1991: 109–24.

Li Siqi, and Yan Xiaolong. "Woguo rushi hou waizi yinhang jianguan fa de chonggou." [The reconstruction of China's regulatory law relating to foreign-funded banks after entry into the WTO] *Shanghai jinrong* [Shanghai Finance] (2002, no. 5): 23–25.

Li Yan. "Zhongguo jiaru WTO yu waizi yinhang de falü guizhi." [China's entering WTO and the supervision of foreign banks] *Shanghai caijing daxue xuebao* [Journal of Shanghai University of Finance and Economics] (2000, no. 4): 45–51.

Liu Jianwen. "Zhongguo suodeshuifa biange de jiben silu." [Basic idea of the reform of income tax in China] *Faxuejia* [Jurists Review] (2004, no. 5): 34–39.

———, and Xiong Wei. "Guomin daiyu yu waizi shuishou youhui zhengce de gaige." [National treatment and the reform of the more favourable tax policy for foreign investment] *Zhongguo faxue* [Chinese Legal Science] (1998, no. 2): 53–59.

Lu jiongxing. "Lun wanshan waishang touzi falü zhidu." [Improving the legal system of foreign merchant investment] *Zhongguo faxue* [Chinese Legal Science] (1996, no. 3): 69–77.

Luo Peixin. "WTO yanjiu lujing tantao." [Study on WTO research approaches] *Jinrong fayuan* [Financial Law Forum], no. 50 (2001): 1–9.

Luo Ying, and Luo Yong. "Zhulu zhongyuan, heyi zhizhi? – qianyi GATS dui zhongguo renmin yinhang jianguan de yingxiang." [How to deal with it? – a preliminary study on the impact of GATS on PBC's banking regulations] *Jinrong fayuan* [Financial Law Forum], no. 50 (2001): 32–40.

Luo Yong, Yuan Kaihong, and Lin Dan. "Rushihou dui woguo waizi zhengche zhong guomin daiyu de chongxin renshi." [Rethinking national treatment in China's foreign capital policy post-WTO] *Guoji maoyi wenti* [Journal of International Trade] (2002, no. 8): 5–8.

Shan Wenhua. "Shichang jingji yu waishang touzi qiye de guomin daiyu yanjiu." [Study on the market economy and national treatment of foreign-funded enterprises] *Zhongguo faxue* [Chinese Legal Science] (1994, no. 5): 23–30.

———. "Waizi guomin daiyu jiben lilun wenti yanjiu." [Studies on basic theoretical issues of national treatment on foreign investment] *Guoji jingjifa luncong* [Chinese Journal of International Economic Law] 1 (1998): 240–67.

Shen Wei, and Tang Huadong. "Lun waishang touzi qiye "chao guomin daiyu" de guominhua." [Nationalization of more favourable treatment of foreign-invested enterprises] *Faxue tansuo* [Law Science Exploration] (1997, no. 1): 23–26.

Sun Nanshen. "Lun WTO xieyi guize zai zhongguo fayuan de shiyong – jianlun rushi dui zhongguo shewai jingji lifa de yingxiang." [The application of WTO rules in China's courts – the implications of entry into the WTO for China's foreign-related economic legislation] *Guoji jingjifa luncong* [Chinese Journal of International Economic Law] 4 (2001): 196–217.

Tang Shuangning, "Jiaqiang jinrong jianguan, yingjie rushi tiaozhan." [Strengthening financial regulation, preparing for the challenge of the entry to the WTO]. In *Zhonghua Renmin Gongheguo Zhongguo Renmin Yinhangfa banbu wu zhounian jinian wenji* [A Treatise to Commemorate the Fifth Anniversary of the PBC Law], the Treaty and Law Department of the PBC (eds). Beijing: Zhongguo jinrong chubanshe [China Finance Publishing House], 2000:63–66.

Wang Cuanli. "WTO xieyi yu sifa shencha." [WTO agreement and judicial review] *Zhongguo faxue* [China Legal Science] (2003, no. 2): 23–33.

Wang Fuquan. "Waishang touzi qiye yu guomin daiyu." [Foreign-invested enterprises and national treatment] *Yatai jingji* [Asian and Pacific Economy] (1994, no. 4): 59–61.

Wang Hui. "Lun woguo yinhangye duiwai kaifang de guomin daiyu wenti." [On the issue of national treatment in the opening of China's banking industry] *Henan zhengfa guanli ganbu xueyuan xuebao* [Journal of the Cadre College of Politics and Law Management in Henan] (2002, no. 3): 65–69.

Wang Li. "Shijie Maoyi Zuzhi Falü Kuangjia xia Zhongguo Jinrong Shichang de Kaifang." [Opening Chinese financial market under the WTO legal framework] *Zhongde faxue luntan* [Jahrbuch des Deutsch-Chinesischen Instituts für Rechtswissenschaft der Universitaten Gottingen and Nanjing]. Vol. 2. Nanjing: Nanjing University Press, 2004: 259–75.

Wang Xuan. "Lun guanshui ji maoyi zongxieding xia de maoyi ziyouhua." [The trade liberalization under the GATT]. *1986 Chinese Yearbook of International Law*, Wang Tieya, and Li Haopei (eds). Beijing: Zhongguo duiwai fanyi chuban gongsi, 1986: 44–64.

Wang Yi. "WTO guomin daiyu zai fuwu maoyi he zhishi chanquan lingyu de shiyong." [The application of national treatment in GATS and TRIPS] *Faxue yanjiu* [Chinese Journal of Law] 26, no. 3(2004): 115–27.

———. "Zhonghua renmin gongheguo zai guoji maoyi zhong de zuihuiguo daiyu wenti" [The People's Republic of China's MFN treatment in international trade]. *1990 Chinese Yearbook of International Law*, Wang Tieya, and Li Haopei (eds). Beijing: Law Press China, 1991: 125–67.

Wu Bin. "Jinrong shichang tuichu falü jizhi de bijiao yanjiu." [The comparative study on the legal system of financial institutions' retreating from market] *The Science of Finance and Economics* (2003, no. 1): 37–41.

Wu Zhipan. "Jinrong fazhi shinian." [Ten years of the financial law] *Zhongguo jinrong* [China Finance] (2005, no. 13): 11–15.

Xia Jinlai, and Ye Bifeng. "Dui WTO tizhi xia guoji maoyi xingzheng susong de sikao." [Thoughts on the administrative litigation of international trade under the WTO regime] *Faxue pinglun* [Wuhan University Law Review] 21, no. 3 (2003): 68–69.

Xu Chongli. "Shichang jingji yu woguo shewai jingji lifa daoxiang." [The market economy and China's legislative direction concerning foreign-related economy] *Faxue yanjiu* [Chinese Journal of Law] (1994, no. 6): 36–43.

———. "Shilun woguo dui waizi shixing guomin daiyu biaozun de wenti." [On the issue of national treatment standards for foreign investment in China] *Guoji jingjifa luncong* [Chinese Journal of International Economic Law]. Vol.1 (1998): 175–201.

Yang Huan, and Zheng Yalan. "Cong shimao zuzhi jinrong fuwu maoyi guomin daiyu kan woguo waizi yinhang lifa." [Observing China's foreign-funded banking legislation from perspective of national treatment in the WTO/GATS] *Guoji maoyi wenti* [Journal of International Trade] (2002, no. 2): 57–61.

Yang Xinyu, Chen Yixin, Song Wenxi, and Li Xiaoning. "Lun shichang jingji de fazhi yuanze." [On the legal principles of the market economy] *Faxue* [Law Science] (1994, no. 1): 4–6.

Yang Zewei and Su Caixia, "Dui Waiguoren Daiyu Wenti de Fansi" [Reflections on the Issue of Foreigners' Treatment], *Zhongyang zhengfa guanli ganbu xueyuan xuebao* [Journal of the Central Cadre College of Politics and Law Management] 13–15 (1998, no. 3).

Yao Meizhen. "Guoji touzi de falü baohu." [Legal protection of international investments]. 1*982 Chinese Yearbook of International Law*, Wang Tieya, and Chen Tiqiang (eds). Beijing: Zhongguo duiwai fanyi chuban gongsi, 1982: 115–44.

Yin Tie'ou. "Shixing duiwai kaifang yilai zhongguo duiwai jingji guanxi he duiwai jingji fazhi jianse gaikuang." [Survey of China's foreign economic relations and foreign economic law since its adoption of the policy of opening to the outside world]. *1989 Chinese Yearbook of International Law*, Wang Tieya, and Li Haopei (eds). Beijing: Law Press China, 1990: 478–89.

Yu Jinsong. "Zhongguo fazhan guocheng zhong de waizi zhunru jieduan guomin daiyu wenti." [Question of national treatment at the stage of foreign capital admittance in the developing process of China] *Faxuejia* [Jurists Review] (2004, no. 6): 12–17.

Yu Meizhen. "Lun woguo liyong waizi zhong shishi guomin daiyu de ruogan wenti" [Relevant issues of implementing national treatment when using foreign investment in China] *Journal of South China Normal University* (Social Science Edition) (1997, no. 1): 9–14.

Zeng Huaqun. "Guoji jingjifa yao yanjiu xinwenti." [Some new problems to be researched in the field of international economic law] *Faxue yanjiu* [Chinese Journal of Law] 26, no. 2 (2004): 135.

Zhang Ge. "GATS guomin daiyu yuanze de falü fenxi ji woguo chuli yuanze." [The legal analysis of GATS national treatment and China's addressing principles] *Nanjing daxue falü pinglun* [Nanjing University Law Review] (Spring 2001): 60–67.

Zhang Naigen. "Lun tiaoyu pizhun de xianfa chengxu xiugai." [On the constitution amendment in treaty ratification process] *Zhengzhi yu falü* [Political Science and Law] (2004, no. 1): 17–19.

Zhao, Weitian. "Tongyi touming yu sifa shencha: jiedu zhongguo rushi yidingshu di er tiao." [Unified, transparent vs judicial review, unscrambling Art. II of the Protocol on the Accession of the PRC] *Guoji maoyi* [Intertrade] (2002, no. 2): 37–40.

———. "WTO buqishi guize de xin fazhan: lun zhongguo rushi yidingshu youguan buqishi guize de guiding." [New development on the rule of non-discrimination of WTO: discussion on the provisions about non-discrimination in the Protocol on the Accession of the PRC] *Zhengfa luntan* [Tribune of Political Science and Law/Journal of China University of Political Science and Law] 20, no. 4 (2002): 23–30.

Zhou Yongkun. "Shichang jingji huhuan lifa pingdeng." [The market economy calling the legislative equality] *Zhongguo faxue* [Chinese Legal Science] (1993, no. 4): 18–25.

Zhu Chongshi, and Guo Junxiu. "Lun jiaru shimao zuzhi hou woguo jinrong fazhi de wanshan." [China's financial legal system after entry to the WTO] *Journal of Xiamen University* (Arts & Social Sciences edition) (2002, no. 6): 71–80.

Chinese Cases Relating to Foreign-Funded Banks

Bank of East Asia v. *Shanghai Xinhongye Real Estate Ltd. et al*. (东亚银行有限公司诉上海新弘业房地产发展有限公司等借款合同案), Overview of Chinese Cases 2004 (《中国审判案件要览, 2004商事审判案例卷》, 国家法官学院和中国人民大学法学院编, 人民法院出版社和人民大学出版社, 2005年第一版, 第77–83页).

Fuxinda (Tianjin) International Trade Ltd v. *Banque LCL Le Credit Lyonnais* (福欣达天津国际贸易有限公司诉法国里昂信贷银行天津分行承担错误通知信用证信息赔偿责任案), Selected Cases of the People's Courts, 2001, No. 3 (《人民法院案例选》2001年第3辑, 人民法院出版社, 2002年版, 第258–64页).

HSBC Xiamen Branch v. *Xiamen Xiangyu Chongli Int'l Trade Company et al.* (香港上海汇丰银行有限公司厦门分行诉厦门象屿崇理国际贸易有限公司等借款合同案), Overview of Chinese Cases 2002 (《中国审判案件要览, 2002年商事审判及行政审判案例卷》, 国家法官学院和中国人民大学法学院编, 中国人民大学出版社, 2003年, 第123–28页).

Jiangsu Huaiyin Foreign Trade Company v. *Nedbank of South Africa* (南非莱利银行以淮阴市外贸公司提起的信用证承兑纠纷属非合同性担保责任争议应由担保人或开证人所在地法院管辖为由提起管辖权异议案), Selected Cases of the People's Courts, 2001, No. 4 (《人民法院案例选》2001年第4辑, 人民法院出版社, 2002年版, 第285–91页).

Wu Weiming v. Citibank Shanghai Branch (吴卫明诉花旗银行上海分行储蓄合同纠纷案), Gazette of the Supreme People's Court 42–46 (2005, no. 9).

Xiamen International Bank v. *Jinjiang Houtai Shoes Ltd, and Jinjiang Xiaosheng Clothing Ltd.* (厦门国际银行诉晋江厚泰鞋业有限公司和晋江晓生服装实业有限公司借款合同纠纷案), Gazette of the Supreme People's Court 71–72 (1998, no. 2).

Shanghai Shenda Joint-Stock Company v. *HSBC Shanghai Branch* (上海申达股份有限公司诉汇丰银行上海分行委托合同案), Overview of Chinese Cases 2002 (《中国审判案件要览, 2002年商事审判及行政审判案例卷》, 国家法官学院和中国人民大学法学院编, 中国人民大学出版社, 2003年, 第219–24页).

Hanli Company v. Chohung Bank of South Korea (邗利公司诉韩国朝兴银行对信用证到期后提交单据未按规定处理仍应支付已提交单据项下的货款案), Selected Cases of the People's Courts, 2000, No. 1 (《人民法院案例选》2000年第1辑, 人民法院出版社, 2000年版).

Standard Chartered Bank (Hong Kong) v. Shandong Cereals & Oil Group Corporation, G G International (Hong Kong) Company Limited (渣打银行香港有限公司与山东省粮油集团总公司和金谷（香港）国际贸易有限公司借款合同案), 山东省高级人民法院, (2006) 鲁民四终字第 17 号.

Korea Exchange Bank v. Huaxia Bank (Qingdao Branch) （韩国外换银行株式会社与华夏银行股份有限公司青岛分行信用证纠纷案）, 山东省高级人民法院, (2009) 鲁民四终字第 38 号.

Agricultural Bank of China (Ningbo Branch) v. Australia and New Zealand Banking Group (Shanghai Branch), (澳大利亚和新西兰银行集团有限公司上海分行与中国农业银行股份有限公司宁波市分行信用欺诈纠纷复议案), 浙江省高级人民法院, (2010) 浙商外复字第 2 号.

Daegu Bank South Korea v. Bank of Communications (Weihai Branch) （韩国大邱银行与威海纺织集团进出口有限责任公司、交通银行股份有限公司威海分行票据付款请求权纠纷案), 山东省高级人民法院, (2009) 鲁民四终字第 74 号.

United Overseas Bank (Shanghai Branch), HSBC (Shanghai Branch) v. Shanghai Golden Landmark Co. Ltd. （大华银行有限公司上海分行、汇丰银行有限公司上海分行为与上海黄金置地有限公司金融借款合同纠纷案), 上海市高级人民法院, (2009) 沪高民四（商）初字第 1 号.

Citibank N.A. v. Trade Mark Appeal Board of State Administration of Industry and Commerce (Citigroup Limited HK as Third Party) （花旗银行与中华人民共和国国家工商行政管理总局商标评审委员会行政诉讼) (香港斯创意有限公司作为第三人), 北京市第一中级人民法院, (2010) 一中知行初字第2885 号.

Citibank N.A. and Citigroup v. Trade Mark Appeal Board of State Administration of Industry and Commerce (CITIC Group as Third Party) （花旗银行、花旗集团公司与中华人民共和国国家工商行政管理总局商标评审委员会行政诉讼) (中国中信集团公司作为第三人), 北京市高级人民法院, (2009) 高行终字第 1207 号.

GATT/WTO Cases

Argentina – Safeguard Measures on Imports of Footwear, WT/DS121/AB/R, adopted January 12, 2000.

Border Tax Adjustments, adopted by the Council December 2, 1970, L/3464, BISD, 18S/97.

Canada – Certain Measures Concerning Periodicals, WT/DS31/R, WT/DS31/AB/R, adopted July 30, 1997.

Canada – Measures Affecting the Importation of Milk and the Exportation of Dairy Products, WT/DS103/AB/R, WT/DS113/AB/R, adopted October 27, 1999.

Canada – Certain Measures Affecting the Automotive Industry, WT/DS139/R, WT/DS142/R, WT/DS139/AB/R, WT/DS142/AB/R, adopted June 19, 2000.

Canada – Term of Patent Protection, WT/DS170/R, adopted October 12, 2000.

European Communities – Regime for the Importation, Sale and Distribution of Bananas, WT/DS27/R, WT/DS27/AB/R, adopted September 25, 1997.

EC – Computer Equipment, WT/DS62/AB/R, adopted June 22, 1998.

EC – Trade Description on Sardines, WT/DS231/R, adopted October 23, 2002.

EC – Conditions for the Granting of Tariff Preferences to Developing Countries, WT/DS246/AB/R, adopted April 20, 2004.

Italian Discrimination against Imported Agricultural Machinery, adopted October 23, 1958, BISD 7S/60.
Japan – Taxes on Alcoholic Beverages, WT/DS8/R, WT/DS/S10/R, WT/DS/S11/R, adopted November 1, 1996.
Japan – Taxes on Alcoholic Beverages, WT/DS8/AB/R, WT/DS10/AB/R, WT/DS11/AB/R, adopted November 1, 1996.
Korea – Definitive Safeguard Measure on Imports of Certain Dairy Products, WT/DS98/R, adopted January 12, 2000.
Korea – Definitive Safeguard Measure on Imports of Certain Dairy Products, WT/DS98/AB/R, adopted January 12, 2000.
Korea – Measures Affecting Imports of Fresh, Chilled and Frozen Beef, WT/DS161/R, adopted January 10, 2001.
Mexico – Measures Affecting Telecommunications Services, WT/DS204/R, adopted June 1, 2004.
US – Section 337 of the Tariff Act of 1930, adopted November 7, 1986, BISD 36S/345, L/6439.
US – Taxes on Petroleum and Certain Imported Substances, adopted June 17, 1987, BISD 34S/136.
US – Gasoline, WT/DS2/R, adopted May 20, 1996.
US – Gasoline, WT/DS2/AB/R, adopted May 20, 1996.
US – Restrictions on Imports of Cotton and Man-Made Fibre Underwear, WT/DS24/AB/R, adopted February 25, 1997.
US – Anti-Dumping Act of 1916, WT/DS136/R, adopted September 26, 2000.
US – Import Prohibition of Certain Shrimp and Shrimp Products, WT/DS58/AB/R, adopted November 21, 2001.
US – Measures Relating Exports Restraints as Subsidies, WT/DS194/R, adopted August 23, 2001.
US – Section 211 Omnibus Appropriations Act, WT/DS176/AB/R, adopted January 2, 2002.
US – Definitive Safeguard Measures on Imports of Circular Welded Carbon Quality Line Pipe from Korea, WT/DS202/AB/R, adopted March 8, 2002.
US – Countervailing Duties on Certain Corrosion-Resistant Carbon Steel Flat Products from Germany, WT/DS213/AB/R, adopted December 19, 2002.
US – Continued Dumping and Subsidy Offset Act of 2000, WT/DS217/AB/R, WT/DS234/AB/R, adopted January 27, 2003.
US – Measures Affecting the Cross-Border Supply of Gambling and Betting Services, WT/DS285/R, adopted April 20, 2005.
US – Measures Affecting the Cross-Border Supply of Gambling and Betting Services, WT/DS285/AB/R, adopted April 20, 2005.
China – Measures Affecting Trading Rights and Distribution Services for Certain Publications and Audiovisual Entertainment Products, WT/DS363/R, adopted January 19, 2010.
China – Certain Measures Affecting Electronic Payment Services, WT/DS413/R, adopted August 31, 2012.

GATT and WTO Documents

JOB (03)/213, *Consideration of Issues Relating to Article XX:2 of the GATS*, Note by the Chairman of the Committee on Specific Commitments (November 20, 2003).

JOB(03)/214, *Consideration of Issues Relating to Article XX:2 of the GATS*, Communication from Switzerland (November 27, 2003).

MTN.GNS/7, *Note on the Meeting of September 15–17, 1987* (October 15, 1987).

MTN.GNS/10, *Note on the Meeting of September 15–17, 1987* (October 15, 1987).

MTN.GNS/15, *Note on the Meeting of May 17, 1988* (June 14, 1988).

MTN.GNS/24, *Note on the Meeting of July 17–21, 1989* (August, 1989).

MTN.GNS/35, *Draft Multilateral Framework for Trade in Services* (July 23, 1990).

MTN/TNC/W/35/Rev.1, *Draft Final Act Embodying the Result of the Uruguay Round of Multilateral Trade Negotiations* (December 3, 1990).

MTN.GNS/W/164, *Guidelines for the Scheduling of Initial Commitments in Trade in Services: Explanatory Note* (September 3, 1993).

MTN.GNS/W/176, *Article XXXIV, Status of Branches as Service Suppliers*, Note by the Secretariat (October 26, 1993).

MTN.GNS/FIN/1, *Note on the Meeting of June 11–13, 1990*, Working Group on Financial Services Including Insurance (July 5, 1990).

MNT.GNS/FIN/2, *Note on the Meeting of July 12–13, 1990*, Working Group on Financial Services Including Insurance (August 10, 1990).

S/C/M/61, Council for Trade in Services, *Report of the Meeting Held on July 17, 2002*, Note by the Secretariat (September 23, 2002).

S/C/M/63, Council for Trade in Services, *Report of the Meeting Held on October 25, 2002*, Note by the Secretariat (November 11, 2002).

S/C/M/65, Council for Trade in Services, *Report of the Meeting Held on February 28, 2003*, Note by the Secretariat (March 21, 2003).

S/C/M/66, Council for Trade in Services, *Report of the Meeting Held on May 14, 2003*, Note by the Secretariat (June 18, 2003).

S/CSS/M/13, Council for Trade in Services, *Report of the Meeting Held on December 3–6, 2001*, Note by the Secretariat (February 26, 2002).

S/CSC/M/15, Committee on Specific Commitments, *Report of the Meeting Held on May 23, 2000*, Note by the Secretariat (June 29, 2000).

S/CSC/W/19, Committee on Specific Commitments, *Revision of Scheduling Guidelines*, Note by the Secretariat (March 5, 1999).

S/CSS/W/39, Council for Trade in Services, *Communication from the European Communities and their Member States – GATS 2000: Financial Services* (December 22, 2000).

S/CSS/W/96, Council for Trade in Services, *Communication from Colombia – Financial Services* (July 9, 2001).

S/C/N/213, Council for Trade in Services, *Notification Pursuant to Article III:3 of the General Agreement on Trade in Services – People's Republic of China* (December 24, 2002).
S/C/N/215, Council for Trade in Services, *Notification Pursuant to Article III:3 of the General Agreement on Trade in Services – People's Republic of China* (December 24, 2002).
S/C/N/221, Council for Trade in Services, *Notification Pursuant to Article III:3 of the General Agreement on Trade in Services – People's Republic of China* (December 24, 2002).
S/C/N/222, Council for Trade in Services, *Notification Pursuant to Article III:3 of the General Agreement on Trade in Services – People's Republic of China* (December 24, 2002).
S/C/N/223, Council for Trade in Services, *Notification Pursuant to Article III:3 of the General Agreement on Trade in Services – People's Republic of China* (December 24, 2002).
S/C/N/224, Council for Trade in Services, *Notification Pursuant to Article III:3 of the General Agreement on Trade in Services – People's Republic of China* (December 24, 2002).
S/C/N/225, Council for Trade in Services, *Notification Pursuant to Article III:3 of the General Agreement on Trade in Services – People's Republic of China* (December 24, 2002).
S/C/W/96, Council for Trade in Services, *Article VI:4 of the GATS: Disciplines on Domestic Regulation Applicable to all Services*, Note by the Secretariat (March 1, 1999).
S/FIN/M/25, Committee on Trade in Financial Services, *Report of the Meeting Held on April 13, 2000*, Note by the Secretariat (May 8, 2000).
S/FIN/M/26, Committee on Trade in Financial Services, *Report of the Meeting Held on May 25, 2000*, Note by the Secretariat (June 29, 2000).
S/FIN/M/27, Committee on Trade in Financial Services, *Report of the Meeting Held on July 13, 2000*, Note by the Secretariat (August 23, 2000).
S/FIN/M/29, Committee on Trade in Financial Services, *Report of the Meeting Held on November 29, 2000*, Note by the Secretariat (March 14, 2001).
S/FIN/M/30, Committee on Trade in Financial Services, *Report of the Meeting Held on April 2, 2001*, Note by the Secretariat (May 8, 2001).
S/FIN/M/36, Committee on Trade in Financial Services, *Report of the Meeting Held on July 22, 2002*, Note by the Secretariat (September 26, 2002).
S/FIN/M/37, Committee on Trade in Financial Services, *Report of the Meeting Held on October 21, 2002*, Note by the Secretariat (October 24, 2002).
S/FIN/M/43, Committee on Trade in Financial Services, *Report of the Meeting Held on December 1, 2003*, Note by the Secretariat (December 4, 2003).
S/FIN/M/47, Committee on Trade in Financial Services, *Report of the Meeting Held on November 23,2004*, Note by the Secretariat (November 26, 2004).
S/FIN/M/50, Committee on Trade in Financial Services, *Report of the Meeting Held on September 19, 2005*, Note by the Secretariat (September 23, 2005).

S/FIN/M/53, Committee on Trade in Financial Services, *Report of the Meeting Held on November 27, 2006*, Note by the Secretariat (November 30, 2006).
S/FIN/M/55, Committee on Trade in Financial Services, *Report of the Meeting Held on November 12,2007*, Note by the Secretariat (December 16, 2007).
S/FIN/M/57, Committee on Trade in Financial Services, *Report of the Meeting Held on December 1, 2008*, Note by the Secretariat (December 4, 2008).
S/FIN/M/58, Committee on Trade in Financial Services, *Report of the Meeting Held on March 31,2009*, Note by the Secretariat (May 7, 2009).
S/FIN/M/61, Committee on Trade in Financial Services, *Report of the Meeting Held on November 7 and 9, 2009*, Note by the Secretariat (March 4, 2010).
S/FIN/M/71, Committee on Trade in Financial Services, *Report of the Meeting Held on October 31, 2011*, Note by the Secretariat (November 4, 2011).
S/FIN/W/18, Committee on Trade in Financial Services, *Communication from the European Communities and their Member States – TRM China – Financial Services* (September 23, 2002).
S/FIN/W/19, Committee on Trade in Financial Services, *Communication from the United States*, Transitional Review Mechanism Pursuant to Section 18 of the Protocol on Accession of the People's Republic of China (October 1, 2002).
S/FIN/W/20, Committee on Trade in Financial Services, *Communication from Canada, TRM China* – Financial Services – *Canada's Questions to The People's Republic of China* (October 1, 2002).
S/FIN/W/21, Committee on Trade in Financial Services, *Communication from Japan*, Transitional Review Mechanism in Connection with Paragraph 18 of the Protocol on the Accession of the People's Republic of China (October 1, 2002).
S/FIN/W/21/Add.1, Committee on Trade in Financial Services, *Communication from Japan*, Transitional Review Mechanism in Connection with Paragraph 18 of the Protocol on the Accession of the People's Republic of China, Addendum (October 14, 2002).
S/FIN/W/30, Committee on Trade in Financial Services, *Communication from Japan*, Transitional Review Mechanism in connection with Paragraph 18 of the Protocol on the Accession of the People's Republic of China (September 29, 2003).
S/FIN/W/32, Committee on Trade in Financial Services, Communication from the European Communities, Transitional Review Mechanism in Connection with Paragraph 18 of the Accession of the People's Republic of China (November 12, 2003).
S/FIN/W/33, Committee on Trade in Financial Services, Communication from Canada, Transitional Review Mechanism in Connection with Paragraph 18 of the Protocol on the Accession of the People's Republic of China (November 12, 2003).

S/FIN/W/34, Committee on Trade in Financial Services, *Communication from the Separate Customs Territory of Taiwan, Penghu, Kinmen and Matsu*, Transitional Review Mechanism in connection with Paragraph 18 of the Protocol on the Accession of the People's Republic of China (November 20, 2003).

S/FIN/W/35, Committee on Trade in Financial Services, *Communication from the United States*, Transitional Review Mechanism in connection with Paragraph 18 of the Protocol on the Accession of the People's Republic of China (November 26, 2003).

S/FIN/W/36, Committee on Trade in Financial Services, *Communication from Japan*, Transitional Review Mechanism in Connection with Paragraph 18 of the Protocol on the Accession of the People's Republic of China (October 28, 2004).

S/FIN/W/37, Committee on Trade in Financial Services, *Communication from Canada*, Transitional Review Mechanism in Connection with Paragraph 18 of the Protocol on the Accession of the People's Republic of China (November 5, 2004).

S/FIN/W/39, Committee on Trade in Financial Services, *Communication from The European Communities*, Transitional Review Mechanism in Connection with Paragraph 18 of the Protocol on the Accession of the People's Republic of China (November 8, 2004).

S/FIN/W/40, Committee on Trade in Financial Services, *Communication from the United States*, Transitional Review Mechanism in Connection with Paragraph 18 of the Protocol on the Accession of the People's Republic of China (November 8, 2004).

S/FIN/W/41, Committee on Trade in Financial Services, *Communication from Chinese Taibei*, Transitional Review Mechanism in Connection with Paragraph 18 of the Protocol on the Accession of the People's Republic of China (November 8, 2004).

S/FIN/W/42, Committee on Trade in Financial Services, *Communication from Australia*, Transitional Review Mechanism in Connection with Paragraph 18 of the Protocol on the Accession of the People's Republic of China (November 17, 2004).

S/FIN/W/44, Committee on Trade in Financial Services, *Communication from the European Communities*, China's Transitional Review Mechanism 2005 (August 2, 2005).

S/FIN/W/45, Committee on Trade in Financial Services, *Communication from the United States*, Transitional Review Mechanism in connection with Paragraph 18 of the Protocol on the Accession of the People's Republic of China (August 23, 2005).

S/FIN/W/46, Committee on Trade in Financial Services, *Communication from Japan*, Transitional Review Mechanism in Connection with Paragraph 18 of the Protocol on the Accession of the People's Republic of China (September 2, 2005).

S/FIN/W/48, Committee on Trade in Financial Services, *Communication from the Separate Customs Territory of Taiwan, Penghu, Kinmen and Matsu*, Transitional Review Mechanism in Connection with Paragraph 18 of the Protocol on the Accession of the People's Republic of China (September 12, 2005).

S/FIN/W/49, Committee on Trade in Financial Services, *Communication from Australia*, Transitional Review Mechanism in connection with Paragraph 18 of the Protocol on the Accession of the People's Republic of China (September 14, 2005).

S/FIN/W/50, Committee on Trade in Financial Services, *Communication from Canada*, Transitional Review Mechanism in connection with Paragraph 18 of the Protocol on the Accession of the People's Republic of China (September 20, 2005).

S/FIN/W/51, Committee on Trade in Financial Services, *Communication from Japan*, Transitional Review Mechanism in connection with Paragraph 18 of the Protocol on the Accession of the People's Republic of China (September 28, 2006).

S/FIN/W/52, Committee on Trade in Financial Services, *Communication from the European Communities*, Transitional Review Mechanism in connection with Paragraph 18 of the Protocol on the Accession of the People's Republic of China (October 11, 2006).

S/FIN/W/53, Committee on Trade in Financial Services, *Communication from the United States*, Transitional Review Mechanism in connection with Paragraph 18 of the Protocol on the Accession of the People's Republic of China (October 18, 2006).

S/FIN/W/55, Committee on Trade in Financial Services, *Communication from Australia*, Transitional Review Mechanism in connection with Paragraph 18 of the Protocol on the Accession of the People's Republic of China (November 16, 2006).

S/FIN/W/56, Committee on Trade in Financial Services, *Communication from Canada*, Transitional Review Mechanism in connection with Paragraph 18 of the Protocol on the Accession of the People's Republic of China (November 22, 2006).

S/FIN/W/57, Committee on Trade in Financial Services, *Communication from the Separate Customs Territory of Taiwan, Penghu, Kinmen and Matsu*, Transitional Review Mechanism in connection with Paragraph 18 of the Protocol on the Accession of the People's Republic of China (October 15, 2007).

S/FIN/W/58, Committee on Trade in Financial Services, *Communication from Japan*, Transitional Review Mechanism in connection with Paragraph 18 of the Protocol on the Accession of the People's Republic of China (October 18, 2007).

S/FIN/W/59, Committee on Trade in Financial Services, *Communication from the European Communities*, Transitional Review Mechanism in connection with Paragraph 18 of the Protocol on the Accession of the People's Republic of China (October 22, 2007).

S/FIN/W/60, Committee on Trade in Financial Services, *Communication from Australia*, Transitional Review Mechanism in connection with Paragraph 18 of the Protocol on the Accession of the People's Republic of China (October 29, 2007).

S/FIN/W61, Committee on Trade in Financial Services, *Communication from the United States*, Transitional Review Mechanism in connection with Paragraph 18 of the Protocol on the Accession of the People's Republic of China (October 29, 2007).

S/FIN/W62, Committee on Trade in Financial Services, *Communication from Canada*, Transitional Review Mechanism in connection with Paragraph 18 of the Protocol on the Accession of the People's Republic of China (October 30, 2007).

S/FIN/W/64, Committee on Trade in Financial Services, *Communication from Japan*, Transitional Review Mechanism in connection with Paragraph 18 of the Protocol on the Accession of the People's Republic of China (November 10, 2008).

S/FIN/W/66, Committee on Trade in Financial Services, *Communication from the European Communities*, Transitional Review Mechanism in connection with Paragraph 18 of the Protocol on the Accession of the People's Republic of China (November 14, 2008).

S/FIN/W/67, Committee on Trade in Financial Services, *Communication from Canada*, Transitional Review Mechanism in connection with Paragraph 18 of the Protocol on the Accession of the People's Republic of China (November 21, 2008).

S/FIN/W/68, Committee on Trade in Financial Services, *Communication from the United States*, Transitional Review Mechanism in connection with Paragraph 18 of the Protocol on the Accession of the People's Republic of China (November 27, 2008).

S/FIN/W/70, Committee on Trade in Financial Services, *Communication from the European Communities*, Transitional Review Mechanism in connection with Paragraph 18 of the Protocol on the Accession of the People's Republic of China (October 21, 2009).

S/FIN/W/71, Committee on Trade in Financial Services, *Communication from Japan*, Transitional Review Mechanism in connection with Paragraph 18 of the Protocol on the Accession of the People's Republic of China (October 22, 2009).

S/FIN/W/72, Committee on Trade in Financial Services, *Communication from the United States*, Transitional Review Mechanism in connection with Paragraph 18 of the Protocol on the Accession of the People's Republic of China (October 23, 2009).

S/FIN/W/79, Committee on Trade in Financial Services, *Communication from Japan*, Transitional Review Mechanism in connection with Paragraph 18 of the Protocol on the Accession of the People's Republic of China (October 3, 2011).

S/FIN/W/81, Committee on Trade in Financial Services, *Communication from the European Union*, Transitional Review Mechanism in connection with Paragraph 18 of the Protocol on the Accession of the People's Republic of China (October 13, 2011).

S/FIN/W/83, S/C/W/344, Committee on Trade in Financial Services, Council for Trade in Services, *Communication from China*, Transitional Review Mechanism in connection with Paragraph 18 of the Protocol on the Accession of the People's Republic of China (October 28, 2011).

S/L/92, *The Guidelines for the Scheduling of Specific Commitments under the GATS: Explanatory Note* (March 28, 2001).

S/WPDR/M/12, Working Party on Domestic Regulation, *Report on the Meeting Held on 3 July 2001*, Note by the Secretariat (August 16, 2001).

S/WPDR/W/14, Working Party on Domestic Regulation, *Communication from the European Communities and Their Member States, Domestic Regulation: Necessity and Transparency* (May 1, 2001).

WT/ACC/7/Rev.2, *Technical Note on the Accession Process*, Note by the Secretariat, Revision (November 1, 2000).

WT/ACC/CHN/1, *Communication from China* (December 7, 1995).

WT/ACC/CHN/49, Working Party on the Accession of China, *Report of the Working Party on the Accession of China* (October 1, 2001).

WT/ACC/CHN/49/Add.2, *The Schedule of Specific Commitments on Services of the People's Republic of China* (October 1, 2001)

WT/ACC/HRV/59, *Report of the Working Party on the Accession of Croatia to the World Trade Organization* (June 29, 2000).

WT/ACC/KGZ/26, *Report of the Working Party on the Accession of the Kyrgyz Republic* (July 31, 1998).

WT/ACC/LTU/52, Working Party on the Accession of Lithuania, *Report of the Working Party on the Accession of Lithuania to the World Trade Organization* (November 7, 2000).

WT/ACC/TPKM/18, Working Party on the Accession of Chinese Taipei, *Report of the Working Party on the Accession of the Separate Customs Territory of Taiwan, Penghu, Kinmen and Matsu* (October 5, 2001).

WT/L/432, *Accession of the People's Republic of China, Decision of 10 November 2001* (November 23, 2001).

WT/L/433, *Accession of the Separate Customs Territory of Taiwan, Penghu, Kinmen and Matsu, Decision of 11 November 2001* (November 23, 2001).

WT/REG109/4, Committee on Regional Trade Agreements, *Free Trade Agreement between the European Communities and Mexico, Services* (March 31, 2003).

WT/REG126/1, Committee on Regional Trade Agreements, *Free Trade Agreement between the EFTA States and Mexico* (August 24, 2001).

WT/REG126/3, Committee on Regional Trade Agreements, *Free Trade Agreement between the EFTA States and Mexico, Goods Aspects*, Communication from the Parties (March 11, 2003).

WT/WGTI/W/124, Working Group on the Relationship between Trade and Investment, *Communication from Japan, Non-Discrimination* (June 28, 2002).

WT/WGTCP/W/221, Working Group on the Interaction between Trade and Competition Policy, *Core Principles in a Trade and Competition Context* (February 6, 2003).

WT/WGTCP/W/222, Working Group on the Interaction between Trade and Competition Policy, *Communication from the European Community and its Member States, Core Principles* (November 19, 2002).

WT/WGTI/W/149, Working Group on the Relationship between Trade and Investment, *Communication from India, Non-Discrimination* (October 7, 2002).

WT/WGTI/W/118, Working Group on the Relationship between Trade and Investment, *Non-Discrimination, Most-Favoured-Nation Treatment and National Treatment*, Note by the Secretariat (June 4, 2002).

Reports and Papers from Governmental Institutions and International Organizations

APEC. *APEC Non-Binding Investment Principles*, Jakarta, November, 1994, 2005/SOM3/IEG2/008.

———. APEC Workshop on Bilateral and Regional Investment Rules/Agreements, May 17–18, 2002, Merida, Mexico, published by the Ministry of Economy, Mexico, for the APEC Secretariat, 2002.

GAO. *Report to Congressional Committees, International Banking: Strengthening the Framework for Supervising International Banks*, March 1994, GAO/GGD-94-68.

———. *Report to the Banking Minority Member,* Committee on Banking, Housing, and Urban Affairs, US Senate, *Foreign Banks: Assessing Their Role in the US Banking System*, February 1996, GAO/GGD-96-26.

———. *Report to Congressional Committees, World Trade Organization: Status of China's Trade Commitments to the United States and other Members*, May 2000, GAO/NSIAD-00-142.

———. *Report to Congressional Committees, World Trade Organization: Analysis of China's Commitments to Other Members*, October 2002, GAO-03-4.

———. Testimony before the Congressional Executive Commission on China, *World Trade Organization: Observations on China's Rule of Law Reforms*, Statement of Susan S. Westin, Managing Director, International Affairs and Trade, June 2002, GAO-02-812T.

OECD. *International Trade in Services: Banking*, Paris, 1984.

———. *National Treatment for Foreign-Controlled Enterprises*, Paris, 1985.

———. *National Treatment for Foreign-Controlled Enterprises*, Paris, 1993.
———. *Recommendation of the Council of the OECD on Improving the Quality of Government Regulation*, adopted March 9, 1995, Paris, OECD/GD(95)95.
———. *Negotiating Group on the MAI, Drafting Group No. 2 on Selected Topics Concerning Treatment of Investors and Investment (Pre/Post Establishment), National Treatment, Non-Discrimination/MFN and Transparency*, DAFFE/MAI/DG2(95)1/REV2, February 15, 1996.
———. Directorate for Financial, Fiscal and Enterprise Affairs, *Commentary to the MAI Negotiating Text* (as of April 24, 1998).
———. *The OECD Declaration and Decisions on International Investment and Multinational Enterprises: Basic Texts*, DAFFE/IME (2000)20.
———. *Overview to the OECD Codes of Liberalization: A Balanced Approach to Liberalization of Capital Movements and Trade in Services – Intergovernmental Co-operation under the OECD Codes of Liberalization*, June 2002.
———. *National Treatment for Foreign-Controlled Enterprises: Decision of the Council, Including Member Countries' Exceptions to National Treatment*, OECD, July 2002.
———. *Fair and Equitable Treatment Standard in International Investment Law, Working Papers on International Investment*, No. 2004/3, September 2004.
UNCTAD. *Bilateral Investment Treaties in the Mid-1990s*, New York and Geneva, United Nations, UNCTAD/ITE/IIT/7, 1998.
———. *Series on issues in international investment agreements, National Treatment*, United Nations, UNCTAD/ITE/IIT/11 (Vol. IV), 1999.
USTR. *US Proposals for Liberalizing Trade in Services: Executive Summary*, USTR Executive Office of the President, Washington, D.C., 20508, USTR Press Release, July 1, 2002.
———. *2002 Report to Congress on China's WTO Compliance*, December 11, 2002.
———. *2003 Report to Congress on China's WTO Compliance*, December 11, 2003.
———. *2004 Report to Congress on China's WTO Compliance*, USTR, December 11, 2004.
———. *2005 Report to Congress on China's WTO Compliance*, USTR, December 11, 2005.
———. *2008 Report to Congress on China's WTO Compliance*, USTR, December, 2008.
———. 2009 Report to Congress on China's WTO Compliance, USTR, December, 2009.
———. 2010 Report to Congress on China's WTO Compliance, USTR, December, 2010.
———. 2011 Report to Congress on China's WTO Compliance, USTR, December, 2011.
———. *2003 National Trade Estimate Report on Foreign Trade Barriers*, March 2003.

US Department of State. *Report of the Commission on Extraterritoriality in China*, Peking, September 16, 1926, Washington, Government Printing Office.
US Department of Treasury. *National Treatment Study* (1998 Report on Foreign Treatment of US Financial Institutions).

Index

For Product Safety Concerns and Information please contact our EU
representative GPSR@taylorandfrancis.com
Taylor & Francis Verlag GmbH, Kaufingerstraße 24, 80331 München, Germany

www.ingramcontent.com/pod-product-compliance
Ingram Content Group UK Ltd.
Pitfield, Milton Keynes, MK11 3LW, UK
UKHW021017180425
457613UK00020B/964